THE

FREEDOM OF SCIENCE

BY

JOSEPH DONAT, S.J., D.D.

PROFESSOR INNSBRUCK UNIVERSITY

NEW YORK
JOSEPH F. WAGNER

𝔑𝔦𝔥𝔦𝔩 𝔒𝔟𝔰𝔱𝔞𝔱

    REMIGIUS LAFORT, D.D.
              Censor

𝔌𝔪𝔭𝔯𝔦𝔪𝔞𝔱𝔲𝔯

    JOHN CARDINAL FARLEY
              Archbishop of New York

NEW YORK, January 22, 1914

AUTHOR'S PREFACE TO THE ENGLISH EDITION

THE present work has already secured many friends in German Europe. An invitation has now been extended for its reception among the English-speaking countries, with the object that there, too, it may seek readers and friends, and communicate to them its thoughts — the ideas it has to convey and to interpret. While wishing it heartfelt success and good fortune on its journey, the Author desires it to convey his greetings to its new readers.

This book has issued from the throes of dissension and strife, seeing the light at a time when, in Austria and Germany, the bitter forces of opposition, that range themselves about the shibboleth *Freedom of Science,* were seen engaging in a combat of fiercer intensity than ever. Yet, notwithstanding, this Child of Strife has learned the language of Peace only. It speaks the language of an impartial objectivity which endeavours, in a spirit of unimpassioned, though earnest, calm, to range itself over the burning questions of the day — over those great *Weltanschauung* questions, that stand in such close relation with the compendious motto: *Freedom of Science.* Yes, *Freedom* and *Science* serve, in our age and on both sides of the Atlantic, as trumpet-calls, to summon together — often indeed to pit in deadly combat — the rival forces of opposition. They are catchwords that tend to hold at fever-pitch the intellectual life of modern civilization — agents as they are of such mighty and far-reaching influences. On the one hand, Science, whence the moving and leading ideas of the time take shape and form to go forth in turn and subject to their sway the intellect of man; on the other, Freedom — that Freedom of sovereign emancipation, that Christian Freedom of well-ordered self-development, which determine the actions, the strivings of the human spirit, even as they control imperceptibly the march of Science. While the present volume is connected with this chain of profound problems, it becomes, of itself, a representation of the intellectual life of our day, with its far-reaching philosophical questions, its forces of struggle and opposition, its dangers, and deep-seated evils.

The Author has a lively recollection of an expression which he heard a few years ago, in a conversation with an American professor, then journeying in Europe. " Here, they talk of tolerance," he observed, " while in America we put it into practice." The catch-word *Freedom of Science* will not, therefore, in *every* quarter of the world, serve as a call to arms, causing the opposing columns to engage in mutual conflict, as is the case in many portions of Europe. But certain it is that everywhere alike — in the new world of America, as well as in the old world of Europe — the human spirit has its attention engaged with the same identical questions — those topics of nerve-straining interest that sway and surge about this same catchword like so many opposing forces. Everywhere we shall have those tense oppositions between sovereign Humanity and Christianity, between Knowledge and Faith, between Law and Freedom; everywhere those questions on the Rights and Obligations of Science, on Catholic Thought, and on Catholic, Doctrinal Beliefs and Duties.

May it fall to the lot of this book to be able to communicate to many a reader, interested in such topics, words of enlightenment and explanation — to some for the strengthening of their convictions, to others for the correction, perhaps, of their erroneous views. At home, while winning the sympathy of many readers, it has not failed to encounter also antagonism. This was to be expected. The resolute championing of the principles of the Christian view of the world, as well as many a candid expression of views touching the intellectual impoverishment and the ever-shifting position of unshackled Freethinking, must necessarily arouse such antagonism. May the present volume meet on the other side of the Atlantic with a large share of that tolerance which is put into actual practice there, and is there not merely an empty phrase on the lips of men! May it contribute something to the better and fuller understanding of the saying of that great English scientist, WILLIAM THOMSON: " Do not be afraid of being free-thinkers! If you think strongly enough, you will be forced by science to the belief in God, which is the foundation of all religion."

Finally, I may be allowed to express my sincere thanks to the publisher for undertaking the work of this translation.

May it accomplish much good.

J. DONAT.

UNIVERSITY INNSBRUCK,
    CHRISTMAS, 1913.

TRANSLATOR'S NOTE

The German original is replete with references to works especially in the German language, the author having with great care quoted title and page whenever referring to an author. Since many of these references are of value only to those familiar with the German, they have been abbreviated or omitted in this English version, whenever they would seem to needlessly encumber its pages.

Those desirous of verifying quotations will be enabled to do so in all instances by a reference to the German original.

CONTENTS

CONTENTS

FIRST SECTION

The Freedom of Science and its Philosophical Basis

THE FREEDOM OF SCIENCE

CHAPTER I

SCIENCE AND FREEDOM

IF a question is destined to agitate and divide for considerable
length of time the minds of men, it must undoubtedly have
its root deep in the entire intellectual life of the times; it must
be anchored in profound philosophical thought, in theories of
life. From this source it derives its power of captivating the
minds. All this applies to the question of the Freedom of Science. If, then, we desire a thorough understanding of this question, we must first of all seek and examine its deeper lying
philosophical basis; we must trace the threads which so closely
unite it to the intellectual life and effort of the times.

But before we begin our study, let us remember a rule of the
great orator and philosopher of ancient Rome; a rule only too
often forgotten in our times: "Every philosophical discussion,
of anything whatsoever, should begin with a definition, in order
to make clear what the discussion is about" (*Cicero*, De Officiis,
I, 2). If we would form a judgment as to the demand of science for freedom, as to the justification of this demand, as to its
compatibility or incompatibility with the duty of faith, the first
question that naturally arises is: What is the purport of this
demand, what does it mean? Only after we have clearly circumscribed this demand can we approach its philosophical presumptions and test its basis.

What, then, do we understand by Science, and what freedom
may be granted to it?

SCIENCE

When a man of Northern or Central Europe hears of science,
his thoughts generally turn to the universities and their teachers.

To him the university is the home of science, there its numerous branches dwell in good fellowship, there hundreds of men have consecrated themselves to its service. In those parts of Europe it is customary for men of science to be university professors. Of what university is he? is asked. Celebrated scientists, like *Helmholtz, Liebig, Hertz, Kirchhoff;* philosophers, like *Kant, Fichte, Schelling, Hegel, Herbart;* great philologists, historians, and so on, were university professors.

For all that, SCIENCE and UNIVERSITY are not necessarily inseparable things. The university needs science, but science does not absolutely need the university. Science was in the world before the twelfth and thirteenth centuries, the time when France and Italy built their first universities; and also since then science has been enriched by the achievements of many a genius who never occupied a university chair. *Pythagoras, Aristotle, St. Augustine* belonged to no universities; *Copernicus, Newton,* and *Kepler* never taught in the higher schools. In the countries of Western Europe and America the man of science and the university professor are to this day not so much identical in person. Therefore, if the freedom of science applies PRINCIPALLY to the higher schools and their teachers, this is not its exclusive application. Science and university are not identical terms.

What, then, is science?

At the sound of this magic word there arises in the minds of many the image of a superhuman being: open on his lap lies the book of wisdom in which all mysteries are solved; in his hand is the flaming torch which enlightens the path down into the lowest depths of research, dispelling all darkness. This, in the minds of many, is what science means. The mere appeal to this infallible being suffices to settle all problems, to silence every contradiction; woe to him who dares open his profane mouth to utter an If or a But!

Were this science, there would be no dispute. We should have to admit that there could be no limit set to the freedom of this being; he must share the privileges of divine Intelligence, for no command to keep silent can be imposed on Infallible Truth; there can be no amendment. But, alas! in the world of reality this personified Science is nowhere to be found, it exists solely in the realm of rhetoric and poetry. Science, as it exists among men, has its seat, after all, nowhere else than in the human mind. It is, indeed, nothing else but THE WELL-ORDERED SUMMARY OF KNOWLEDGE AND OF THE RESEARCH FOR THE CAUSES OF THINGS. Natural science is the summary of knowledge and research in the realm of natural phenomena, arranged in an orderly way, as a text-book will give it; that is, an investigation of phenomena and their causes. A mere description of natural phenomena, without any explanation, or reference of them to the laws of nature, would indeed be teaching about nature, but not natural science. Similarly, the science of history is the well-ordered summary of knowledge and research in the domain of human events, derived from their sources, with the statement of facts according to cause and effect.

And not all this knowledge is certain, and free from doubt. The modern conception of science, as we now have it — the ancients had a much narrower conception — includes certain as well as uncertain knowledge, results and hypotheses, and even the activity of research, together with its methods. Astronomy was thus in *Ptolemy's* time the summary of what was then known with more or less certainty about the stars; included in this, as is well known, was the opinion that the sun circles around the earth. And the philosophy of *Aristotle* embraced his philosophical ideas about God, the world and man; hence many errors. Further, when speaking of science in general, we mean the whole number of the individual sciences. It is the freedom of science in this sense that we have to investigate here. The individual sciences are distinguished one from another principally by the subjects of which they treat. Astronomy is distinguished from palæontology and philosophy by the fact that it treats of the stars, not of fossils, or of the fundamental truths of reason.

From this brief analysis of concepts it is clear that science and scientific research are not superhuman beings, but an activity or condition of the human mind, distinguished from the ordinary thought of the individual only by system and method, and, commonly, by greater thoroughness and by the united effort of many. IT IS SUBJECT TO ALL THE LIMITATIONS OF THE HUMAN MIND.

What follows from this? Two things. Let us at once make a brief reference to both of them, because in our discussion they are of the greatest importance.

Since, then, science is an activity of the human mind, it must, like it, always and everywhere be SUBJECT TO THE TRUTH and SUBJECT TO GOD. Subject to the Truth: whenever science comes in contact with it, it must reverently bow to the truth. And subject to God: if God is the Creator of man and of his spiritual and bodily activity, He is also the master of his whole being, and man is subject to Him in all his activity and development, therefore in his intellectual life, and in his artistic and scientific pursuits. Everything is and remains the activity of the *creature*. As gravitation rules the entire planet and its material activity, attracts it towards the sun and makes it circle around it, so does the law of dependence on God rule the whole life of the creature. Man cannot therefore, even in his scientific research, ignore his Creator, cannot emancipate himself from His authority; and if God has given a revelation and demands faith, the man of science, too, must believe. There cannot be an emancipated, free, science in this sense.

Another consequence is this: since science is an activity of the human mind, it shares all its IMPERFECTIONS AND WEAKNESSES. It is truly flesh of its flesh. The fruit cannot be more perfect than the tree that produces it, nor the flower better than the plant on which it blossomed. Now, as the human mind is throughout limited in its nature, so is it also in its research. It is not given to man to soar aloft on eagle wings to the heights of knowledge, thence to gaze upon truth with unerring intuition; the ascent must be slow, with constant dangers of stumbling, even of falling headlong. To these dangers must be added his latent likes and dislikes, which imperceptibly guide his thought, especially in forming opinions on questions of the world and of life, which the human heart cannot view with indifference: they influence his thought. Hence ignorance, darkness, and error, everywhere accompany the

investigator individually, and science as a whole, all the more
the loftier the questions that present themselves.

Already the philosopher of the dim past gave expression to the complaint, that our reason is no more capable of knowing the divine than
the eyes of the owl are of seeing in broad daylight. It is *Aristotle* who
so complains. And the great *Newton*, in the evening of his life, thus
estimates the worth of his knowledge: " What the world may think
about my labour, I do not know; I feel like a child that plays on the
strand of the sea: now and then I may perhaps find a pebble or shell
more beautiful than those of my playmates, while the boundless ocean
lies ever before me with its undiscovered treasures " (apud *O. Zoeckler*,
Gottes Zeugen im Reich der Natur (1906), 173). The same sorrowful
plaint is heard from all serious investigators, especially those in the
domain of the natural sciences, who should have more reason than others
to be proud of their achievements. " However great the amount of
human knowledge may seem to the multitude," writes the well-known
chemist *Schoenbein*, " the most experienced scientist feels the incomplete-
ness and patchwork of it, and realizes that man so far has been able to
learn but infinitely little of what nature is, and of what can be known."
" The more exact the investigation," says the geologist *Quenstedt*, " so
much the more obscure is its beginning. Indeed, the deeper we think
to have understood the single parts, the further the original plan of
the Creator seems to escape us " (cf. *Kneller*, Das Christentum und
die Vertreter der neueren Naturwissenschaften (1904), 208, 281).
" Although science," so we are assured by another modern savant,
" has brought to light many a treasure, still, compared with what we
do not yet know, it is as a drop to the ocean. In all our knowledge there
will always be the danger of error." We are probably not very far in
advance of the time of *Albrecht von Haller*, who said: " We, all of us,
err, only each errs in a different way. Every passage that has been illuminated by science is surrounded by dense darkness; beyond the visible
lies the invisible." And Prof. *J. Reinke* continues: " As early as the
day of *Socrates*, the beginning of philosophy was to know that we know
nothing; the end of philosophy, to know that we must believe: such is
the inevitable fate of human wisdom " (Naturwissenschaft und Religion, in Natur und Kultur IV (1907), 418, 425. Printed also separately). Some years ago Sir *W. Ramsay*, a noted scientist, concluded a
discourse on his scientific labour with the words: " When a man has
reached the middle of his life, he begins to believe that the longer he
lives the less he knows! This is my excuse for having molested you
for an hour with my ignorance " (Einige Betrachtungen ueber das
periodische Gesetz der Elemente. Vortrag auf der 75. Versammlung
Deutscher Naturforscher und Ærzte zu Cassel (1903)).

If science, then, can only with difficulty lift from visible nature the
veils that hide the truth — and even this is often beyond its power — no
wonder it is confronted with still greater obstacles when it approaches
the truths that are beyond visible nature. Moreover, it is an old truth
that here it is led not by reason only, but also, and even more ener-

getically, by self-interest. "Most men," says *Cicero*, "are swayed in their judgments by either love or hatred, likes or dislikes " (De Oratore, II, 42).

If this is the nature of human science, its adepts would be badly deceiving themselves, if, in the pride of learning, they would reject every correction, even proudly pushing aside the hand of God that reaches down into the darkness of man's intellectual life to offer its guidance. He who realizes that he is in danger of losing his way in the dark, will not reject a reliable guide; and he who fears to stumble will not refuse a helping hand. Self-knowledge is the sister of wisdom, and the mother of modesty.

FREEDOM

Such, then, is science: not the goddess that emanated from the head of immortal Jove, but the offspring of the puny mind of man, bone of his bone and flesh of his flesh. And this science cries for freedom. It would be free and act freely; it urges its claim in the name of truth, which must not be slighted; in the name of the progress of civilization, which must not be hindered.

FREEDOM clearly means nothing less than to be untrammeled and free from restraint, from fetter and check, in action, thought, and desire. The prisoner is free when his chains drop off, a people is free when it has cast off the yoke of serfdom, the eagle is free and can spread out its wings in lofty flight when not bound down to the earth. Science, therefore, should be free in its activity from bond, fetter, and restraint. Does this mean it must be free from ALL restraint and law? Should the historian be given the right to make *Solon* a member of the French Academy, or of the heroes of Troy mediæval knights? Should the scientist be given the right to break every rule of logic, to ignore all progress, and perhaps in his capriciousness return to the four elements of *Aristotle*, or the astronomical chart of primitive ages? Nobody demands this. No, science must be bound by the TRUTH. Freedom indeed should not mean lawlessness. Science remains bound by the general laws of logic, and by positive facts. Truth is the irremovable barrier set in restraint of the freedom of everything, even of scientific thought. The freedom of science therefore can only be freedom from UNREASONABLE restraint and fetters; from such that hinder it unreasonably in its inquiry after the truth, and in the communication of the results of its investigation. IT SHOULD BE FREE, NOT FROM THE INTERNAL BONDAGE OF TRUTH, BUT FROM THE RESTRAINT BY EXTERNAL AUTHORITY, the restraint which would hinder it, in an IMPROPER WAY, from approaching those questions, and using those methods, that lead to the discovery of truth, and from acknowledging the results it has found to be true; or which would unlawfully keep it from making known, for the benefit of others, the results of its investigation. It should be free from any unjust restriction, imposed by state or Church, by popular opinion, by party spirit, by hampering protectorate, or servility of any kind.

From any UNJUST restriction, we said. For this is clear: if under certain circumstances there might be warrant for a JUST restriction by external authority, such a restriction could not be refused in the name of freedom. So long, then, as we understand by freedom a LAWFUL freedom, there cannot be included in this the freedom from EVERY external authority, but only from UNLAWFUL interference. There is, then, the question whether there may be a legitimate restraint, imposed by external authority, which man must not evade, and what the nature of such restraint may be.

We must, moreover, take into consideration two elements, which are distinguished in the above definitions, both belonging to the modern idea of scientific freedom. We will call them FREEDOM OF RESEARCH, and FREEDOM OF TEACHING. The investigator and the scientist claim the one; the teacher, the other. Searching after truth, and communicating the truth found, are, as is known, the principal occupations of science. The scientist should first of all be an investigator. He should not be content to appropriate to himself the knowledge of others, he should also make his own additions to knowledge. He is also commonly a teacher, by word of mouth, as at the university, or by his writing, in his literary activity. Research, as such, imparts directly a certain knowledge only to the investigator;

it is of a private nature and as such does not reach beyond him. But by teaching, his ideas are communicated to others, and then begin to influence their thought, will, and action, often very strongly. Teaching is a social factor; with it are bound up the weal and woe of others. Suppose a man of influence conceives in his study the idea that monogamy is an infringement upon the universal rights of man; should he be given without any ado the right of disseminating, by teaching, the imagined results of his investigation, to the confusion of men, and with serious danger to the peace of society?

We shall therefore have to distinguish between freedom of research and freedom of teaching. The neglect of this distinction causes not a little confusion; thus, if one complains of his convictions being trammeled or his liberty of conscience being violated, when he is hindered from immediately proclaiming whatever he calls his convictions. Private opinion, and the public propaganda of this opinion, are evidently very different things. It may be that an opinion seems to me the right one, but, in spite of that, public dissemination of it may, always or under certain circumstances, mean danger to my fellow-men. If I am for this reason prevented from publishing it, I am not thereby hindered from giving it my own private assent. It is, moreover, quite clear that the state — we disregard here religious authority — cannot at all directly restrict research, which is something personal. It can only impose restrictions on the communication of one's ideas by teaching them to others, which is a social function.

From these few remarks will be followed the impropriety of the following, or similar, observations: " The fostering of science and its teaching are not separate functions . . . to insinuate a twofold function of freedom, viz., that of the savant and that of the teacher, would be to dissolve the unity of the moral personality " (*W. Kahl*, Bekenntnissge-bundenheit und Lehrfreiheit (1897), 22). It is not at all double-dealing if some one does not publicly proclaim one's private knowledge. Is it double-dealing, is it a violation of " the unity of the moral personality," if one is, and must be, silent about official secrets? And if one does not tell, and is not allowed to tell, official secrets, if one prevents an anar-chist from spreading his revolutionary ideas, is this a violation of the unity of the moral personality? It is true that " to deny one's con-victions is a violation of one of the most indubitable principles of moral

conduct " (*K. v. Amira,* Die Stellung des akademischen Lehrers zur
Freiheit in Forschung und Lehre. Beilage der Muenchener Neuesten
Nachrichten. 9. Juli, 1908). But it is logically incorrect to conclude
therefrom that the freedom of teaching should not be restricted. To
keep silence is not denying one's convictions. Later on, when speaking
of freedom in teaching, we shall return to this thought and deal with
it more thoroughly.

So far there can be no serious diversity of opinion. Freedom
from unjust restraint is demanded, and rightly demanded, for
science. The very object of science requires it. In scientific
research man's power of discernment should freely develop;
his inclination towards truth should exert itself; and by communication of acquired knowledge mankind should advance in
mental and material culture.

The bud bursts forth and freely unfolds its splendour; the
butterfly grows unhindered in beauty; the tree, too, wants freedom, in order to develop its boughs and branches according to
its nature, and if you try to bind and tie it, it resists as much
as it can. Just so is freedom needful for the development
of the noblest aspirations of human nature, for its progress
in knowledge. Every friend of humanity, every one who loves
his own kind, must be in sympathy with its progress. Who
will not rejoice to see the mind of man happily trace the
laws of nature, laid down by the Spirit of God in the stillness
of eternity when as yet there was no creature to heed, the laws
He then placed in nature in order that the reasonable creature
might discern the marks of his Creator? Who would not rejoice
to see man, diligently following the facts of history and studying the works of literature and art, find therein the ideas of
God reflected, as the rays of the sun in the trembling drop of
dew, and, finally, trying to solve the difficult problems of life?
To this end has the Creator enkindled in the mind of man a
spark of His own intelligence; to this end has He put in him a
desire to inquire and learn, a desire which has exerted itself
most in the noblest of men. Man is destined to find his ultimate gratification in beholding the Eternal Truth and Beauty, a
vision which will be the completion of human science and culture, the highest perfection of created life. Thus man's noble
desire for knowledge and truth must develop, it must be able to

produce leaves and blossoms.   For this he needs freedom, free air, and free light.

If science is to attain its high purpose, it must have freedom also to impart the knowledge acquired.   It should indeed further the progress of mankind.   By its discovery it should enhance the beauty of human life, should enrich the treasure of human knowledge, should promote education and morality, to the honour of the Creator.   For this end, too, freedom is necessary: freedom to impart newly acquired knowledge, else there would be no pleasure in work, stagnation rather than progress.

CHAPTER II

TWO VIEWS OF THE WORLD AND THEIR FREEDOM

THERE can, then, be no difference of opinion on this matter among sober-minded men: science must be free from all unjust hindrances and restraint. But we have not yet finished. We have not even proceeded very far on our way. The further question at once presents itself: Which are those unjust hindrances and restraints that scientific research and teaching may reject? May there not perhaps be such which it must respect? There is little meaning in the cry: Freedom! Freedom! This attractive word, which always finds an enthusiastic echo in man, may easily prove a misleading catchword, and become a dangerous weapon of the thoughtless and the unscrupulous.

The question is not, whether our science, or, to speak more generally, our intellectual life, must be free — of that there can be no doubt. No life can spring up and thrive without due freedom. The question is: WHAT SORT OF FREEDOM? how can it be more precisely defined? We all, indeed, demand freedom for the citizen; but what kind of freedom? He should be free from the fetters of tyranny and despotism. Do we also demand that he be free from the laws of the state? By no means! On the contrary, he must be subject to these, for the very reason that he is a citizen and not the inhabitant of an uncivilized world. We demand freedom for the artist; he should not be bound by the tyranny of fashion. Do we also demand that he be exempt from the laws of beauty and art? Not at all. He must subject himself to these if he means to be an artist and not a quack. That would not be true freedom, but lawlessness and license, the privilege of barbarism. Freedom therefore is a very ambiguous word.

There are TWO KINDS OF FREEDOM, LAWFUL and UNLAWFUL: the latter is freedom from just laws, the former from unjust laws.

We ask again, what is that lawful freedom which man may claim for his scientific activity? In other words, what are the restraints which he may reject as unjust, and as enslaving the mind? — Here the ways part. Here, too, our question goes deeper, and touches something which moves men's minds very powerfully. Two different views of the world, two opposite conceptions of man and his thought, come here in collision.

The Christian View of the World and its Freedom

On the one hand there is the Christian view of the world: it is essentially also the one which appears self-evident to every unbiassed mind. In this view man is a CREATURE, LIMITED IN EVERY WAY, THEREFORE IN MANY WAYS DEPENDENT UPON external rules, forces, and authorities. To God alone is it reserved to be infinite, and, therefore, to possess in Himself all perfection, goodness, and truth; for which reason there is nothing above Him on which He could be dependent. This is not the case with man. As a creature man is subject to his Creator. The latter is master over man's life and therefore at the same time its ultimate aim. For this reason religion is of obligation to man, that is, he must honour God as He demands it; if God requires faith in a revelation, if He established a Church and duly authorized it to guide us, we must submit to it. In the same way the intellect of man is bound by the laws of objective truth, which is not of his making, but presents itself to him as a norm: he must always be subject to it whether he wishes or not. Man is, finally, a factor in social life; he lives in the family, state, and Church, in the great society of mankind; upon them he is dependent for his education and development. And society requires that man be subject to a ruling authority, that in many things his own interests be subordinated to the welfare of the community.

This is the order that God has established and wishes observed. Hence all human authority is a participation in God's supreme government. Thus it comes about that limits may be set to the scientist's free expression of his views, if the interest of the community require it.

Man is, nevertheless, free. But his freedom does not mean complete independence; nor freedom from all restraint, but only from those external restraints which are opposed to his nature and position, which hinder his legitimate development and activity. He possesses freedom, but only such a freedom as is his due, by which he can unfold and develop his physical and mental powers. To keep his place of subordination to, and dependence on, these higher authorities and powers of truth and order, tends not to injure but to improve his being, not to dwarf but to develop his personality; for they are sources of life to him, they impart to his existence order and harmony, they raise him above himself and his own littleness, they free him from the prison of his own narrowness and selfishness, from the chains of his unruly desires. If a man emancipates himself from these bonds, which he ought to bear, he has freedom of course, but an unnatural freedom, which will be harmful and perhaps ruinous to him.

Take the tree, for instance. It should have freedom for its natural growth. If you force it to creep along the ground instead of growing upward, if you deny it air and light, you infringe on the freedom it should have. Still it cannot have absolute freedom, for it is dependent on the ground from which it derives its nourishment, dependent on the laws of light and atmosphere and gravitation, on the laws of season; it must adapt itself to climate and soil. It may not say to the light: Away with you! — a stunted growth and deformity would be the result of such emancipation. It may not say to the ground: Away with you! — a sad but quick death would be its fate. It has its freedom, and in this freedom it grows and thrives. If it desires greater freedom, it would be an unnatural one, and it would tend, not to its development, but to its destruction.

Such is the Christian view of man and his thought. Here, then, there is but one question to solve: Are the external restraints imposed on me in my investigation and teaching against my nature; against the right of my mind to truth; against my position in human society? If so, then I reject them, because they mean serfdom, not duty; unjust bonds, not natural restraint. But if not, then I do not refuse them my submission. Freedom I want, but only the freedom of man.

Here we pause. Suffice it at present to have formulated the question; we shall return to this topic later and discuss it at greater length.

THE MODERN IDEA OF FREEDOM

The Christian view of man and his freedom, which to past ages appeared self-evident, has grown obscure to many minds, and given place to another, a more modern view.[1]

For the modern man, freedom, especially freedom of intellectual life, means INDEPENDENCE FROM EXTERNAL TIES, FROM ALL AUTHORITY, or, to express it positively, absolute right of self-determination, AUTONOMY. He does not recognize any law or rule which he has not imposed upon himself. In civil life, of course, it is a principle that man must submit to external, legal restraint in many things that do not directly concern his own person, but only so far as is necessary in order that others, too, may enjoy the same freedom; but also here every citizen must be able to share in the legislation, according to the rules of constitutional or republican government. But he must be free from every external restraint in whatever touches the core of his personality, his feeling, desire, thought, and the expression of his thought.

It should now be clear, from what has been said, what is meant by FREEDOM OF SCIENCE. It means independence from every external authority and restraint in research and teaching, the unhindered development and assertion of one's own intellectual personality. Man must let himself be directed only by his own judgment and his instinct for the truth, or his personal need, without heeding dogmas, Church laws, tradition, or any other external norm whatsoever. This is particularly true in the DOMAIN OF PHILOSOPHY AND RELIGION, in questions regarding the world and life, and in fundamental social ques-

---

[1] Whenever we use here the word "modern," we do not take it in the sense of "present," — the Christian view of the world is also a present one, and is still of the utmost importance, — but in the sense of "new" in contrast to the time-honoured and inherited.

tions. This is principally, and almost exclusively, the field in which an authoritative influence of the Church, or state, or society in general, is to be feared. Hence the importance of the question of the freedom of science in this field.

This is also the manner in which the advocates of modern freedom of science unanimously describe it.

For the academic teacher, says *G. Kaufmann*, there are "strictly speaking only the barriers drawn by his own instinct for the truth. It is in this sense that we demand freedom of science to-day for the university teacher. The freedom of the scientist and of the academic teacher must not be limited by patented truth, nor by faint-hearted consideration" (Die Lehrfreiheit an den deutschen Universitaeten im neunzehnten Jahrhundert (1898), 36). The first resolution proposed at the *Second Conference of German University Teachers*, at Jena, in September, 1908, was this: "The purpose of scientific research, and the communication of its results, demand that it be independent of every consideration foreign to scientific method itself." Of this resolution we have from another source the following explanation: "Therefore, it should be independent especially of tradition and the prejudices of the masses, independent of authority and social bodies, independent of party interest." (This was the addition to the thesis as originally formulated by Prof. *von Amira*. Beilage der Muenchener Neuesten Nachrichten, July 9, 1908.) And Prof. *F. Paulsen* writes: "No thought can be commanded or forbidden the academic teacher or his audience" (Die deutschen Universitaeten und das Universitaets-studium, 1902, 288).

A. Harnack likewise teaches that "In regard to research and knowledge there must be unlimited freedom," especially in matters of religion. Here "man must fully understand his own innermost being; the soul must recognize its own needs and the indicated way to their satisfaction. This it can do only when it is entirely free." "The fear that thereby the door to serious error is thrown open should not in the least deter it, for the most serious error of all is the opinion that man should not enjoy perfect freedom in the determination of his state" (Neue Freie Presse, 7 Juni, 1908).

The same demands are made by free-thinkers, who are always and everywhere in favor of free science. The *International Congress of Free-thinkers*, held at Rome in June, 1904, thus defines free-thought: "Since free-thought cannot concede to any authority whatever the right to oppose human reason, or even to supersede it, it demands that its advocates reject directly not only any compulsory belief, but also every authority that tries to enforce its dogmas, even though such an authority be based on revelation, or though it command obedience to dogmas or a-priori principles of philosophy, or to the decisions of public authority or the vote of a majority." — We shall have frequent occasion to speak of this freedom in these pages.

Hence it is easily seen that this view differs from the one we considered before. Freedom from ALL external restraint has superseded freedom from UNJUST restraint. The presumption has found acceptance that every interference by authority is unjust, a violation of the natural rights of man and his thought. On what is this presumption based? In other words: What are the philosophical premises of modern freedom of science? We shall be occupied with this question now for some time. For only after we have attentively considered it, can we gain an intelligent idea of the nature of this freedom, of its methods, and of the justice of its claims. Advocates of this view not infrequently think they have exhausted its meaning when they have protested against ecclesiastical encroachments, when they have held forth against Syllabus and Index. Of the deeper thoughts it contains they have scarcely any idea.

THE HUMANITARIAN VIEW OF THE WORLD

We may distinguish a twofold basis for this view, a general and a particular one. The latter, which is connected with the former, is subjectivism in thought. The former, the more GENERAL, at the same time the REAL BASIS OF THE MODERN FREEDOM OF SCIENCE, is that particular view of man and his position in the world, which we may call the theory of humanitarianism. We are familiar with this word — it has its history. The word of itself conveys a good meaning: it means human nature and dignity, thought and desire worthy of man, nobility of culture. During the Renaissance the so-called " humanists " identified culture with knowledge of the ancient classical literature. Many of them, however, added to the admiration of classical literature also preference for pagan tastes, to the contempt of the Christian spirit. Since that time the word HUMANITARIAN has never lost its unchristian sense; it has ever been made the motto of men who emancipated themselves from God and Christianity. Hence it is extensively the motto of our times.

It has changed the position of man. It has forgotten that man is a created, limited, even a fallen being, withal destined for eternal existence. To it man is everything; man left to himself and to his life in this world, severed from God and his

eternal destiny, an ABSOLUTE, PURELY WORLDLY BEING. No
longer does he look up to Heaven, no longer does he get
from above his laws, his hope for help, and strength, and
eternal life. He is his own and only end: he and his earthly
happiness and advancement. In himself alone he sees the source
of his strength, in himself he finds his law, to himself alone is he
responsible, the inherited corruption of his nature he has
forgotten. What God once was to our fathers — the end and
rule of their life — that now is Man to their sons. The
anthropocentric has succeeded the theocentric view of the
world. *Diis extinctis successit humanitas* (Man has succeeded
the fallen gods). "Out of the corrupted nations and decaying religions let there arise a more beautiful humanity!" is
the radical cry of this humanitarian religion.

When in 1892 the battle for a new school law was raging in Prussia, *Caprivi,* the Chancellor of the Empire, said:
"It is here question of a contrast between Christianity and
atheism. Essential to man is his relation to God." Scarcely
had these words been uttered when a champion of modern
thought, Prof. *Fr. Jodl,* took up his pen and wrote: "No
sharper contrast with the convictions of the modern world is
imaginable than that expressed by the words of the imperial
Chancellor, 'essential to man is his relation to God.' To
this sentence, which might be expected in a speech of Cromwell,
or in a papal encyclical, rather than from a statesman of modern
Germany, liberalism must with all possible emphasis oppose
this other sentence: What determines the real worth of a man,
is, first and last, his relation to humanity" (Moral, Religion
und Schule, 1892, 14 f.). *Diis extinctis successit humanitas.*
We shall not deny that the modern spirit is a complicated structure: but neither can any one deny that its chief characteristic is the humanitarian view, with its emancipation from
God, its decided emphasis of the things of this world, and
its boundless overestimation of man.

An attentive observer of these days, should he chance to come
from an old, Catholic town, and saunter with observant eye
through one of our great modern cities, particularly a Protestant one, would behold a vivid realization of this modern view

of the world. The most prominent feature of the Catholic town of old was the House of God. It towered high above the city, its spires reached heavenward; the houses of the faithful clung around the House of God like chicks about the mother hen. The mere sight told the beholder that here dwelt a people whose thoughts were directed towards the other world; over their lives ruled the sacred peace of eternity.

But here all is different. Here the most prominent feature is no longer the House of God; worldly edifices have usurped its place; railroad depots, barracks, city-hall and court-house dominate the city. The state house bears no longer on its front the Christian motto, *Nisi Dominus custodierit* ("Unless the Lord keep the city he watcheth in vain that keepeth it"). It would be considered a degradation should the state base its existence upon religion. Should, then, the observer enter the legislature he would learn the modern principles of state wisdom. The state as such has no relation to religion; the principle is the separation of state and Church. In the public squares he beholds mighty monuments, erected, not to religious heroes and leaders, as perhaps of old, but to great men of the world, champions of national progress. At their feet lie wreaths of homage. They have brought modern humanity to its full stature, maturity, and self-consciousness. Here it is Man who is standing everywhere in the foreground. "It is I," says he, "that lives here. Here I have pitched my tent, from this earth come all my joys, and this sun is shining upon my sorrows."

Our observer, wandering about, finds everywhere magnificent state-schools, scientific institutes, splendid colleges and universities. In years gone by a cross or a word of divine wisdom was probably found here somewhere. It is seen no more. Often it would seem that we can almost hear the words: "We will not have this One rule over us." Here a new race is being reared, which no longer follows blindly the "old tradition," it believes in its own self and its own reason; culture and science take the place of the old religion. He finds but few churches; and where found they are mostly overshadowed by great palaces, and — mostly empty. The modern man passes them by. He has no longer any understanding for the truths of the Christian religion. It fails to satisfy him because it does not appeal to modern ways of thinking and feeling, because it does not symbolize the humanitarian creed. His desire is no longer for Heaven; his aspirations are earthward. " The life beyond concerns me little: my joys come from this world." Contemplating modern civilization he exclaims, with the king of Babylon: " Is not this the great Babylon, which I have built to be the seat of the kingdom, by the strength of my power, and in the glory of my excellence? " (Dan. iv. 27). The doctrine of a nature corrupted by original sin, of a darkened intellect that needs divine revelation, of a weakened will that needs strength from above, of sin that demands atonement, — all this has become meaningless to him, it offends his higher sentiments, his human dignity. He has no longer any understanding for a Saviour of the world, in whom alone salvation is to be sought, much less for a Cross. This sign of redemption, as a certain herald of modern thought remarked, weighs like a mountain upon the mind of our day. He has no longer any understanding for the saving institution of the Church, by whom he should be led: she is to him an institution of intellectual serfdom. He makes his own religion, free from dogma, just as his individuality desires, just as he " lives " it.

Should our observer, while visiting the Protestant city, make a final visit to its university, he will find there the thoughts, which hitherto he had but vaguely felt, clothed in scientific language. There they meet his gaze, defined sharply on the pedestal of Research as the Modern Philosophy, protected, often exclusively privileged, by the state license of teaching. It is the modern scientific view of the world, the only one that men of modern times may hold. From here it is to find its way to wider circles.

" Man," we are told by a pupil of *Feuerbach*, in accord with his master's teaching, " man is man's god. And only by the enthronement of this human god can the super-human and ultra-human God be made superfluous. What Christianity was and claimed to be in times gone by, that now is claimed by humanity." " The being which man in religion and theology reveres," continues *Jodl* with *Feuerbach*, " is his own being, the essence of his own desires and ideals. If you eliminate from this conception all that is mere fancy and contrary to the laws of nature, what is left is a cultural ideal of civilization, a refined humanity, which will become a reality by its own independent strength and labour" (*Ludwig Feuerbach*, 1904, 111 f., 194). "The greatest achievement of modern times," says another panegyrist of emancipated humanity, " is the deliverance from the traditional bondage of a direct revelation. . . . Neither revelation nor redemption approach man from without; he is bound rather to struggle for his perfection by his own strength. What he knows about God, nature, and his own self, is of his own doing. He is in reality ' the measure of all things, of those that are, and why they are; of those that are not, and why they are not.' Of his dignity as an image of God, he has therefore not lost any-thing; on the contrary, he has come nearer to his resemblance to God, his highest end, by his consciousness of being self-existent and of having the destiny to produce everything of himself; from a receptive being he has become a spontaneous one; he has at last come to a clear knowledge of his own real importance and destiny " (*Spicker*, Der Kampf zweier Weltanschauungen, 1898, 134).

Hence "not to make man religious," to quote again the above-men-tioned exponent of modern wisdom of life, "but to educate, to promote culture among all classes and professions, this is the task of the present time." "Religion cannot therefore be the watchword of a progres-sive humanity; neither the religion of the past nor the religion that is to be looked for in the future, but ethics " (*Jodl*, ibid., 108, 112). Ethics, to be sure, the fundamental principles of which are not the com-mandments of God, by the keeping of which we are to reach our eternal happiness, but human laws, which are observed for the sake of man. "Morality and religion," we are told, "shall no longer give us a narrow ladder on which we, each one for himself, climb to the heights of the other world; we are vaulting a majestic dome above this earth under which the generations come and go, succeeding each other in continuous procession. . . . The day will come when the rays of thought which are now dawning upon the highest and freest mountain-tops will bring the light of noonday down to mankind." Woe to us, if from these high mountain-tops, where the bare rocks no longer take life and fecundity from the heavens, the sad desert of estrangement from God should extend into the fresh green of the valleys!

The central ideas of the humanitarian view of the world appear again, though under different form, among Freemasons and free-thinkers, agitators for free religion and free schools. It is well known that Freemasonry has emblazoned "humanity" upon its standard. "One word of the highest meaning," so wrote an official authority some years ago, "contains in itself the principle, the purpose, and the whole tenor of Freemasonry, this word is humanity. Humanity is indeed everything to us." "What is humanity? It is all, and only that, which is human" (Freiburger Ritual, 24. *Pachtler*, Der Goetze der Humanitaet, 1875, 249 f.). "That which is essentially human is the sublime, divine, and the only Christian ideal," adds another authority, addressing the aspirant to Freemasonry. "Leave behind you in the world your different church-formulas when you enter our temple, but let there always be with you the sense for what is holy in man, the religion which alone makes us happy " (Latomia, 1868, p. 167, *Pachtler*, 248). As early as 1823 the " Zeitschrift fuer Freimauerei " wrote: " We should be accused of idolatry should we personify the idea of humanity in the way in which the Divinity is usually personified. This is indeed our reason for withholding from the eyes of profane persons the humanitarian cult, till the time has come when, from east to west, from noon to midnight, its high ideal will be pondered and its cult propagated everywhere " (*Pachtler*, 255).

The time has already come when "the rays of thought that dawned upon the mountain-tops" are descending into the valley. The Twenty-second Convention of German Free-religionists, at Goerlitz, at the end of May, 1907, passed this resolution: " The Convention sees one of its chief tasks in the alliance of all anti-clericals and free-thinkers, and tries by united effort to obtain this common end and interest by promoting culture, liberty of mind, and humanitarianism." There was, moreover, taken up for discussion the thesis: " Free-religionists reject the teaching that declares man lost by original sin, unable to raise himself of his own strength and reason, that directs him to revelation, redemption, and grace from above."

This view of the world finds its most characteristic expression in PANTHEISM, which, though expressed in various and often fantastic forms, is eminently the religion of modern man. From this gloomy depth of autotheism the apotheosis of man and his earthly life, the modern consciousness of freedom, draws its strength and determination.

To find this modern view of man expressed in the language of consistent radicalism, let us hear *Fr. Nietzsche,* the most modern of all philosophers. His ideal is the transcendental man, who knows that God is dead, that now there is no bar to stepping forth in unrestricted freedom to superhuman greatness and independence. To this " masterman," who deems himself superior to others, everything is licit that serves his egotism and will, everything that will promote his interest to the disadvantage of the rabble; probity is cowardice! " But now this god is dead. Ye superior men, this god was your greatest danger." Thus spoke Zarathustra. " Only since this god is buried do you begin to rise. Now at length the great Noon is in its zenith. Now the superior man becomes master. Onward and upward, then, ye superior men! At last the mountain of man's future is in travail. God is dead; let the superior man arise and live." (Also sprach Zarathustra, W. W. VI, 418.) And, in the consciousness that the Christian religion condemns this self-exaltation, he breaks out in this blasphemous charge: " I call Christianity the one great curse, the one great internal corruption. . . . I call it the one immortal, disgraceful, blot on mankind " (Antichrist, W. W. VIII, 313). This is independent humanity in the cloak of fanaticism. *Nietzsche* has carried the modern view of the world to its final consequences; the autonomous man has developed into the god-like superman who carries into effect the behest: Ye shall be as gods; his code of ethics is that of the autocrat who is above the notions of good and bad.

And " let no one deceive himself," writes an intelligent observer of the times, " the spirit of our time is attuned to *Nietzsche's* idea. Consciously or unconsciously this sentiment dominates more minds than many a man learned in the wisdom of the schools may dream of. Did *Nietzsche* create this spirit? Certainly not: he grew out of it, he has only given it a philosophical setting. *Nietzsche* would never have caused that tremendous sensation, never have gathered around him his enthusiastic followers, had not the soil been prepared. As it was, he appeared to " his " men as the Messiah " in the fulness of time." He, too, in his own way " loosened the tongue of the dumb and opened the eyes of the blind." The veiled anti-Christian spirit, the unconscious religious and ethical nihilism, which no one before dared profess openly, though it was hatching in the minds, now had found its " master," its " scientific system " (*Von Grotthuss,* Tuermer, VII, 1905, 79). It is, asserts *Wundt,* " the new ideal of free personality, dependent on precarious moods and chance influences, that has found in *Nietzsche's* philosophy a fantastic expression " (Ethik, ed. 3, 1905, p. 522).

The Autonomous Man

Now we have a clearer idea of modern freedom. It is known as autonomism. The individual wants to be a law to himself, his own court of last appeal; he wants to develop his personality, feeling, desires, and thought, independently of all authority. Too long, it is said, have man's aspirations been directed upward, away from things of this world, to a supernatural world.

Religion and Church seek to determine his thought and desire, to subject him to dogma. Too long has he clung like a child to the apron-strings of authority. Man has at last awoken to self-consciousness and to a sense of his own dignity, after a period of estrangement, so to say, from himself; he has become himself again, as the poet sang when the century of the " illuminati " was closing:

> " How beautiful, with palm of victory,
> O man, thou standest at the century's close,
> The mightiest son thy Time has given birth,
> By reason free, by law and precept strong,
> Alike in meekness great and treasure rich,
> So long unknown concealed within thy breast."

Yes, man has discovered the treasure that long lay hidden in his breast, the seed and bud that longed to burst forth into life and blossom. Now the motto is: Independent self-development; no more restraint, but living out one's personality. The eagle is not given wings to be bound down upon the earth; nor does the bud come forth never to unfold. Full freedom, therefore, too, for everything human! And modern man leaps to the fatal conclusion: therefore all interference of external authority is unjust, is force, constraint upon my being; the same error that boys fall into when life begins to tingle with its fulness of strength. Being ignorant of their nature, they feel any kind of dependence a chain; only themselves, their judgments and desires, are law. Just so modern man, 'in his deplorable want of self-knowledge, fails to see how he is cutting himself off from the source and support of life; how he is pulling himself out by the roots from the soil whence he derives his strength; how, left to his own littleness, he withers away; how, abandoned to his own diseased nature, he condemns himself to intellectual decay.

Autonomism, individualism, independent personality — these have become the ideals that permeate the man of this age, and influence the thought of thousands without their knowing it.

The well-known, Protestant, theologian, *A. Sabatier*, writes: " It is not difficult to find the common principle to which all the expressions and tendencies of the spirit of modern times can be reduced in any field whatever. One word expresses it — the word, 'autonomy.' By autonomy I understand the firm confidence, which the mind of man has attained in his present stage of development, that he contains in himself his own rule of life and norm of thought, and that he harbours the ardent desire of realizing himself by obeying his own law" (La Religion de la Culture moderne, 10).

"Modern times," writes *R. Eucken,* "have changed the position of the human subject . . . it has become to them the centre of his life and the ultimate end of his endeavours" (Zeitschrift fuer Philosophie und philosophische Kritik, 112 (1898), 165 s.). Still clearer are the following words of *G. Spicker:* "Man depended formerly either on nature or on revelation, or on both at once; now it is just the opposite: man is in every way, theoretically as well as practically, an autonomist. If anything can denote clearly the characteristic difference between the modern and the old scholastic view, it is this absolute, subjective, standpoint." "As we in principle do not intend to depend on any objectivity or authority, there is nothing left but the autonomy of the subject" (Der Kampf zweier Weltanschauungen (1898), 143, 145).

A noted apostle of modern freedom exclaims enthusiastically:

"This after all is freedom: an unconditional appreciation of human greatness, no matter how it asserts itself. This greatest happiness, as *Goethe* called it, the humanists have restored to us. Henceforth we must with all our strength retain it. Whoever wants to rob us of it, even should he descend from heaven, is our deadliest enemy." (*H. St. Chamberlain.*)

It is true, of course, that man should strive for perfection of self in every respect; for the harmonious development of all the faculties and good inclinations of his own being, and, in this sense, for a nobler humanity; he should also develop and assert his own peculiar disposition and originality, so far as they are in order, and thus promote a healthy individualism. But all this he should do within the moral bonds of his created and limited nature, being convinced that only by keeping within the right limits of his being can he develop his ability and personality harmoniously; he dare not reach out, in reckless venture after independence, to free himself from God and his eternal end, and from the yoke of truth; he dare not transform the divine sovereignty into the distorted image of created autotheism.

He who professes a Christian view of the world, can see in such a view of man and his freedom only an utter misunderstanding of human nature and an overthrow of the right order of things. This overthrow, again, can only produce calamity, interior and exterior disorder. Woe to the planet that feels its orbit a tyrannical restraint, and leaves it to move in sovereign freedom through the universe! It will move along free, and free will it go to ruin. Woe to the speeding train that leaves its track; it will speed on free, but invariably dash itself to pieces! A nature that abandons the prescribed safeguards can only degenerate into a wild sprout. We shall see how these principles have actually become in modern intellectual life the principles of negation and intellectual degeneration.

St. Augustine states the history of mankind in the following, thoughtful words: "A twofold love divides mankind into the City of the World and the City of God. Man's self-love and his self-exaltation pushed to the contempt of God constitute the City of the World; but the love of God pushed to contempt of self is the foundation of the City of God." (*Fecerunt itaque civitates duas amores duo, terrenam scilicet amor sui usque ad contemptum Dei, coelestem vero amor Dei usque ad contemptum sui.* De civ. Dei XIV, 28.) Thus *St. Augustine,* while contemplating the time when the war between heathenism and Christianity was raging. The same spectacle is presented to our own eyes to-day, probably more thoroughly than ever before in history.

THE PERIOD OF MAN'S EMANCIPATION

The modern view of man and his freedom has shaped itself gradually in recent times; the present is ever the child of the past. The most important factor in this development was undoubtedly the REFORMATION. It emancipated man in the most important affair, religious life, from the authority of the Church, and made him independent. "All have the right to try and to judge what is right and wrong in belief," so *Luther* told the Christian nobility of the German nation; "everybody shall according to his believing mind interpret the Scriptures, it is the duty of every believing Christian to espouse the faith, to understand and defend it, and to condemn all errors." Protestantism means even to the modern man "the think-

ing mind's break with authority, a protest against being fettered
by anything positive, the mind's return to itself from self-
alienation" (*Schwegler,* Geschichte der Philosophie (1887),
167) : "it puts out of joint the Christian Church organization,
and overturns its supernatural foundation, quite against its will,
but with an actual, and ever more plainly visible, effect" (*E.
Troeltsch,* Die Bedeutung des Protestantismus fuer die
Entstehung der modernen Welt (1906), 29).

The first step towards full autonomy was taken with energy;
the emancipation from external authority then progressed rapidly in the domain of politics, sociology, economy, and especially
of religion, to the very elimination of everything supernatural.
There came the English individualism of the seventeenth century. The liberty of "individual conviction," termed also
"tolerance," in the sense of rejecting every authoritative interference in the sanctuary of man's thought and feeling, was
extolled; of course at first only as the privilege of those who
were intellectually superior. Soon the Deism of a *Herbert of
Cherbury* and *Locke* was reached; it was the religion of
natural reason, with belief in God and the obligation to moral
action. Whatever is added by positive religions, and therefore
by the Christian religion, is superfluous; hence not dogma, but
freedom! *Locke,* indeed, denied to atheists state toleration; but
J. Toland already advised full freedom of thought, even to the
tolerance of atheism. In the year 1717 FREEMASONRY came into
existence in England. *Adam Smith* originated the idea of a
liberal political economy which frees the individual from all
bond, even in the economic field. The views prevailing in
England then exert great influence in France. *Rousseau* and
Voltaire appear.

In France and Germany the enlightenment of the eighteenth
century makes rapid strides in the direction of emancipation.
"The enlightenment of the eighteenth century," writes *H.
Hettner,* "not only resumes the prematurely interrupted work
of the sixteenth century, the Reformation, but carries it on independently, and in its own way. The thoughts and demands of the
'enlightened' are bolder and more aggressive, more unscrupulous
and daring. . . . With *Luther* the idea of revelation remained

intact; the new method of thought rejects the idea of a divine revelation, and bases all religious knowledge on merely human thought and sentiment. . . . It is only the free, entirely independent thought that decides in truth and justice, moral and political rights and duties. Reason has regained its self-glory; man comes to his senses again" (Literaturgeschichte des 18. Jahrhunderts II (1894), 553). *Kant* gave it a philosophical setting.

Then the FRENCH REVOLUTION breaks into fierce blaze, writing on the skies of Europe with flaming letters the ideas of emancipated humanity; the adherents to the old religion are sent to the guillotine. On August 27, 1789, the proclamation of the "rights of man" is made. "The principles of 1789," as they are now called, henceforth dominate the nineteenth century. The system which adopted these principles called itself, and still calls itself, LIBERALISM.

Liberalism as a principle — we are speaking of the principles of liberalism, not of its adherents, who for the most part do not carry out these principles in their consequences, and occasionally do not even grasp them completely — tried to accomplish man's utter emancipation from all external and superior authority. It sought to accomplish this in the political field, by instituting constitutional, and, wherever possible, a republican form of government; in the field of economy, by granting freedom to labour and possession, to capital and commerce; but especially in the field of morals and religion, by emancipating thought and science, and the entire life of man, — school, marriage, state, — from every religious influence and direction, and in this sense it aimed at humanizing the whole life of man. This is its purpose. To achieve this, it aims at establishing itself in the state, by gaining political power through the aid of compulsory laws, of course against all principles of freedom; it tries to attain this by compulsory state-education, by obligatory civil marriage, and so on. At first there appeared only a moderate liberalism, which gradually gave place to a more radical tendency, striving more directly and openly toward the enfeeblement and, if possible, the destruction of the Christian view of the world and its chief representative, the Church. In 1848 the well-known materialist *K. Vogt* said at the national assembly in Frankfort: "Every church is opposed to a free development of mankind, in that it demands faith above all. Every church is an obstacle in the way of man's free intellectual development, and since I am for such intellectual development of man, I am against every church" (cf. *Rothenbuecher,* Trennung von Staat und Kirche (1908), 106).

In the field of economics, every one can see how liberalism has failed. In some countries people were ashamed to retain its name any longer. It suddenly disappeared from public life, and gave place to its translation, — free thought. This shows that nobody cares to boast of its success. All barriers of safety had been removed in a night; crises, confusion, and the serious danger of the social question were the consequence. In the field of actual economics it became clear that the principle of unlimited freedom could not be carried out, because it was utterly ruinous, and it really means a complete misunderstanding of human nature. Therefore liberalism has disappeared from this field, leaving to others to solve the problem it created, and to heal the wounds it inflicted. It is otherwise in the field of theoretical economics. Here it still strives to dominate, often more thoroughly than before, no matter what name it may assume. The consequences do not appear so gross to the eyes as they would in the tangible sphere of sociology. Especially science it wants to hold in subjection to its principles of freedom in undiminished severity.

That freedom which is identified with absolute independence from all authority, especially in the intellectual sphere, we shall here know as Liberal freedom, in contradistinction to Christian freedom, which is satisfied with independence from unjust restraint.

In the foregoing discussion it has been shown how deeply the liberal idea of freedom is imbedded in the unchristian philosophical view of the world. The inevitable result is a freedom of science which considers every authoritative interference in research and teaching as an encroachment upon the rights of free development in man's personality, especially in the sphere of philosophy and religion. Moreover, the humanitarian view of the world, insisting on the independence of man and his earthly life, naturally demands the exclusion of God and the other world, it orders the rejection of " dualism " as unscientific, and the adoption of the monistic view in its stead; an autonomous science can hardly be reconciled with a superior, restricting authority. Later on we shall demonstrate that the main law of modern science is that the supernatural is inadmissible. Furthermore, since science is not a superhuman being, but has its seat in the intellect of man, subject to the psychology of man, every one who knows the heart of man will suspect from the outset that man cannot stop at merely ignoring, but will often proceed to combat and explain away faith, the Church, and all authority that might be considered an oppressor of the truth. This undue love of liberty will of itself become a struggle for freedom against the oppressor. How far this is actually the case we shall have occasion to discuss later on.

We have heard *Nietzsche's* haughty and proud boast. Shortly after the philosopher had penned these words he was stricken (1889) with permanent, incurable insanity, with which he was afflicted till his death in 1900. The " transcendental man " was dethroned. The strength of the Titan was shattered. He that said with *Prometheus,* I am not a god, still I am in strength the equal of any of them, received the ironical answer, " Behold he has become as one of us " (Gen. iii. 22). He that cursed Christian charity towards the poor and suffering, was now cast helpless upon charity. His grave at Roecken, the place also of his birth, is a sign of warning to the modern world.

To the believing Christian a different grave opens on Easter day. From it comes the risen God-man; in His hand the banner of immortal victory. It points the way to true human greatness, to a superior humanity according to the will of God. Man longs for perfection; he longs to go beyond the narrow limits of his present condition. But modern man wants to rise to greatness by his own strength, without help from above; he would rise with giant bounds, without law. In his weakness he falls; error and scepticism and the loss of morality are the bitter fruit. Another way is pointed out by the great Friend of Man. Humanity is to be led on the way of progress by the hand of God, by faith in God, supported by His grace; thus man shall participate in God's nature, shall one day attain his highest perfection in eternal life, far beyond the limits of his present condition. "I am the way, the truth, and the life."

CHAPTER III

SUBJECTIVISM AND ITS FREEDOM

THE tendency of the modern intellect to independence in its own peculiar sphere of thinking and knowing, cannot fail to work itself out energetically. In this sphere it leads naturally to that view of human reasoning called subjectivism: the thinking or reasoning subject is its own law, the autonomous creator and guide of its thought. Herein lies the ESSENTIAL PRESUMPTION, the very core, of the liberal freedom of science. Wherever we turn we meet subjectivism with its autonomous rejection of all authority, its arbitrary separation of knowledge from faith, its agnosticism, its relativity to truth as the moving factor of, and the ostensible warrant for, this freedom, especially in the sphere which it considers peculiarly its own, philosophy and religion. Only when we look closer into its philosophical premises will it be possible to form a judgment of the "scientific method" it employs in this, its peculiar, sphere, and of the justice of its claim to be the sole administrator of man's ideal possessions, and to be altogether "independent of every view not conforming to this scientific method." Before considering subjectivism let us by way of preface set down a few considerations on the nature of human, intellectual perception.

OBJECTIVISM AND SUBJECTIVISM

It always has been, and still is, the firm conviction of unbiassed men, — a conviction which irresistibly forces itself upon us, — that in our intellectual perception and thought we grasp an OBJECTIVE, EXTERIOR ORDER OF THINGS, AN EXISTENCE DISTINCT FROM OUR THOUGHT; of this objective reality we reproduce an image in our minds, and thus grasp it intellectually. *Cognitio est similitudo rei,* says the old school; that is, Knowledge is the reproduction of an objective reality, which thus becomes the criterion of cognition. The reproduction is a counterpart of the original. In this perfect resemblance of our cognition to the objective reality there has ever been recognized the TRUTH of knowledge.

When the thinking mind has arrived at the mathematical truth that the circumference of a circle is the product of the diameter multiplied by *Ludolph's* number, it knows — unless indeed it has lost its natural candour — that it has not of itself produced this result of reasoning, but that it has recognized in it an objective reality of truth, distinct from its own thought, and has reproduced that truth in itself. And because this reproduction corresponds to the reality, it is called true cognition. Similarly, when the intellect expresses the general law of causality, namely, everything that happens has a cause, the intellect is again convinced that it has not of itself produced this result of reasoning, but has only reproduced it by assimilating to itself an objective truth which is necessarily so and cannot be otherwise, and which the mind must assimilate if it wants to think aright. This is true not only when the mind is dealing with concrete things, but also when it would give expression to general principles, as in the present instance; these, too, are not subjective projections, but are independent of the thinking subject, and are eternal laws.

This view of the nature of human cognition and thought has gradually undergone an essential change, not indeed with those outside the influence of philosophical speculation, but with the representatives of modern philosophy, and those subject to its influence. Objectivism has been superseded by subjectivism. Its principle is this: cognition, imagination, and thought are not the intellectual apprehension of an objective world existing independent of us, of which we reproduce in ourselves a counterpart. No, THE MIND CREATES ITS OWN RESULTS OF REASON AND COGNITION; the objects before us are the creatures of the imagining subject. At the utmost, we can but say that our reasoning is the manner in which a hidden exterior world appears to us. This manner must necessarily conform to the peculiarity of the subject, to his faculties and stage of development; but the exterior world as it is in itself we can never apprehend. *Descartes,* starting with the premise that consciousness is the beginning of all certainty, was the first modern philosopher to enter upon the way of subjectivism. He was followed by *Locke, Berkeley,* and *Kant.* It is due to them that in the modern theory of cognition the fundamental principle of idealistic subjectivism, no matter how difficult and unreasonable it may appear to an ordinary thinker, has obtained so many advocates who, nevertheless, cannot adhere to it, but contradict it at every step.

" The world," *Schopenhauer* is convinced, " is the projection of my idea. . . . No truth is more certain, more independent of all others, less in need of proof, than this, that all there is to be known, hence the whole world, is an object only in relation to a subject, a vision of the beholder; in a word, the projection of my own idea. Hence the subject is the bearer of the world" (Die Welt als Wille und Vorstellung, I, §§ 1–2). " It is evidently true that knowledge cannot go beyond our consciousness, and hence the existence of things outside of our sphere of consciousness must, to say the least, remain problematical " (Der Gegenstand der Erkenntniss, 1892, p. 2). In like manner *O. Liebmann* says: " We can never go beyond our individual sphere of ideas (projection of our ideas), even though we apprehend what is independent of us, still the absolute reality of it is known to us only as our own idea " (Zur Analysis der Wirklichkeit, 1900, p. 28). Therefore " the contrast between ' I ' and the world," says *E. Mach,* " between feeling or apprehension and the reality, falls away " (Die Analysis der Empfindungen, 2d ed., 1900, p. 9). And a disciple of *Mach* says: " It is important to hold fast to the idea that a self-existent, divine Truth, independent of the subject, objectively binding, enthroned, so to say, above men and gods, is meaningless. . . . Such a Truth is nonsense " (*H. Kleinpeter,* Kantstudien, VIII, 1903, p. 314).

None of these representatives of worldly wisdom are able to fulfil the first duty of the wise man: " Live according to what you teach." Even the sceptic *Hume* has to admit that in the common affairs of life he feels himself compelled of necessity to talk and act like other people.

Subjectivism is really nothing but SCEPTICISM, for it eliminates the knowableness of objective truth. But it is a masked — if you will, a reformed — scepticism. Cognition is given another purpose; its task is not at all, so it is said, to reproduce or assimilate a world distinct from itself, but to create its own contents. The very nature of cognition is reversed.

The Autonomy of Reason

It was *Kant,* the herald of a new era in philosophy, who gave to this gradually maturing subjectivism its scientific form and basis. At the same time he gave prominence to that element of subjectivism which seems to give justification to freedom of thought, to wit, autonomism, the creative power of the intellect which makes its own laws. Independence of reason and free thought have become catchwords since *Kant's* time. They are a precious ingredient of the autonomy of modern man.

When the flaming blaze of the French Revolution was reddening the skies of Europe, and inaugurating the restoration of the rights of man, *Kant* was sitting in his study at Königsberg, his heart beating strongly in sympathy with the Revolution, for he saw in it a hopeful turn of the times. An old man of nearly seventy, he followed the events with most passionate interest. *Varnhagen* records in his Memoirs, based on the stories of *Staegemann,* that, when the proclamation of the Republic was announced in the newspapers, *Kant,* with tears in his eyes, said to some friends: " Now can I say with Simeon, ' Now dost Thou, O Lord, dismiss Thy servant in peace, because mine eyes have seen Thy Salvation ' " (*H. Hettner,* Literaturgeschichte des 18. Jahrh. III, 4th ed., 3, 2, 1894, p. 38). While on the other side of the Rhine the Jacobins were doing their bloody work of political liberation, the German philosopher, the herald of a new era and an ardent admirer of *Rousseau,* sat in his study labouring for man's intellectual liberation. To give man the right of autonomous self-determination in action and thought was the work of his life. Autonomy was indeed to him " ' the source ' of all dignity of man and of every rational nature " (Grundlegung zur Metaphysik der Sitten, II). And hence it was that his ardent followers beheld in him " the first perfect model of a really free German, one who had purged himself from every trace of Roman absolutism, dogmatism, and anti-individualism " (*H. St. Chamberlain,* Die Grundlagen des 19. Jahrh., 8th ed., 1907, II, 1127).

In his " Grundlegung zur Metaphysik der Sitten " (The Foundation of the Metaphysics of Ethics) and " Kritik der prak-

tischen Vernunft" (Critique of Practical Reason) *Kant* sought
to establish AUTONOMY IN MORAL LIFE and action. Man himself,
his practical reason, is the ultimate foundation of all moral obligation; did man lead a good life out of obedience to God it
would be a heteronomy unworthy of the name of " moral."
" The autonomy of the will," he teaches, " is the sole principle
of all moral laws and the duties allied to them; all arbitrary
heteronomy, on the contrary, far from having any binding force,
is contrary to the principle of morality of the will " (Kritik der
prakt. Vern., Elementarlehre, I, 1, 4. Lehrsatz). Or, as amplified by a faithful interpreter of the master: " In the moral world
the individual should be not only a member but also a ruler;
he is a member of the moral order when he obeys its law; he
is its ruler when he enacts the law. . . . The distinction between autonomy and heteronomy separates true from false ethics,
the system of *Kant* from all other systems. All moral systems,
except that of *Kant,* are based on the principles of heteronomy;
they can have no other. And critical philosophy was the
first to grasp the principle of autonomy" (*Kuno Fischer,*
Geschichte der neuen Philosophie, IV, 2d ed., 1869, p. 114 *seq.*).
Kant's just man no longer prays " Thy will be done "; he iden-
tifies the law with himself. *Nietzsche's* transcendental man is
seen in the background.

AUTONOMY OF THOUGHT is the result of the " Critique of
Pure Reason," and in spite of its inconsistency of expression,
its involved sentences, its extremely tiresome style, it is and
will long continue to be the text-book of modern philosophy.
According to *Kant* our cognition consists in our fashioning the
substance of our perceptions and reasoning after innate, purely
subjective, views and conceptions. Time and place, and especially the abstract notions of existence and non-existence, necessity, causality, substance, have no truth independent of our
thought; they are but forms and patterns according to which
we are forced to picture the world. Their first matter is supplied by sense experience, such as sound, colour, feeling;
but these, too, according to *Kant,* are not objective. Nothing
then remains to our cognition that is not purely subjective,
having existence in ourselves alone. Our cognition is no longer

a reproduction, but a creation of its object; our thought is no longer subject to an external truth that may be forced upon it. "Hitherto," says *Kant,* "it has been generally supposed that our cognition must be governed by objects. . . . Let us see if we cannot make better headway in the province of metaphysics by supposing that objects must be governed by our cognition" (Kritik der Reinen Vernunft, Vorrede zur zweiten Ausgabe).

This is, indeed, nothing but a complete falsification of human cognition. It is evident to an unbiassed mind that there must be a reason for everything, not because I so think, but I think so because such is the fact; that the multiplication table is right, not because I think so, but I must multiply according to it simply because it is right. My thought is subject to objective truth. But *Kant's* autonomy means emancipation from objective truth, and hence, though *Kant* himself held fast to the unchangeable laws of thinking and acting, he energetically opened the way for subjectivism with all its consequences. This was *Kant's* doing, and history credits him with it. It was one of those events which have made men famous: the giving to the ideas and sentiments of a period their scientific formula, and thereby also their apparent justification.

Schiller wrote in 1805 to *W. von Humboldt:* "The profound fundamental ideas of ideal philosophy remain an enduring treasure, and for this reason alone one should think himself fortunate for having lived at the present time. . . . Finally, we are both idealists, and should be ashamed to have it said of us that things made us and not we the things." *Fr. Paulsen* gives expression to the opinion of many when he says: "*Kant* gives to the intellect the self-determination that is essential to it, and the position in the world which it deserves. He has raised the intellect's creative power to a position of honour: the essence of the intellect is freedom" (Immanuel Kant, 1898, p. 386). "The autonomy of reason . . . we cannot give up" (*Kant*, Der Philosoph des Protestantismus, in Philosophia militans, 2d ed., 1901, p. 51). "It is indeed the offspring of Protestantism." "To me it is beyond doubt," *Paulsen* continues, "that the fundamental tendency of primitive Protestantism has here been carried out in all clearness" (Ibid. 43). *Luther,* too, found in the heart of the individual the unfailing source of truth. For that reason *Kant* has been called the philosopher of Protestantism.

Hence the well-known historian, *J. Scherr,* may not be wrong when he calls the philosophy of *Kant* "the foundation of granite whereon is built the freedom of the German intellect."

Now, indeed, we easily understand the demand for freedom of thought. It is unintelligible how an external authority, a divine revelation or infallible Church, could have ever approached man, assured him of the truth of its teaching, and laid upon him in consequence of this testimony the obligation of accepting it as true. " An external authority," we are assured, " be it ever so great, will never succeed in arousing in us a sense of obligation; its laws, be they ever so lofty and earnest, will be deemed arbitrary, simply because they come from without" (*Sabatier,* La Religion et la Culture moderne, apud *Fonsegrive,* Die Stellung der Katholiken gegenueber der Wissenschaft, Deutsch von *Schieser* (1903), 10). Man accepts only what he himself has produced, what is congenial to his individuality, what is in harmony with his personal intellectual life. In the place of truth steps " personal conviction," the shaping of one's views and ideals; in the place of unselfish submission to the truth steps the " development of one's intellectual individuality," the " evolution of one's intellectual personality "; in a word, free-thought. Exterior authority can no longer impose an obligation. " Is there on earth," asks *Paulsen,* " an instance where authority can decide for us in matters of belief and thought? " And he answers: " There is none; there cannot be on this earth an infallible teaching authority." And why not? " Philosophy and science must refuse to recognize such an authority. . . . If I could believe all that the Church or the Pope teaches, this one thing I could never believe, that they are infallible; it would include a resolution, once for all, to renounce my own judgment regarding whatever they declare true or false, good or bad; it would be the utter renunciation of the use of my reason and conscience." (Ibid. 51–53. We shall often cite the testimony of *Paulsen* for the purpose of illustrating modern thought, partly because he is no longer living, partly because he is quite an outspoken representative of the modern view of the world, though generally regarded as moderate. Moreover, he is without doubt one of the most widely read of the modern German philosophers.)

The demonstration of all this is quite unique. Here it is in brief: Were there an infallible authority, one which necessarily taught the truth, then thought and science would be irrevocably subjected to this authority: that will not do; therefore there is no such authority. Or thus: Were there an infallible teaching, then we should have to accept it without contradiction: that is impossible; therefore there is no infallibility. Hence it is clear, the protest against an infallible authority, even though divine, — for the argument holds good also in regard to such an authority, — is not based on the impossibility of teaching the truth, for the authority is supposed to be infallible, but on man's refusal to be taught. And this refusal is made in accordance with that sovereign freedom of thought which is the natural offspring of subjectivism; the principal renunciation is based on its denial of objective truth. IT IS THE REJECTION OF THE TRUTH.

" In advanced progress," *Paulsen* continues, " the individual is also separating himself from the intellectual mass of the people in order to enjoy a separate mental existence. . . . The individual is beginning to have his own ideas about things; he is no longer satisfied with the common opinions and notions about the world and life which have been dealt out to him by religion and mythology: all philosophy begins with freeing the individual from common notions." " If the individual ideals of a personality, gifted with extraordinary power of mind and will, happen to come in conflict with the objective morality of the time, then there results one of those struggles which cause the dramatic crises of history. They who thus struggled were the real heroes of mankind. They rose against the conventional and indifferent ideals which had grown obsolete, against untrue appearances, against the salt that had lost its savour; they preached a new truth, pointed out new aspirations and ideals which breathed a new strength into life and raised it to a higher plane " (System der Ethik, 8th ed., 1906, I, 372 f.).

Truly encouraging words for the modern agitator and reformer. To summon the courage to rise above the level of the masses, to feel within himself the centre of gravity, and to fashion his thoughts regardless of the whole world, this is nothing less than the beginning of philosophy and wisdom. And should he feel himself strong-minded he may simply change all moral and religious values which do not square with his individual judgments. " To remain faithful to one's own self," we are told again, " that is the essence of this ideal bravery. No one can possess this virtue who does not feel within himself the centre about which life gravitates; whoever pursues exterior things as his ultimate end cannot penetrate to interior freedom. *Spinoza,* by life and teaching, is a great preacher of this freedom" (Ibid. II, p. 27). Self-consciousness as arrogant as that of a pantheist like *Spinoza,* who indeed did not pursue " exterior things as the ultimate end," nor God either; the self-consciousness in which man feels himself the centre about which world and life revolve; the will which now directs thought on its way, — these are the life-nerves of autonomous free-thought.

In fact, inclination and will, not objective truth, are the measure and norm of free-thought. This *Paulsen* again expresses with astonishing candour. According to him, intelligence is after all nothing else than a transformation of the will, this doctrine is rooted in the more modern voluntaristic monism, and is akin to subjectivism. If our cognition itself forms its object, then the real concept of cognition has been lost to us, and in its place we have the will determining the action even of the intellect. *Paulsen* says emphatically, "Intelligence is an instrument of the will in the service of preservation of life. . . . Perhaps it can be said that even the elementary formations of thought, the logical and metaphysical forms of reality, are already codetermined by the will. If the forms of abstract thought are at all the result of biological evolution, then this must be accepted: they are formations and conceptions of reality, which have proved effective and life-preserving, and have therefore attained their object. The principle of identity is in reality not a mere statement, not an indicative, but an imperative: A is A; that is, what I have put down as A shall be A and remain A. . . . If this be so, if thought and cognition be determined fundamentally by the will, then it is altogether unintelligible how it might finally turn against the will, and force upon it a view against its will" (*Kant's* Verhaeltniss zur Metaphysik, 1900, p. 31 f.). We have to do here with a confusion of ideas possible only when correct reasoning has sunk to a surprisingly low level. To think with the will, to draw conclusions with intention, is degenerate thinking. But now we understand better what is meant by autonomy of thought. It gives man license to disregard by shallow reasoning everything that clashes with his own will. " What I have put down as A shall be A and remain A! "

It is now clear that subjectivism and autonomism in thinking are rooted in the positive disregard of objective truth, in the refusal of an unconditional subjection to it; they mean EMANCIPATION FROM THE TRUTH. Here we have the most striking and DEEPEST DIFFERENCE between modern subjectivistic and Christian objective thought. The latter adheres to the old conviction that our thoughts do not make the truth, but are subject to an objective order of things as a norm. For this reason autonomous freedom and subjective caprice, a manner of reasoning that would approach truth as a lawgiver, and even change it according to time and circumstance, are unintelligible in the Christian objective thought. This thought submits unselfishly to truth wherever met, be it without a divine revelation or with it, if the revelation be but vouched for. And the reward of this unselfishness is the preservation of the truth.

But subjectivism, with its freedom, leads inevitably to the loss of the truth; it is scepticism in principle. In fact, if my thoughts are not a counterpart of an objective world, but only a subjectively produced image; not knowledge of an external reality, but only a figment of the imagination, a projection, then I can have no assurance that they are more than an empty dream.

THE MODERN SEPARATION OF KNOWLEDGE AND FAITH

Of course it would be too much to expect that subjectivism in modern thought and scientific work should go to the very limit, viz., to disregard all reasoning, to advance at will any theory whatever, to silence disagreeable critics by merely referring to one's autonomy in thinking, and denying that any one can attain to absolute truth. Errors in empirical speculation never prosper as others do; the power of natural evidence asserts itself at every step, and tears down the artificial cobwebs of apparently scientific scepticism. It asserts itself less strongly where the opposing power of natural evidence is weaker, than is the case in matters of actual sense-experience. Here indeed one sees the objective reality before him, which he cannot fashion according to his caprice. The astronomer has no thought of creating his own starry sky, nor does the archæologist wish to create out of his own mind the history of ancient nations. They both desire to know and to reveal the reality. But in the SUPRASENSIBLE SPHERE, in dealing with questions of the whence and whither of human life, where there is question of religion and morals, there autonomy and scepticism assert themselves as though they were in their own country, there the free-thinker steps in, boasting of his independence and taking for his motto the axiom of ancient sophistry: the measure of all things is man.

Here at the same time the natural product of subjectivism, sceptic agnosticism, has full sway. In such matters, we are told, there is no certain truth; nothing can be proved, nothing refuted: they are all matters of FAITH — not faith, of course, in the Catholic sense. The latter is the acceptance by reason of recognized divine testimony, hence an act of the intellect. The modern so-called faith, on the contrary, is not an act of the intellect, but is supposed to be a vague FEELING, a want, a longing and striving after the divine in one's innermost soul, which divine is then to be grasped by the soul in some mysterious way as something immediately present in it. This feeling is said to emerge from the subconsciousness of the soul, and to raise in the mind those images and symbols which we encounter in the doctrines of the various religions, varying according to times and men. They are only the symbols for that unutterable experience of the divine, which can be as little expressed by definitions and tenets as sounds can by colour. It is a conviction of the ideal and divine, but different from the conviction of reason; it is an inner, actual experience. Hence there can no longer be absolute religious truth, no unchangeable dogmas, which would have to be adhered to forever. In religion, in views of the world and life, the free feeling of the human subject holds sway, a feeling that experiences and weaves together those thoughts and ideals that are in accord with his individuality. This is the modern doctrine.

The dark mysticism of the ancient East and the agnosticism of modern times here join hands. This modern method of separating knowledge and faith is, as we all know, a prominent feature of modern thought. Knowledge, that is, cognition by reason, is said to exist only in the domain of the natural sciences and history. Of what may be beyond these we can have no true knowledge. Here, too, *Kant* has led the way; for the important result of his criticism is his incessant injunction: we can have true knowledge only of empiric objects, never of things lying beyond the experience of the senses; our ideas are

merely subjective constructions of the reason which obtain weight
and meaning only by applying them to objects of sense experiment. Hence God, immortality, freedom, and the like, remain
forever outside the field of our theoretical or cognitive reason.
Nevertheless *Kant* did not like to drop these truths. Hence he
constructed for himself a conviction of another kind. The
" practical reason " is to guide man's action in accomplishing the
task in which her more timid sister, theoretical reason, failed.
And it does it, too. It simply " postulates " these truths;
they are its " POSTULATES," since without them moral life and
moral order, which it is bound to recognize, would be impossible. No one knows, of course, whether this be truth, but it
ought to be truth. *Stat pro ratione voluntas.* The Gordian knot
is cut. " It is so," the will now cries from the depths of the
soul, " I believe it "; while the intellect stands hesitatingly by
protesting " I don't know whether it is so or not." Doubt
and conviction embrace each other; Yes and No meet peacefully.
" I had to suspend knowledge," *Kant* suggests, " in order to
make room for faith " (Kritik der reinen Vernunft, 2. Vorrede).
" It is an exigency of pure practical reason based on duty," he
further comments on his postulate, " to make something the
highest good, the object of my will, in order to further it with
all my power. Herein, however, I have to assume its possibility,
and therefore its conditions, viz., God, freedom, and immortality, because I cannot prove them by speculative reason, nor yet
disprove them." Thus " the just man may say I wish that
there be a God; I insist upon it, I will not have my faith taken
from me " (Kritik der prakt. Vernunft, I. Teil, 2. Buch, 2
VIII).

Others have followed the lead of *Kant.* For philosophers,
Protestant theologians, and modernists, he has become the pilot
in whom they trust.

" *Kant's* critical philosophy," says *Paulsen*, " gives to knowledge
what belongs to it — the entire world of phenomena, for the freest investigation; on the other hand, it gives to faith its eternal right, viz.,
the interpretation of life and the world according to their value "
(Immanuel Kant, 1898, 6). " Faith does not simply rest upon proofs,
but upon practical necessity "; " it does not come from the intellect,
but from the heart and will " (Einleitung in die Philosophie, 10th ed.,

1903, 271, 269). " Religion is not a science, hence it cannot be proved nor disproved." Therefore man's view of the world does not depend on the intellect, but solely on his will. . . . The ultimate and highest truths, truths by which man lives and for which he dies, have not their source in scientific knowledge, but come from the heart and from the individual will." In a similar strain *R. Falkenberg* writes: ." The views of the world growing out of the chronology of the human race, as the blossoms of a general process of civilization, are not so much thoughts as rhythms of thinking, not theories but views, saturated with appreciations. . . . Not only optimism and pessimism, determinism and doctrine of freedom, but also pantheism and individualism, idealism and materialism, even rationalism and sensualism, have their roots ultimately in the affections, and even while working with the tools of reason remain for the most part matters of faith, sentiment, and resolve " (Geschichte der neuen Philosophie, 5th ed., 1905, p. 3).

You may look up any books or magazines of modern philosophy or Protestant theology, and you will find in all of them " that faith is a kind of conviction for which there is no need of proof " (*H. Luedemann*, Prot. Monatshefte IX, 1905, 367). This emotional faith has been introduced into Protestant theology especially by *Schleiermacher*. It is also this view of the more recent philosophy that the modernists have adopted. They themselves confess: " The MODERNISTS in accord with modern psychology distinguish clearly between knowledge and faith. The intellectual processes which lead to them appear to the modernists altogether foreign to and independent of one another. This is one of our fundamental principles " (Programma dei Modernisti (1908), 121).

Religious instruction for children will then have to become altogether different. The demand is already made for " a recast of thought from the sphere of the intellect into the sphere of affection." Away, so they clamour, away with the dogmas of creation, of Christ as the Son of God, of His miracles, as taught in the old schools! For all these are religious ideas. Pupils of the higher grades should be told " the plain truth about the degree of historicity in elementary religious principles. . . . The fundamental idea of religion can neither be created nor destroyed by teaching, it has its seat in sentiment, like — excuse the term — an insane idea " (*Fr. Niebergall*, Christliche Welt, 1909, p. 43).

This dualism of " faith " and knowledge is as untenable as it is common. It is a psychological IMPOSSIBILITY as well as a sad DEGRADATION OF RELIGION.

How can I seriously believe, and seriously hold for true, a view of the world of which I do not know whether it be really true, when the intellect unceasingly whispers in my ear: it is all imagination! As long as faith is a conviction so long must it be an activity of the intellect. With my feeling and will I may indeed wish that something be true; but to wish simply that there be a God is not to be convinced that there actually is a God. By merely longing and desiring I can be as little convinced as I can make progress in virtue by the use of my feet, or repent of sins by a toothache. It is μετάβασις εἰς ἄλλο γένος. A dualism of this kind, between head and heart, doubt and belief, between the No of the mind and the Yes of the heart, is a process incompatible with logic and psychology. How could such a dualism be maintained for any length of time? It may perhaps last longer in one in whom a vivid imagination has dimmed the clearness of intellect; but where the intellectual life is clear, reason will very soon emancipate itself from a deceptive imagination. One may go on dreaming of ideal images, but as soon as the intellect awakens they vanish. Hallucinations are taken for real while the mind is affected, but they pass away the moment it sees clearly.

Kant himself, the father of modern agnostic mysticism, has made it quite clear that his postulates of faith concerning the existence of God and the immortality of the soul, have never taken in him the place of earnest conviction. Thus in the first place *Kant* holds that there are no duties towards God, since He is merely a creature of our mind. "Since this idea proceeds entirely from ourselves, and is a product of ours, we have here before us a postulated being towards whom we cannot have an obligation; for its reality would have to be proved first by experience (or revealed)"; but "to have religion is a duty man owes to himself." Again, he dislikes an oath, he asks whether an oath be possible and binding, since we swear only on condition that there is a God (without, however, stipulating it, as did *Protagoras*)." And he thinks that "in fact all oaths taken honestly and discreetly have been taken in no other sense" (Metaphysik der Sitten, II, § 18, Beschluss).

PRAYER he dislikes still more. "Prayer," he says, "as an internal form of cult, and therefore considered as a means of grace, is a superstitious delusion (feticism). . . . A hearty wish to please God in all our actions, that is, a disposition present in all our actions to perform them as if in the service of God, is a spirit of prayer that can and ought to be our perpetual guide." "By this desire, the spirit of prayer, man seeks to influence only himself; by prayer, since man expresses himself in words, hence outwardly, he seeks to influence God. In the former sense a prayer can be made with all sincerity, though man does not pretend to assert the existence of God fully established; in the latter form, as an address, he assumes this highest Being as personally present, or at least pretends that he is convinced of its presence, in the belief that even if it should not be so it can do him no harm, on the contrary it may win him favour; hence in the latter form of actual prayer we shall not find the sincerity as perfect as in the former. The truth of this last remark any one will find confirmed when he imagines to himself a pious and well-meaning man, but rather backward in regard to such advanced religious ideas, surprised by another man while, I will not say praying aloud, but only in an attitude of prayer; any one will expect, without my saying so, that that man will be confused, as if he were in a condition of which he ought to be ashamed. But why this? A man caught talking aloud to himself raises at once the suspicion that his mind is slightly deranged; and not altogether wrongly, because one would seem out of mind if found all alone making gestures as though he had somebody else before him; that, however, is the case in the example given " (Religion innerhalb der Grenzen der blossen Vernunft, 4. Stueck, 2, § 4, Allgemeine Anmerkung). Thus it happens that in his opinion those who have advanced in perfection cease to pray.

Nor does it seem that *Kant* is serious about his postulate of the IMMORTALITY of the soul. Asked by *Lacharpe* what he thought of the soul, he did not answer at first, but remarked, when the question was repeated: "We must not make too much boast of it" (*H. Hettner*, Literat. Gesch. des 18. Jahrh., III, 4. ed., 3, p. 26. From *Varnhausen's* Denkwuerdigkeiten).

Thousands have with *Kant* destroyed their religious conviction by a boastful scepticism, and, like him, finally given it up to replace its lack by artificial autosuggestions.

And is not the religious life of man thereby made completely valueless? The highest truths on which the mind of man lives, and which from the first stage of his existence not only interested but deeply stirred him, become fiction, pictures of the fancy, suggestions of an effeminate mind, that cannot make a lasting impression on stronger minds. And how can the products of autosuggestion give comfort and strength in hours of need and trial? It is true they do not impose any obligations. Every one is free to form his own notions of life; they are not to be taken seriously anyway, whether they be this or that; they are all equally true and equally false. Buddhism is just as true as Christianity, Materialism as true as Spiritualism, Mohammedanism as true as Quakerism, the wisdom of the Saints as true as the philosophy of the worldly. " The most beautiful flower is growing on the same soil (that of the emotions) with the rankest weed " (*Hegel*). The decision rests with sentiments which admit of no arguing. Thus all is made over to scepticism, to that constant doubting which degrades

and unnerves the higher life of modern times, to that MODERN
AGNOSTICISM which, though bearing the distinction of aristo-
cratic reserve, is in reality dulness and poverty of intellect; not
a perfection of the human intellect, but a hideous disease, all the
more dangerous because difficult to cure. It is the neurasthenia of the intellect of which the physical neurasthenia of our
generation is the counterpart.

The distinguishing mark between man and the lower animals
has ever been held to be that the former could knowingly step
beyond the sphere of the senses, into that world of which his
intellect is a part. The conviction has always prevailed that
man by means of his own valid laws of thought, for instance, the
principle of causality, could safely ascend from the visible world
to an invisible one. Thus also the physician concludes the interior cause of the disease from the exterior symptoms, the
physicist thus comes to the knowledge of the existence of atoms
and ions which he has never seen, and the astronomer calculates
with *Leverrier* the existence and location of stars which no eye
has yet detected.

One thing has certainly been established: a FREE SENTI-
MENT can now assert itself with sovereignty in the most important spheres of intellectual life, without any barriers of
stationary truths and immovable Christian dogmas; one is now
free to fashion his religion and ideals to suit the *individuum
ineffabile*. The latter asks no longer what religion demands
of him, but rather how religion can serve his purposes. " For
the gods," it is said, " which we now acknowledge, are those
we need, which we can use, whose demands confirm and
strengthen our own personal demands and those of our fellow-
men. . . . We apply thereby only the principle of elimination
of everything unsuitable to man, and of the survival of the fittest,
to our own religious convictions"; " we turn to that religion
which best suits our own individuality" (*W. James*). Arrogant doubt can now undermine all fundamental truths of Christian faith until they crumble to pieces; beside it rises the free
genius of the new religion, on whose emblem the name of God
is no longer emblazoned, but the glittering seal of an independent humanity.

RELATIVE TRUTH

Freedom of thought appears still more justified when we take a further step which brings us to the CONSEQUENCE OF SUBJECTIVISM; *i. e.*, when we advance so far as to assert that there are no unchangeable and in this sense no absolute truths, but only temporary, changeable, relative truths. And modern thought does profess this: there is no absolute truth, no *religio et philosophia perennis;* different principles and views are justified and even necessary for different times and even classes. This removes another barrier to freedom of thought, viz., allegiance to generally accepted truths and to the convictions of bygone ages.

The logicalness of this further step can hardly be denied. If the human intellect, independent of the laws of objective truth, fashions its own object and truth, especially in things above the senses, why can it not form for itself, at different periods and in different stages of life, a different religion and another view of the world? Cannot the human subject pass through different phases? He indeed changes his costume and style of architecture; why not also his thoughts? Every product of thought would then be the right one for the time, but would be untenable for a further stage of his intellectual genesis and growth, and would have to be replaced by a new one. The nature of subjectivistic thought is no longer an obstacle to this. Besides, we have the modern idea of EVOLUTION, already predominant in all fields: the world, the species of plants and animals, man himself with his whole life, his language, right, family, all of them the products of a perpetual evolution, everything constantly changing. Why not also his religion, morality, and view of the world? They are only reflexes of a temporary state of civilization. Hence also here motion and change, evolution into new shapes!

Therefore, so it is said, we have now broken definitely with the "dogmatic method of reasoning" of the belief in revelation, and of scholastic philosophy which adhered to absolute truth. They are replaced by the historical-genetical reasoning of the *saeculum historicum* which "has discarded absolute truth: there are only relative, no eternal truths" (*Paulsen,* Immanuel Kant, 1898, 389). We are further assured that "this treatment of the history of thought prevails in the scientific world; the Catholic Church alone has not adopted it. She still clings to dogmatic reasoning, and that is natural to her; she is sure that she is in possession of the absolute truth" (Idem, Philosophia militans, 2d ed., 1901, 5). Outside of this Church every period of time is free to construct its own theories, which will eventually go with it as they came with it.

We meet this relative truth, and all the indefinable hazy notions identified with it, IN ALL SPHERES.

The modern history of philosophy and religion concedes to every system and religion the right to their historic position: they are necessary phases of evolution. The notion of immutable problems and truths by which any system of thought would have to be measured has been lost. "The appearance and rejection of a system," says *J. E. Erdmann*, "is a necessity of world-history. The former was demanded by the character of the time which the system reflected, the latter again is demanded by the fact that the time has changed" (Grundriss der Geschichte der Philosophie, 3rd, I, 1878, 4). And Professor *Eucken* says: "Despite all its advantages, such a view and construction of life is not a definite truth, it remains an attempt, a problem that always causes new discord among minds" (Grundlinien einer neuen Lebensanschauung, 1907, 2). "Thus, if according to *Hegel* the coming into being constitutes the truth of being, the ideals and aims also must share in the mobility, and truth becomes a child of the times (*veritas temporis filia*). That apparently subjects life to a full-blown relativism, but such a relativism has lost all its terror by the deterioration of the older method of reasoning. For agreement with existing truth is no longer its chief object." (Geistige Stroemungen der Gegenwart, 1904, p. 197). The new theory of knowledge assures us quite generally: "It is a vain attempt to single out certain lasting primitive forms of consciousness, acknowledged constant elements of the mind, to retain them. Every 'a-priori' principle which is thus maintained as an unalienable dowry of thought, as a necessary result of its psychological and physiological 'disposition,' will prove an obstacle of which the progress of science will steer clear sooner or later" (*E. Cassirer*, Das Erkenntnissproblem in der Philosophie und Wissenschaft der neueren Zeit, 1906, 6).

That this relativism is also laying hand, more and more firmly, upon modern ethics is well known. One often gets the conviction that, as *E. Westermark* teaches, "there is no absolute standard of morality," that "there are no general truths," "that all moral values," as Prof. *R. Broda* writes, "are relative and varying with every people, every civilization, every society, every free person" (Dokumente des Fortschritts, 1908, 362).

Thus modern subjectivism has lost all sense for definite rules of thought; in its frantic rush for freedom and in its confused excitement it seeks to upset all barriers. Now, of course, we may disregard convictions thousands of years old, by simply observing that they suited former ages but not the present; that they perhaps suit the uneducated but not the educated. Henceforth one may also reject the dogmas of CHRISTIANITY by merely pointing out that they were at one time of importance, but are not suited to the modern man. That is an idea readily grasped, one which has already become quite general with those who are mentally tired of Christianity. What is demanded is a further evolution also of the Christian religion, a continuous cultivation of freer, higher forms, an undogmatic Christianity without duty to believe, without a Church: nothing else, in the end, but a veiled humanitarian religion.

"It will be difficult for coming generations to understand," says *Paulsen*, in the same sense, "how our time could cling in religious instruction with such peace of mind to a system which, having originated several centuries ago under entirely different conditions of intellectual life, stands in striking contrast to facts and ideas accepted by our time everywhere outside the schools." Hence a revision of the fundamental truths of Christianity is needed. Away with everything supernatural and miraculous, obedience to faith, original sin, redemption: all this sounds strange to the modern man. "So there remains but one way: to adapt the doctrine of the Church to the theories and views of our times" (System der Ethik, 8th ed., 1906, II, pp. 247, 250). And *Eucken* says similarly: "We can adopt the doctrinal system of the Church only by retiring from the present back to the past" (Zeitschr. fuer Philosophie u. Phil. Kritik 112, 1898, 165). Therefore we demand evolution of the Christian religion! "Let us not blindly follow antiquated doctrines disposed of by science," we are exhorted. "Let there be no fear lest our belief in God and true piety suffer by it! Let us remember that everything earthly is in continual motion, carried along by the rushing river of life." Onward, therefore, to advancement! . . . cheerfully avowing the watchword: "evolution of religion" (*Fr. Delitzsch*, Zweiter Vortrag ueber Babel u. Bibel, 45. thousand, 1904, 42).

Modern Protestant theology has achieved a great deal in this direction; its evolution has progressed to a complete disintegration of Christianity, by adapting it to modern ideas so thoroughly that there is not a single thought left which this Christianity, reduced to meaningless words, might not accept.

This is the relativism of the present subjectivistic reasoning and its consequences.

Now, it is true that there is room for a certain relativity and evolution in the field of thought and truth. There is a relative truth in the sense that our knowledge of it is never exhaustive. Even the eternal truths of the Christian religion we always know only imperfectly, and we ought to perfect our knowledge continually; established facts of history can also be known, if studied, in greater detail. Thus there is progress and evolution. But from this we may not conclude that there can be no fixed truths at all. In the astronomy of to-day one can surely have the conviction that the fundamental truths of *Copernicus's* System of the Universe must remain an unchangeable truth, and that the time will never come when we shall go back to the obsolete doctrines of old *Ptolemy,* who made the sun revolve around the earth. Is astronomy therefore excluded from progress and evolution? It is moreover true that the individual as well as the community pass through an intellectual evolution in the sense that they gradually increase their knowledge and correct their errors, that literature and the schools gradually enhance the energy and wealth of our ideas and thoughts.

But a progressive change of the laws of thought, to the effect that we must now hold to a proposition which at another time we should naturally reject as untenable, can be maintained only upon the supposition that the thought of evolution has driven all others out of the intellect. It would be absurd to hold that the same view could be true at one time and false at another, that the same views about the world and life could be right to-day and wrong to-morrow, to be accepted to-day and rejected to-morrow. A view is either true or false. If true, it is always true and warranted. Or was old *Thales* right when he declared the world to consist of water; were *Plato* and *Aristotle* right in maintaining that it consisted of ideas, or forms, with real existences; was *Fichte* and his time right with his Ego, and are finally *Schopenhauer, Wundt,* and *Paulsen* right in claiming the world to be the work of the will? Were our heroic ancestors right, as the theories of evolution claim, in holding that trees are inhabited by ghosts; were then the Greeks right with their idea of a host of gods dwelling in the Olympus; and later

on, was the civilized world right in holding that there is but one
God, a personal one; and, after that, are many others of to-day
right when they tell us that the world, and nature itself, is god?
These are conclusions that threaten confusion to the human
brain. And yet they are the logical consequences of "relative
truth," and any one reluctant to accept these consequences
would prove thereby that he has never realized what absurdities
are marketed as relative truth.

Or shall we give it up, as entirely impossible, to judge of
the truth or falseness of doctrines and views? Are we to
value them only so far as they are adapted to a period, and as
moulding and benefiting that period? This opinion indeed is
held. "The values of science and philosophy," says *Paulsen,*
"of our arts and poetry, consist in what they give us; whether
a distant future will still use them is very questionable.
Scholastic philosophy has passed away; we use it no longer;
that is, however, no proof against its value; if it has made the
generations living in the latter half of the Middle Ages more
intelligent and wise . . . then it has done all that could right-
fully be expected of it; having served its purpose, it may be laid
with the dead: there is no philosophy of enduring value."
"Whatever new ideas a people produces from its own inner
nature will be beneficial to it. Nature may be confidently expected to produce here and everywhere at the right time what
is proper and necessary " (System der Ethik, 8th ed., 1906, I,
339, *seq.,* II, 241).

We have here a very deplorable misconception of the real value
of truth, degrading it to suit passing interests and to promote
them. This also is in conformity with subjectivism. But
what could be answered to the straight question: suppose
the opinions which some prefer to call "false " are more useful
and valuable than "truth "? None but *Nietzsche* had the
courage to say that "the falsity of a judgment is not yet a
sufficient prejudice against it; here our new speech will
perhaps sound strangest. The question is: How far is that
judgment life-promoting, life-sustaining, preservative, even creative of species, and we are inclined, on principle, to say that the
falsest judgments are to us the most indispensable " (Jenseits

von Gut und Boese, I, 4, W. W. VII, 12.) The view that doctrines and opinions become especially or exclusively true and
valuable by their usefulness for practical life, has become in our
times the principle of pragmatism.

What others thought out only half way, *Nietzsche* reasons out
to the end.

To what lengths this contempt of objective truth may lead a man of
such an honest character as *Paulsen*, is learned from his advice to
the modern Protestant preacher who can no longer believe what he
has to preach to his orthodox congregation: he may speak just as
suits his congregation, orthodox as well as unorthodox, according to
the principles of relative truth. " Let us assume," he says, " that his
congregation is of a remote country village, where not the slightest
report of the happenings in theology and literature has penetrated,
where the names of *Strauss* and *Renan* are as little heard as those
of *Kant* and *Schleiermacher*. Here the Bible is still taken to be the
literal Word of God, transmitted to us by holy men commissioned to
do it. In this case the preacher may speak without scruple of that book
in the same way as his present hearers are used to. Would he
thus be saying what is wrong? What is meant by saying the Bible
is the Word of God? The same preacher, if transferred to other surroundings where he has to address readers of *Strauss* and *Kant*, may
change his manner of speaking without changing his view or without
violating the truth one way or the other. He would be speaking to
them from their own point of view. . . . Again, should the same
preacher publish his philosophical scientific research, he could speak of
Holy Scripture in an entirely different way. . . ." And he adds:
" Some have taken exception to this opinion." Surely not without
reason!

A justification of this counsel was attempted in these words:
" Just as the electric incandescent light and the tallow-candle may
exist side by side, and as each of them may serve its purpose in its
proper place, so there exist also side by side various physical and
metaphysical ideas and fundamental notions: the scientist and the
philosopher and the old grandmother in her cottage on the remote
mountain-side, cannot think of the world in the same way " (Ethik
II, 240–244). But the argument, if it should prove anything, must
be formulated thus: "As the incandescent light can at the same time be
a tallow-candle, just so can two different and opposite views about one
and the same thing be at the same time both right."

Thus, thanks to the science of modern subjectivism, every
fixed and unchangeable truth, especially in the sphere of philosophy and religion, is removed, and with it also every barrier to
freedom of thought in science as well as elsewhere. The human

intellect in its autonomous self-consciousness may not only reject those truths which are proposed by revelation or the Church; it may not only experience its views of religion and the world by giving free activity to its feelings, it also knows that to be no longer satisfied with the old truths means to be progressive.

Above we have sketched the deeper-lying thoughts on which the liberal freedom of science is based; it is the humanitarian view of the world with its emancipation of man, and autonomous scepticism in thought, joined to that sceptical disregard of truth which once the representative of expiring pagan antiquity comprised in the words: *Quid est veritas?* Now we also understand better the liberal science which often claims the privilege of being " the " science, and which only too often likes to put down as unwarranted and inferior every other science that does not pursue its investigations in the same way. We understand its methods of thought in philosophy and religion, for which it claims an exclusive privilege; we can also form a judgment of its claim to be the leader of humanity in place of faith.

No doubt there are many who are flirting with this freedom without accepting its principles entirely. They do not reason out the thing to the end, they argue against the invasion of the Church into the field of science, and point to *Galileo;* they denounce Index and Syllabus, and then believe they therewith exhausted the meaning of freedom of science. That the real matter in question is a view of the world diametrically opposed to the Christian view, that a changed theory of cognition is underlying it, is by many but insufficiently realized.

This freedom is not acceptable to one who professes the Christian view of the world. He will not offer any feeble apology to the eulogist of this freedom, as, for instance: Indeed you are quite right about your freedom, but please remember that I, too, as a faithful Christian am entitled to profess freedom. No; the answer can only be: Freedom, yes; but THIS freedom, no. A wholly different view of the world separates me from it. I see in it not freedom but rebellion, not the rights of man but upheaval, not a real boon of mankind but real danger.

The principle of liberalism has in the field of social economy already done enough to wreck man's welfare. It has here proved its incompetence as a factor of civilization. That in science also, where it is active in the field of philosophy and religion, liberalism is the principle of overthrowing true science, without any appreciation for truth and human nature, that it is a principle of intellectual pauperism and decay, that it despoils man of his greatest treasures, inherited from better centuries — this we shall prove conclusively.

It is difficult to say how long the high tide of liberalism will sweep over the fields of modern intellectual life before it subsides. One thing, however, is certain, that just so long it will remain a danger to Christian civilization, and to the intellectual life of mankind.

SECOND SECTION

Freedom of Research and Faith

CHAPTER I

RESEARCH AND FAITH IN GENERAL

INTRODUCTION

WHEN the youth growing to maturity begins to feel the development of his own strength, it may happen that he finds his dependence on home unbearably trying. Perhaps he will say, " Father, give me the portion of substance that falleth to me," and then depart into a strange country.

The men of Europe have for centuries lived in the Christian religion as in their fathers' house, and have fared well. But to many children of our time the old homestead has become too confining. Modern man, we are told, has at last come to his senses. He wants to develop his personality, thoughts, and sentiments freely, independently of every authority. He turns his back on his father's house. His parting words are the accusation: The old Church " opposes the modern principles of free individuality, the right to drain the cup of one's own reason and personal life, and it sets itself against the whole of modern feeling, investigation, and activity " (*Th. Ziegler,* Gesch. der Ethik, II, 2d ed., 1892, p. 589).

We are already acquainted with this freedom. We approach now the main question: What is the true relation of the freedom, which man may rightly claim for his scientific activity and reason, to external laws and regulations? Is man really justified to reject them all on the plea that they degrade his intellect and are an obstacle to his development, or does this rejection but manifest an error into which his desire of freedom has decoyed him? This is the question, it will be remembered, that we reached soon in the beginning of our investigation. We have already found the categorical answer — an emphatic rejection of such justification; we also traced the hypotheses on

which the answer rests. We now return to the question to
discuss it in principle. We begin with the freedom of scientific
RESEARCH, in order to take up afterwards the freedom in
TEACHING.

What are those external powers that may interrupt or caution the scientist in his investigations and problems? Here we
do not yet consider the scientist as a teacher, communicating to
the public the result of his investigation, his ideas and views,
from the university chair to his scientific audience, or to a
wider circle of hearers by means of publications; we here regard
him in his private study only, in the pursuit of which he perhaps encounters new questions, and new solutions suggest themselves to him. What freedom can he and must he enjoy here?
This private freedom must evidently be judged from a point of
view other than that from which the freedom in teaching should
be judged. With the latter, the interests of his contemporaries
must be taken into account, and the question must be considered,
whether they suffer by such teaching. The freedom of the
scientist is greater than that of the teacher. Moreover, research is the principal and most important activity of science:
nothing, surely, is taught that has not been previously investigated. If, therefore, research is in any way restricted, so also is
teaching; but not *vice versa*. Are there, then, exterior authorities that may restrain research and reasoning, and what are
they?

One who lives in the Christian world knows at once of what
authority to think. It is not the state. The state cannot directly influence the private work of the student; if it may exert
its influence directly upon anything, it is only upon freedom in
teaching. No, the authority to think of is the authority of
the faith, revealed religion and its guardian, the Church.

Of course, this is not the only authority. Even if a revelation
from heaven had not been given us, yet those GENERAL CONVIC-
TIONS OF MANKIND, common to all nations and times, of the
immutability of the laws of thought and morality, of the existence of a supramundane God, of the retribution for moral
conduct to be made in the world to come, of the sanctity of
state-authority, of the necessity of private property, and others,

would ever remain most revered utterances of truth. No one
would be allowed to contradict this avowal of all mankind,
relying on his own reasoning, which he calls science, and give
the lie to the reasoning of all other men, in order to make
his own reason the sole measure of truth.

But for the present let us pass over the natural authority
of mankind, of its convictions and traditions. It is surpassed
and replaced by the AUTHORITY OF FAITH which belongs to OUR
CHRISTIAN RELIGION. The latter comes to us claiming to possess the only true view of the world, and laying upon us the
obligation of accepting it. It has even the courage to put its
anathema upon propositions which the scientist may call science;
it dares write out a list of the propositions which it condemns
as untenable. Against this authority the protest is raised:
Where is freedom of research, if one cannot even indulge
in his own ideas, if the intellect is to be cropped and fettered?
What is to become of frank, unprejudiced investigation, if I am
from the outset bound to certain propositions, if from the outset
the result at which I must arrive is already determined? It is
intellectual bondage that the man of faith is languishing in.
Thus reads the indictment; thus sounds the battle-cry. Is the
indictment justified? Can and shall science take faith as
a guide in many instances without detriment to its own innate
freedom? And where, and when?

First, the more general question: Is freedom of research
compatible with the duty to believe, or do they exclude each
other in principle?

WHAT FAITH IS NOT

What, then, is faith, and what does the duty to believe demand of us?

Here we meet at once with a false proposition which the opponents of the Christian faith will not abandon. To them faith
is always a blind assent, in giving which one does not ask, nor
dare ask, whether the proposition be true — A BELIEF WITHOUT
PERSONAL CONVICTION. According to them the believer holds
himself " captive to the teaching of his Church. He cannot reflect personally, but follows blindly the lead of authority and

force of habit." Thus " Catholicism is the religion of bondage "
(*W. Wundt,* Ethik, 3d ed., 1903, II, 255, 254). To them it is but
an " uncritical submission to the existing authority, uninfluenced
either by the testimony of the senses or the reflection of
the intellect " (*K. Menger,* Neue Freie Presse, 24 Nov., 1907).
The campaign for liberal science is denouncing those who
" even to-day dare to demand blind faith," " without proof or
criticism," faith in the " word of the Popes and men pretending to be interpreters and emissaries of God, men who have
proved their incompetence and inability by the physical and
religious coercion to which they have subjected mankind "
(*T. G. Masaryk,* V boji o nábozenstvi, The Battle for Religion,
1904, p. 10, 23).

To be sure, if the Christian faith were such, it would be intellectual slavery. If I am compelled to believe something of
which I cannot know the truth, this is coercion, and conflicts
with the nature of the intellect and its right to truth. Infidelity
would then be liberation. But faith is *not* that.

As a rule this view is based on a presumption, which has
already been extensively discussed, viz., that faith and religion
have nothing at all to do with intellectual activity, but are
merely the PRODUCT OF THE HEART, a sentimental, freely acting notion; for, of metaphysical objects no human intellect
can form a certain conviction. It is subjectivism that leads to
this view. According to it the subject creates its own world of
thought, free in action and feeling, not indeed everywhere, — in
the sphere of sense-experience the evidence of the concrete is
too great, — but at least in the sphere of metaphysical truth.

Such modes of expression find their way also into Catholic
literature and language; even here we meet with the assertion
that religion is a matter of the heart, and for that very reason
has nothing to do with science. On the whole it is a remarkable
fact that among believing men many expressions are current
that have been coined in the mint of modern philosophy, and
have there received a special significance. They are used without
real knowledge of their origin and purposed meaning; but the
words do not fail to colour their ideas, and to create imperceptibly a strange train of thought.

One who is of the opinion that religion and views of the world are but sentiment and feeling, which change with one's personality and individuality, can, of course, no longer understand a dogmatic Christianity and the obligation to hold fast to clearly defined dogmas as unchangeable truth. I can hold dogmas and doctrinal decisions to be unquestionably true only when I can CONVINCE MYSELF OF THEIR CREDIBILITY by the judgment of my reason. If I cannot do that, and am still bound to believe them, without the least doubt, then such obedience is compulsory repression of the reason. Then it would indeed be necessary for the Church, as *Kant* says, " to instil into its flock a pious dread of the least deviation from certain articles of faith based on history, and a dread of all investigation, to such a degree that they dare not let a doubt rise, even in thought, against the articles proposed for their belief, because this would be tantamount to lending an ear to the evil spirit " (Religion innerhalb der Grenzen der blossen Vernunft, 3. Stueck, 2. Abtlg.). Fixed dogmas may then at the very most, according to the great master of modern thought, be of pedagogic value to a minor, until he be grown to maturity. But to more advanced minds must be unconditionally conceded the freedom to construct dogmas as they think best, viz., as symbols and images for the subjective thought they underlie. This also, as is well known, is an article of Modernism, which here again follows in the steps of *Kant*.

" Ecclesiastical faith," says *Kant*, " may be useful as a vehicle to minors who can grasp a purely rational religion only through symbols, until in the course of time, owing to the general enlightenment, they can with the consent of everybody exchange the form of degrading means of coercion for an ecclesiastical form suitable to the dignity of a moral religion — that of free faith." " The membranes," he says in another place, " in which the embryo first shaped itself into man must be cast off, if he is to see the light of day. The apron-strings of sacred tradition with its appendages, viz., the statutes and observances which at one time did good service, can gradually be dispensed with; they may even become a harmful hindrance when one is growing to manhood."

Of course, to him who takes the position of *Kant's* DUALISM OF BELIEF AND RATIONAL JUDGMENT, freedom from every authority in matters of faith, and in this sense tolerance, will appear to be self-evident. Whatever has nothing to do with knowledge, but is merely the personal result of an inner, subjective experience, cannot be offered by external authority as matter for instruction. The sole standard for this belief is the autonomous subject and its own needs. In this sense *Harnack* tells us: "The kernel of one's being is to be grasped in its own depths and the soul is merely to recognize its own needs and the road traced out for their gratification. This can only be done with the fullest freedom. Any restraint here is tantamount to the destruction of the problem; any submission to the teaching of others . . . is treason to one's own religion" (Religioeser Glaube und freie Forschung. Neue Freie Presse, 7. Juni, 1908). To have one's religion determined by any authority, even a divine one, would be treason to the sovereignty of man!

Viewed from this standpoint, the RECONCILIATION BETWEEN FAITH AND SCIENCE is no longer a problem. And they congratulate themselves on the solution of this vexing question. Now, they say, deliverance from an oppressive misery has been found, now the peace sought for so long is restored. A fair division has been made: two worlds, the world of the senses, and the world above sense experience. One belongs to science, where it now rules supreme; the other belongs to faith, where it can move freely, undisturbed by, and even unapproachable to science. Just as the stars in the sky are inaccessible to the custodian of civil order, — he can neither support them nor hinder them, nor pull them down, — just so the realm of faith is inaccessible to science: peace reigns everywhere.

Cheered on by this treaty of peace, *Paulsen* writes: "Thus critical philosophy has solved the old problem of the relation of knowledge to faith. *Kant* is convinced that by properly setting the limits he has succeeded in laying the foundation for real and enduring peace between them. In fact, upon this in the first place will rest the importance and vitality of his philosophy. It gives to knowledge, on the one hand, what belongs to it for unlimited research, the whole world of phenomena; on the other hand it gives to faith its eternal right, the interpretation of life and the world from the view-point of values. There can be no doubt that herein lies the cause of the great impression made by *Kant* upon his time; he appeared as the liberator from unbearable suspense" (Immanuel Kant, 1898, 6).

To a critical observer, such peace-making is utterly incomprehensible. They probably did not consider that in this way RELIGION AND FAITH were not liberated, but DISPOSSESSED; not brought to a place of safety, but transferred from the realm of reality into the realm of fancy. Similarly an aggressive ruler might address a neighbouring prince thus: We cannot agree any longer, let us make peace: you retain all your titles, and I shall see to your decent support, but you will have to lay down your crown and sovereignty and leave the country — in this way we can have peace. Religion, once the greatest power in the life of man, for the sake of which man made sacrifices and even laid down his life, has now become a matter of sterile devotion; it may, moreover, no longer claim power and importance; it is now reduced to a poetic feeling, with which one can fill up intellectual vacancies. No longer is man here for religion's sake; religion is here for man's sake. A buttonhole flower, a poetic perfume to sprinkle over his person. For he does not want to give up religion entirely. "We are the less inclined to give up religion forthwith, since we are prone to consider a religious disposition as a prerogative of human nature, even as its noblest title." Thus *D. F. Strauss,* when he asked of those who sympathized with his opinions, Have we still religion? (Der alte u. neue Glaube, II, n. 33). Of course religion has now become something quite different; it has been CONSIGNED TO DEEP DEGRADATION.

To be sure, feeling is of great importance in religion. Dissatisfaction with the things of this earth, man's longing for something higher, for the Infinite, his craving for immortality, for aid and consolation — are all naturally seeking for religious truths. If these are known, they in turn arouse fear and hope, love and gratitude; they become a source of happiness and inspiration. But these feelings have no meaning unless we are certain that there exists something corresponding to them; much less could they of themselves be a conviction, just as little as hunger could convince us that we have food and drink. If one cannot perceive that there is a God, a Providence, a life beyond, then religion sinks to the level of a hazy feeling, without reason and truth, which must appear foolish to men who think, —

as "the great phantasmagoria of the human mind, which we call religion" (*Jodl,* Gedanken über Reform Katholizismus, 1902, 12), — which departs from the sphere of rational intellectual life, and which many have even begun to contemplate from the view-point of psychopathology. It is only due to the after-effect of a more religious past that religion is suffered to lead still a life of pretence: moral support in struggles it can give no more, nor comfort in dark hours, much less may it presume to guide man's thought. It stands far below science.

Despair of the possibility of knowing higher truths is confronting us, the disease of deteriorating times and intellectually decaying nations. But just as Christianity, once in youthful vigour, went to the rescue of an old World dying of scepticism, just as the Catholic Church has ever upheld the rights of reason, especially against Protestantism, which from its beginning has torn asunder faith and knowledge: so the Catholic Church stands to this day unaffected by the doubting tendency of our times, upholding the rights of reason. It also upholds faith. But its faith has nothing to do with modern agnosticism.

What Faith Is

What, then, according to Catholic doctrine, is faith and the duty to believe?

Let us briefly recall to mind the FUNDAMENTAL TENETS of the CHRISTIAN RELIGION. It tells us that even in the Old Testament, but more especially in the New, through His Incarnate Son, God has revealed to man all those religious and moral truths which are necessary and sufficient for the attainment of his supernatural end. Some of them are truths which reason by itself could not discover; others it could discover, but only by great labour. And this divine revelation demands belief. Belief is natural to man. The child believes its parents, the judge believes the witnesses, the ruler believes his counsellors. God wished to meet man in this way, and to give him certainty in regard to the highest truths.

But revelation was to be an heritage of mankind, it was to be transmitted and laid unadulterated before all generations. For this reason it could not be left unprotected to the vicissitudes of time, or the arbitrary interpretation of the individual. It would have utterly failed in its purpose of transmitting sure knowledge of certain truth, — the history of Protestantism proves this, — had it been given merely with the injunction: Receive what I have committed to your keeping, and do with it what you please. No, it had to be made secure against subjective, arbitrary choice.

To this end Christ established an international organization, the CHURCH, and committed to it His Gospel as a means of grace, together with the right and sacred duty to teach it to all men in His Name, to keep inviolate the heirloom of revelation, defending it against all error. " Going, therefore, teach ye all nations " (Matt. xxviii. 19), was His command. " Go ye into the whole world and preach the Gospel to every creature; he that believeth and is baptized shall be saved, but he that believeth not shall be condemned " (Mark xvi. 15). " He that heareth you, heareth Me, and he that despiseth you, despiseth Me " (Luke x. 16). " Behold, I am with you all days, even to the consummation of the world " (Matt. xxviii. 20). He gave His divine aid to the Church, in order that she might INFALLIBLY keep His doctrine to the very end of time.

Thus the divine revelation and the Church approach all men with the duty to believe: " he that believeth shall be saved, " God gravely commands; " and if he will not hear the Church, let him be to thee as the heathen and publican " (Matt. xviii. 17). They lay their teachings before the human intellect, bidding it retain them as indubitable truth, upon their infallible testimony, yet only after convincing itself that God has really spoken, and that this Church is the true one, which cannot err. And only after having convinced itself of the credibility of the proposed teaching is it obliged to believe. Hence, according to the Christian mind, faith is the REASONABLE CONVICTION OF THE TRUTH OF WHAT IS PROPOSED FOR BELIEF, BY REASON OF AN ACKNOWLEDGED INFALLIBLE TESTIMONY.

The Catholic dogma we find explained in the definition of the Vatican Council, which had to expose so many errors that are liable in our days to confuse the faithful in their notions of faith and Church. " This faith," says the Vatican Council (Sess. III, chap. 3), "which is the beginning of human salvation, the Catholic Church teaches to be a supernatural virtue, by which, through the inspiration and co-operation of the grace of God, we believe to be true what He has revealed, not on account of the intrinsic truth of it, perceived by the natural light of reason, but on the authority of God who gives the revelation, who can neither deceive nor be deceived. . . . Nevertheless, in order that the service of our belief might be in accord with reason (' a reasonable service ') God willed to unite to the internal helps of the Holy Ghost external proofs of His revelation, to wit, external works divine, especially miracles and prophecies, which, clearly demonstrating God's omnipotence and infinite knowledge, are most certain signs of divine revelation and are suited to the intelligence of all." The Council adds expressly the canon: " If any one say that divine revelation cannot be made credible by exterior signs, and that men ought therefore to be moved to belief solely by their interior experience or individual inspiration, let him be anathema." We have here stated the Catholic dogma as unanimously taught by all Christian centuries, by all Fathers and theologians.

Hence, the act of faith by which I believe that the Son of God became man, that I shall rise from the dead, is first of all a JUDGMENT OF THE REASON, not an act of the will, or a feeling of the heart. It is, moreover, a CERTAIN rational judgment upon weighty reasons, not, indeed, such which I draw from intellectual knowledge, but those which rest upon the infallible testimony of God. The act of faith agrees therefore with assent to historic truth in that it is of the same kind of knowledge, but upon the authority of infallible testimony. Just as I believe that Alexander once marched victoriously through Asia, because there is sure testimony to that effect, so I believe that I shall rise from the dead, because God has revealed it. The difference being that in the former case we have only human testimony, whereas in the latter God Himself speaks. Thus, according to Catholic teaching, faith and knowledge may be distinct from each other, but in a sense quite different from that of the representatives of modern, sentimental faith. The latter understand knowledge, in this connection, to be any judgment of the reason based upon evidence, and they deny that faith is such; but to a Catholic, faith, too, is a JUDGMENT OF THE REASON, and in this sense true knowledge; only it is not knowledge in the more common sense of a cognition derived from one's own mental activity WITHOUT the external means of authority.

As we have heard from the Vatican Council, it is the recognized fact of divine revelation which bestows upon the matter of faith its certainty in reason. Hence the knowledge of this fact must precede faith itself. But the knowledge must be certain, not merely a belief, for it is the very presupposition of belief, but a knowledge, derived from the intellect, which may at any time be traced back to scientific proofs if there is the requisite philosophical training. So long as man is not certain that God has spoken, he cannot have faith according to the Catholic view. One of the sentences condemned by *Innocent XI.,* to say nothing of other ecclesiastical testimonies, is this: " The assent of supernatural faith, useful for salvation, can exist with merely probable information of the fact of revelation, even with the fear that God has not spoken." And very recently there has been condemned also the proposition: " The assent of faith ultimately rests upon a sum of probabilities " (Decretum Lamentabile, July 3, 1907. Sent. 25).

It cannot be our task here to show at length how the Christian arrives at this certain knowledge. Our present purpose is only to state the Catholic concept of faith. We have already heard the Vatican Council refer to miracles and prophecies. To most of the faithful the chief fact that offers them this security is the wonderful phenomenon of the CATHOLIC CHURCH itself, which proposes to them the doctrines of faith as divine revelation.

Thus again the Vatican Council defines clearly: " To enable us to do our duty in embracing the true faith and remaining in it steadfastly, God has through His incarnate Son established the Church and set plain marks upon His institution, in order that it may be recognized by all as the guardian and interpreter of revelation. For only the Catholic Church possesses all those arrangements, so various and wonderful, made by God in order to demonstrate publicly the credibility of Christianity. Indeed the Church of itself, because of its wonderful propagation, its pre-eminent sanctity and inexhaustible fecundity in everything good, its Catholic unity and invincible duration, is a grand permanent proof of its credibility and irrefutable testimony in behalf of its divine mission. Thus, like a ' standard unto the nations,' it invites those to come to it who have not yet believed, and assures its children that the faith they profess rests upon a most firm foundation."

The Catholic looks with pride upon his Church: she has stood all the trials of history. He sees her endure, though within harassed by heresies and endangered by various unworthiness and incapacity of her priests, and attacked incessantly from without by irreconcilable enemies, yet prevailing victoriously through the centuries, blessing, converting nations and beloved by them; while by her side worldly kingdoms, supported by armies and weapons, go down into the grave of human instability. The most wonderful fact in the world's history, contrary to all laws of natural, historical events, — here a higher hand is plainly thrust into human history; it is the fulfilment of the divine promise: "I am with you all days, even to the consummation of the world." "The gates of hell shall not prevail against it." He sees the Saints, who, have lived in this Church and have become saints through her, those superhuman heroes of virtue, who far surpass the laws of human capacity.

In the most widely different states of life in the Church he sees virtue grow in the degree in which one submits to her guidance. He witnesses the remarkable spectacle, that everything noble and good is attracted by the Church, and their contrary repelled. He sees the miracles which never cease in her midst. Finally he beholds her admirable unity and vigorous faith; she alone holding firm to her teaching, not compromising with any error; she alone holding fearlessly aloft the principle of divine authority, and thus becoming a beacon to many who are seeking a safe shelter from spiritual ruin. In addition we finally have that harmony and grandeur of the truths of faith, and — perhaps not in the last place — that calm and peace of mind, produced in the faithful soul by a life led according to this faith, by prayer and the reception of the Sacraments. This is a clear proof that where the Spirit of God breathes there cannot be the seat of untruth.

These are sufficient proofs to produce even in the uneducated, and in children, true and reasonable certainty, provided they have had sufficient instruction in religion. It must, however, be emphasized that this conviction produced by faith need NOT FIRST BE GAINED BY SCIENTIFIC INVESTIGATION of the motives of faith, or by minute or extensive theological studies. A wrong notion of human knowledge frequently leads to the opinion that there is no true certainty at all unless it is the result of scientific study — a presumption on which is based the claim of freedom of science to disregard any conviction, be it ever so sacred, and the claim that it is reserved to science alone to attain the sure possession of the truth. Later on we shall dwell more at length upon this important point. Let it suffice here to remark that the intellect can attain real certainty even without scientific research; most of our convictions, which we all hold unhesitatingly as true, are of this kind. They constitute a belief that is based upon the real knowledge of the reason, which knowledge is not, however, so clear and distinct that it could be demonstrated easily in scientific form.

The certainty of faith, therefore, is based upon the knowledge that God Himself vouches for the truth of the teachings of faith. This relieves the faithful from the necessity of obtaining by his own reflection an insight into the intrinsic reasons of the why and the wherefore of the proposed truth, and to examine in each instance the correctness of the thing. He knows that God has revealed it, that His infallible Church vouches for it; hence it is credible and true; that suffices for him, just as trustworthy evidence suffices for the historian concerning facts which he himself has not observed.

Let no one say that faith is a BLIND BELIEF and blind obedience, and that dogmatic Christianity, or, to use another phrase, " the religion of the law, demands first of all obedience: it is true it would like, besides that, an interior assent for its thoughts and commandments, but where this is lacking the law itself furnishes the ways and means to compensate the lack of this internal assent, if only obedience is there" (*A. Harnack,* Religioeser Glaube u. freie Forschung. Neue Freie Presse, June 7, 1908). Nor let any one say that free research has " at least this advantage over dogma, that its claims can be proved, which is not true of the other's claims " (*J. H. van't Hoff,* ibid., Dec. 29, 1907). These are misrepresentations.

There is no obedience to faith which is not INTERNAL ASSENT AND CONVICTION, and there is no clinging to dogmas which is not based on motives of faith, or which could not at any time be subjected to scientific investigation. If the term " blindness of belief " were intended to express only that the believer holds the revealed doctrine to be true, not because he has discovered its truth by his own reasoning, but on the authority of God, then we might suffer the misleading word. But it is utterly false in the sense that the believer has no conviction at all. Even though others have it not, the faithful Catholic, the believing Christian, has it, and it is personal conviction. He has convinced himself that God has spoken, and of the credibility and hence the truth of the revealed doctrine, by his own reason, and this is why he assents.

Still greater is the misrepresentation of the real motive of faith, if it is held to be the opinion of the Pope or of Roman Prelates. *Wundt* thus misstates the Catholic position: "Not every one can acquire knowledge. But any one can believe. The enlightened leaders of the Church, and the Church herself first of all, have knowledge, and by dint of authority determine what is to be believed" (Ethik, 3d ed., 1903, I, p. 342). According to the popular scientific propaganda of unbelief, we have to deal in the Church merely with "ignorant monks, Asiatic patriarchs, and similar dignitaries, some very superstitious, who, for instance, assembled in the third century and decided *by vote* that the Gospel is the word of God; we have to deal with men who have proved their incapacity and incompetence" (*Masaryk*, Im Kampfe um die Religion, 1904, pp. 22–23).

Any one who shares such ideas about the supernaturalness of the Catholic Church has, of course, forfeited his claim to understand Catholic life and faith. The Catholic believes in his Church, not on any account of Asiatic patriarchs and superstitious dignitaries, but because she is led by the Holy Ghost, and the Pope must believe the same as the humblest of the faithful: neither the Pope himself relies upon his own judgment, nor does the Catholic who trusts in the word of the Pope.

We add a few remarks which may further illustrate the action of faith.

The knowledge of the fact of revelation, hence of the credibility of the truths revealed, is certain, as shown above. Nevertheless, IT DOES NOT COMPEL reason to assent. Under ordinary circumstances it would be impossible to think of one's own existence, of the elementary laws of mathematics, without being constrained by the evidence to give direct internal assent. But insight into the truth of a thing is not always of this high degree of clearness. In such cases it is an empirical law of the mind that reason discerns of itself the LOGICAL necessity, that is, if it desires to proceed according to the merits of the case, without, however, acting under PHYSICAL constraint. There remains then the determination, the command of the will. This is generally true of many judgments about natural things, but especially true of belief. The knowledge of the fact of revelation is true and certain, though it might be still clearer. The truths offered by divine revelation are too deep for us to comprehend them fully; they imply questions and difficulties for us to ponder. We feel the physical possibility of pondering these difficulties, although we see at the same time that the difficulty is exploded by the certainty of the fact of revelation; but we remain FREE in giving our assent.

Herein lies the possibility of MERITORIOUS faith, the possibility of the creature rendering to God the free tribute of his free submission. At the same time it opens the possibility of turning voluntarily to doubts, and of submitting to them more and more, till the mind becomes clouded and ensnared by error. Thus, since faith depends on free will, the will is strictly commanded to impel the intellect to assent and cling to faith and to put aside doubts. God has revealed the truths of faith that they may be firmly believed.

Hence faith is a product of the will also, and may become part and parcel of the sentimental life. Firmly believed, revealed truths engender in man love and gratitude, fear and hope. And being beautiful and comforting, they are embraced fervently by the heart, and become objects of desire, sources of comfort and happiness. Nevertheless they are in themselves, and remain, rational judgments, based upon insight and knowledge; just as the fond recollections of home are and remain acts of cognition, though our affections are twined round those reminiscences like wreaths of evergreen.

What has just been said illustrates also another point, — the RELATION OF FAITH TO GRACE. The Vatican Council says: "Faith is a supernatural virtue by which, through the inspiration and co-operation of the grace of God, we believe to be true what He has revealed." Faith is called a gift of God, a work of grace. But this must not mislead us to think that it is a mystical process, taking place in the human mind, indeed, but not moving along the natural course of human cognition, but along quite a different course: perhaps an immediate mystical grasp of the revealed truth, while natural intelligence stands aside, not understanding it. This would be returning to our starting point, — making faith anything but a judgment of the reason. It is a common doctrine of theology that the process of faith differs nothing in kind from the natural process of human intellect in its apprehension of the truth. It is belief on grounds recognized as sufficient motives for assent.

What then does grace do? Two things. First, it elevates the act of the soul in the process of believing to a higher sphere. Just as sanctifying grace elevates the soul itself to a supernatural sphere, permitting it to partake of the nature of God, so does the grace of faith raise the acts of the soul to the supernatural order. The KIND of cognition, however, remains the same: just as a ring does not alter its form by being golden instead of silver.

In the second place, grace is ASSISTANCE: it enlightens the intellect that it may be able to see more clearly, not giving to motives of faith an importance which they have not of themselves, but helping the intellect to see them as they are; removing the troubles and dangers of doubt which beset the mind, so that it may retain that calmness which generally accompanies the possession of the truth. The pledge of this assistance is given the Christian at baptism and with each increase of sanctifying grace. But the actual effect of grace depends on many conditions. If one omits prayer and neglects religious duties, deafens one's ear to the word of God, incurs knowingly unnecessary dangers to faith, forsakes the path of virtue, then grace may withdraw to a considerable extent; doubts become stronger, intellectual darkness and confusion increase, and man goes on apace towards infidelity.

This is the Catholic doctrine concerning faith.

FAITH AND REASON

But to return to our question: In what relation do faith and the duty to believe stand to freedom of research? We said that freedom of research consists in exemption from all unjust external restraint, that is, from those external hindrances to the action of the human intellect which prevent it from attaining its natural end. Now what is this natural end? The answer will make clear what restraint and laws must be respected by the human mind, and which may be rightly rejected.

On the coat-of-arms of Harvard University is written the beautiful word " Truth." Upon the human mind, too, is inscribed the word *Veritati* — FOR THE TRUTH. The human mind exists for the sake of truth; for the truth it reasons and searches; it is its natural object, as sound is the object of the human ear, and light and colour the object of the eye. And truth attracts the mind strongly. The child wants the truth, and tries to get it by its many questions; the historian wants the truth, and tries to get it by his incessant searching and collecting. " I can hardly resist my craving," *William von Humboldt* confesses, " to see and know and examine as much as possible: after all, man seems to be here only for the purpose of appropriating to himself, making his own property, the property of his intellect, all that surrounds him — and life is short. When I depart this life I should like to leave behind me as little as possible unexperienced by me " (apud *O. Willmann,* Didaktik als Bildungslehre, 3d ed., II, 1903, p. 7). The great physicist, *W. Thomson,* a few years ago closed a life of eighty-three years — he died in December, 1907 — devoted to the last to unabated search for the truth. It is true not all are called to labour in this field like *W. Thomson.* But every one who has capability may and should help to promote the noble work. Only they are excluded who do not want to look for the truth, or who are even ready, for external considerations, to pass off falsehood for the truth, unproved for established results. " I know of nothing," says the ancient sage, *Plato,* " that is more worthy of the human mind than truth " (Rep. VI, p. 483 c.). And so the poet *Pindar* sings: " Queen Truth, the mother of sublime Virtue."

If this is the aim of the human mind and its science, there is but one freedom of research, the FREEDOM FOR THE TRUTH, the right not to be hampered in searching for the truth, not to be forced to hold as true what has not been previously vouched for to the intellect as true; in a word, the freedom to wear but one chain, the golden chain of the truth. Hence, if the scientist should be compelled by party interest, or public opinion, to pursue a course in science which he cannot acknowledge as the right one; if the younger scientist should feel constrained to conform the results of his research to the pleasure of his older colleagues or of men of name, against his own better judgment, then he would be deprived of his rightful freedom of searching for the truth, and of deciding for himself when he has found it. But there is one sort of freedom the scientist should never claim — FREEDOM AGAINST THE TRUTH, freedom to ignore the truth, to emancipate himself from the truth. He is bound to accept every truth, sufficiently proved, even religious dogmas, miracles too, provided they are authenticated. Not freedom, but truth, is the purpose of research: emancipation from the truth is degeneration of the intellect, destruction of science.

What, then, does the duty to believe require of the faithful Christian? He is required, first of all, to assure himself of the certain credibility of those truths which he is required to believe, and here authentic proofs are offered him. On his perception of the credibility of these truths, he ought to assent to and accept God's testimony. Hence there should be no coercion to believe without interior conviction, no obstacle put in the way of recognizing the truth. WHERE, THEN, IS HERE ANY OPPOSITION TO THE LAWFUL FREEDOM OF RESEARCH, to the right of unimpeded search for the truth? How is reason hindered in its search for the truth when truth is offered it by an infallible authority? We have here no opposition to the laws of reason, but due honour to its sacred rights; no bondage, but elevation and enrichment, completion and crowning of its thought, for the highest truth has been communicated to the reason that it may be of one mind with that Infinite Wisdom which has shaped reason for the truth, and from which it obtains its light as the planet from the sun around which it revolves.

Therefore, it cannot be said that "the Catholic resolves to believe as true what the Church teaches in the Apostles' Creed, but were he offered anything else as Church doctrine he would accept it as well. Hence these doctrines do not express his own personal opinions, they are something extraneous to him."

(*W. Herrmann,* Roemische u. evangelische Sittlichkeit, 3d ed., 1903, p. 3). No, what the Catholic, what any true Christian, believes by faith, that is his innermost conviction, as it is the firm conviction of the historian that what he has drawn from reliable sources is true. — But what if the contrary were offered him? Well, this assumption is absurd; and why? Because God and His Church are infallible, and an infallible authority cannot speak the truth and its contrary at the same time. Much less than a reliable historical witness can testify to the truth and its contrary at the same time.

This same conviction gives to the faithful Christian the firm assurance that no certain result of human research will ever come in conflict with his faith, just as the mathematician does not fear that his principle will ever be contradicted by any further work. Truth can never contradict truth. " Thus we believe and thus we teach and herein lies our salvation." It is the very old conviction of the faithful Christian " that philosophy, that is, the study of wisdom, and religion are not different things." *Non aliam esse philosophiam, i.e., sapientiae studium et aliam religionem (Augustinus,* De Vera Religione, 5). It is precisely this that enables the believing scientist to devote himself with great freedom and impartiality to research in every field, and to acknowledge any certified result without fear of ever having to stop before a definite conclusion.

Such is the PEACE BETWEEN FAITH AND SCIENCE according to Christian principles. They are not torn apart, but join hands peacefully, like truth with truth, like two certain convictions, only gained in different ways. Similar is the peace and harmony between the results of various sciences, as physics and astronomy, geology and biology, which results, though arrived at by different methods, are still not opposed to each other, because they are both true.

The authority of faith, however, must be INFALLIBLE; the authority of a scientist, a school or the state, can never approach us with an absolute obligation to believe it, because it cannot vouch for the truth. To the Catholic his Church proves itself infallible; hence everything is here logically consequent. Protestant Church authorities have not infallibility, nor do they claim it. Hence their precepts, are seen more and more opposed. Hence to the Protestant the firm attachment of the Catholic to his Church must ever remain unintelligible, and it is regrettable that Catholics take instruction from Protestants about their relation to their Church.[1]

We must go a step further. If there is a divine revelation or an infallible Church — we speak only hypothetically — then no man and NO SCIENTIFIC RESEARCH CAN CLAIM THE RIGHT to contradict this revelation and Church. Scientific research is not the hypostatized activity of a superhuman genius, of a godlike intelligence. No, it is the activity of a human intellect, and the latter is subject to God and truth everywhere. There can be no freedom to oppose the truth; no privilege not to be bound to the truth but rather to have the right to construct one's views autonomously.

But here lies the deeper reason why to-day thousands to whom *Kant's* AUTONOMISM IN THOUGHT has become the nerve of their intellectual life, will have nothing to do with guidance by

---

[1] The difference between the Protestant and the Catholic manner of reasoning is stated by the convert, Prof. *A. von Ruville*, as follows: " My mind had harboured up to now the characteristically Protestant thought that I, from my superior mental standpoint, was going to probe the Catholic Church, that I was going to pass an infallible judgment on her truth or untruth, and this in spite of my being ready to acknowledge the truth in her. But now I became more and more conscious of the fact that it was the Church who had a right to pass judgment on me, that I had to bow to her opinion, that she immeasurably surpassed me in wisdom. Many details, which I was inclined to criticize, demonstrated this to me, for in every instance I recognized that it was my understanding that was at fault, and that what appeared to me as an imperfection was rooted in the deepest truth. In this way I was gradually brought to the real Catholic standpoint, to accept the doctrines immediately as Truth, because they proceeded from the Church, and then to endeavour to understand them thoroughly, and to reap from them the fullest possible harvest of Truth. Formerly, with regard to Protestant doctrines, I always retained my independence and the sovereignty of my judgment. Why should I not have had my own opinion, when every denomination and every theologian had an individual opinion? How different with the Catholic Church. Before her sublime, never varying wisdom, as it is proclaimed by every simple priest, I bowed my knees in humility. Compared to her experience of two thousand years my ephemeral knowledge was a mere nothing " (Back to Holy Church, by Dr. *Albert von Ruville*, pp. 30, 31).

revelation and Church. They can no longer understand that their reason should accept the truth from an external authority, not, indeed, because they would not find the truth, but because they would lose their independence.

It was *Sabatier* who maintained that " an external authority, no matter how great one may think it to be, does not suffice to arouse in us any sense of obligation." And *Th. Lipps* says on this further: " If obedience is taken in its narrower sense, that is, of determination by the will of another, then no obedience is moral." " In brief, obedience is immoral — not as a fact but as a feeling, betokening an unfree, slavish mind " (Die ethischen Grundfragen, 2d ed., 1905, p. 119). And *W. Herrmann* assures us, " We would deem it a sin if we dared treat a proposition as true of which the ideas are not our own. If we should find such a proposition in the Bible, then we may perhaps resolve to wait and see whether its truth cannot be brought home to us after we have obtained a clearer and stronger insight of ourselves. But from the resolution to take that proposition as true without more ado, we could not promise ourselves anything beneficial."

It is for the sovereign subject himself to decide whether the ideas offered are compatible with the rest of his notions. A truth offered from without is acceptable to the subject only when, and because, he can produce of himself at the same time what is offered; but he cannot accept the obligation of SUBMITTING to that truth in obedience to faith. " There is no infallible teaching authority on earth, nor can there be any. Philosophy and science would have to contradict themselves to acknowledge it," says another champion of *Kant's* freedom (*Paulsen,* Philosophia militans, 2d ed., p. 52). Hence the reason why there cannot be any infallible authority is, not because it does not offer the truth, but because the human intellect must not be chained down.

Now, this is no longer true freedom, but rebellion against the sacred right that truth has over the intellect. It is rebellion against the supreme authority of God, who can oblige man to embrace His revelation with that reason which He Himself has bestowed upon man. It is a misconception of the human mind, for it is by no means the source of truth and absolute knowledge, but weak and in need of supplement. Many truths it cannot by itself find at all, while in the quest for others it needs safe guidance lest it lose its way. If it refuses to be supplemented

and guided from above, it demands the freedom of the weak
vine allowed to break loose from the needed support of the tree,
the freedom of the planet allowed to deviate from its orbit
to be hopelessly wrecked in the universe. The barrenness and
disintegration in the ideal life of our own unchristian age,
are clear testimony that freedom is not only lawlessness but
a sin against one's own nature.

Or, do they seek to save themselves by asserting that a divine
revelation and the founding of an infallible Church are IM-
POSSIBLE? Very well, then, let them prove it. On this the
question hinges. If they can prove it to us, that very moment
we shall cease to be faithful Catholics, and Christianity will have
been the most stupendous lie in history. But if the reverse is
the case, then all declamations in the name of free research fall
to the ground.

This impossibility, however, could only be proved by the aid
of a presumption. This presumption is ATHEISM, which denies the existence of a personal God, or at least doubts it. If it
is admitted that there is a personal God, then it is self-evident
that He can give a revelation, and. found an infallible Church,
and can oblige all to believe. But herewith collapses also the
liberal principle that, in reasoning, one may reject an external
authority. Hence the principle of liberal freedom in science
can only then be taken seriously, when one advances to atheism.
Then, of course, they will say with *Nietzsche:* God is dead;
long live the transcendental man!

Our assertions are proved by experience. At the end of the
eighteenth century the enlightenment began by excluding all revelation; but it was desired to retain the rational truth of God's
existence. Since then, liberal science has been aiming at atheism
in philosophy, whether open or masked. And if we follow up
the career of men who have left their faith, we shall soon find
that if they do not seek peace in the sheltering harbour of
thoughtlessness, they have reached the terminal station of atheism. There is no stopping on this incline.

Since it is the express fundamental principle of the liberal
freedom of research, that science is not bound to any external
authority, it is evident that it is nothing else but the refusal

to submit to God's authority, hence, also, to submit to truth
if it appears as revelation. For, either it is admitted that
if there is a divine revelation, we have to give it our assent —
and in this event liberal freedom of science would have to be
abandoned, — or this liberal freedom is adopted in real earnest
— then it must be admitted that it is tantamount to RADICAL
APOSTASY AND DEFECTION FROM THE TRUTH. If a man wishes
to be a faithful Christian and at the same time to uphold the
liberal freedom of science, then he has never made clear to
himself what he wishes.

Ecce ancilla Domini. Thus spoke the Mother of the Lord,
when she heard the message that she was to receive the
Word of the eternal Father in her bosom. This word of
humility and submission was the condition under which she
could receive in herself the eternal Wisdom of the Father.

Behold, the Handmaid of the Lord! This word of humility
and submission to God must also be spoken by the creature's
intelligence, if it desires by faith to share in God's truth. Without humility of mind a faithful attachment to God is impossible;
pride and arrogance lead to desertion of God, faith, and truth.
Multum errant, quoniam superbi sunt, says *Augustine* of
the erring companions of his youth. Only if there is humility
does God's wisdom cross the threshold of the creature's mind,
only if there is humility can it be said of man: *Et verbum
caro factum est et habitat in nobis, plenum gratiae et veritatis.*

CHAPTER II

THE AUTHORITY OF FAITH AND THE FREE EXERCISE OF RESEARCH

Preliminary Remarks

WE must not stop at what we have just said in general about the relation between the freedom of research and the obligation to believe. We must go further into detail, in order to give a more exact explanation of how and where the authority of faith clashes with research and restrains it. Is it true that the believing scientist cannot move freely in his research, that there are barriers on all sides which he may not overstep? Is it true that the Church may prescribe for the Catholic scientist what he is allowed to defend and approve, what he ought to refute and reprove, suppress or advocate, so that his eyes must ever be turned towards Rome, to inquire and ascertain what might there be approved? And what a chain of proscriptions of free thinking is attached to the name of Rome! Index, Syllabus, *Galileo* — link after link is added to this chain of miserable slavery!

We shall say something more about this chain later on. First we must consider the principal question: Where and how do faith and science come in contact? And what we are going to say we shall condense into four points. Thus freedom of science will be more precisely defined; it will be shown what freedom revelation, and especially the guardian of revelation, the Church, offers to science: there can be no doubt that its natural freedom of exercise must be left to science intact.

We shall deal in the first place with the PROFANE SCIENCES, and, at least for the present, leave aside the discussion of theology, since it is clear that theology, being the science of faith, must assume a peculiar position in regard to the authority of faith: theology, moreover, is a special mark for attack; accordingly we shall deal with it particularly later on. However, the principles to be cited, being of a general nature, refer also to the science of faith, and for this reason we shall have occasion to refer to them.

1. *Authority of Faith and Private Authority*

We often meet with the most inconceivable notions. We are told quite seriously that the Church teaches, and that the Catholic has therefore to believe, that the earth is a flat disc surrounded by the sea, as the ancients believed; above it is a vault, below it hell-fire; that the earth stands still and the sun and stars revolve about it, just as *Ptolemy* of Egypt taught; that God created the whole world just as it is now in exactly six days of twenty-four hours each; that He made the sun and moon, just as they are now illuminating the skies; that the strata, just as they now look when bared by the geologist's hammer, even the coal-fields and petrified saurians and fossils — all were made, just as they now are, well nigh six thousand years ago. The Scriptures teach this, the Fathers of old and the theologians believe this: and that is where the Catholic must get his science. And then they are astonished, and consider dogma retreating before science, when they see other notions prevailing, when they see Catholic scientists defend without prejudice the evolution of the solar system, and even the system of the whole universe, from some primitive matter, or assume an organic evolution, as far as science supports it (cf. *Braun,* Ueber Kosmologie u. Standpunkt christlich. Wiss., 2d ed., 1906, etc.). They would be still more astonished perhaps to learn that similar ideas had long ago been proposed by *St. Augustine* and *St. Thomas* (cf. Summa c. G. l. 3, c. 77; *Knabenbauer,* in Stimmen a. M. Laach xiii, 75 *seq.*).

A distinction must be made between the teaching of the Church and the private views of individuals, schools, or periods. Only the teaching of the Church is the obligatory standard of Christian and Catholic thought, not the opinion of individuals. Hence not everything that Catholic savants have held to be true belongs to the teaching of the Church. Only when theologians unanimously declare something to be contained in the deposit of revealed truth, or the teaching of the Church, — only then is their teaching authoritative; not because it is the teaching of theologians, but because it is contained in revelation or the teaching of the Church. Else the maxim holds good: *Tantum valet auctoritas, quantum argumenta.* Nor is all that which a former age found in Holy Scripture, therefore to be believed as revealed truth, to the exclusion of all other interpretations.

The foregoing may be elucidated by the examples given above. When Holy Writ describes in figurative language and Oriental, demonstrative style, how God created the heaven and earth, the sun and moon, the sea and its contents, it means to teach us religious truths: that God is the First Cause of everything, and hence that the sun and moon, for instance, are not uncreated deities, as the Egyptian believed them to be. The narrative need not be taken in a literal sense, as if God immediately formed everything in the exact condition as it now appears to us; it may be interpreted in the sense that God let the present condition of things gradually grow out of the forces and materials and plan of nature He created, the result of a lengthy evolution. When our Lord tells us in the gospel that His Father in heaven feeds the birds of the air and clothes the grass of the field, we know that this is to be understood as a mediate action of God, which He exercises through the instinct of animals and through natural forces which He created for the purpose. Now when former ages, reading the narrative of Genesis, generally understood an immediate creation of the world, because the knowledge of nature at the time did not admit of any other interpretation, it is by no means necessary to conclude from it that every other interpretation must be rejected as against the Bible, or that the Church herself has prescribed this literal interpretation as the only correct one. As is known, *St. Augustine,* the greatest Father of the Church, had another very liberal explanation of the Genesis narrative, and the Church has never censured him. (He taught that the whole world had been created at one time, and that the six days of the Mosaic narrative were the logical divisions of an account of the various orders of creatures.) And now the interpretations vary greatly. The passages in Scripture, in which, according to popular modes of expression, the sun is said to rise and set and revolve about the earth, the latter standing in the centre of the world — these, too, were interpreted literally in the days of the Fathers: there was no cause for interpreting them otherwise; but it was only due to defective knowledge of nature at the time. These temporary errors remained till corrected by research in the field of the natural sciences: had the discoveries been made sooner, the errors, too, would have disappeared sooner.

The Church knows, and the holy Fathers knew, that it is not the purpose of Holy Writ to teach profane sciences, but to instruct in faith and morals; if it speaks of other matters, it is but occasionally, and then in the idiom of common life, which is not the same as the scientific language of the specialist. Indeed, the Bible does not intend to give scientific instruction in such matters, nor could it have done so at a time when men were not ripe for such enlightenment.

Thus *St. Augustine* insists that the Spirit of God who spoke through the authors of Scripture did not intend to instruct men in matters which do not serve for salvation, and hence he objects to the Scriptures being taken literally in regard to such matters, because the Bible adapts itself to man's manner of speech: a distinction is to be made between letter and sense ("Multi multum disputant de iis rebus, quae majore prudentia nostri auctores omiserunt, ad beatam vitam non profuturas discentibus . . . Breviter dicendum est, . . . Spiritum Dei, qui per ipsos loquebatur, noluisse ita docere homines nulli saluti profuturas," De Gen. ad lit., II, 9, n. 20. Cf. De Gen. contra Manich. 1, 5, n. 3; 11, n. 17). He further cautions Bible students against putting their own interpretation upon obscure passages and then claiming it to be dogma, because one may easily go astray and thus make the Scriptures appear ridiculous. "In rebus obscuris atque a nostris oculis remotissimis, si qua inde scripta etiam divina legerimus, quae possint salva fide, qua imbuimur, alias atque alias parere sententias, in nullam earum nos praecipiti affirmatione proiciamus, ut si forte diligentius discussa veritas eam recte labefactaverit, corruamus, non pro sententia divinarum scripturarum, sed pro nosctra ita dimicantes, ut eam velimus scripturarum esse, quae nostra est" (De genesi ad lit. I, 18 n. 37). "Plerumque accidit, ut aliquid de terra, de coelo, de ceteris mundi huius elementis . . . etiam non christianus ita noverit, ut certissima ratione et experientia teneat. Turpe est autem nimis et perniciosum ac maxime cavendum, ut christianus de his rebus quasi secundum christianas literas loquentem ita delirare quilibet infidelis audiat, ut, quemadmodum dicitur, toto coelo errare conspiciens, risum tenere vix possit" (Ibid. I, 19 n. 39). Cf. also I, 21. *St. Thomas of Aquin* also expresses himself in this sense: " Multum autem nocet, talia, quae ad pietatis doctrinam non spectant, vel asserere vel negare, quasi pertinentia ad sacram doctrinam . . . Unde mihi videtur tutius esse, ut haec, quae philosophi communius senserunt et nostrae fidei non repugnant, neque sic esse asserenda ut dogmata fidei, licet aliquando sub nomine philosophorum introducantur, neque sic esse neganda tamquam fidei contraria, ne sapientibus huius mundi contemnendi doctrinam fidei occasio praebeatur " (Opusc. X. ad Jo. Vercel. Proem.).

The doctrine of the CHURCH concurs with this, as laid down in numerous documents, many of them quoting the above-mentioned words of *St. Augustine.* It also insists that the interpretation of the Fathers be only taken as a standard of the Church's explanation of the meaning of Scripture when they are unanimous on the meaning of a passage relating to faith and morals; but not to other things (cf. Encycl. Providentissimus, Denz. 10 ed., n. 1947, 1944; Conc. Trid., sess. IV., Conc. Vat. sess. III., c. 2, Denz. nn. 786, 1788).

Now if one simply opens Holy Scripture, takes up some passage at random, explains it in its most literal sense, and then insists that this is the evident meaning, and goes on to assert with the same insistence that this is the interpretation of the Church, and a part of the faith of Catholics in regard to the natural sciences, then of course it is very easy to make out contradictions between faith and science: but such efforts cannot claim to be scientific. It is not necessary to know theology and the principles of Catholic exegesis; but it is not proper that those who are ignorant of these matters pass judgment on them, not even in the name of objective research.

Hence we may easily see what we should think of a writer who asserts that the examination of the Christian-Catholic idea of the world leads to the following results: " The Books of Moses, inspired by divine revelation, are the golden key to the understanding of the whole history of creation. Other Scriptural passages of the Old and New Testaments, the writings of the Fathers, etc., are to be considered as supplementary to these. According to these authorities the earth is a flat disc, surrounded by the sea. Above it arches the firmament of heaven, with its great lights for day and night. Below it are purgatory and hell. All this is not the gradual outgrowth of lengthy evolution, but was created by God out of nothing in a few days, about six thousand years ago, of which four thousand are reckoned before Christ and two thousand after Christ. Although modern science has long since established that the Biblical narrative is of no worth, nothing but an imperfect reproduction of older myths, the Catholic Church continues to teach it literally to this very day, spreading it broadcast by thousands and thousands of catechisms, and insisting on it being learned as a part of religious instruction in all schools, and to be accepted as the revealed truth" (*L. Wahrmund*, Katholische Weltanschauung und freie Wissenschaft, 1908, p. 14. The scientific value of this work has been considered by *L. Fonck*, Katholische Weltansch).

"Clericalism," we are told, "stands on a rigidly fixed view of the world, corresponding in part to the childhood of mankind, to the dawning of civilization. . . . Philosophy, built upon the results of progress, since it is unceasingly forcing its way ahead, cannot remain in accord with the notions belonging to a remote past, partly to Babylonian and Egyptian civilization, partly to the thought of nomadic times." It is then pointed out how this view of the world on which clericalism, that is, the Catholic Church, is based, has already been overthrown in many instances. "The geocentric position, the doctrine of our earth being the centre and man the ultimate aim of the universe, must needs be abandoned by the world of scientists, in view of the new system of Copernicus; the doctrine also of the earth being a disc must be abandoned in consequence of the voyage of Columbus, and subsequent discoveries, which make it certain that the earth is a globe" (Prof. *K. Menger*, Die Eroberung der Universitaeten. Neue Freie Presse, Nov. 24, 1907). It is surprising what little knowledge suffices to warrant writing about theological matters in the name of "objective research."

These passages, in regard to their scientific contents and manner, recall vividly an American work that appeared some time ago, and reached many editions. It is entitled, "A History of the Conflict Between Religion and Science," by *J. W. Draper*. The book was answered by a competent authority, *De Smedt*, S. J., "L'Eglise et la Science," 1877.

It seems *Draper's* arguments have since become a pattern for many. He, too, maintains that Holy Writ has always been declared by the Church and the Fathers to be a source of profane science. This, he states, is true especially of *St. Augustine*. We read: "The book of Genesis . . . also in a philosophical point of view became the grand authority of Patristic science. Astronomy, geology, geography, anthropology, chronology, and indeed all the various departments of human knowledge, were made to conform to it. . . . The doctrines of *St. Augustine* have had the effect of thus placing theology in antagonism with science. . . ." "No one did more than this Father to bring science and religion into antagonism; it was mainly he who diverted the Bible from its true office — a guide to purity of life — and placed it in the perilous position of being the arbiter of human knowledge. . . ." "What, then, is that sacred, that revealed science, declared by the Fathers to be the sum of all knowledge? . . . As to the earth, it affirmed that it is a flat surface, over which the sky is spread like a dome. In this the sun and moon and stars move, so that they may give light by day and by night to man. . . . Above the sky or firmament is heaven; in the dark and fiery space beneath the earth is hell. . . ." (pp. 57–63).

By reading again what we said above, especially the urgent admonitions of *St. Augustine* not to look upon the Scriptures as a text-book of profane science, one will be able to appreciate the scientific quality of the book in question.

The fancy of this writer has distorted Christianity and the Church into a monster that has nothing more important to do than to tread down and crush science and civilization. A few examples will suffice to show how he proves the CONTRADICTIONS BETWEEN FAITH AND SCIENCE. The Christian religion teaches that man is subject to death as a penalty for original sin: prior to that sin death had no power over Adam and Eve. It is claimed that this is a contradiction of science. But how? Long before Adam, thousands of animals and plants had died, the author asserts. " The doctrine declared to be orthodox by ecclesiastical authority is overthrown by the unquestionable discoveries of modern science. Long before a human being had appeared on earth millions of individuals, nay, more, thousands of species and even genera had died " (p. 57). The author has completely missed the point. The matter in question is not the death of animals and plants, but the death of man. The infallibility of the Pope is refuted by the fact that he failed to foresee the result of the war between France and Germany. " Notwithstanding his infallibility, which implies omniscience, His Holiness did not foresee the issue of the Franco-Prussian war " (p. 352, also p. 362).

How high his historical statements are to be rated is shown by the assertion that *Cyril of Alexandria* had much to do with the introduction of the worship of the Virgin Mary (p. 55) ; that auricular confession was introduced by the Fourth Lateran Council in 1215 (p. 208). He asks when the idea originated that the Pentateuch was written by Moses under divine inspiration, and he finds that " not until after the second century [of the Christian era] was there any such extravagant demand on human credulity " (p. 220). It would seem incredible that any one could write such stuff.

The author says in his preface: " I had also devoted much attention to the experimental investigation of natural phenomena, and had published many well-known memoirs on such subjects. And perhaps no one can give himself to these pursuits, and spend a large part of his life in the public teaching of science, without partaking of that love of impartiality and truth which philosophy incites " (VIII–IX). We do not care to argue with the author about his experience in experimental research, nor about his love for the truth, but he himself has shown superabundantly that they have not sufficed to keep him clear from scientific shallowness and the grossest blunders. Nevertheless, it seems that his scientific ability obtained for him in the consideration of many the weight of an authority. *Haeckel*, in his " Weltraetsel," refers repeatedly to the book, and recommends " its truthful statements and excellent discussion " to his readers (Weltraetsel, 17. Kap., Wissenschaft u. Christentum).

Such is the fashion in which contradictions between faith and science, and the Church's hostility towards scientific research, are proved.

The result is that we must distinguish clearly between dogmas of faith and private opinions or interpretations. Of course it may frequently happen, and has happened, that the Christian savant is too timorous, and looks askance at the discoveries of science, and even thinks he ought to resist them, because he is afraid that religious truth might be opposed by them. Nor can it be said that this timidity is altogether without excuse, for there was hardly one scientific discovery of the nineteenth century that was not immediately grasped and exploited by eager enemies of the Christian religion. Too often has science been made the menial of infidelity, and the assertion has been untiringly repeated that science and faith cannot agree. No wonder, then, that timid souls become suspicious, that they are prone to resist the whole theory of evolution in a lump, instead of trying to distinguish between what is of scientific value in it, and what is misused for the purpose of denying creation.

Nevertheless, such narrow-mindedness is strongly to be censured. It has often caused the reproach, that Catholics lack the freedom to admit scientific discoveries. They forget the wise admonition of the prince of mediæval theologians, that it were advisable, in regard to scientific views which have nothing to do with religion, neither to set them down as truths of faith, nor either to reject them as contrary to faith lest occasion be given to think contemptuously of the faith. As long as men are and men think, narrow-mindedness will never be lacking. Hence if the believing scientist wants to know whether he is running counter to faith in any particular, he has to ascertain from theological text-books what the Church declares to belong to faith, what explanation of Holy Scripture is unconditionally binding, and not what is the individual opinion of theologians, much less what some pious nurse is telling the little ones.

This is the first rule concerning the relation between faith and science: it states what the scientist is *not* tied down to.

2. *Science Retains its Method of Research*

But when and how may the scientist be restricted? Here we come to the second point: the directions which faith may give to the profane sciences are in themselves not of a positive but of a NEGATIVE KIND; revelation and Church cannot tell the scientist what he is to assert or defend in the field of the profane sciences, but only what propositions he must AVOID. Thus every science is left free to pursue its own method of research. It is not difficult to understand this.

Faith draws from divine revelation; profane sciences, as such, do not draw from divine revelation, but only from experience and reason. Philosophy would cease to be philosophy and become theology did it demonstrate the immortality of the soul by revelation. The anthropologist would cease to be an anthropologist and become a theologian if he would attempt to prove the common origin of mankind by Holy Scripture.

In other words, the profane sciences are distinguished from faith and theology by their formal object, by the end they have in view, by the scientific method with which they handle their subject. Theology, of course, uses revelation extensively; and in this it differs from the other sciences. Hence faith cannot command the anthropologist to defend also in profane science the common origin of the human race from Adam and Eve, because it is held to be a revealed truth. He must say: I believe as a Christian that this is true, established by divine revelation, and no science will ever prove the contrary; but whether I can positively defend this fact as resulting from anthropology, depends on my ability to corroborate it by the methods of this science, that is by the testimony of profane history. And just as little could the historian be required to obtain historical results of which he cannot produce the evidence according to his method.

Therefore faith can only tell the profane scientist that he must not assert anything which is held by faith to be erroneous; that it is false to say there is nothing but force and matter, that the human soul ends in death, or that the various families of the human race have not a common origin. As soon as the scientist knows by faith that a thing is false, he is bound to refrain from asserting it: bound in the first place by the duty to believe, but also by the principles of his own science, which is to find not error, but truth, which forbids to assert what has been proved to be erroneous. Perhaps his own means will not enable him to prove the truth independently of revelation; then from the standpoint of his science he must say, *Non liquet*.

The position of the Catholic Church agrees with these principles. She knows, and emphasizes that science has its own method, and hence a natural right and freedom to proceed in its own field according to its method. The Church rejects but one kind of freedom, viz., the freedom to propound a doctrine proved by faith to be erroneous. "The Church by no means forbids these disciplines to use in their own field their own principles and method," declares the Vatican Council. "But, while acknowledging this lawful freedom, the Church takes care to prevent them from taking up errors in opposition to divine teaching, or from creating confusion by transgressing their limits and invading the realm of faith " (Vat. sess. III, ch. 4. Cf. also the letter of *Pius IX.*, "Gravissimas," of Dec. 11, 1862, to the Archbishop of Munich, Denz. n. 1666, *seq.*).

These few remarks show the lack of intelligence in the charge that " Catholic philosophy starts from dogmas and revelation," or that the Church would dictate to scientists everything they should teach; that, according to its principles it could claim the right " to impose upon a physicist of *Zeppelin's* era the task of proving the Ascension of Christ or the Assumption of Mary by aërostatic rules." This is simply gross ignorance or misrepresentation.

3. *Restraint Only in the Province of Revelation*

In what matters may faith and the Church be a guide to research in this negative sense? In all fields, or only some? Evidently only in their own sphere. But to the sphere of faith belongs only what is contained in divine revelation, viz., the truths of RELIGION AND MORALITY, as laid down in Scripture and tradition, the truths of God and His work of salvation, of man and his way to his eternal destiny, of the means of grace, and of the Church. Whatever lies outside of that sphere does not belong to the province of faith. This is true also of the teaching authority of the Church. The purpose of the Church is to guard faithfully the treasure of divine revelation and to transmit it in an authoritative manner to mankind; hence her authority in teaching is confined to what is contained in revelation, and what is necessary for an efficient custody and transmission of it to mankind. Hence she may declare certain truths as revealed, she may reject opposing errors, she may condemn books offensive to faith, she may approve or reject systems of ethics. But she cannot set up wholly new religious truths or revelations. *Depositum custodi* — this is the purpose of the Church. Still less are matters of an entirely profane nature subject to the teaching authority of the Church. Profane sciences can therefore receive direction from faith only in those matters which at the same time belong to the province of faith.

What follows from this? It follows that ALMOST ALL THE PROFANE SCIENCES ARE INCAPABLE OF BEING INSTRUCTED OR RESTRICTED BY FAITH, because their province lies outside that of faith, and does not come in touch with it: they are left to themselves to correct their errors. When the astronomer in his observatory watches the movements of the planets, and bases thereon his mathematical calculations, when the physicist or chemist in his laboratory observes the laws of nature or makes new discoveries, when the pathologist studies the symptoms of diseases in organisms, no warning voice interrupts their work of study. Of course when they deny the creation, the possibility of miracles, then they conflict with faith; but then they have ceased to be naturalists, they have become philosophers. When the botanist or zoölogist in his laboratory is studying plants and animals and collecting his specimens, when the palæontologist is excavating and examining his fossils, they enjoy perfect freedom: all this has nothing directly to do with faith. And there is no warning sign set up for the geographer or geologist when settling the orographical or hydrographical conditions of countries or measuring geological strata; no danger signal disturbs the linguist in establishing the grammar of unknown languages, nor the archæologist or the historian, when they discover new documents or decipher inscriptions. Nor does anybody interrupt the mathematician in his calculations.

What unnecessary worry, then, for the representatives of mathematics, geology, palæontology, and chemistry to write burning protests against the fetters of dogma in the interest of their scientific activity! And it is superfluous worry for professors of the technical arts to get excited by imagining that electricity and steam must be treated according to ecclesiastical precepts. Nor is there need of emphasizing the statement that there cannot be a Catholic chemistry, geography, or mathematics — it is self-evident.

Hence almost the entire province of the profane sciences, which are the pride of our age and occupy the foremost position in our universities, with their laboratories, institutes and observatories and meteorological stations, are free and perfectly undisturbed by faith. If accordingly any one should be of the opinion that the Christian-minded scientist were hindered in his scientific research, he would have to consider him an unhampered investigator at least in this vast field.

Most in touch with faith comes PHILOSOPHY. Not in the vast field of logic, of empirical psychology, in questions concerning the essence of bodies and their forces, in matters of mere history of philosophy; but in questions of views of the world and life, in metaphysics and ethics, it does. These, the highest questions, bearing on the direction and pursuit of human life, matters that most occupy the human mind, are at the same time subjects of revelation; God Himself has deigned to teach the truth in these matters, to make them safe for all time against the error of the mind of man. Here philosophers encounter danger-signals. They hear, what their reason even tells them, that it is erroneous to think there is no world of spirits, no God above nature, no immortality, no life hereafter, no providence. Nor could one say that philosophy is the loser by being kept from error which endangers human life. Nowhere are errors so apt to occur as in questions which are outside the sphere of immediate experience; nowhere are self-deceptions more common than there, where disposition and character continually influence the mind.

A modern representative of philosophy, *E. Adickes,* writes as follows: " In the course of this history (of metaphysics) there have been given long since all the principal answers that are at all possible to all metaphysical questions. The building up of metaphysical systems can and will proceed, nevertheless, and their multiplicity will remain. . . . Of course, progress will not be gained thereby: results will not gain in certainty, contradictions and mysteries do not diminish."

" If the greatest of the ancient Greek natural scientists, physicians, and geographers should rise again they would be amazed at the progress made in their sciences; like beginners they would sit at the feet of teachers of our day, they would lack the most elementary ideas; they would first have to learn what every grammar-school boy knows, and much of what they once considered achievements would be disclosed to them as deception or mere hypothesis. On the other hand a *Plato*, an *Aristotle*, a *Zeno* or *Epicurus*, might readily take part in our discussions about God and the soul, about virtue and immortality. And they could safely use their old weapons, the keenness of which has suffered but little from the rust of time and the attacks of opponents. They would be astonished at the little progress made, so that now, after two thousand years, the same answers are given to the same questions" (Charakter und Weltanschauung, 1905, p. 24).

A science which must make such a confession has no reason to reject with haughty self-confidence the intimations of a divine revelation.

The SCIENCE OF HISTORY again has not the duty of praising everything that has happened within the Catholic Church or else to repress it; no, only the truth is desired. But it must not start out with the assumption that God's influence in the world, a divine revelation, miracles, and a supernatural guidance of the Church, are impossible; nor must it attempt to construe history according to that assumption. Hence it must not undertake to explain the religion of the Jewish nation, or the origin of Christianity, by unconditionally ignoring everything supernatural, and attempting to eliminate it by prejudiced research and by means of natural factors, whether they be called Babylonic myths or Greek philosophy or anything else; it must not impugn the credibility of the Gospel, claiming that reports of miracles must be false; it must not write the history of the Church and deliberately ignore its supernatural character, as if it were the violent struggle of a federation of priests for universal rule. Assured results undoubtedly are arrived at in history less frequently than in other sciences; it offers full play to suppositions, hypotheses, constructive fancy, the influence of ideas inculcated by education and personal views of the world, especially when summing up facts. Hence here more than anywhere else must moral character and unselfish love of the truth stand higher than the desire for freedom.

The HISTORY OF RELIGION and ANTHROPOLOGY must be forbidden to assume that the human mind is but a product of animal evolution, that therefore religion and morality, family and state life, reason and language, and the entire intellectual and social life have necessarily evolved from the first stages of animal life. If we add that JURISPRUDENCE in its highest principles comes in touch with faith, and that it also must not dispute the divine right of the Church, we have mentioned the most important sciences and instances in which the investigator must take faith into consideration.

We now understand in what sense we may rightly speak of a " CHRISTIAN PHILOSOPHY AND SCIENCE " or of a " CATHOLIC SCIENCE OF HISTORY." Surely not in this sense that philosophy and history have to draw their results from Holy Scripture or from the dogmatical decisions of the Church; nor in the sense that they have to make positive defence for everything that the Church finds it necessary to prescribe. The sense is merely this: they guide themselves by faith, as we said above, by refraining from propositions and presumptions proved by faith to be false. In a large measure this is also the meaning of the often-misrepresented term, CATHOLIC UNIVERSITY. In the reverse sense we may speak of a liberal science. It is that science which in the field of philosophy and religion guides itself by the principles of liberalism and the principle of liberal freedom and the rejection of faith. But to speak of a Catholic, Protestant, Liberal chemistry or mathematics, has no sense at all, because these disciplines, like most other profane sciences, have no direct connection with Catholicism, Protestantism, or Liberalism.

That we have stated correctly the ATTITUDE OF THE CATHOLIC CHURCH is evidenced by more than one official document. In the decree of the Holy Office of July 3, 1907, the so-called Syllabus of *Pius X.*, the following (5.) proposition is condemned: " Inasmuch as the treasure of faith contains only revealed truths, it does not behoove the Church under any consideration to pass judgment on the assertions made by human sciences." Similarly was the proposition (14), likewise condemned in the Syllabus of *Pius IX.*: " Philosophy must be pursued without any regard to supernatural revelation. "

These condemnations stirred up anger: " Now, " it was said, " the Church wants to subject the whole of human knowledge to her judgment: this is unbearable insolence." But what follows from these condemnations? The opposite truth asserted in them is this: the Church in one respect must pass judgment on the assertions made by human science, namely, in so far as they come in conflict with the doctrines of faith. The only freedom rejected by the Council is the freedom to contradict revealed truth: it must not be held " that human science may be pursued with freedom, that its assertions can be considered true and must not be rejected by the Church even if they contradict a revealed doctrine " (sess. III, ch. 4, can. 2). The Church does not want to judge on matters of profane science; but she claims the right, due to her as guardian appointed for the preservation of the pure faith, to raise her warning voice when, for instance, natural science transgresses its limits and trespasses on the province of religion by denying the creation of the world. It is but self-defence against an attack upon her inviolable domain. But she does not claim the authority to sit in judgment upon the results of astro-physics, upon the atom-hypothesis, or its opposite; or on the acceptance of a theory about ions or earthquakes.

Another question may be touched upon : Is the CATHOLIC HISTORIAN free to proceed steadily in the search after historic truth, even where he discovers facts which do not reflect honour on his Church? And where it is a question of uncertain, private revelation, of doubtfulness of relics and other sacred objects exposed for public worship, may he proceed undisturbed with his critical research, or is he restrained by ecclesiastical authority?

Should the Catholic meet with dark passages in the history of his Church, then every well-meaning observer will demand that he display in the treatment of such matters a pious forbearance for his Church. His respect for her will dictate this. Unsparing criticism and hunting for blemishes and shadows must be excluded. But he cannot on this account be bound to pass by the unpleasant facts he may meet in his researches, or to cloak or deny them against his better knowledge. He knows that the divinity of his Church shows itself to best advantage just because, notwithstanding many weaknesses and faults, past and present, she passes unvanquished and imperishable through all storms, — a token of the supernatural origin of her strength and power of endurance.

It was this very thought that moved *Leo XIII.* to open the Vatican Archives for freest research to friend and enemy, — the clearest proof that could possibly be given that the Church does not fear historical truth. In his letter of admonition, of August 18, 1883, urging the fostering of historiography, the same Pope gives the following rules for the Catholic scientist : " The first law of history is that it must not say anything false ; the second, that it must not be afraid of saying the truth, lest a suspicion of partiality and unfairness arise." An excellent example of the application of these rules is found in *L. v. Pastor's* " History of the Popes," especially in what he says about *Alexander VI.* and *Leo X.*

In his historical investigation of private revelations, such as those of *St. Gertrude, St. Mechtild, Bl. Juliana of Liège,* or of relics and objects of veneration, the historian is likewise not restricted by Church-direction. Having merely the task of preserving the treasure of the faith received from Christ and the Apostles, the Church in her function as Teacher never vouches for the divine origin of new, private revelations, nor for the accuracy of pious traditions of another kind. True, she decides authoritatively whether private revelations contain anything against faith and morals, but she decides nothing more. If she accepts such revelations or traditions as genuine, she claims for the facts in question only that human faith which corresponds to their historical proof.

This is clearly stated by the recent encyclical *Pascendi:* " In judging of pious traditions, the following must be kept in mind: the Church employs such prudence in treating of these matters that she does not allow such traditions to be written about except with great precaution and only after making the declarations required by *Urban VIII.;* and even then, after this has been properly done, the Church by no means asserts the truth of the private revelation or of the tradition, but merely permits them to be believed, provided there be sufficient human reasons. It was in this sense that the Sacred Congregation of Rites declared thirty-one years ago: ' These apparitions are neither approved nor condemned by the Holy See; it merely permits them to be believed in a natural way, provided the tradition on which they rest be corroborated by credible testimonies and documents.' Whoever follows this maxim is safe. The veneration of such things is always conditional, it is only relative, and on the condition that the tradition be true. In so far only is the veneration absolute as it relates to the Saint to whom the veneration is paid. The same applies to the veneration of relics." (*Benedict XIV.* says of private revelations: " Praedictis revelationibus etsi *approbatis,* non debere nec posse a nobis adhiberi assensum fidei catholicae, sed tantum fidei humanae juxta regulas prudentiae, juxta quas praedictae revelationes sunt probabiles et pie credibiles." De Serv. Dei beatificatione, III, c. ult. n. 15).

Hence the historian is free to investigate such traditions critically, provided, of course, that he does not violate the reverence due to sacred things.

4. *Infallible and Non-Infallible Teachings*

Now to consider a last point.   Does it not rest entirely with
the pleasure of ecclesiastical authority, as would seem from what
has been said above, to suppress at any time the results, or at
least the hypotheses, of scientific research by pointing to puta-
tive truths of faith presumed to be in opposition?   Then, of
course, the scientist would be at the mercy of a zealous ecclesiastical authority.   Or will it perhaps be said that this authority
is infallible in its every decision?   Think of *Galileo,* of the
interdict against the Copernican view of the world, and you will
be able fully to appreciate the danger alluded to!

We shall later on return to the famous case of *Galileo.*   For
the present we only call attention to a distinction which must
not be overlooked, the distinction between infallible teachings
and those that are not infallible.[1]

According to Catholic teaching, the universal teaching body of
the Church, when declaring unanimously to be an object of
faith something relating to faith and morals, is endowed with
INFALLIBILITY, and also when in its daily practice of the faith
it unanimously professes a doctrine to be a truth of faith.   This
infallibility is also possessed by the Pope alone when, acting in
his capacity as Supreme Teacher of the Church in matters of
faith and morals, he intends to give a permanent decision for the
whole Church (ex cathedra).

Besides these infallible teachings there are also NON-INFALLI-
BLE teachings, and they are the more frequent.   Such are, first
of all, the ordinary doctrinal utterances of the Pope himself in
his regular supervision of the teaching of doctrine: these in-
structions and declarations are of a lower kind than those per-

---

[1] Infallible teachings are often also called dogmas.   But they are not
always dogmas in the strict sense.   In the strict sense dogmas are such
truths as are contained in divine revelation, and are proclaimed by the
infallible teaching authority of the Church to be believed as such by
the faithful.   In a broader sense those tenets are often called dogmas
which are presented by revelation or by the Church as infallible truths.
In this sense all teachings of faith clearly found in Holy Scripture are
dogmas, even if not declared by the Church.   In this sense Protestants,
too, believe in revealed dogmas.

emptory ones that are pronounced ex cathedra: he is infallible only in the utterance of these ultimate, supreme decisions, the chief bulwark, as it were, erected against the floods of error. Decisions ex cathedra are very rare. Encyclical letters, too, are, as a rule, not infallible. It is self-evident that the theological opinions and statements of the Pope as a private person, not as Supreme Head of the Church, do not belong here at all. They have no official character and are in no way binding.

Among decisions that are not infallible are further included, in various degrees, the doctrinal utterances of Bishops, of particular synods, and especially those of the Roman Congregations. The latter are bodies of Cardinals, delegated by the Head of the Church, as highest Papal boards, to co-operate with him in the various offices of administration. Of these, the Congregation of the Holy Office and that of the Index may also render decisions on doctrinal questions. Although the Congregations act by virtue of their delegation from the Pope, and publish their decrees with his consent, the decisions are not decisions of the Pope himself, but remain decisions of the Cardinals. Much less can the infallibility of the Pope pass over to them: it is his personal prerogative, the aid of the Holy Ghost is promised to him, and protects his judgments under certain conditions against error.

But the Catholic owes submission also to the non-infallible teachings; and not only an outer submission, a reverent silence, that offends not either verbally or in writing against the decision rendered, but he owes also his inner assent. But it cannot be that unconditional inner assent which he owes to the infallible decision, for this he holds to be irrevocably certain; nor is his assent to non-infallible decisions a real act of faith. He is not given any unconditional guarantee of the truth. An error is, of course, most unlikely, but not absolutely impossible. Hence the faithful Catholic should always be ready to accept such decisions in as far as they are warranted by recognized truth. This applies to all kinds of doctrinal teaching, but of course in different ways, corresponding to the degree of authority, — for instance, Papal decisions are of higher authority than those of the Congregations, — yet it applies also to the doctrinal decisions of the Congregations, because they are the ordinary teaching organs of the Church.

When the Congregation of the Index, 1857, had forbidden the works of *Guenther* and many thought they could evade the decision, *Pius IX.* wrote, June 15, to the Archbishop of Cologne: "The decree is so far-reaching that nobody may think himself free not to hold what we have confirmed." Similar was what the Pope had written to the Archbishop of Mecheln after the condemnation of the ontological errors of *Ubagh.* The Motu proprio of *Pius X.* of November 8, 1907, speaks similarly of the obligation of submission to the decisions of the Papal Biblical Commission relating to doctrines, and to the decrees of Congregations when approved by the Pope. (Cf. also the Syllabus of Pius IX., sent. 22.)

Theologians agree that this requisite internal assent is not the same as irrevocable assent. This was also declared by *Pius IX.* in his letter to the Archbishop of Munich-Freising, saying that this inner submission is by no means faith; and no theologian will ascribe infallibility to a mere congregational decree. (See on this point: *e. g. Grisar,* Galileistudien, 1882, 171 *seq.* Cr. *Pesch,* Theol. Zeitfragen, Erste Folge, 1900, III. *Egger,* Streiflichter ueber die freiere Bibelforschung, 1889.)

It would be erroneous to think that only in recent times, after the embarrassment caused by the regrettable *Galileo* decision the subtle distinction had been invented that congregational decisions are not binding on Catholics with absolute force. This was taught by theologians long before the *Galileo* case caused any excitement. In this sense the celebrated writer on Moral Theology, *Lacroix,* said: "The declarations of none of these Congregations are infallible. . . . No infallibility is promised to the Congregation in so far as it is viewed as separate from the Pope" (Theologia Moralis, 1729, I, n. 215). *Raccioli,* soon after the *Galileo* trial, wrote: "The Holy Congregation of Cardinals as separate from the Pope cannot give to any proposition the proper authority of faith." And he adds: "There being extant no decision of the Pope, or of a Council directed and confirmed by him, the proposition of the sun moving and the earth standing still cannot on the strength of a congregational decree be considered a truth that must be believed" (Almagestum novum, 1651, I, 52).

The obligation to give interior assent also to an authority not infallible, cannot seem strange if this authority offers a guarantee for the truth commensurate to the assent demanded. We certainly ask of a child to receive the instruction from his parent and teacher with internal assent, so far as the latter does not run counter to its instinct for the truth, else the education of the child and the needful influence over its intellectual life would be impossible. Upon the Church has been bestowed by her divine Founder the task of guiding the faithful authoritatively in the educational matters committed to the Church, and not only in their youth but throughout their lives. This guidance in religion and morality would be impossible if the faithful could constantly deny their internal assent to the instruction of the Church, which is given generally in a form that is not infallible. The full power of the Church to teach with authority implies a corresponding duty of the faithful to assent to her teachings as far as this is possible. Does not the scientific specialist think himself obliged to accept a proposition on the strength of a certain authority, even if the latter's infallibilty is not established? He reads in his scientific periodical and finds in it the report of special researches made by a colleague. He cannot examine them over again, yet he accepts them because of the reliability of his colleague, in which he sees the guarantee of truth. Likewise, only more so, does the Catholic owe it to his sense of truth to impose upon himself an assent even where the representatives of the teaching authority of the Church are not endowed in their decision with the gift of infallibility. For he knows that even in such teachings the Church is commonly under the guidance of the Holy Ghost, who will seldom tolerate error. He is promised to the teaching Church for the safe guidance of the faithful; these declarations are, however, the ordinary doctrinal utterances of that ecclesiastical office. And the Holy Ghost cannot permit that the teaching authority should by a wrong decision forfeit the confidence it enjoys.

Moreover, this authority ranks very high even when looked at from a purely human standpoint. Those who are invested with it are mostly men of great learning, competent to give such doctrinal decisions by virtue of their experience and position, and learned advisers are at their side. They are guided by the tradition and wisdom of a universal Church, which measures its history by thousands of years; the decisions, too, are for the most part but the application or repetition of previous doctrinal utterances. Besides, there is the hesitating caution which advances to a decision only after long deliberations, and in undemonstrated matters usually refrains from decision; a caution which has increased still more in recent times, since so

many subtle questions have arisen on the boundaries of science
and faith. It is also known that many inquisitive eyes are constantly turned on Rome, and a single wrong decision might entail most disagreeable consequences for friend and foe. The
pressure must be very great before a much-disputed question is
taken up at all.

Of course it is by no means impossible that difficulties may
pile up in such a way that an error may really be made. History
knows of such a case. But the very fact that the one case of
Galileo is always quoted, and, therefore, that in the long history
of the Congregations this is considered to be almost the only
case of importance, is a proof how carefully the Congregations
proceed, and that supernatural aid is granted them. An institution which in the course of its long existence had to reply to
innumerable questions and against which only one wrong decision of importance can be pointed out, must necessarily be
an exemplary institution. An institution so free from human
error must surely be guided by the Holy Ghost. Compare with
this the many cases in which science has had to correct itself,
had to abandon its long-championed propositions as untenable.

Thus, in a given case, the decision is not difficult for the
Catholic. On one side stand the representatives of a science
which has erred, very often, incomparably more frequently than
the ecclesiastical teaching authority, and which lacks the
special aid of God. On the other side is the ecclesiastical authority, which has almost never erred, and which
enjoys special divine aid; moreover, it examines into its questions with greater caution and care, because it has more to lose.
In addition it is almost invariably able to point to a large
number, and frequently the majority, of savants who indorse its
decisions, because these mostly concern disputed questions not
yet scientifically determined. Hence the Catholic will find
no difficulty in presuming that the decision is in accord with
the truth; the more so because, as a rule, he himself is unable
to examine scientifically both sides of the question.

Should any one, nevertheless, be clearly convinced, by substantial and valid reasons, that there has been prejudgment, then
he would not be any longer obliged to give it his interior

assent: truth before all else. It would be easy, too, by presenting reliable information to an authoritative quarter, to secure the triumph of the truth. However, in this case a man must be ever on his guard against the tendency to overrate his own arguments. In excitement he easily thinks himself to be certainly in the right, but when considering the matter quietly before God and his conscience, he will rarely come to the conclusion that it would be wise to set his judgment above the decision. In the case of *Galileo* the decision of the Congregation was by no means opposed by a clear conviction of the truth of the opposite.

Take, for instance, a more recent decision of the Congregation, forbidding craniotomy. It has often been denounced. The question was submitted to the Congregation of the Holy Office whether it were permissible to teach that craniotomy is allowable in case the mother cannot give birth to the child, and that both will have to die unless the child be killed and removed by a surgical operation. The Congregation answered twice in the negative, in May and August, 1889. Neither craniotomy, nor any operation implying the direct murder of the child or mother can be taught to be permissible. The reason on which the answers were based is that the direct murder of an innocent person in order to save human life is never allowable; and this applies to the murder of a child, which has as much right to its life as any other person. In the case of craniotomy we have the direct murder of the child. We, too, shall have to admit, if we judge according to the objective morality of the action, that the Congregation is in the right; though it may seem hard to let both mother and child die rather than take a life directly, we shall have to admit that it is more in accord with the sanctity of the moral law than the opposite, though the latter may seem preferable to medical practice. Viewed in the interest of truth and the purity of the moral law, it is gratifying to know that there is a court courageous enough to uphold this law always and everywhere, even when it becomes hard.

So much about assenting to doctrinal decisions that are not infallible.

In regard to INFALLIBLE decisions, the Catholic knows that there are certain truths which no result of science can contradict. To these decisions he owes unconditional submission, and he gives it with conviction: he knows the promise, " I am with you always, even unto the consummation of the world." New decisions of this kind are very rare. When the dogma of the Infallibility of the Pope was proclaimed in 1870, the fear was frequently expressed that the Head of the Roman Church would hasten to make the fullest use of this prerogative, by erecting theological barriers at all nooks and corners in the realm of thought. The fear did not come true; it was unfounded.

A Protestant scientist wrote recently: "Those who thought *Doellinger's* prediction of a prolific crop of dogmas would come true were disappointed. There has been no new dogma pronounced since 1870, although there were many pious opinions that certain circles would have been only too glad to see confirmed. On looking calmly at the dogma of infallibility it is seen that it was, after all, not so bad as had been feared during the first excitement" (*K. Holl*, Modernismus, 1908, p. 9, Religionsgesch. Volksbuecher, IV, 7, Heft).

We may get a good idea of the precaution taken prior to the proclamation of an infallible decision by perusing the History of the Vatican Council, published by *Granderath,* in three volumes. He describes the proceedings with conscientious objectiveness. He shows how minutely all questions had been previously studied, with all the available means of scientific investigation, and how minutely and freely they were discussed by the most venerable representatives of the Catholic world.

Cardinal *Gibbons,* Archbishop of Baltimore, gave his impressions of the Vatican Council as follows:

"I happened to be the youngest Bishop that attended the Council of the Vatican, and, while my youth and inexperience imposed on me a discreet silence among my elders, I do not remember to have missed a single session, and I was an attentive listener at all the debates. . . . I think I am not exaggerating when I say that the Council of the Vatican has been excelled by few, if any, deliberative assemblies, civil or ecclesiastical, that have ever met, whether we consider the *maturity* of years of its members, their *learning,* their *experience* and *piety,* or the widespread influence of the *Decrees* that they framed for the spiritual and moral welfare of the Christian Republic.

"The youngest Bishop in the Council was thirty-six years old. Fully three-fourths of the Prelates ranged between fifty-six and ninety years. The great majority, therefore, had grown gray in the service of their Divine Master. Several Fathers of the Church, bent with age, might be seen passing through St.

Peter's Basilica to the council chamber every morning, leaning
with one hand on their staff, the other resting on the shoulder
of their secretary.   One or two blind Bishops could be observed, guided by their servants, as they advanced to their posts
with tottering steps, determined to aid the Church in their declining years by the wisdom of their counsel, as they had consecrated to her their vigorous manhood by their Apostolic labours.

"But to the gravity of years the members of the Council generally united profound and varied learning. . . .

"They were men, too, of world-wide experience and close observation.   Each Bishop brought with him an intimate knowledge of the history of his country and of the religious, moral,
social, and political condition of the people among whom he lived.
One could learn more from an hour's interview with this living
encyclopædia of divines, who were a world in miniature, than
from a week's study of books. . . . The most ample liberty of
discussion prevailed in the Council.   This freedom the Holy
Father pledged at the opening of the synod, and the pledge was
religiously kept.   I can safely say that neither in the British
House of Commons, nor in the French Chambers, nor in the
German Reichstag, nor in our American Congress, would a
wider liberty of debate be tolerated than was granted in the
Vatican Council.   The presiding Cardinal exhibited a courtesy
of manner and a forbearance even in the heat of debate that was
worthy of all praise.   I do not think that he called a speaker
to order more than a dozen times during the eighty-nine ses-
sions, and then only in deference to the dissenting murmurs
or demands of some Bishops.   A Prelate representing the smallest diocese had the same rights that were accorded to the highest
dignitary in the Chamber.   There was no limit prescribed as
to the length of the speeches.   We may judge of the wide scope
of discussion from the single fact that the debate on the Infallibility of the Pope lasted two months, occupying twenty-five ses-
sions, and was participated in by one hundred and twenty-five
Prelates, not counting one hundred others who handed in written observations.   No stone was left unturned, no text of Sacred
Scripture, no passage in the writings of the Fathers, no page
of Ecclesiastical History bearing on the subject, escaped the

vigilant investigations of the Bishops, so that the whole truth of God might be brought to light. . . .

"The most important debate in the Council was that on the Infallibility of the Pope. It may be proper to observe here that the discussion was rather on the expediency or opportuneness of defining the dogma than on the intrinsic truth of the doctrine itself. The number of Prelates who questioned the claim of Papal Infallibility could be counted on the fingers of a single hand. Many of the speakers, indeed, impugned the dogma, not because they did not personally accept it, but with the view of pointing out the difficulties with which the teaching body of the Church would have to contend in vindicating it before the world. I have listened in the council chamber to far more subtle, more plausible, and more searching objections against this prerogative of the Pope than I have ever read or heard from the pen or tongue of the most learned and formidable Protestant assailant" (North American Review, April, 1894).

Obedience of Faith and Freedom of Action

In looking back at what has been said, we see the justice of the question: where is here any real injury to lawful freedom in thought and scientific research? In most of the profane sciences the scientist receives no directions from the authority of faith; he is altogether free, as long as he keeps within his province. In some matters he is given a list of errors to beware of: these are in the first place the great questions concerning views of the world and life, of which, after all, it is very difficult to obtain scientific knowledge. But here he knows, through the conviction he has of the truth of his faith, that he is offered the truth free from error and prejudice.

It is true, adhering to a religious authority implies restraint. But it is only the restraint of truth. Truth does not lose its claim upon the mind because it is offered to the latter by a supernatural authority; much less does the Creator lose the right to the tribute of homage of his rational creature; and this tribute is rendered by voluntary submission to the revealed truth. Upon the Church, however, has been laid the task of preserving unadulterated the legacy of her Founder from generation to generation. She is responsible before God and history for the faithful presentation of the most sacred inheritance of mankind. Therefore the Church must raise her voice when the puny thoughts of men, called science and progress, rise against the saving truth to disparage, to falsify, to annihilate it. IT IS NOT SCIENCE THE CHURCH OPPOSES, BUT ERROR; not truth, but the emancipation of the human mind from God's authority, an emancipation that is trying to hide its real self under the guise of scientific truth.

"The Church," says the Vatican Council (Sess. III, ch. 4), "having received with her apostolic office to teach, the obligation of preserving the legacy of the faith, has also the God-given right and duty to condemn what is falsely called science, ' lest any one be cheated by philosophy and vain deceit.' " That the denial of the faith is flippantly called science does not alter the case. What determines the attitude of the Church is not eagerness to rule, not a propensity to apply force to the mind, but loyalty to her vocation. If it is disagreeable for any superior to have to correct those under him, then it requires an heroic strength and courage to cry out time and again to the whole world and its leading minds, *Errastis,* you have erred! It requires heroism to reject, to oppose and condemn, time and again, propositions sailing under the flag of progress, light and enlightenment, in spite of the protest of those concerned, who denounce whatever opposes them as darkness and retrogression. How much easier it would be to fawn upon the pet ideas of the age, Neo-protestantism and Modernism, and thus to gain their approval, than to hear repeatedly the distressing words, "We will not have her to rule over us — *crucifige, crucifige!* "

But why not let SCIENCE CORRECT ITSELF? Why these violent condemnations and indictments? Science, by virtue of its instinct for the truth will by itself find the way back, when it has gone on the wrong track; only be patient. Science has in itself the cure for all its defects. Has it not already all by itself overcome numerous errors in the course of the centuries? Indeed, were there nothing at stake but scientific theories they might be readily left to themselves: the loss to mankind would not be great. But here there are more important issues at stake. The protection of the faith, of truths of the vastest importance for Christian life and the souls of men. And it is the duty of the Church to protect her charges from going astray, from dangers to salvation. How many thousands of them would suffer harm before it would please science to correct its heresies! It often takes a long time to pull down the idols placed upon pedestals, and then it may be only to erect another idol. How long will it take modern philosophy to agree that the will of man is free, that there is a substantial immortal soul, that a Creator of the world dwells above the heavens? Is the Church to wait till the men of science make up their minds to desist from denying the existence of a personal God, and to bow before the Creator of heaven and earth? Should she meanwhile look on calmly how such ruinous doctrines are pervading and penetrating society deeper and deeper? Souls cannot wait thus to suffer shipwreck. Finally, the duty to believe remains the same for all, for the scientist, too — he is not free to delay his assent until he has exhausted all his antagonistic scientific experiments.

To be sure, the scientist is restricted in so far as he is not allowed to pursue any and every hypothesis, regardless of the immutable truth; he may no longer follow every scientific fashion. But is this a real detriment to the human intellect and science? Has not every science to bear RESTRAINT FROM OTHER SCIENCES at all times? The adherent of *Darwin's* theory of natural selection needs a billion years for his slow evolution; but the geologist tells him that neither the formation of the earth's surface nor the strata or sub-strata have taken so long in formation — he corrects him. When the philosopher, drawing the logical deductions from his materialistic views of the world, assumes that the first living being sprang from lifeless matter, the naturalist informs him that this is contradicted by facts — there never has been a case of spontaneous generation. The naturalist is corrected by the better experiment of men of his profession, the scientific author is corrected by his critic. Hence if a man submits to the guidance of other men of his profession, if one science accepts direction from another science, without any one seeing any injury to freedom therein, why, then, should it be mental oppression for God's infallible wisdom to call out through His Church to the fallible human mind: this is error, I declare it so? When the guide-post points out to the traveller that he is on the wrong way, will the wanderer indignantly resent the correction as an interference with his freedom of action? Is the railing along the steep precipice, to guard against falling down, an interference with liberty? Is the lighthouse, warning the sailor of cliffs and shoals, any interference with his freedom?

Generally those who oppose the Christian and Catholic duty to believe use the following argument: Where there is restraint and dependence there is no freedom; the Christian, and especially the Catholic, is restrained and dependent; hence he is not free: consequently he has no true science, because there can be no true science without freedom. In the same way it may be argued: The civilized nation is restrained in various ways by the civil order, therefore it is not free. The careful writer of scientific works is tied down on all sides by the rules of logic, by the dictates of good style, by scientific usages: hence he is not free.

Let us not lose sight of the question. It cannot be denied that the man who does not bother about faith has a greater outer freedom than the man who does. We speak purposely of outer freedom. It is quite another question, where real internal freedom exists, *i. e.,* freedom from the fetters of one's own inclinations and prejudices, — in the religiously disciplined mind, or in the other. Here we speak of inner freedom. Obviously it is greater in the former. The deer in the forest is freer in his movements than the cautious mountain-climber, who keeps to marked roads and paths, so as to journey safely, yet the latter is not without freedom. Nor will any one deny that the Australian bushman enjoys a greater outer freedom than the civilized white, restrained by laws, by rules and regulations, by standards of decency. And the busy writer of many things and everything, who in his writing never pays any attention to logic, to scientific form, to style and tact, has more freedom than one who strictly conforms to all these.

EVERY CIVILIZATION, CULTURE, AND EDUCATION IMPLIES RESTRICTION OF FREEDOM, and the more the rejection of dependence and laws increases the nearer we approach the state of uncultured and barbarous nations. The same applies to intellectual culture. The higher it is, the more learning and mental culture a man has, the greater the number of truths, principles, and intellectual standards he carries within him. By these he is bound if he wants to advance into the higher spheres of intellectuality. And the more the intellect rejects laws and standards the more unregulated and dull its intellectual life will become. The more one knows the more strictly is he bound to truth in every respect; the less one knows the freer he is to commit errors. This is no advantage, it is the privilege of the ignorant and untrained mind. The believer is bound by religious truth in the same way as one who knows the truth is bound by it, while one who is ignorant of it is not.

It is certainly not impossible for the obedience of faith to create INTELLECTUAL CONFLICT. There may be cases when scientific views look probable to the scientist, while they contradict a doctrine of faith or an ecclesiastical decision. The roads may even cross more radically. It may happen that his views and books are condemned, forbidden by the Church.

If the conflicting doctrine should be an INFALLIBLE one, the decision of the believing scientist is soon reached. He knows now what to think of his hypothesis, that it is not true progress but aberration, and consistency with his own conviction moves him to desist. Thus the philosophical errors of modern times are opposed almost throughout to infallible dogmas, for the most part fundamental doctrines of the Christian religion. This is also the legal right under which revelation and the Church approach the scientist with the demand not to permit his views to go contrary to faith, because there can never be a contradiction between faith and reason. "There can never be a contradiction between faith and reason," the Vatican Council teaches; "the apparent conflict is due either to the doctrine not being understood and interpreted in the sense of the Church, or to erroneous opinions that are mistaken for conclusions of reason" (Conc. Vat. sess. III, cp. 4). If the Catholic finds his position opposed to NON-INFALLIBLE decisions, then he will re-examine his views in unselfish impartiality before God. If he must calmly tell himself that his arguments are not so weighty as to be able to stand up before so high an authority, guided by the Holy Ghost, then he will forego the gratification of holding fast to his own opinions, and will remind himself that true wisdom knows the fallibility of the human mind, and is ever ready to take advice from a divinely guided authority. Perhaps he will recall the words of the great *St. Augustine:* " Better bow before an incomprehensible but saving symbol than entangle one's neck in the meshes of error " (De doctr. Christ. III, 13). This Christian self-denial surpasses in beauty even science itself, and sheds upon it a greater splendour.

The great *Fénelon,* proceeding to his pulpit in the cathedral of Cambrai, on Annunciation day in 1699, was handed by his brother the Roman brief condemning twenty-three propositions of *Fénelon's* " Maximes des Saints." The Bishop took the writing, calmly ascended the pulpit and announced it forthwith, and preached a sermon on the submission due to ecclesiastical superiors, at which the whole congregation was greatly moved. A few days later he announced in an episcopal letter to his diocese his submission, " simple, absolute, and without a shadow of reservation." By this deed, an heroic act of obedience, *Fénelon* is placed higher in history than by his brilliant works, than by the honour of having been the illustrious tutor of the Dauphin of France.

Antonio Rosmini-Serbati in August, 1849, received official notice of the condemnation of two of his works by the Congregation of the Index. He immediately sent in his submission: " With the sentiments of a true and obedient son of the Apostolic See, that I have always been by the grace of God and wish ever to be, and have ever acknowledged myself, I now declare clearly and sincerely, without reservation, my submission, in the most complete manner, to the condemnation of my writings." Both the condemnation and the submission were soon made the target of attack by the Liberal press. *Rosmini* replied in an admirable open letter: " To my great sorrow I have seen several articles in different newspapers which dare criticize the Holy Congregation of the Index for condemning my writings. Inasmuch as I have submitted to the decree of the said Congregation with all sincerity, and with full interior and exterior obedience as becomes a true son of the Church, every one will easily understand how much I regret these articles and disapprove of them. Yet I deem it not superfluous to declare expressly that I reject those articles entirely and that I do not accept the praise for me which they offer. With regard to other newspaper writers, who are censuring me and even insulting me for having done what it was my duty to do, in submitting to the condemnation, as though I had committed a crime, I can only say that I greatly pity them, and that they would fill me with contempt could I deem it permissible to despise any one " (apud *J. Hilgers*, Der Index der verbotenen Buecher, 1904, 413).

A *Fénelon* or a *Rosmini*, bowing with the humility of the Christian savant to the judgment of their Church, have thereby forfeited nothing of their intellectual fame in the eyes of earnest critics, but, on the contrary, have greatly increased the respect for their noble character.

Even should the future prove as scientifically correct that which the believing scientist does not as yet clearly see, that he was scientifically in the right, no considerable damage would result to science. Providence, which guides human affairs, will protect science for its noble modesty in submitting meanwhile to an authority appointed by God. As a matter of fact, science cannot be shown ever to have suffered any real loss by such submission, not even in the *Galileo* case, as we shall see further on. On the other hand, countless are the errors and injuries which have befallen human thought and belief, and which the Church has warded off from those who yielded to her guidance. Of course the submission may become difficult if a man clings to his views, or has already publicly proclaimed them. Then, indeed, a bitter struggle may ensue. A number of scientists have failed to stand the test and have left to posterity the ill-fated name of apostates. The Church regrets such cases; but the deposit of faith is too precious to be endangered for the sake of any individual.

For this reason the Church is and must be CONSERVATIVE; for this reason she may have to warn against the dissemination of propositions which may not in themselves be false, but fraught with danger for the time being. She cannot take part in any hasty effort to make experiments, risking everything inherited in order to try something new.

During the nineteenth century the United States was repeatedly the scene of communistic experiments. Daring adventurers assembled people and founded settlements on communistic principles, private property being abolished. In 1824 *Robert Owen* founded a colony in Indiana, which soon grew to nine hundred members, living in the fashion of athe-istic communism. In 1825 the colony adopted its first constitution, which within the following year suffered six complete revisions. In June of the second year the last members of the colony ate their farewell dinner together. The experiment had come to a speedy termination. A Frenchman, *Etienne Cabet*, founded, in 1848, a new colony in Texas, called Icaria. Soon it numbered 500 members. Each family had its small homestead. Children were educated by the community. Amusement was provided for by a band and a theatre; a library supplied more intellectual wants. But soon it all fell into decay. *Cabet* departed and died. In 1895 the newspapers reported the dissolution of the last remnant of the colony. Such is the fate of experiments.

Daring adventurers may undertake them. The lecturer at college, too, will be readily pardoned for his eagerness to take up the cudgel in defence of what is new in his profane science: he may easily correct himself. But the Teacher of the Centuries and of the Nations, in the sphere of religion and morals, has not the right to experiment. Here, where mistakes may entail the direst consequences, the rule must be: slowly onward, to keep the whole from ruin. Cardinal *Benedict Gaetani*, later Pope *Boniface VIII.*, once praised Rome for having *pedes non plumeos sed plumbeos* — not winged feet, but leaden heels.

Sentiments of the kind just set forth are of course possible only in conjunction with the belief in a revelation and in the supernatural character of the Church, where the interests of faith come first, and must be unconditionally preserved. He who lacks this conviction, he to whom the Church is but a human institution, founded in the course of time, tending perhaps to oppose truth and science for fear they might endanger the submission of minds — to such a one the Catholic's confident devotion to his Church, and consciousness of unimpaired freedom at the same time, will be unintelligible; and the inflexibility of the Church in defending the faith will pass his comprehension. And woe to the Church when her position toward science is being tried before this court: only harsh denunciations are to be expected where the judge does not understand the matter he undertakes to decide.

Nor do we attempt to bridge the chasm that separates the two views of the world which we here again encounter, the one, which rejects the supernatural world, the other, the view of the believing Christian. We have but endeavoured to show that FAITH DOES NOT RESTRAIN THE MENTAL FREEDOM OF ONE WHO IS CONVINCED OF THE TRUTH OF HIS FAITH. Submission to the authority of faith is the consequence of his conviction. This is the question to be decided: Either there is a revelation and a Church founded by God, or there is not. If such there be, or if it is only possible, then modern freedom of thought, with its demand of exemption from all authority, is against reason and morality. If there is not, then this should be proved. It can be done consistently only by acknowledging atheism. For if there is a personal God, then He can give a revelation and found a Church, and demand submission from all. Since the days of *Celsus* to this day the attempt to demonstrate that the convictions of a faithful Christian are unjustifiable has proved futile.

Obedience of Faith and Injury to Science

While all this is true, yet one may not share this conviction, nor rise to the certainty that there is a supernatural world whence the Son of God descended to teach man and to found an infallible Church. Still, to be fair, he must admit that no real danger to freedom of research and progress of science results from submission to faith, as shown above.

In the first place it must be admitted that the assertion is still unproved, that a positive result of research has ever come in hopeless conflict with a dogma of faith; hence that science has been prevented from accepting this result. No such case can be found. The condemnation of the Copernican view of the world will be considered presently; we pass over the fact that at the time of its condemnation it was not a positive result of science: the main point is that the condemnation was not an irrevocable dogma of faith, but only the decision of a Congregation, which was withdrawn as soon as the truth was clearly demonstrated. Besides, science has suffered no injury from that decision.

In general, where there is real contradiction between science and faith, the matters in question are invariably HYPOTHESES. Is it more than an hypothesis, and a very doubtful hypothesis at that, that the world and God are identical, that there is an eternal, uncreated course of the world, that miracles are impossible? That what is said about the natural origin of Christianity, the origin of the Jewish religion from Babylonian myths, the origin of all religions from fear, fancy, or deception, is it anything more than hypothetical? The false systems of knowledge, subjectivism, and agnosticism — are they more than hypotheses? Ask their originators and champions; they will admit it themselves; and if they will not admit it, others will tell them that their propositions are not only hypotheses, but often quite untenable. There is hardly a single hypothesis which has not its vehement opponents. That the serious conflict between dogma and science is waged only in this field could be proved by abundant examples. Besides, is it not the philosophical axiom of modern freedom of thought, that in the sphere of philosophy and religion there is no certain knowledge, but only supposition?

Can hypotheses claim to rank as assured results of research which should be universally accepted? Why should it not be allowed to contradict them, to oppose them with other suppositions? Is it not in the interest of science that this be done, that they be subjected to sharp criticism, lest they gradually be given out for positive results? Is it not a shameful trifling with the truth, when a *Haeckel* deceives wide circles by pretending that most frivolous hypotheses are established results of science? Is it not misleading when modern science treats the rejection of a supernatural order as an established principle?

And how often the hypotheses of profane sciences change! "Laymen are astonished," says *H. Poincaré*, "that so many scientific theories are perishable. They see them thrive for a few years, to be abandoned one after the other; they see wrecks heaped upon wrecks; they foresee that theories now fashionable will after a short while be forgotten, and they conclude that these theories are absolute fallacy. They call it the bankruptcy of science" (Wissenschaft u. Hypothese, German by *F. Lindemann*, 2d ed., 1906, 161). The conclusion is certainly unjustified, but the fact itself remains. Is it then a loss to science when faith opposes in the field of religion these variations of opinion with fixed dogmas? Or are these perhaps of less worth, or less certain than their contraries? Is the dogma of the existence of God of less value than atheism? Is the conviction of the existence of a world of spirits less substantial than the philosophy of materialistic monism? Is the doctrine of the origin of the human soul from the creating hand of God found inferior to the notion that the soul has developed from the lower stages of animal life? Should the holy teaching of Christianity, doctrines believed by the best periods in the world's history, believed in and professed by minds like those of an *Augustine*, a *Thomas*, and a *Leibnitz;* doctrines that since their appearance on earth have always attracted the noble and good, and repelled chiefly the base and immoral; doctrines that still wait for their first unobjectionable refutation — should such doctrines be less sure than the innumerable, ever-changing suggestions of unregulated thought, apparently directed by an aversion to everything supernatural?

ERRAVIMUS

Yet another fact may be pointed out. It is an undeniable fact that science, after straying for some time, is not unfrequently COMPELLED TO RETURN TO WHAT IS TAUGHT BY FAITH AND THE CHURCH, thus confirming the truth of the faith. Frequently the new theory has come on like a tornado, sweeping all minds before it. But the tempest was soon spent, the minds recovered their balance and the hasty misjudgment was recognized.

Not long ago, when materialism revelled in its orgies, especially in Germany, when *Vogt, Buechner,* and *Moleschott* were writing their books, and science with *Du Bois-Reymond* was hunting *Laplace's* theory in the evolution of the world, the Syllabus, undaunted, put its anathema upon the (58.) proposition: "No other forces are acknowledged but those of matter." The summer-night's dream came to an end, and people rubbed their eyes and saw the reality they had lost a while. The materialism of the 60's and 70's has been discarded by the scientific world, and finds a shelter only in the circles of unschooled infidelity. *J. Reinke,* in the name of biology, bears testimony in the words: "In my opinion materialism has been disposed of in biology; if, nevertheless, a number of biologists still stand by its colours, this tenacity may be explained psychologically; for, in the apt words of *Du Bois-Reymond,* in the domain of ideas a man does not willingly and easily forsake the highway of thought which his entire mental training has opened up" (Einleitung in die theoretische Biologie, 1901, 52).

A few decades ago a number of scientists declared it impossible that the different races could have descended from one pair of ancestors, as taught by faith: the difference between the various families being too great and radical, it was said; the difference being rather of species than of race. Moreover, there was announced the discovery of people without religion, without notions of morality and family life; of tribes incapable of civilization and culture; it was asserted in the early days of *Darwin* enthusiasm that there had been discovered a race of men that clearly belonged to the species ape. Assertions of this kind have gradually ceased. Now the different human races are considered to belong to the same species, and their common parentage is considered possible from the view-point of the theory of evolution. The anthropologist *Ranke* expresses his opinion thus: "We find the bodily differences perfectly connected by intermediate forms, graded to a nicety, and the summary of the differences appears to point to but one species. . . . This is the prevalent opinion of all independent research of anatomically schooled anthropologists" (Der Mensch, 2d ed., II, 1894, 261). Ethnology denies the existence of nations or tribes without religion (*Ratzel*, Voelkerkunde, I, 1885, 31). *Peschel* says: "The statement that any nation or tribe has ever been found anywhere on earth without notions and suggestions of religion can be denied emphatically" (*O. Peschel*, Voelkerkunde, 6th ed., 1885, 273). "The more recent ethnology knows of no tribes without morality, nor does history record any" (*W. Schneider*, Die Naturvoelker, 1886, II, 348). Until a short time ago it was believed that the derivation of man's life from inferior stages of animal life would not be difficult to prove; but at present, while many still adhere to the theory that man has developed from the brute, the conviction is steadily gaining ground that it cannot be scientifically proved and that it becomes more and more difficult to disprove man's higher origin. Unable to withstand the force of facts, one hypothesis gives place to another: what had to be found could not be found, living or extinct links between the brute and man refused to appear anywhere, and those which people thought they had found, turned out to be unsuitable. *Kohlbrugge* concludes his criticism of the recent theories of the evolution of the body of man from lower animals with the confession: "The above summary is enough to convince everybody that we do not know anything distinct about the great problem of evolution; we have not yet seen its face. All must be done over again" (Die Morpholog. Abstammung des Menschen, 1908, 88). *Virchow* said at the anthropological congress of Vienna, 1889: "When we met at Innsbruck twenty years ago Darwinism had just finished its first triumphal march through the world, and my friend *Vogt* became its ardent champion. We have searched in vain for the missing link connecting man directly with the ape."

What has become of those anatomic-morphologic links between man and beast, the *pithecanthropus erectus*, the man dug out at Neandertal, Spy, Schipka, La Naulette, and Krapina, and shown with great confidence to the world? What has become of the prehistoric man, said to belong to the glacial period of Europe, and to have ranked far below the present man? *J. Kohlmann* writes: "I wish to state that I thoroughly adhere to the theory of evolution, but my own experience has led me to the result that man has not changed his racial characteristics since the glacial period. He appears on the soil of Europe physically complete, and there is no ape-man to be found" (apud *Ranke*, Ibid. 480). Prof. *Branco*, director of the Palæontological Institute of Berlin, says: "Palæontology tells us nothing about the missing link. This science knows of no ancestors of man" (at the 5th international Zoological Congress, 1901, *Wasmann*, Die mod. Biolog. 3, p. 488). And the palæontologist *Zittel* says: "The missing link between man and ape, though a postulate of the theory of evolution, has not been found" (*Ranke*, l. c. 504). *E. Grosse* concludes his studies on evolution with the significant words: "I began this book with the intention of writing a history of the evolution of the family, and I finish it convinced that at present the writing of that history is impossible for me or for anybody else" (Die Formen der Familie, 1896, Vorwort). *Ranke* is perfectly right in saying that "it behoves the dignity of science to confess that it knows nothing of the origin of man" (Thuermer V, 1902, I. Heft).

A century ago or so, ridicule was heaped in the name of science on the description in the Bible of the last day: "The stars shall fall," "and the powers of heaven shall be moved," "the elements shall be melted with heat, and the earth shall be burnt up " (Matt. xxiv. 29 *seq.*; Luke xxi. 25 *seq.*; Mark xiii. 24 *seq.*; 2 Pet. iii. 10). Then the assertion that stones could fall from the skies caused a smile, but now science has come to the general knowledge that this is not only possible, but perhaps really will be the end of all things, if once our earth on its journey through unknown spaces of the universe should collide with a comet or get into a cosmic cloud of large meteors. (Cf. the graphic description in *K. Braun,* Ueber Kosmogonie, 3d ed., 1905, p. 381 *seq.*)

An example of another kind: It is not so long since Protestant, liberal Bible-criticism and its history of early Christian literature, in the endeavour to remove everything supernatural from the beginning of Christianity, regarded the New Testament and the oldest Christian documents as unreliable testimony, even forgeries, and for this reason placed the date of their origin as late as possible. But now they have to retrace their steps.

A. Harnack writes: " There was a period — the general public is still living in it — when the New Testament and the oldest Christian literature were thought to be but a tissue of lies and forgeries. This time has passed. For science it was an episode in which much was learned of which much must be forgotten. The result of subsequent research overreaches in a ' reactionary ' effect what might be termed the central position of modern criticism. The oldest literature of the Church is in the main and in most details true and reliable, that is, from the literary and historical point of view. . . . I am not afraid to use the word ' retrogressive ' — for we should call a spade a spade — the criticism of the sources of the earliest Christianity is beyond doubt moving retrogressively towards tradition " (Chronologie der Alt-Christ. Literatur I, 1897, VIII). In a more recent work the same savant writes: " During the years from 30 to 70 all originated in Palestine, or, better, in Jerusalem, what later on was developed. This knowledge is steadily gaining and replacing the former ' critical ' opinion that the fundamental development had extended over a period of about a hundred years " (Lukas der Arzt, 1906, Vorwort). This retrogression is continued still farther in his later work, " Neue Untersuchungen zur Apostolgesch. u. zur Abfassungszeit der synopt. Evang., 1911," in which *Harnack* draws very near to the Catholic view regarding the date of writing of the Acts of the Apostles, as also regarding *St. Paul's* attitude towards Judaism and Christian-Judaism, and departs from the modern Protestant view (cf. pp. 28–47, 79 *seq.*, 86, 93 *seq.*). " Protestant authorities on church-history," he says elsewhere, " no longer take offence at the proposition that the main elements of Catholicism go back to the Apostolic era, and not only peripherically " (Theol. Literar. Zeitung, 1905, 52).

In a speech, much commented on, which he made at his university January 12, 1907, Prof. *Harnack,* discussing the religious question in Germany, called attention to the fact that there has been quite a marked return to the Catholic standpoint: " From the study of Church history we find that we all have become different from what our fathers were, whether we may like it or not. Study has shown that we are separated from our fathers by a long course of development; that we do not understand their ideas and words at all, much less do we use them in the sense they used them." He then draws out the comparison more particularly: "*Flacius* and the older Protestants denied that *Peter* had ever been in Rome at all. Now we know that his having been there is a fact well evidenced in history." The motto of the older Protestants was that the Scriptures are the sole source of revelation. "But now, and for a long time past, Protestant savants have realized that the Scriptures could not be separated from tradition, and that the collecting of the New Testament Scriptures was a part of tradition." "Protestants of the sixteenth century taught justification by faith alone, without works. In the absence of confessional controversy, no evangelical Christian would now find fault with the teaching which declares only such faith to be of any worth which shows itself by the love of God and of the neighbour" (Protestantismus u. Katholizismus in Deutschland, Preussisch. Jahrbücher 127. Bd., 1907, 301 *seq.*).

Many similar instances of science confessing Erravimus in regard to the Christian or Catholic position could be cited. They are an admonition to be modest, not to overrate the value of a scientific proposition, and not, with supreme confidence and infallibility, to brand it as an offence against the human intellect to let one's self be guided by the principles of faith.

Moreover, it has often happened that science emphatically and sneeringly rejected propositions, and called them false and absurd, which to-day are considered elementary.

Newton, in 1687, had correctly explained the revolution of the moon around the earth, and of the planets around the sun, as the co-operation of gravitation and inertia, and thence concluded also the elliptic form of the orbits of planets previously discovered by *Kepler*. *Leibnitz* rejected this theory, *Huygens* called it absurd, and the Academy of Paris as late as 1730 still favoured the theory of revolution of *Descartes;* it was only about the year 1740 that it was generally accepted. *Huygens,* himself, had formed in 1690 his theory about light-waves. For a long time it was misunderstood. Only in 1800, or somewhat later, it received its merited acknowledgment, but noted physicists like *Biot* and *Brewster* rejected it still for some time and held to the theory of emission. "Even in the intellectual world the law of inertia holds good" (*Rosenberger,* Gesch. der Physik, III, 1887, 139).

The great discoverer *Galvani* complained of being attacked from two opposite sides, by the scientists and by the ignorant: "Both make fun of me. They call me the dancing master of frogs. Yet I know I have discovered one of the greatest forces of nature."

When *Benjamin Franklin* explained the lightning-rod to the Royal Academy of Sciences, he was ridiculed as a dreamer. The same happened to *Young* with his theory of the undulation of light. " The Edinburgh Review " proposed to the public to put *Thomas Grey* in a strait-jacket when he presented his plan for railroads. Sir *Humphry Davy* laughed at the idea of illuminating the city of London by gas. The French Academy of Sciences actually sneered at the physicist *Arago* when he proposed a resolution to merely open a discussion of the idea of an electric telegraph (*Wallace,* Die wissensch. Ansicht des Uebernatuerlichen, 102 *seq.*).

Until about a hundred years ago scientists almost universally thought it impossible for a stone to fall from the skies — not to mention a rain of stones. Of the big meteor that fell at Agram in 1751 the learned Vienna professor, *Stuetz*, wrote in 1790 as follows: "That iron had fallen from the skies may have been believed in Germany in 1751 even by its enlightened minds, owing to the uncertainty then prevailing in regard to physics and natural history. In our times, however, it were unpardonable to consider similar fairy tales even probable." Some museums threw away their collections of meteors, fearing they would appear ridiculous by keeping them. In that very year, 1790, a meteor fell near the city of Juillac in France, and the mayor of the town sent a report of it to the French Academy of Sciences, signed by three hundred eye-witnesses. But the wise men of the academy knew better. Referee *Bertholon* said: "It is a pity for a town to have so foolish a mayor," and added: "It is sad to see the whole municipality certifying by affidavit to a folk-saga that can only be pitied. What more can I say of an affidavit like that? Comment is self-evident to a philosophically trained mind who reads this authentic testimonial about an evidently false fact, about a physically impossible phenomenon." *A. Deluc*, in other respects a sober-minded man, and a scientist, even remarked that should a stone like that fall before his feet, then he would have to admit that he had seen it, but nevertheless would not believe it. *Vaudin* remarked: "Better to deny such incredible things than to have to try to explain them." Thus taught the French Academy of that time (apud *Braun*, Ueber Kosmogonie, 3d ed., 1905, 378 *seq.*). And now science is teaching the contrary. Everybody knows that such falling meteors are not only possible, but that they fall about seven hundred times a year on our earth.

Do not these examples bear a striking resemblance to the attitude of many of the representatives of modern science towards facts and truths of our faith?

This has not been said with a view of detracting from the

reputation of science. Not at all. It has fallen to the lot of man to be subject to error. The above was said to recall that fact. Science is not so infallible as to be able to claim the right to ignore, in religious and ethical questions, faith and the Church, and even to usurp the place of the faith given by God, in order to lead its disciples upon the new paths of a delivered mankind.

CHAPTER III

UNPREPOSSESSION OF RESEARCH

What it Is

IN the year 1901 a case, insignificant in itself, caused great excitement in and even beyond the scientific world. What had happened? At the University of Strassburg, in a territory for the most part Catholic, no less than one-third of the students were Catholic, yet of the seventy-two professors sixty-one were Protestant, six Israelites and but four Catholics (according to the report of the Secretary of State, *Koeller,* in the 115th session of the Reichstag, January 11, 1901). The government resolved, in view of the state of affairs, to give more consideration, when appointing professors, to the Catholic members of the university. Even the non-Catholic members of the Bundesrat desired it. A vacancy occurring in the faculty of history, the government, besides appointing the Protestant professor proposed by the faculty of philosophy, decided to create a new chair to be filled by a Catholic.

The appointment of a Catholic professor of history was regarded as seriously endangering science. The storm broke. The venerable historian, *Th. Mommsen,* who had been a champion of liberty in the revolution of 1848, promptly gave the alarm. In the Munich " Neueste Nachrichten " there appeared over his signature an article that created a general sensation. " German university circles," he said, in his solemn protest, " are pervaded by a feeling of degradation. Our vital nerve is unprejudiced research; research that does not find what it seeks and expects to find, owing to purposes, considerations, and restraints that serve other, practical ends extraneous to science — but finds what logically and historically appears to the conscientious scientist the right thing, truthfulness. The appointment of a college teacher whose freedom is restricted by bar-

riers is laying the axe to the root of German science. The call
to a chair of history, or philosophy, of one who must be a Catholic or a Protestant, and who must serve this or that confession,
is tantamount to compelling him to set bounds to his work
whenever the results might be awkward for a religious dogma."
And he concludes with a ringing appeal for the solidarity
of the representatives of science: "Perhaps I am not deceived in the hope of having given expression to the sentiments
of our colleagues." This statement of the famous scientist,
conceived in the temper of his days of '48, was soon softened,
if not neutralized, by a subsequent statement from his pen. But
the spark had already started the fire. From most universities
there came letters of approval and praise of his courageous
stand, in behalf of the honour of the universities and of German science. On the other hand, some gave vent to their regret
of his hot-spurred action. Since then the song of unprejudiced
science has been sung in countless variations and keys, ending
as a rule with the chorus: Hence the believing, especially
Catholics, cannot be true scientists. For this was the central idea
of *Mommsen's* protest, and in that sense it had been understood.

For the sake of clearness we shall condense the substance of
the thought into a brief form: The vital nerve of science, the
condition under which alone it can exist, is unprepossession, that is, a straightforward honesty that knows of no
other consideration than to aim at the truth for its own sake.
The believer, the Catholic, cannot be unprepossessed, because
he must pay regard to dogmas and Church-doctrine and pre-
cept. Therefore he is wanting in the most essential requisite
of true science. Hence college professors of a Catholic conviction are anomalous: they have no right to claim a chair
in the home of unprepossessed science. For reasons of expediency it may be advisable to appoint some of them, but they
cannot be regarded as sterling scientists. Catholic theology,
building upon faith, is not science in the true sense of the word,
and deserves no place in a university. A Catholic university, a
home of scientific research built upon a Catholic foundation, is
something like a squared circle. It may be that Catholic
scientists, too, have their achievements, but they cannot be

expected to be possessed of that unflinching pursuit of the truth which must be part of the man of science.

These are thoughts which have petrified in the minds of many into self-evident principles, with all the obstinacy of intolerance. It is not difficult to recognize in it the old reproach we have already dealt with, it is here in a slightly different form. The believing scientist is not free to search for the truth, being tied down by his duty to believe. Science, however, must be free. Hence the believer cannot properly pursue science.

Freedom of science and science unprepossessed are related terms and are often used synonymously. Therefore, in putting the probe to the often-repeated demand for unprepossession, we shall meet with ideas similar to those we have already discussed, only in a slightly different shape.

What, then, is that unprepossession which science must avow? Can the Catholic, the believing scientist, possess it? Unprepossessed research — " I don't like the expression," says a representative of free-thought, " because it is a product of that shortcoming which has already done great damage to free-thought in its struggle with the powers of the past" (*Jodl*). Hence we have reason to fear that the confidence with which this word is used is greater than the clearness of thought it represents.

What is meant by saying that science must be UNPREPOSSESSED? Undoubtedly it means that science should make no presuppositions, it must enter upon its work free from prejudice and presumption. And what is presumption? Evidently something presumed, upon which the research is to rest the level and rule of its direction: the supposition being taken for granted, without express proof. What I have expressly proved in my process of thought is no longer a supposition to the structure of thought, but a part of that structure.

Is the scientist, however, to allow no presumption at all? That would be impossible. When making his calculations the mathematician presupposes the correctness of the multiplication table. Or is he first to prove that twice three are six? He could not do it, because it is immediately self-evident. In his optical experiments in the laboratory, in drawing inferences as to the nature of light from different indications, the physicist presupposes that senses are able to observe the facts correctly, that everything has its respective reason, that nothing can be and not be, at the same time, under the same conditions. Can he or must he try first to prove it? He must presume it because it is beyond a doubt, and because it cannot be proved at all, at least all of it cannot. The astronomer, too, makes unhesitating use of the formulas of mathematics without examining them anew; every natural scientist calmly presupposes the correctness of the results established by his predecessors and goes on building upon those results: he may do so because he cannot with reason doubt them. Hence presumptions are common; they may be made when we are convinced of their truth; they must be made because not everything can be proved. Much cannot be proved because it is immediately self-evident, as, for instance, the ability to recognize the true or the elementary principles of reasoning; many other things cannot always be proved minutely, because not every scientist cares to begin with the egg of Leda. He that wants to build a house builds upon a given base; if he will not accept it, if he desires to dig up the fundament to the very bottom, in order to lay it anew, he will be digging forever, but the house will never be built.

Hence to say that science must be unprepossessed cannot mean that it must not make any presupposition. What, therefore, does it mean? Simply this: SCIENCE MUST NOT PRESUME ANYTHING TO BE TRUE WHICH IS FALSE, NOR ANYTHING AS PROVED WHICH IS STILL UNCERTAIN AND UNPROVED. Whatever the scientist knows to be certain he may take as such, presuming it as the foundation and direction of further work; and what he knows to be probable he may suppose to be probable.

In so doing he in no way offends against the ideal that should be ever-present to his mind — the truth, because he merely allows himself to be guided by the truth, recognized as such. And the sequence of truth cannot but be truth, the sequence of certainty cannot but be certainty. But should he presuppose to be true what is false and unproved, and the uncertain to be certain, then he would offend against truth, against the aim of every science.

Hence if the critic of the Bible presupposes miracles and prophecies to be impossible, inferring therefrom that many narratives in Holy Writ cannot be authentic, but must be legends of a later period, he is making arbitrary presuppositions, he is not an unprepossessed scientist. Likewise, if an historian presupposing God's supernatural providence over the world to be impossible, and, in building upon this basis, comes to the conclusion that the Christian religion grew from purely natural factors, from Oriental notions and myths, from Greek philosophy and Roman forms of government, he again makes unproved suppositions. If the natural philosopher assumes that there cannot be a personal Creator, and infers from it that the world is of itself and eternal, he has forfeited the claim of being an unprepossessed scientist, and by making in any way his own pet ideas the basis of his research he is violating the demands of unprepossession; the results he arrives at are not scientific results, but the speculations of an amateur.

UNPREPOSSESSION AND RELIGIOUS CONVICTION

Is it possible for the Christian scientist who adheres to his faith, to be unprepossessed, as demanded by science? According to all that has been said hitherto about the relation of science to faith, the answer can be only in the affirmative. The believing Christian and Catholic looks upon the doctrines of faith taught him by revelation and the Church as an ESTABLISHED TRUTH. What to me is true and certain I can take for the true and certain basis and standard of my thought. This is demanded by unprepossession — nothing more.

Considering the immense extent of the sciences, the profane sciences will but seldom, and in but few matters, have occasion to presuppose truths of faith in the above-mentioned way; and only in a negative form at that. We have previously shown that the profane sciences must never take truths of faith for a positive basis to build upon; they must regard the doctrines of revelation only in so far as it is not allowed to teach anything in contradiction to them. And with this demand they will meet in rare instances only, because, if not overstepping their province, they will very seldom come in touch with faith (cf. pp. 88–96). When *Kepler* was studying his planetary orbits, and *Newton* discovered the law of gravitation, both worked independent of the Christian view of the world which they both professed; it was in no way a necessary presupposition to their research. When *Scheiner* discovered the sun-spots, and *Secchi* classified the spectra of the stars, they were not doing so as Jesuits nor as Catholics; as Mohammedans or atheists they might have made the same discoveries. Steam engines and railways, *Volta's* electricity, cathode-rays and X-rays, all discoveries that the nineteenth century can boast of, do not depend directly on any special view of the world.

And if the believing scientist does take his faith for a guide in some matters, when in all his researches in the history of the Christian religion and the Church he presupposes that God's miraculous interference is not impossible, because the contrary would offend not only against his faith, but also against his common sense; when in pondering the ultimate reasons of all things he allows himself to be influenced by the idea that atheism is false, or at least not proved — for that there is a God both his faith and his reason tell him — then these presumptions are by no means inadmissible. The naturalist, too, presupposing certain results of science to be true, takes care not to get into conflict with them, and he will soon correct himself should he arrive at different results. If a mathematician should arrive at results conflicting with other proved results, he would infer therefrom that his calculation was faulty; why, then, cannot the Christian now and then be led by the truths of his faith, of which he is certain, without by doing so offending against the spirit of scientific truthfulness?

Or may he not do so just because they are RELIGIOUS truths, vouched for by a supernatural authority? As a fact many of them are established also by the testimony of reason. This is shown by the examples just mentioned. However, the question is not how a truth is vouched for, but whether it be a truth or not. If the scientist is assured that something is unquestionably true, then he owes it to the spirit of truthfulness to accept it. In doing so he will in no way be unfaithful to his scientific method; the truths of faith are to him not a source of proofs for the results of his profane science, but only hints, calling his attention to the fact that certain propositions are not proved, that they are even false.

Much less is in historical questions the Catholic obliged to defend or praise everything of advantage to his Church, whether true or not. Hence

Mommsen is grossly mistaken when he states in his letter of protest mentioned above: " The appointment of a historian or philosopher, who must be a Catholic or a Protestant and who must serve his confession, evidently means nothing else but to prohibit the Protestant historian from presenting the powerful mental structure of the papacy in its full light, and the Catholic historian from appreciating the profound thought and the tremendous importance of heresy and Protestantism." The Catholic is only bound to the truth.

Or are the Christian truths of faith perhaps regrettable errors, hence presumptions that should not be made? If so, demonstrate it. Hitherto such demonstration has not succeeded. So long as the creed of the believing Christian cannot be refuted convincingly, he has the right to cling to it in the name of truth.

Or can we not have reasonable certainty at all in religious matters? Are they the undemonstrable things of an uncontrollable sentiment? To be sure, this is asserted often enough, explicitly or by insinuation. If this were true, then of course duty of faith and true unprepossession could not go together; one would be regarding as the truth things of which one cannot be convinced. But this is also an unproved assumption: it is the duality of subjectivism and agnosticism, the fundamental presumption of liberal freedom of science, which we have already sufficiently exposed.

However, let us assume again the position of those who do not feel themselves personally convinced of the truth of the Christian dogmatic faith, or of the Catholic Church. But the Catholic is FIRMLY CONVINCED thereof and, if need be, will make sacrifices for this conviction, as millions have done. Hence, can any one forbid him to think and judge according to his conviction? Would they who differ from his opinion for this very reason force him to think against his own conviction? Would not that indeed be " seduction to sin against the Holy Ghost "? If the jurist or historian has formed the conviction that *Mommsen* is on historical questions concerning Roman law an authority, who may be followed without scruple, and he does so without re-examining the particular points, will this be looked upon as an offence against unprepossession? If, then, the Catholic is certain that he may safely trust to revelation and the Church — and there is no authority on earth of more venerable standing, even if viewed from a purely natural point — will he alone be accused of mental blindness and lack of freedom?

Or may the scientist have NO VIEW OF THE WORLD at all, because he might be influenced thereby in certain directions? The champions of this demand will surely not admit that they have not a definite view of the world. By no means! We know very well that just those who are most vehement in urging unprepossessed science have a very pronounced notion of the world, we know also that they are resolutely propagating that notion. Yet nothing is said against a scientist who is a monist, or who starts from agnosticism. It seems they intend to exclude one view only, the positive religious view. Yet not even this one wholly. No one finds the Jew who adheres to his religion unfit for scientific research. Of course not. Protestants, too, find favour: according to the statutes of some German universities Protestants only may be professors there. Neither *Mommsen* nor any other herald of unprepossession deems it necessary to defend science against these institutions and usages. It is plain what is meant by the popular cry for science unprepossessed: The man of science may be anything, sceptic or atheist, pagan or Hottentot, only he must not be a faithful Catholic. Is this fair? Is this the spirit of truth and justice with which they claim to be filled?

What has just been said about the Catholic being excluded, could easily be exemplified by a lengthy list of facts. But we shall pass them over. We shall note one utterance only, from the pen of a non-Catholic writer. The renowned pedagogue, *Fr. W. Foerster*, says in the preface to the second edition of his book on " Sexual Ethics and Sexual Pedagogy ": " Special exception has been taken to the catholicizing tendency of my book, and not infrequently the author has without further ado been made out an orthodox Catholic. For many years past I have been in a position to gain interesting information concerning the incredible bias of many champions of unprepossessed research. To them it is an a-priori dogma that everything represented by the Catholic Church is nonsense, superstition, bigotry. They are past comprehending how an unprejudiced man, simply by concrete experience, unprepossessed research and serious pondering in the field of pedagogy, could be brought to affirm that certain notions of the Roman Catholic Church are the unavoidable consequence of a penetrating knowledge of soul and life. This cannot be admitted by the non-Catholic: for him the truth must cease where the Catholic faith begins; he dares not assent to anything, else he will no longer be taken for a reputable scientific man."

The bluster about unprepossession proceeds from SHALLOW-NESS AND DISHONESTY. The most varied presumptions, that have nothing to do with science and the pursuit of the truth, may pass without notice; only when Christian and Catholic religious convictions, resting upon divine authority, are encountered, then tolerance gives way to excitement, a hue and cry is raised, the gate is shut, and entrance to the scientific world denied.

Philosophers arise, and each philosophizes according to his manner. *Fichte* says: "What philosophy to choose depends on the kind of a man one is." The historian enters. It is reported that *Treitschke* said: "If I cannot write history from my own view-point, with my own judgment, then I had rather be a soapmaker." According to trustworthy testimony, the well-known Protestant historian, *Giesebrecht,* used to preface his lectures in Munich with the words: "I am a Prussian and a Protestant: I shall lecture accordingly" (Hochschulnachrichten, 1901, 2, p. 30). Even here there are no objections in the name of Unprepossession. "Science," says *Harnack,* "will tear off the mask of the hypocrite or plagiarist and throw him out of the temple, but the queerest suppositions it must let pass if they go by the name of convictions, and if those who harbour them are trying to demonstrate them by scientific means."

Therefore the convictions, or, to speak with *Harnack,* the "prejudices," of the Catholic "certainly deserve as much consideration and patience as the velleities, idiosyncrasies, and blind dogmas which we have to meet and refute in the struggle between intellects" (Internationale Wochenschrift, 1908, 259 *seq.*). "Science has been restricted," the same authority also admits, "at all times; our progeny will find even modern science in many ways not ruled by pure reason only" (Dogmengesch. III, 3d ed., 1907, 326).

And what is to be said of those more serious suppositions, unproved and unprovable, which guide modern science wherever it meets philosophical-religious questions? That truly dogmatic rejection of everything supernatural and transcendental, that obstinate ignoration of a personal God, the rejection of any creative act, of any miracle, of any revelation, — a presupposition directly raised to a scientific principle: the principle of causality. Later on we shall make an excursion into various fields of science, and we shall show clearly how this presumption is stamped upon entire branches of science. Those solemn assurances of persevering unselfishness in desiring nothing but the truth; the confidence with which they claim a monopoly of the instinct for the truth, all this will appear in quite a strange light, the twilight of dishonesty, when we examine the documents and records of liberal science itself. We shall see sufficiently how truthful the self-confession of a modern champion of liberal science really is: " The recently coined expression, ' science unprepossessed,' I do not like, because it is a product of that shortcoming which has already done so much damage to free thought in its struggle with the powers of the past — because that word is not entirely honest. None of us sits down to his work unprepossessed " (*F. Jodl*, Neue Freie Presse, November 26, 1907). Here we shall touch upon only one more question.

The Duty to Believe and Scientific Demonstration

But cannot the believing Christian submit to scientific investigation the doctrine of faith itself, which he must without doubt hold to be true? This must surely be allowed if he is to convince himself scientifically of the truth of it. Indeed, this is allowed. He may critically examine everything to the very bottom, even the existence of God, the rationality of his own mind. But how can he, if no doubt is permissible? To examine means to search doubtingly; it means to call the matter in question — this, too, is right. It is, on the one hand, a doctrine of the Catholic Church that they who have received faith through the ministry of the Church, that is, they that have been made familiar with the essential subjects of the faith and the motives of their credibility by proper religious instruction, must not doubt their faith. They have no reasonable excuse for doubting because they are assured of the truth of the faith. We have discussed this point before.[1]

As a matter of course only voluntary doubts are excluded, doubts by which one assents deliberately and wilfully to the judgment that perhaps not all may be true that is proposed for our belief. Involuntary

---

[1] " They that have received the faith through the ministry of the Church can never have just cause for changing their faith or calling it into doubt " (Sess. III, ch. 3). The Vatican Council did not thereby mean to say that an exceptional case could not happen where some one, without fault of his own, might fall away from his faith, either on account of insufficient religious instruction, or of natural dullness or exceptional misfortunes in the circumstances of life in which he may be placed. The theologians who worded the decision also say that the Council did not intend to condemn the opinion expressed by many older theologians, that under certain conditions an uneducated Catholic might be led in such way into error as to join another faith without committing a sin " (cf. *Granderath*, Const. Dog. ss. oec. Concl. Vat. 69).

doubts are neither excluded nor sinful. These are apparent counter-arguments, objections, difficulties against the faith, which occur to the mind without getting its conscious approval. They are not unlikely, because the cognition of the credibility of Christian truths, while it is certain, is yet lacking in that obvious clearness which would render obscurity and counter-argument impossible; the assent to faith is free. Doubts of this kind are apt to molest the mind and buzz round it like bothersome insects, but they are not sinful because they do not set aside the assent to faith any more than the cloud that intervenes between us and the sun can extinguish its light. The assent to faith is withdrawn only when the will with clear consideration approves of the judgment that the doubt may be right.

But what about doubts which one cannot solve? Would we not owe it to truth and probity to withhold assent to faith for a while?

The answer lies in the distinction of a twofold solution of difficulties. It is by no means necessary, nor even. possible, to solve directly all objections; it suffices to solve them indirectly, that is, by recognizing them as void; since faith is certain, whatever is contrary to it must be false. If one is convinced by clear proofs of the innocence of a defendant he will not be swayed in his assurance, no matter how much circumstantial evidence be offered against the defendant. He may not be able to account directly for one or the other remarkable coincidence of circumstances, but all the arguments of the other side are to him refuted, because to him the defendant's innocence is a certainty. Thus the faithful Christian may hear it solemnly proclaimed as a scientifically established fact that miracles are impossible, because they would be tantamount to God making correction on His own work, because they would imply a self-contradiction, or they would be against the law of preservation of energy; he hears of atrocities in the history of the Church, of the Inquisition, of the Church being an enemy of civilization — he knows not what to say: but one thing he knows, that there must be an answer, because he knows, enlightened by faith, that his belief cannot be false. Nowhere is it demanded that all objections be directly answered, in order that the conviction be true. If I, with the whole world, am convinced that I am able to recognize the truth, must I therefore carefully disentangle all the cobwebs ever spun about the truth by brooding philosophical brains? If I am in the house, safe from the rain, must I, in order to keep dry, go out and catch every drop of rain that is falling? Such doubts may indeed harass the untrained mind, may even confuse it. This is the juncture where grace comes in, the pledge of which has been received at baptism, bringing enlightenment, peace, assurance; then we learn from others and from ourselves that faith is also a grace.

Nevertheless a scientific examination of the foundations and truths of faith is allowed and wholesome. Nearly all the theological works written by Catholics since the days of *Justin* and *Augustine* are nothing but examinations of this kind. At every examination one proceeds ˙with doubt and question. This is admitted; but this doubt must be merely a methodical one, not a serious one, nor need it be serious. These two kinds of doubt must be clearly distinguished. In case of a serious doubt I look upon the matter as really dubious, and withhold my assent. I am not yet convinced of its truth. This kind of a doubt is not allowed in matters of faith and it is the only one that is forbidden. In case of a methodical doubt I proceed as convinced of a truth, but I do not yet see the reasons plainly, and would like to be fully conscious of them. Evidently there is no need of casting aside the convictions I have hitherto held, and of beginning to think that the matter is by no means positively established.

For instance, I am convinced that a complicated order must be the work of intellect; however, I would like to find the proof of it. Hence I proceed as if the truth were yet to be found. But it would evidently be absurd to think in the meantime that such admirable order could be the result of blind accident. Or, I am convinced that there must be a source for every event: I desire to find the demonstration of it. In the meantime shall I think it possible for another Nova Persei to be produced in the sky without any cause? Or, investigating to see whether I am capable of recognizing the truth, shall I seriously become a sceptic till I am convinced that I ought not to be such? As soon as I really doubt that I can recognize anything at all as true, obviously I cannot proceed any further. *Kant* begins his "Critique of Pure Reason" with this doubt, and many imitate him, but only by evident inconsistency are they able to continue their researches by means of reason. Scientific examination does not consist in repudiating a certainty held hitherto, in order to arrive at it anew; it consists in bringing to one's clear consciousness the reasons for that certainty, and in trying to formulate those reasons precisely. To investigate the light it is evidently not necessary first to extinguish it.

Thus the believing Christian may most certainly probe into his religious conviction without interfering with his adherence, and by doing so proceed unprepossessed in the fullest sense, for unprepossession does not mean the rooting up of all certainty. At the threshold of wisdom does not sit Scepticism.

What Unprepossession is Not

But the deeper, modern meaning of unprepossession is precisely the right to doubt seriously everything, especially the truths of the Christian faith; this is the freedom demanded. Scepticism, the stamp of our time.

Many a misconception may have contributed to the definition of this unprepossession. For instance, overlooking the important difference between methodical doubt and serious doubt.

Then there is the erroneous opinion that we should and could proceed everywhere in the same way as in the natural sciences. Almost parallel with the progress in the natural sciences grew the doubt of the correctness of the ancient physical and astronomical notion of the world; piece after piece crumbled away under the hand of research; new truths were discovered. In just admiration of these results it was concluded that all provinces of human cognition should be "researched" in the same way, not excepting religion and theories of the world; here, too, science should cast a radical doubt upon everything and discover truth — as if here we had to deal with matters similar to astronomy and physics, in the state they were centuries ago; as if all mankind was still ignorant of the truth and science had to discover it.

This right to doubt is claimed especially in the higher questions of religion. Certain cognition by reason is, after all, impossible here, such is the presumption, and therefore, first of all, it is the right and duty of man, as soon as he has attained his intellectual maturity, to shape by doubt his views of the world to the satisfaction of his mind and heart, to win them by a struggle; nor is this true only in the case of the single individual, but also of entire generations. To see problems everywhere, not to have any convictions, this is taken to be true unprepossession.

" Man must learn," so we are told, " that there is no absolute miracle, not even in the domain of the religious life, which supernaturally offers truth at a point or by an institution, but that every man and every era as witnessed by the authority of history must conquer truth by themselves for their own sake and at their own risk" (*E. Troeltsch*, Internationale Wochensch. 1908, 26). Thus the mind of man cannot slake its thirst for positive truth at the divine fountain of revelation, but only by search and research. Such is the cheerful message of this science. "Amid grave crises," we are told again, "a new concept of science has forced its way to the front since the beginning of the eighteenth century and conquered the universities." "Science is not a finished system, but a research to be forever under examination" (*A. Harnack*, Die Aufgabe der theol. Facultaeten, 1901, 17).

Research without ever arriving at the sure possession of the truth, this is now the meaning of science, especially of philosophy. Hence there cannot be a philosophy conclusive and immutable, and any point which seems established may at any time be revised according to new perceptions. "There is no question that may not be asked; none which in the abstract could not just as well be denied as affirmed. In this sense philosophy is unprepossessed" (*Paulsen,* Die deutschen Universitaeten, 1902, 304 *seq.*). The highest achievement it declares itself capable of, is not to point out the truth to its disciples, for it does not know the truth itself, but only this: "We expect, or at least we should expect, that during the years of study the mind give itself earnestly to philosophy, and strive for a firm grasp of ideas. The great pathfinders in world thought, *Plato, Aristotle, Spinoza, Kant,* and whoever may be ranked with them, remain the living teachers of philosophy." Thus we hold those great intellectual achievements, *Plato's* doctrine and ideas, *Spinoza's* atheistic pantheism, *Aristotle's* objectivism and *Kant's* subjectivism, with other views of the world of most variegated patterns, all contradicting and excluding one another, all dubious, none sure. What would be said of an astronomy that could do nothing better than fix the telescope on the different stars and then tell its disciples: Now look for what you please, ideas of *Ptolemy* or *Copernicus; Aristotle's* theory of the spheres or *Newton's* theory of gravity; each has its points, but of none can it be said it is certain! Such an astronomy would probably be left to its deserved fate.

In the most important points of religion mankind has ever, even in pagan times, recognized the truth, albeit imperfectly. This is evinced by the conviction that there exists a personal

God and a hereafter; convictions which can be proved historically. God's revelation has provided those who desire to believe with a fuller knowledge of the truth: heaven and earth will pass away, but these words will not pass away. But what is already in our safe possession cannot be once more discovered by research. What has already been found is no longer an object of research. Mankind's lot would be a sad one indeed were this unprepossessed science in the right; if in the most important questions of life it were condemned forever to tantalizing doubt. God's providence has ordained matters more kindly for humanity.

On the other hand, it is a poor science that has nothing to offer but an eternal query for the truth. A poor science, that with self-consciousness promises enlightenment and what not, but finally can give nothing but ceaseless doubt instead of truth, tormenting darkness instead of cheerful light. Why, then, research where nothing can be found? Why raise searching eyes to the sky when the stars do not show themselves? What kind of progress is this when science does nothing further than dig forever at the foundation? The great *St. Augustine* has long also passed judgment on this kind of science: " Such doubting is abhorred by the City of God as false wisdom, because among the things which we grasp with our intellect and reason there is a knowledge, limited, it is true, because the soul is weighed down by a perishable body, as the Apostle says: *ex parte scimus* — but which has full certainty " (De Civitate Dei, XIX, 18).

AN ERRONEOUS SUPPOSITION

The errors just dealt with, and the demand that scientific research must doubt everything, is based on a supposition often stated expressly as a principle, and which appears quite plausible even to a mind not trained in philosophy. It says: There is but one certainty, the scientific certainty; the certain possession of the truth can be obtained only by scientific research. To rid the world of error, we are told, " there is but one way, viz., scientific work. Only science and scientific truth are able to dispose of error " (*Th. Lipps,* Allgemeine Zeitung, Muenchen,

August 4, 1908). " Truth is scientific truth, based on criticism, hence the religion of modern man must also rest on critical truth. . . . There is no other authority but science " (*Masaryk*, Kampf um die Religion, 13).

This sort of speech we hear from the college chair as the slogan for education and enlightenment: any one deficient in science or in education belongs more or less to the unthinking mass who have no convictions of their own, but submit blindly to impressions and authority.

Such unclarified conceptions, with their inferences, are even met with where they would not be expected, for instance, we read: "What the average individual needed was a good shepherd, a shepherd's devotion and love, that uplifts and urges onward; it was authority, Church-ministry and care of souls, that was needed. The Church is an organized pastorate, for the average individual likes to go with the flock. The chosen are they who feel within themselves the great question of truth as the care of their heart and task of their life, who experience its tremendous tension, and who are struggling to the end with the intellectual battles provoked by this question of truth. The average people, *i. e.*, the many, the great majority, need something steady to which they can cling — persons and teachers, laws and practice." And why this uncharitable distinction between people belonging to the flock and the chosen ones, as if the Church and its ecclesiastical functions were only appointed for the former? Particularly because "without methodical scientific work man cannot attain to the truth" (*H. Schell*, Christus, 1900, 125, 64).

Thus science may summon everything before its forum, no one having a right to interfere; in the superiority bestowed by the right of autocracy it may sweep aside everything that is opposed to it, no matter by what authority. Hence science must be free to jolt everything, free to question the truth of everything, which it has not itself examined and approved. This is the fundamental supposition of modern freedom of science; also a fatal error, betraying a woeful ignorance of the construction of the human intellect, in spite of all its pretentiousness. As a rule we have a true certainty in most matters, particularly in philosophical-religious convictions, a certainty not gained by scientific studies; by aid of the latter we may explain or strengthen that certainty, but we are not free to upset it.

We cannot avoid examining this point a little closer. There is a twofold certainty, one, which we shall call the NATURAL certainty, is a firm conviction based on positive knowledge, but without a clear reflexive consciousness of the grounds on which the conviction is actually resting. Reason recognizes these grounds, but the recognition is not distinct enough for reason to become conscious of them, to be able to state them accurately and in scientific formulas. SCIENTIFIC certainty is a firm conviction, with a clear consciousness of the grounds, hence it can easily account for them. Natural certainty is the usual one in human life; scientific certainty is the privilege of but a few, and even they have it in but very few things.

Everybody has a positive intellectual certainty that a complicated order cannot be the result of accident, and that for every event there must be a cause, though not every one will be able readily to demonstrate the truth of his certainty. But if the philosopher should look for the proof, he would do so in no other way than by reflecting upon his natural and direct knowledge, and by trying to become conscious of what he has thus directly found out. To illustrate by a few examples: We are all convinced of the existence of an exterior world, and any one who is not an idealist will call this conviction a reasonable certainty, and yet only a few will be able to answer the subtle questions of a sceptic. This certainty again is a natural but not a scientific one. How difficult it is here also for reason to attain scientific certainty, how easy it is to go astray in these researches, is proved by the errors of idealism so incomprehensible to the untrained natural mind. Let us ask, finally, any one: Why must we say: ' *Cæsar* defeated *Pompey*,' but not ' *Cæsar* defeated of *Pompey* '? He will tell us this is nonsense; maybe he will add that the genitive has another meaning. But should I ask further how the meaning of the genitive differs from that of the accusative, as both cases seem to have often the same meaning, I shall get no answer. There is a certitude, but only a natural one. Even if I should ask modern students of the psychology and history of languages, like *Wundt*, *Paul*, or whatever their names may be, I should not get a satisfactory answer either. The whole logic of language, with its subtle forms and moods of expression — how difficult for scientific research! And yet the mind of even a child penetrates it, and not only a European child, but the Patagonian and negro child, who is able to master by its intellectual power complex languages, with four numbers, many moods, fourteen tenses, etc.

These examples will suffice, though volumes of them could be written. They show us clearly a twofold certainty. The difference between the natural and scientific certainty is not that the former is a blind conviction formed at random, but only that one is not clearly conscious of the reasons on which it rests, whereas this is the case in scientific certitude. We see further the untrained power of the intellect manifest itself in natural knowledge and certainty; for this purpose it is primarily created; philosophical thought is difficult for it, and many have no talent at all for it. It is also unfailing in apprehending directly things pertaining to human life. Here the mind is free of that morbid scepticism of which it too easily becomes a prey when it begins to investigate and probe scientifically. What it there sees with certainty cannot always be found here distinctly, and thus the mind begins to doubt things it was hitherto sure of, and which often remain instinctively certain to the mind despite its artificial doubts. Now we can also understand why philosophers so often have doubts which to the untrained look absurd, and why philosophers differ in their opinions on most important things, whereas mankind guided by its natural certitude is unanimous in them.

This certainty is destined to be the reliable guide of man through life. It precedes science, and can even exist without it. Long before there was a science of art and of jurisprudence the Babylonians and Egyptians had built their monuments, and *Solon* and *Lycurgus* had given their wise laws. And long before philosophers were disputing about the moral laws, men had the right view in regard to virtue and vice (cf. *Cicero,* De Oratore, I, 32). The same certitude is also destined to guide man in the more important questions, in the questions of religion and morality. The Creator of human nature and its destiny, who implanted instinct in the animal to guide it unconsciously in the necessities of life, has also given to man the necessary light to perceive with certainty truths without which it would be impossible to live a life worthy of man.

It is just this natural knowledge and certitude that gives man certainty of divine revelation, after God vouchsafed to give it to mankind for its unfailing guidance and help. For revelation was not only intended for theologians, Bible critics, philosophers, and Church-historians, but for all. And God has taken care, as He had to do, that man has ample evidence that God has spoken, and that the Church is the authorized Guardian of this revelation, even without critical research in history and philosophy. We have elsewhere briefly stated this evidence in the words of the Vatican Council.

This evidence is seen in the invincible stability of the Church and its unity of faith, the incontestable miracles never ceasing within it, the grand figures of its Saints and Martyrs, virtue in the various classes, a virtue increasing in proportion to the influence the Church exerts, the spectacle that everything truly noble is attracted by the Christian faith and the contrary repulsed. In addition the intrinsic grandeur and harmony of the truths of faith, above all the unique figure of Christ, with His wonderful life and sufferings, also the calm and peace of mind effected in the soul of the faithful by living and thinking in this faith; all these tell him that here the spirit of God is breathing, the spirit of truth. The natural light of his intellect, further illuminated by grace, suffices to give him a true intellectual certainty of his faith, based upon these motives and similar ones, even without scientific studies. The calmness of the mind that holds fast to this faith, the compunction and unrest which follow defection from the faith, both so characteristic of Catholics, prove that their minds embrace the truth in their faith.

Hence it betrays little philosophical knowledge of the peculiarity of man's intellectual life, if infidelity approaches an inexperienced, believing student, perhaps even an uneducated labourer, with the express assurance that his faith hitherto has been but a blind belief, an unintelligent following of the lead of a foreign authority, with the distinct admonition to turn his back on the faith of his childhood.

What has been said above makes it clear why a Catholic is not permitted to have a serious doubt about his faith under the pretext that he ought first to form a certain conviction all for himself by scientific investigation. He has it already, if we presuppose sufficient instruction and normal conditions; he may raise his natural certitude to a scientific one by study if he has the time and talent for it, but he must not condition his assent upon the success of his scientific investigations. He has certitude; he has no right to demand scientific knowledge as a necessary condition, because it is not required for certitude, and also because it lies altogether outside of the conditions of human life. It would amount simply to shaking off the yoke of truth. The Church teaches as follows: " If any one says that the condition of the faithful and of those who have not yet come to the only true faith is equal, so that Catholics can have a just cause for suspending their assent and calling in question the faith which they have received by the ministry of the Church until they have completed the scientific demonstration of the credibility and truth of it, let him be anathema."

How high this wisdom rises above the limited thought of a science that imagines itself alone to be wise! Sad indeed would be the lot of mankind could it attain to certain truth in the most important questions of life only by lengthy scientific investigations. The overwhelming majority of mankind would be forever excluded from the certain knowledge that there is a God, an eternity, liberty, that there are immutable moral laws and truths, on the value of which depends the woe and weal of humanity.

Behold the wisdom of the world that is put before us: " In order to arrive at a definite conclusion by our own philosophical reasoning (on the existence of God and the possibility of miracles) what a multitude of things must be presupposed! " Thus we are informed in a philosophical novel of modern times which aims at proving the incompatibility of the Catholic duty to believe with the freedom of the intellect [Katholische Studenten, by *A. Friedwald* (nom de plume). An explanation of the ideas contained in it is given by the Academia 18, 1905-6, December and March. The ideas found in the novel are also advanced by *A. Messer*, Einfuehrung in die Erkenntnistheorie, 1909, p. 158 *seq.*]. And Prof. *Rhodius*, who put the ideas of the novel in formulas, teaches: "The question whether our knowledge could penetrate beyond what we know by our experience and even our senses, is answered, as you know, in the negative by a noted philosophical school. Hence, before attacking those metaphysical questions regarding the existence of God and His relations to the world, we must first try to have definite views as to the essence of human knowledge, of its criterion, its scope, and of the degrees of its certainty. But these preliminary questions of theoretic knowledge, how difficult and perplexing they are! You probably have not the faintest idea into what a mass of individual problems the main questions must be dissected, nor what a multitude of heterogeneous views are struggling here against one another " (p. 181).

Consider how shortsighted a wisdom is manifested by these words. Is it seriously intended to summon the peasant from his plough, the old grandmother from behind the stove, and lead them into the lecture rooms of the university in order that they might there listen to lectures on phenomenalism, and positivism, and realism, and criticism, until their heads are swimming? Or else can they not hope to arrive at the truth? Do they seriously think that the truth asked for by every man, the truth in the most vital questions of mankind, is the exclusive privilege of a few college professors? And how very few. More than twenty-four hundred years have elapsed since the days of *Pythagoras*, and yet modern philosophy still stands before the first preliminary question in all knowledge, whether a man can know what the eye does not see. "Many views are at variance there." If this be the only way for mankind to reach certain truth, then we are indeed in a pitiful plight!

We esteem philosophy and its subtle questions, and we heartily wish our Catholic young men in college to obtain a more thorough philosophical training. But if, involved in theories, one will lose his insight into the world and human life to such a degree as to make of the "wisdom of the world " an isolated narrow speculation which boasts of being alone able to discover the higher truths, while withering in neurasthenic doubt — such wisdom should be left to its deserved fate, sterility.

Or should it be possible to the ideal of Protestantism — and therefore also of the modern spirit — to console mankind by pointing out that the knowledge of the question which concerns us most deeply, "the knowledge of God and the knowledge of good, remains but a leading idea and problem, though we are confident of advancing nearer to its solution "? Is thus mankind to be eternally without light in the most important questions and problems? Every little plant and animal is equipped by nature with everything it needs — and man alone to, be a failure? The young shoots of the tree strive to bring forth blossoms and fruit, and succeed; the bird flies off in the fall in quest of a new home, and finds it; hunger and thirst demand food and get it; only the aim of the human mind shall never be fulfilled — he alone shall ever pine without hope! — *Dicentes se esse sapientes stulti facti sunt.* What a difference between such principles and the grand thoughts of Christianity! A difference like that between peace and eternal restless doubt, like that between man's dignity and man's degradation, between man's short-sightedness and the wisdom of God.

Hence the result of our discussion is: independent of science mankind has its positive convictions, independent of science it finds here rest and gratification in its longing for truth. Scientific study and research are for the purpose of setting these truths in a brighter light, of defending the patrimony of mankind. But the fosterer of science must not claim the freedom to ignore these positive convictions in himself and in others, to endanger the patrimony of mankind by doubts and attacks instead of protecting it, much less must he condemn the human mind to the eternal labour of *Sisyphus,* to the eternal rolling of a huge stone which, recoiling, must always be lifted anew.

CHAPTER IV

ACCUSATIONS AND OBJECTIONS

AMONG the notable facts in history one stands out prominently, it is more remarkable than any other, and evokes serious thought. It is the fact that the Christian religion, especially its foremost representative, the Catholic Church, concerning which every unbiassed critic is bound to admit that none has made more nations moral, happy and great than this Church; that nowhere else has virtue and holiness flourished more than in her; that no one else has laboured more for truth and purity of morals; that nevertheless there is not, and never was, an institution which has more enemies, which has been more persecuted, than the Catholic Church. This fact will suggest to every serious-minded critic the question, whether we have not here focussed that tremendous struggle, which truth and justice have ever waged in the bosom of mankind against error and passions — an image of the struggle raging in every human breast. The Church recognizes in this fact the fulfilment of the prophecy of her Founder: " And ye shall be hated by all men for my name's sake " (Luke xxi. 17). And the Church may add, that in her alone this prophecy is being fulfilled.

THE ENEMY OF PROGRESS

In her journey through the centuries the Church has had to listen to many accusations because she, the keeper of the truth entrusted to her care, has refused to respond to the demand to accept unconditionally the ideals devised by existing fashions. *Cantavimus vobis et non saltastis* (we have piped to you and you have not danced). Therefore the Church has been called reactionary; the heretics of the first centuries of Christianity denounced her as the enemy of the higher gnosis; a later period

denounced her as an enemy of the genuine humanism, in the
eighteenth century she was denounced as the enemy of enlightenment, to-day she is denounced as the enemy of progress. Again
the Church is accused before the judicial bar of the children of
the age. They desire to eat plentifully from the tree of knowledge, but the Church, they say, prevents them. They wish to
climb the heights of human perfection, to ascend higher than any
preceding generation, but the Church holds them back. She
will keep them in the fetters of her guardianship. And with
a keen, searching eye the smart children of our age have looked
the old Church over, taking notice of everything, anxious to put
her in the wrong.

Their charges do not fail to make an impression, even on the
Church herself. She wishes to justify herself before the plain-
tiffs, and still more before her own children who trust in her.
Thus she has not hesitated in declaring loudly on most solemn
occasions that SHE IS NOT AN ENEMY OF NOBLE SCIENCE and of
human progress, and with great earnest she takes exception to
this charge.

No wonder, one might say, that the Church makes such assurances. It is time for her to realize that unless she can clear
herself from it this accusation will be her moral ruin at a time
when the banner of progress is held aloft, and when even the
Catholic world shares in that progress. True, but let us not
forget this: if there is anything characteristic of the Catholic
Church it is her frankness and honesty. She is not afraid to
proclaim her doctrines and judgments before the whole world;
she leaves her Index and Syllabus open for inspection, openly
avowing that she is the irreconcilable enemy of that emancipated
freedom proclaimed by modern liberalism as the ideal of the age.
It is the honesty which she inherited from her Founder, who told
the truth to friend and enemy, to His disciples and to the
Scribes, to *Nicodemus,* that lonely night, and to *Caiaphas.* With
the same straightforwardness the Church declares that she
feels not enmity but sympathy toward civilization. A fair-
minded critic will admit here again that the Church is in
earnest. " Far from opposing the fostering of human arts and
sciences, the Church is supporting and promoting them in

various ways," declares the Vatican Council. "The Church does not underrate nor despise their advantages for human life: on the contrary, it avows that they, coming as they do from God, the Master of the sciences, also lead to God by aid of His grace, when properly used" (Sess. III, c. 4). The Church has put this accusation on the list of errors of the age condemned by *Pius X.* (Sent. 57). She feels the charge as an injury.

THE TESTIMONY OF HISTORY

Nevertheless, in anti-ecclesiastical circles it is taken very often for an established fact that the Roman Church has ever tried her best to hamper the progress of science, or has suppressed it, or at least scowled at it. How could it be otherwise? they say. How could she favour the progress made in enlightening reason or in advancing human knowledge? Must she not fear for its intellectual sway over men whom she keeps under the yoke of faith? Must she not fear that they might awaken from the slumber in which they were held prisoners by the suggestive force of her authority, held to be transcendental; that they might awaken to find out the truth for themselves? And what is the use of science? He that believes will be saved: hence faith suffices. If we wish to hear the accusation in the language of militant science, here it is: "Outside the monastic institutions no attempt at intellectual advancement was made (in the Middle Ages), indeed, so far as the laity were concerned, the influence of the Church was directed to an opposite result, for the maxim universally received was, that 'ignorance is the mother of devotion'" (*J. W. Draper,* History of the Conflict between Religion and Science).

This is the train of thought and the result of anti-ecclesiastical a-priorism and its historical research. Are the plain facts of history in accord with it? The first and immediate task of the Church is certainly not to disseminate science: her task, first of all, lies in the province of morals and religion. But as she is the highest power of morality and religion, she stands in the midst of mankind's intellectual life, and cannot but come in contact with its other endeavours, owing to the close unity

of that life. Hence, let us ask history, not about everything
it might tell us in this respect, but about one thing only.

We do not wish to show how the Church, headed by the
Papacy, has become the mother of Western civilization and
culture. Nor shall we enumerate the merits of the Church
in art, nor point out the alertness she has certainly shown,
in her walk through the centuries, by taking up the intellectual
achievements of the time and assimilating them with her moral
and religious treasure of faith, withal preserved unchanged. The
old Church had done this with the treasures of ancient learning
and science; "this spirit of Christianity proved itself by the
facility with which Christian thinkers gathered the truth contained in the systems of old philosophy, and, even before
that, by assimilating those old truths into Christian thought, the
beginning of which had already been made in the New Testament. They were appropriated, without hesitating experiment,
without wavering, and were given their place in a higher order "
(*O. Willmann*, Gesch. des Idealismus, 2d ed., II, 1907, 67).
This, she unceasingly continues to do, as proved by the high
standard of Catholic life and Catholic science at the present, a
fact not even disputed by opponents. We point only incidentally
to THE FOUNDATION AND THE FOSTERING OF PRIMARY SCHOOLS
by the Church. It is an historical fact that public education
began to thrive only with the freer unfolding of the Church.

The first elementary schools were those of the monasteries. Later
on there were established after their pattern the cathedral and chapter
schools, then the parish schools. Still later there came the town and
village schools — all of ecclesiastical origin, or at least under the
direction of the Church and in close connection with her. As early
as 774 we find an ecclesiastical school law, to the effect that each
Bishop should found an ecclesiastical school in his episcopal town and
appoint a competent teacher to instruct "according to the tradition
of the Romans." *Eugene II.* ordained in 826 anew that efficient
teachers should be provided for the cathedral schools wherever needed,
who were "to lecture on the sciences and the liberal arts with zeal."
"All Bishops should have the liberal arts taught at their churches,"
was a resolution of the Council held in Rome in 1079 by *Gregory VII.*
We read in the acts of the Lateran Synod of 1179: "Inasmuch as it
behooves the Church, like a loving mother, to see to it that poor children who cannot count upon the support of their parents should not
lack opportunity of learning to read and make progress, there should
at every cathedral church be given an adequate prebend to the teacher

— who is to teach the clerics of this church and the poor pupils gratuitously " (*E. Michael*, Gesch. des Deutschen Volkes II, 1899, 370). School education flourished more and more; in the thirteenth century it was in full bloom. In Germany even many unimportant places, market towns, boroughs, and villages had their schools at that time. In Mayence and its immediate neighbourhood there were, in the twelfth and thirteenth centuries, seven chapter schools; at Muenster at least four schools; the clerical schools at Erfurt had an attendance of no less than 1,000 pupils. About the year 1400 the diocese of Prague alone had 460 schools. In the middle Rhine district, about the year 1500, many counties had an elementary school for every radius of two leagues; even rural communities with 500 to 600 inhabitants, like Weisenau near Mainz, and Michaelstadt in Odenwald, did not lack schools " (*J. Janssen*, Gesch. des Deutschen Volkes, 15th ed., 1890, 26; cf. Michael, l. c. 402, 417–419; *Palacky*, Gesch. v. Boehmen, III, 1, p. 186). Even in far-off Transylvania there was, as early as the fourteenth century, no village without a church and a school (*K. Th. Becker*, Die Volksschule der Siebenbuerger Sachsen, 1894, y; Michael, 430). There is no doubt that this flourishing state of schools was due in the first place to the stimulus, support, and unselfish effort of the Church.

But we will not dwell longer on this subject. We wish, however, to point out more plainly something more closely related to our subject, viz., THE ATTITUDE OF THE CHURCH TOWARDS THE UNIVERSITIES, at a time when the most prominent nurseries of science were first coming into existence and beginning to flourish, when they began to exert their influence upon the civilization of Europe. Here, in the first place, it should become clear whether it be true that the Church has ever looked upon the progress of science with suspicion or even suppressed it. History teaches, in this instance again, that no one has shown more interest, more devotion, more readiness, to make sacrifices in promoting the establishment and growth of the university, than the Church.

When, in the twelfth and thirteeenth centuries, the thirst for knowledge, stronger than at any time in history, made itself felt in the Christian countries of Europe, there were erected in the universities great international homes of science, so as to gratify the deeply felt need of education. And thousands hastened to these places to acquire the knowledge of the period, overcoming all difficulties, then much greater than now. A recent writer remarks about this not without reason: " The academic instruction met on part of the thronging thousands with a psychic disposition more favourable than at any other time. In a way it was here a case of first love " (*W. Muench,* Zukunftspaedagogik, 1908, 337). At the universities of the Middle Ages there were taught theology, ecclesiastical and civil law, the liberal arts, and medicine. But not in the manner that all four faculties were everywhere represented. Theology especially was quite frequently lacking, though the aim was to have all sciences represented. What since the beginning of the thirteenth century was first of all understood by a university were *studia generalia* — then the usual name for universities, in contradistinction to *studium particulare.* Universities enjoyed the privilege of having their academic degrees honoured everywhere, and their graduates could teach anywhere. The universities were of an international character. Hence it happened that at the German universities there were sitting in quest of knowledge by the side of Germans also foreign youths, from Scotland, Sweden, and Norway, from Italy and France, all contending for academic honours — a moment which unquestionably contributed in no small degree to the improvement of education.

Prior to the Reformation, universities were not state institutions, as they are at present in Europe, but free, independent corporations. They were complete in themselves, they made their own statutes, had their own jurisdiction, and many other privileges. The modern university enjoys but a small remnant of those ancient prerogatives. In a public speech, made in the presence of the Duke of Saxony, the Leipsic professor, *Johann Kone,* could say in 1445: " No king, no chancellor, has any right to interfere with our privileges and exemptions; the university rules itself, and changes and improves its statutes according to its needs " (*Janssen,* l. c. 91).

Up to the year 1300 there were no less than 23 universities established in Italy, 5 in France, 2 in England, 4 in Spain, and 1 in Portugal. " Had all intentions been realized, Europe would have had by the year 1400 no fewer than 55 universities, including Paris and Bologna. But of 9 of them there are extant only the charter deeds that were never executed. At any rate, there were 46 of them, of which 37 or 39 existed at the turn of the fourteenth century; a considerable number, which was not known till recent years" (*Denifle*). Germany, Austria, and Hungary shared in 8: Prague, Cracow, Vienna, Fuenfkirchen, Ofen, Heidelberg, Cologne, and Erfurt. Within fifty years, from 1460 to 1510, no less than 9 universities were founded in Germany — a clear proof of the generous enthusiasm for science of that period.

By their fostering and founding of universities, secular princes have won the lasting gratitude of posterity, and so have the municipalities of a later period for showing an even greater zeal than those princes. But it was indisputably the Church that bestowed upon these homes of learning and culture the greatest benevolence and support for their foundation and maintenance.

In the first place, history shows that the majority of them were founded by PAPAL CHARTERS. Since universities were understood to have the power of conferring degrees of international value, they had to be universally acknowledged; this could be effected only by an authority of universal recognition; hence by the Roman-German Emperor — as the supreme prince of the world-wide Christian monarchy, or by the Pope, who was considered in the first place. He was the general Father and Teacher of Christendom; this is why Papal charters were so zealously sought after, in addition to imperial charters. Of the 44 universities called into existence before the year 1400, 31 were founded by Papal charters. A similar condition prevailed in the fifteenth century and afterwards, up to the Reformation. This was no interference in foreign affairs: such an interpretation would have caused just surprise in the Middle Ages. That the highest spiritual power on earth should have the first claim in education was a matter of general concession. And certainly the manner in which the Church made use of this right, to speak with an historian of the universities, forms "one of the most important, and by no means least inglorious, parts of an activity so manifold and difficult" (*V. A. Huber,* Die Englischen Universitaeten, I, 1839, p. 14).

These Papal charters breathe a warm BENEVOLENCE for science. Everywhere we find the wish expressed, that studies thrive in those places which are most suitable for the effectual spread of science, and that the different countries have a sufficient number of scientifically trained men.

Read, for instance, the charter given by Pope *Boniface VIII.* to Pamiers and Avignon, or the Letter of Privileges granted to Coimbra by *Clement V.* (apud *Denifle,* 793, 524), or *Pius II.'s* Bull founding the university of Basle. The Pope says here about the aim of science: " Among the various blessings to which man may by the grace of God attain in this mortal life, the last place is not to be given to persevering study, by which man may gain the pearl of the sciences, which point out the way to a good and happy life, and by their excellence elevate the learned men above the uneducated. Science makes man like to God, and enables him to clearly perceive the secrets of the world. It aids the unlearned, it elevates to sublime heights those born in the lowliest condition." " For this reason the Holy See has always promoted the sciences, given them homes, and provided for their wants, that they might flourish, so that men, well directed, might the more easily acquire so lofty a human happiness, and, when acquired, share it with others." This was the longing desire that led to the opening at Basle of " a plentiful spring of science, of whose fulness all those may draw who desire to be introduced into the study of the mysteries of Scripture and learning." Even prior to this, the same Pope had written to the Duke *Louis of Bavaria:* " The Apostolic See desires the widest possible extension of science," which, " while other things are exhausted by dissemination, is the only thing that expands the more the greater the number of those reached by it " (apud *Janssen,* l. c., p. 89).

But the Church was not satisfied with granting charters. She also gave very SUBSTANTIAL MATERIAL AID to most of the universities. The Popes maintained two universities at Rome, one of them connected with the Papal Curia, a sort of court-school. It was founded by *Innocent IV.,* in order that the many who came to the Papal court from all parts of Christendom might satisfy also their thirst for knowledge. Theology, law, especially civil law, medicine, and languages, including Oriental languages, were taught there. Besides this there was another university at Rome, founded by *Boniface VIII.* for a similar purpose: it did not flourish long, though in 1514 it counted no less than eighty-eight professors. Many attempts to found or support universities would have proved abortive had not the Popes provided for the salaries of professors by prebends and stipends, and by allotting to that end a portion of the income of priests and churches. Bishops, too, proved themselves zealous patrons of the universities (*Paulsen,* Gesch. des gelehrten Unterrichts, 2d ed., I, 1898, p. 27).

Thus, to cite a few examples of German universities, there was in 1532, with the consent of the Archbishop *Arnest,* a contribution raised by the clergy for the endowment of the university of Prague, to which the various cloisters and chapters, especially those at Prague, contributed. With the money thus raised the Archbishop purchased property, the income from which was to provide salaries for the professors. Twelve professors received from *Urban V.* the canonicates of the church of All Saints (*Denifle,* 598). Erfurt university was given 4 canonicates, Cologne 11, Greifswald still more. Similarly Tuebingen, Breslau, Rostock, Wittenberg, and Freiburg were cared for (*Kaufmann,* Die Gesch. der Deutschen Universitaeten, II, 1896, p. 34, *seq.*). Vienna found a benefactor in the pastor of Gars, who on October 13, 1370, founded a purse for 3 sublectors and 1 scholar. Heidelberg received 10 canonicates. Its great benefactor was the learned *Johann von Dalberg,* first curator of the university, and later Bishop of Worms. Under him Heidelberg reached the zenith of its lustre, and laid the foundation of almost all that has won it the reputation it at present enjoys. By his co-operation the first chair of Greek was founded; to him the foundation of the college library is due, which later on gained world-wide fame under the name of "Palatina." He further collected a private library, rich in Latin, Greek, and Hebrew books, the use of which was open to all scientists. "The Rhenish Literary Society" attained its greatest prominence under his direction (*Janssen,* l. c. 100–105). Ingolstadt, too, obtained its needed income by the donation of rich church-prebends, to such an extent that the "endowments netted the university about 2,500 florins," a very large sum for that time (*Kaufmann,* l. c. 38). *Prantl* also admits in regard to Ingolstadt: "The Papal Curia did its best to furnish the university" (Gesch. der Ludwig-Maximilian in Ingolstadt, 1872, I, 19, apud *Janssen,* l. c. p. 9).

It is true, the Church then owned much property. But it is just as true that she was ever ready to support science and colleges out of this property. Pope and clergy were also taking incessant pains to make it possible for POOR STUDENTS to attend the university, not only for theological students, but for those of all the faculties, to give an opportunity to rich and poor alike to enjoy the advantages of higher education. Stipends and legacies of this kind are numerous. Even in our own days many a son of an *alma mater* owes the stipend he enjoys to endowments made by the Church. In the course of time there were established at most of the universities so-

called COLLEGES for the purpose of offering shelter and maintenance to poor students.

These colleges contributed essentially to the flourishing condition
of the university. Thus *Albrecht v. Langenstein* suggested, at the founding of Vienna university, to the Duke, *Albrecht of Austria*, the establishment of such colleges, inasmuch as the continuance of the university
was dependent on them, and stated that Paris owed its prosperity to
them (*Denifle*, 624).

The Popes set here the best example. *Zoen*, Bishop of Avignon, had
provided in his testament that eight students from the province of
Avignon should be maintained at Bologna by his successors from their
estates at Bologna. These estates, however, were sold later on. *John
XXII.* then interfered in favour of the students injured thereby and annulled the deed of purchase. The income was set aside and increased to
an amount sufficient for thirty scholars; later on the Pope endeavoured
to raise their number to fifty. At the same celebrated academy, which,
next to Paris, had long been a beacon of science sought from near and
afar, *Urban V.* founded a home for poor students and directed the appropriation of 4,000 gold ducats a year for it. From June 16, 1367, to June
15, 1368, the home received an appropriation of 5,908 ducats in gold and
155 baskets of cereals. His successor, *Gregory XI.*, set himself to the
task of completing the work begun. Out of the income of the Church
he ordered appropriated in the future 1,500 ducats a year for thirty
students, of whom one half were to study Canon Law, the other half
Civil Law. He then decreed the purchase of a home for 4,500 ducats
in gold, and ordered to pay out immediately 4,000 florins in gold for
the next school year. Besides the college named, *Urban V.* had founded
one at Montpellier for medical students, and another, which had its seat
at first at Trets, later at Monosque. During his pontificate this Pope
maintained no less than 1,000 students at various institutions. Toulouse
also had several colleges for poor students, founded by high princes
of the Church. In the year 1359 *Innocent VI.* devoted his own home
at Toulouse with all its possessions and its entire income to twenty
poor students, ten of whom were to study Canon Law and ten Civil
Law. For their further maintenance he ordered given to them, besides
other things, 25,000 florins in gold "manualiter" (*Denifle*, 213 *seq.*,
308 *seq.*, 339).

Finally, nearly all universities, whether they owed their existence to ecclesiastical or civil power, received many and far-
reaching PRIVILEGES from the Popes. Not the least one was for
clerical students the dispensation to free them from the requirement of residence for the enjoyment of their benefices,
which made it possible for them to study in remote university towns, where they were free to study not only theology,
but other sciences as well. This dispensation was quite common.

Furthermore, the Popes protected in the most energetic way the universities in their privileges and freedom every time they were applied to for aid.

This happened, for instance, at Bologna. The students there had their free guilds. The municipal authorities began to restrict their privileges by forbidding native students under heavy penalties to study outside of Bologna, which was later on extended to the alien students. The professors sided with the city. *Honorius III.* in 1220 called upon the latter to repeal those statutes; if they wanted to confine the students to the city, it should be done by clemency, not with severity and coercion. The city relented. But we see again in 1224 the students appeal, for the third time since 1217, to the Pope, begging for protection. The tension had grown; the city was actually beginning to use force. *Honorius* sharply rebuked the city for this action, threatening excommunication if the authorities continued to suppress freedom. The city yielded completely, and the freedom of the students was saved, thanks to their protector. Later on the Popes had to interfere again. *Clement V.* had already ordered the Bishops to protect the students at Bologna. His successor, *John XXII.*, received complaints that privileges of students in Italy were being violated by authorities and citizens of the city. Against the Podesta of Bologna especially complaints were made. The Pope, in 1321 and 1322, bade the Bishops and Archbishops to take measures against those who *directe et indirecte impedire dicuntur, ne ad praedictum studium valeant declinare contra apostolica et imperialia privilegia.* He appointed at Bologna a special protector and conservator of the university. Some years after, when the Podesta declined to take the *juramentum de observandis statutis ejusdem studiis factis et faciendis,* he was commanded to take the oath.

At Orleans there was a flourishing law school; especially its *jus civile* was famous. Professors and students were granted by *Clement V.* the privilege of an autonomous university with the right of free corporation, with the power to suspend lectures in case they could get no satisfaction for any wrong done them. These privileges were a thorn in the eye of the city; its citizens even allowed violence to be done the university. Then *Philip the Fair* interfered, but in a way which indicates that he did not know sufficiently the university life of the Middle Ages. Moreover, he annulled the granted free fellowship, and put professors and the students under civil supervision. But this was not tolerated in those days. The king had at the same time given many privileges, but they were disregarded. In 1316 professors and students left Orleans and the university ceased to exist. The first act of *John XXII.* upon ascending the Papal throne was to restore this school, the French king himself having begged his support in the matter. The king's suggestion to take the privilege of free fellowship from the professors and students was rejected by the Pope. The Pope reaffirmed all privileges granted to the university, whereupon the professors and students returned, to inaugurate the most brilliant epoch of their college.

Considering these facts, one may subscribe to the judgment of *Denifle* which he pronounces at the conclusion of his thorough treatise on the universities of the Middle Ages: " So far as the foundation of the universities can be spoken of, its merit belongs to the Popes, to secular rulers, clergy, and laity. But that the lion's share belongs to the Popes every one must admit who has followed my presentment, which is exclusively based on documents, and who examines history with impartiality " (Ib. 792 *seq.*). Even *Kaufmann,* who is very unfavourably disposed towards the Church, cannot deny that " numerous Popes have shown warm interest for the fostering of sciences during those centuries, and were for the most part themselves prominent representatives of science " (Ib. 403).

That the mediæval universities in some points, though not in all, were inferior to modern universities, was not their fault. No good judge of human conditions could expect it to be otherwise. The experience and efficiency of the mature man is not attained at once, but only after the exertions and experiments made by him during the period of youth and development. At a time when all the experiences in the field of school legislation, which are the property of the present day, had yet to be collected, when the relation between lower and higher schools had not been regulated in all respects, at that time it was not possible to be in the position we are in to-day. Future critics of our times will see in our present educational systems many gross defects, which often are not hidden even to our own eyes. But it would be arrogance for them to belittle our efforts, the fruits of which they will once enjoy without any merit on their part. The university of yore conformed to the educational purposes of that period; it was the focus of intellectual life, perhaps to a larger degree than is the case to-day. This suffices. Moreover, the number of professors was quite considerable, that of the students even more so. In Bologna in 1388 the number of professors was 70, not including the theologians, among them 39 jurists; in Piacenza there were from the years 1398 to 1402 71 professors; among them were 27 teachers of Roman law and 22 teachers of medicine (*Denifle,* 209, 571).

In regard to the zeal displayed by the Church in promoting universities, it might be objected that she was caring in the first place for THEOLOGY, not for the other sciences, and that the universities then had chiefly been established for theological students. This, however, is not the case. The universities especially favoured by the Popes were first of all law schools, chiefly of civil law, or medical schools. Those at Bologna, Padua, Florence, and Orleans were principally law schools; in Italy, in general, chief attention was paid to jurisprudence, particularly to Roman law. Montpellier was essentially a medical college; it attained during the thirteenth century preponderance even over Salerno. The assertion has been made that the vigorous life at this medical college was owing to its independence of Rome (*Haeser,* Lehrbuch der Geschichte der Medizin, 1, 655. Cfr. *Denifle,* 342). But *Denifle* has proved that " clerical organs have been the moving spirits of the medical college at Montpellier."

Nor did the Papal charter deeds exclude any profane science. The common formula, which always prevails, authorizes to teach indiscriminately *in jure canonico et civili necnon in medicina et qualibet alia licita facultate.* Only one science was frequently excepted, and that was just theology. Of the forty-six high schools that had been established up to the year 1400, about twenty-eight, therefore nearly two-thirds, excluded by their charter the teaching of theology. At first a number of universities sprang up merely as law schools, others as medical schools, and there was then no need to include the science of theology in the schedule of studies. Furthermore, Paris was ever since the twelfth century looked upon as the home and the natural place for theology (*Denifle,* 703 f.). Hence the benevolence of the Church towards the universities was not merely determined by selfish interest.

Or was it, nevertheless? May the Church not have bestowed so much care on the homes of science in order to increase her own influence thereby, and also with an eye to the future? This assertion has been made. But this assertion is an injustice and it is against the testimony of history. The Popes very often issued their charter deeds only then, when request was made

by worldly rulers and by the cities themselves. Hence there
was no hurried self-assertion. And the Church has never denied
the right to worldly powers to found their own high schools.
The theologians of the thirteenth century expressedly declared
it to be the duty of princes to provide for institutions of learning (Cfr. *Thomas of Aquin,* De regimine principum, I, 13; Op.
contra impug. relig. 3).

Thus up to the year 1400 nine high schools had received no charters
at all, ten only imperial charters or charters from their local sovereigns.
If the Popes had cared only about their influence, why then did they
treat such colleges with the same benevolence? Spain's first college
was founded at Palencia in the years 1212–1214 by *Alfonso VIII.*
without asking the Pope. When soon afterwards it was in trouble
it was *Honorius III.* who aided *Alfonso's* successor in restoring it,
by assigning some ecclesiastical income to its professors. When
the college was nearly wrecked and Rome once more applied to for help,
Urban IV. lent an aiding hand because he did not want *ut lucerna
tanta claritatis in commune mutorum dispendium sic extincta re-
maneat. Frederick II.* had founded a university of his own. When
it failed it was *Clement IV.* who urged *King Charles* of Anjou to re-
establish it. *In eodem regno facias et jubeas hujusmodi studium
reformari (Denifle,* 478, 459). This is not the language and action
of one who is only ruled by the passion to spread his own influence, and
not guided by benevolence for science.
   But it is true, in supporting the higher schools the Church did
not aim at science as its ultimate object; it was her view that science
should serve the material welfare of man, but still more the highest
ethical and religious purpose of life. This in general was the conception of the entire Middle Ages. At that time it would have been considered curious to seek a science ultimately for its own sake.

And the universities repaid the Church by gratitude and devotion. The effort has been made to demonstrate that the
modern separation of science from religion had already begun
in the Middle Ages, and had showed itself everywhere; this
tendency for autonomy " appeared at first only timidly and in
manifold disguises " (*Kaufmann,* 14). How easy it is to find
such disguises may be shown by an example. The university
of Paris had after the death of *St. Thomas* asked for his remains. *Kaufmann* holds that the notion of the autonomy
of science had found sharp expression in the memorandum wherein the university stated the motive of its request.
Now how does this harmless document sound? " Quoniam

omnino est indecens et indignum ut alia ratio aut locus quam omnium studiorum nobilissima Parisiensis civitas quae ipsum prius educavit nutrivit et fovit et post modum ad eodem doctrinae monumenta et ineffabilia fomenta suscepit ossa . . . habeat . . . Si enim Ecclesia merito ossa et reliquias Sanctorum honorat nobis non sine causa videtur honestum et sanctum tanti doctoris corpus in perpetuum penes nos habere in honore." Evidently the university requests the relic for itself, or rather for the Parisiensis civitas, not in opposition to the Church, but in opposition to other cities, altera natio aut locus. I wonder if the Parisian admirers of St. Thomas ever dreamed that they would one day be put in the light of forerunners of liberal science, because of their pious application for the bones of their great teacher? This is tantamount to carrying one's own idea into the fact. *Denifle,* probably the most competent judge of the affairs of mediæval universities, writes as follows: " If we weigh the different acts which suggest themselves to us in these various foundations, and if we compare them with one another, there is revealed to us, in the realm of history of the foundation of mediæval universities, a wonderful harmony between Church and State, between the spiritual and material. This is the reason why the universities of the Middle Ages appear to us as the highest civil as well as the highest ecclesiastical teaching institutions. Fundamentally, they are the product of the Christian spirit which penetrated the whole, wherein Pope and Prince, clergy and laity, each held the proper position " (l. c. p. 795).

One consequence of this relation between the universities and the Church was that " they attained their greatest prosperity as long as the unity of Church and faith remained unimpaired, and that, at the time of the Reformation, they all sided with the Church with the exception of two, Wittenberg and Erfurt. Torn away from their ecclesiastical and established basis only by violent means, they were led to the new doctrine, but really succumbed to it only when their freedom had been curtailed and they had been reduced to state institutions " (*Janssen,* l. c. p. 91). They had been, as the learned *Wimpheling* wrote at the close of the sixteenth century, " the most favoured daughters

of the Church, who tried to repay by fidelity and attachment
what they owed to their Mother " (De arte impressoria, apud
Janssen, l. c. 91).

A False Progress

Hence history cannot subscribe to the accusation that the
Church is the enemy of progress. How then does it happen that
this accusation is made so frequently? The idea suggests itself
that there may be here a different meaning given to the word
" progress," that the Church opposes a certain kind of progress
which her enemies call " the " progress. And this is the actual
fact. If we examine the proofs which are to show the hostile
attitude of the Church, we meet at every step *Galileo,* the Copernican system, the Syllabus, and Index. But this appears only on
the surface, which hides beneath it something that is easily overlooked by the cursory glance. And this is the precise definition
of scientific and civilized progress. Progress has ever been
an ideal of powerful attraction. The noblest and best of men
have ever displayed the most earnest endeavour onward and
upward. In our times, however, this ideal comes forward differently garbed, in the name of the new view of the world, and
resolutely censures as reactionary everything that will oppose it.
What is this definition?

Since the THEORY OF EVOLUTION of *Lamarck* and *Darwin*
entered biology, it has also more and more invaded other branches
of science. The principle is now that everywhere, in the organic
or inorganic world and in the whole province of human life
there is a gradual growth and change — nothing permanent,
nothing definite and absolute. Uninterrupted evolution hitherto; hereafter restless development; especially in the greatest good belonging to human life, thought, philosophy, and
chiefly religion. Here, too, there are no forms nor dogmas
which evolution in its continual development does not evolve
and elevate. This idea of evolution is supplemented by subjectivism with its RELATIVISM OF TRUTH: all views, especially
philosophical and religious " Truths," are no longer the reproduction of objectively existing things, but a creation of the

subject, of his inner experience and feeling; hence each age must proceed to new thought of ITS OWN.

"The methods of scientific research," we are told, "are determined by the idea of evolution, and this applies not only to natural sciences but also to the so-called intellectual sciences, — history, philology, philosophy, and theology. The idea of evolution influences and dominates all our thoughts: without it progress in the field of scientific knowledge is quite impossible." We read, for instance, in the modern history of philosophy: "The rise and fall of a system is a necessary part of universal history; it is conditioned by the character of its time, the system being the understanding of that time, while this understanding of the time is conditioned by the fact that the time has changed." At *Roscellin's* time the nominalists were intellectually inferior; but where there is question of undermining the militant Church of the Middle Ages the nominalists will be considered to have been the greater philosophers. In this the realists "by the futility of their struggle proved that the time for nominalism had arrived, hence that whoever favours it understands the time better; that is, more philosophically. After the beginning of the Renaissance we notice an attempt at philosophizing in such a way as to ignore the existence of divine wisdom taught by Christianity. The pre-Christian sages had done so: to philosophize in their spirit was therefore the task of the time, and those who had a better understanding of the time philosophized that way better than by the scholastic method; though their method may appear reactionary to unphilosophical minds" (*J. E. Erdmann*, Grundriss der Gesch. der Philosophie, 3d ed., I (1878), 4, 262, 434, 502). This is a frank denial of any truth in philosophy: the more neological and modern a thing is, the more truth there is in it! Realism was right in *Roscellin's* time, but a later period had to sweep it away. The Christian religion was right for the Middle Ages, but when the Greek authors began to be read again it was no longer modern.

Apostasy from the faith is considered a mark of progress. "Italian natural philosophy," we are told, "reached its pinnacle with *Bruno* and *Campanella*, of whom the former, though the older, appears to be more progressive on account of his freer attitude towards the Church" (*R. Falkenburg*, Gesch. der neueren Philosophie, 5th ed. (1905), page 30, *seq.*). Hence evidently further development of Christianity, too, is demanded. According to subjectivistic views it was hitherto only an historical product of the human intellect: hence onward to new and higher forms corresponding to modern thought and feeling, onward to a new Christianity without dogmas and authority! " "Break up those old tablets," spoke *Zarathustra*.

Such is progress in thought and science, for which the way must be opened. That the immutable dogmas of Christianity, that the task of the Catholic Church to preserve revelation intact, are incompatible with it, that the Church appears reactionary, and as an obstacle to this progress, is now self-evident. Here we have the DEEPER CONTRAST BETWEEN PROGRESS, IN THE ANTI-CHRISTIAN SENSE, AND THE ESSENCE OF CHRISTIANITY in general, and, especially, of the CATHOLIC CHURCH.

"It is frankly admitted that the issue is the struggle between the two views of the world — between the Christian, conservative dogmatism and the anti-dogmatic evolutionary philosophy" (Neue Freie Presse, Jun. 7, 1908). Faith according to its very essence is immutable and stationary, science is essentially progressive: they had therefore to part in a manner which could not be kept a secret. "A divine revelation must necessarily be intolerant of contradiction, it must repudiate all improvement in itself" (J. Draper, History of the Conflict between Religion and Science, VI). "The great opposition between the rigid dogmatism of the Roman Catholic Church and the ever progressing modern science cannot be removed" (Academicus, 1. c. 362). So say the opponents of the Church.

There is no error, says *St. Augustine,* which does not contain some truth, especially when it is able to rule the thought of many. Hence its capacity to deceive. The same is true in the present case.

There is evolution and progress in everything, or at least there should be. The individual gradually develops from the embryo into a perfect form, though it becomes nothing else than what it had formerly been in its embryonic state. Mankind advances rapidly in civilization; we no longer ride in the rumbling stage-coach but in a comfortable express train, and the tallow candle has been replaced by the electric light. Thus we demand progress also in knowledge and science, and even in religion. Many things that were obscure to older generations have become clear to us; we have corrected many an error, made many discoveries which were unknown to our ancestors. Many doctrines of faith, also, appear to our eyes in sharper outlines than before; of many we have a deeper understanding, discovered new relations, meanings, and deductions. Thus there is progress and development everywhere.

But it would be erroneous to conclude from all this that there cannot be any stable truths and dogmas, that progress to new and different views and doctrines is necessary. By the same right we might conclude that the main principles of the Copernican system cannot be immutable, because they would hinder the progress of science. Progress certainly does not consist in throwing away all certainty acquired, in order to begin anew. Or does it really belong to progress in astronomy to again give up *Copernicus,* to go back to *Ptolemy* and let the sun and all the stars revolve again around the earth? Does not progress rather consist in our studying these astronomical results more closely, in building up the details, and, first of all, in trying to solve new problems?

The champion of the faith will reply: Just as established results do not hinder the progress of science, just so do the doctrines of faith not form an obstacle to progress and evolution. The fixed doctrines of the faith themselves, in themselves and in their application to the conditions of life, offer rich material for the growth of religious knowledge. And there is the immense field for progress in the profane sciences. If any one should say that the believing scientist, who is bound by his dogmas, can do nothing further but reiterate his old truths, one might in turn argue: Then the astronomer bound by the fundamental rules of the Copernican system could have only the monotonous task of drawing over and over again the outlines of his system, while the mathematician who holds the multiplication table to be an unalienable possession would not be allowed to do aught but to repeat the multiplication table.

Or the argument may be put thus: We have made great progress in the material province of civilization, in science and art; "can an old religion suffice under these new and improved conditions, a religion which originated at an age when these conditions did not exist? This contradiction is shocking. . . . Progress in culture demands progress in religion. . . . We want a more perfect religion, a higher religion" (*Masaryk,* Im Kampf um die Religion, 1904, 29). Note the logic of this demonstration. We no longer light our rooms by the dim light of a small oil lamp, we walk no longer at night through dark narrow lanes, but through brightly illuminated avenues, does it follow from this that it can no longer be true that Christ is the Son of God, nor that He has worked miracles, or founded a Church, and a new religion is therefore necessary? We have made progress in our knowledge of history; we know a good deal of Rome and Carthage, of the civilization of ancient Egypt and of Greece, and of their mutual relations; we have other fashions of life than our fathers had, we build and paint differently — our political life, too, has grown more complicated; does it follow from all this, that it cannot be true that we are created by God, that we must believe a divine revelation, hence a new religion is necessary? Progress and evolution to consist in ever abandoning the old and advancing to new and different views — this is ABSURD. Absurd, in the first place, because it is no PROGRESS at all, but a retrogression, a hopeless alternation of forwards and backwards. There can be no progress if I am always withdrawing from my old position; progress is possible only by retaining the basis established and then advancing therefrom. And EVOLUTION is not a continuous remodelling and shaping anew, but a continuance in growth. Evolution means that the embryo unfolds, and by retaining and perfecting the old matter gradually becomes a plant; evolution is in the progress from bud to blossom; but not in the changing mass of clouds, swept away to-day by the current wind and replaced to-morrow by other clouds. An absurdity, also, for the reason that it violates all laws of reason, that once there was a revelation of God to be believed, but that this is no longer true.

Furthermore, the demand to follow always " the ideas of the period " suggests the question: Who is to represent the period? Who represented Greece, the sophists or *Plato?* Who was representative of the first days of Christianity, the Roman emperors or the martyrs? Will not the passage in *Goethe's* Faust apply in most cases: " What they call the spirit of the times is but their own mind wherein the times are reflected "? True, if progress is taken to be the overstepping by human reason of the eternal standards of immutable truth and the barriers of faith, if it is to be the attempt at emancipation from God and religion, then there is no more resolute foe of progress than the Christian religion, than the Catholic Church. But this is not progress but loss of the truth, not higher religion but apostasy, not development of what is best in man, but retrogression to mental disintegration by scepticism.

The Syllabus

In the eyes of many it is especially the Syllabus of *Pius IX.*
by which the Catholic Church has erected a lasting monument to
its enmity to civilization. It is the Syllabus, we are told, in
which *Pius IX.* has " ex cathedra condemned the freedom of
science " (*W. Kahl,* Bekenntnissgebundenheit und Lehrfreiheit,
1897, 10) ; " in which modern culture and science is being
cursed " (*Th. Fuchs,* Neue Freie Presse, Nov. 25, 1907) ; in
which " the most general foundations of our political order, the
freedom of conscience, are rejected " (*G. Kaufmann,* Die Lehrfreiheit an den deutschen Universitaeten, 1898, 34) ; " in which
it has simply anathematized the achievements of the modern
concept of right " (*F. Jodl,* Gedanken über Reformkatholizis-
mus, 1902, 5) ; the Syllabus " strikes blows against the autonomy
of human development of culture, it is a *non possumus,* I cannot
make peace, I cannot compromise with what is termed progress,
liberalism, and civilization." The Syllabus is a favorite stock
argument of professional free-thinkers and agitators, and the
one with which they like to open the discussion. For this reason
we must say a few words about it.

When a Syllabus is spoken of without any distinction, the
Syllabus of *Pius IX.* is meant. It is a list of eighty condemned propositions which this Pope sent on December 8,
1864, to all the Bishops of the world, together with the encyclical letter " Quanta Cura." *Pius IX.* had, prior to this, and on
various occasions, denounced these propositions as false and to
be repudiated. They were now gathered together in the Syllabus. They represent the PROGRAM OF MODERN LIBERALISM in
the province of religion and in politics in relation to religion.
They are repudiated in the following order: Pantheism; liberal freedom of thought and of conscience as a repudiation of the
duty to believe; religious freedom as a demand of emancipation
from faith and Church; religious indifferentism; the denial of
the Church and of her independence of the state; the omnipotence of state power, especially in the province of thought. The
single propositions are not all designated as heretical, hence the
contrary is not always pronounced to be dogma; they are re-

jected in general as "errors." It is not necessary to discuss
here the question whether and to what extent the Syllabus is
an infallible decision. Suffice it to say it is binding for believing
Catholics.

Has the Catholic any reason to be ashamed of the Syllabus?
It was a resolute deed. A deed of that intrepidity and firm
consistency which has ever characterized the Catholic Church.
With her fearless love of truth the Church has in the Syllabus
solemnly condemned the errors of the modern rebellion against
the supernatural order, of the naturalization and declaration
of independence of the human life. For this reason the Syllabus
is called an attack upon modern culture, science, and education,
upon the foundations of the state. Is this true?

It is, and it is not. All that is good and Christian in modern culture is not touched by the Syllabus; it strikes only at
what is anti-Christian in our times and in the leading ideas
of our times. It does not condemn freedom of science, but only
the liberal freedom which throws off the yoke of faith; it does
not repudiate freedom of religion and conscience, but the LIB-
ERAL freedom which will not acknowledge a divine revelation
nor take the Church as a guide. Not the foundations of modern
states are attacked, but only the liberal ideas of emancipation
from religion, and of opposition to the Church. The Church
proclaims to the world only what has been known to all Christian centuries, that, just as the single individual is bound to
have the Christian belief and must lead a Christian life, so are
nations and organized states; that the human creature is subject
to the law of Christ in all its relations. Nor does she contend
against genuine progress in science, education and in the material domain, but merely against liberal progress towards the
irreligious materialization of life.

This emancipation from the Christian faith poses mostly
under the attractive and deceptive name of "modern progress." Indeed, it has ever been the pretension of liberalism
to look upon itself as the sole harbinger of civilization, to claim
the guidance of intellectual life for its aim, and to stigma-
tize as a foe of culture any one that opposes the dissemination of
its anti-Christian humanism. It is also an expert in giving

to words a charm and an ambiguous meaning that deceive. Emancipation from religion is "progress" and "enlightenment." Everything else is reactionary. Its infidelity is freedom of conscience and thought. Everything else is "bondage." Only its secular schools, its civil marriage, its separation of Church and State are "modern." Everything else is obsolete, hence no longer warranted. For the Church to defend her rights is arrogance; when the Church uses her God-given authority for the good of the faith, she practises intellectual oppression; the Catholic who lets himself be guided by his Church is called unpatriotic, bereft of his civil spirit.

What striking contrast to the honesty in which the Church presents her doctrines frankly before the whole world, without disguise or artifice. The reason is that she has sufficient interior strength and truth to render it unnecessary for her to take refuge in disguise or present the truth in ambiguity.

The clearest evidence of the Church's hostility to culture is the condemnation of the 80th thesis of the SYLLABUS, so it is said. It is the thesis that the Pope can and must reconcile himself to, and compromise with, progress, liberalism, and modern civilization. This is a condemned proposition, hence the contrary is true: the Pope of Rome cannot, and must not, reconcile himself, nor compromise with, liberalism and modern civilization. Here we have the frankly admitted hostility against progress, education, and science — it is the watchword of the Papacy.

This conclusion can be arrived at only by pushing aside all rules of scientific interpretation. What progress is this, with what civilization can the Papacy not be reconciled with? The progress of modern liberalism. The heading of the paragraph containing this proposition states expressly that "errors of modern liberalism" are to be condemned. This becomes clear by the Allocution "Jamdudum cernimus" of March 18, 1861, from which this condemnation is taken. There it is stated: "It is asked that the Pope of Rome reconcile himself with progress, to liberalism as they call it, to the new civilization, and compromise with them. . . . But now we ask of those inviting us to be reconciled with modern civilization, whether the facts be such as to tempt the Vicar of Christ on earth . . . to connect himself with the civilization of to-day without the greatest injury to this conscience . . . a civilization that has caused the dissemination of numerous despicable opinions, errors, and principles in conflict with the Catholic religion and its doctrines." Of course a civilization cut off from any true Christianity by education and science, by family life and political life, a progress, trying to stop the activity of the Church in every sphere and attacking her in their speech, in newspapers, and in schools, cannot demand of the Papacy to join hands with them. No Christian, whether Catholic or Protestant, can profess this "progress." We have here at the same time a specimen of how they proceed in interpreting the propositions of the Syllabus in order to discover in them all possible absurdities. Many propositions are short sentences taken from the work of an author, or from previous Papal declarations. Hence they must be understood in the sense of those sources. Furthermore, attention must be paid to what is specially emphasized. Then, again, we must remember that by repudiating a proposition only the contradictory is asserted, but not the contrary; to conclude this would be to conclude too much. For instance, the seventy-seventh condemned proposition reads: "In our times it is no longer to any purpose that the Catholic religion should be the sole religion of the state to the exclusion of all other confessions." According to some, *e. g.*, *Frins*, the contradictory is thus formulated: "In our times also it is still to the purpose. . . ." According to others, however, *e. g.*, *Hoensbroech* and *Goetz:* "In our times also it is beneficial. . . ." Thus while *Hoensbroech* and *Goetz* make the ecclesiastical doctrine appear to read that it would be beneficial to hold fast to the Catholic as the sole religion of the state under all circumstances even to-day, the actual opposite is the doctrine, that this may be yet to the purpose under certain circumstances. While no reasonable man could object to the latter, the former is eagerly exploited against the Church (*Heiner*, Der Syllabus, 1905, p. 31, *seq.*; cf. *Frins*, Kirchenlex, 2d ed., XI, 1031; *Hoensbroech*, l. c. 25; *Goetz*, Der Ultramontanismus, 1905, 148).

Of course it may be taken for granted that the Syllabus is distasteful to modern liberalism, which is branded there as one of the errors of the day. Yet the Church cannot be censured for not becoming unfaithful to her vocation of preserving the patrimony of Christianity to mankind, or for acting as the invincible defender of the Christian religion in the universal struggle between truth and error, even though the latter pose with great assurance.

THE CONDEMNATION OF MODERNISM

The great excitement caused in intellectual circles by the Syllabus of *Pius IX*. was aroused again, though not with the same intensity, when some years ago the news of another Syllabus was circulated through the world, and the excitement increased when the rumour was followed by the publication of the encyclical "Pascendi Dominici gregis." Indeed, the new event was not very unlike the former: in the 60's Rome's sentence was directed against the Modernism of that period, which called itself liberalism. The excitement caused by its condemnation was more intense, because it struck directly at the principles governing the liberal politics against the Church, which principles were claimed to be the foundation of the modern state. Now the Modernism repudiated by the Church's voice was nothing more than the old humanistic, fundamental, errors of liberalism, but put in the form of a religious and philosophical view of the world, and in Catholic garb: it meant man detached from everything supernatural, and dependent alone on himself in his intellectual life, more especially in his religious life.

Now, as then, similar charges were raised: The Church is the irreconcilable foe of modern achievements and the opponent of them; " the encyclical aims at modern intellectual life in all its phases and forms " (XX. Jahrh., 1908, 568). Now, as then, we have the same ambiguity of the terms "modern " and " progress."

What was condemned by the Church? The document " Lamentabili sane exitu," issued by the teaching authority of the Church on July 3, 1907, is entitled " A Decree of the Holy Congregation of the Roman and General Inquisition or the Holy Office," which has to watch over the unadulterated preservation of the faith. The decree soon was christened the " New Syllabus," because of its similarity with the Syllabus of *Pius IX*. In a similar way it condemns sixty-five propositions against the inspiration and the historical character of Holy Scripture, against the divine origin of revelation and of faith, against the divinity of Christ, His Resurrection and His atoning death, against the Sacraments, and against the Church. These are component parts of the philosophical religious system of thought which soon after was set forth and condemned by the encyclical " Pascendi," of September 8, 1907.

Modernism is essentially philosophy, combining modern AGNOSTIC-AUTONOMOUS SUBJECTIVISM with EVOLUTIONISM, and applied to the Christian religion, which thereby becomes disfigured beyond recognition. Its chain of thought, excellently stated by the encyclical, starts with the proposition that the supernatural is beyond the knowledge of man, and hence man

cannot know anything of God. The faith which unites us to
God is nothing but a feeling, born of a blind impulse, which
may be considered a divine revelation. If this religious feeling
is expressed in forms, the result is " doctrines of faith "; for
Christian " dogmas " are this and nothing more, images and
symbols of the noble and divine, hence they are of human
origin and are changeable according to the disposition and the
degree of learning of the individual, as well as of the times.
There is no dogmatic Christianity, in the sense of an immutable religious doctrine, nor is there any absolutely true
religion, for religion is but a variable feeling, that has nothing
to do with cognition and knowledge. For this reason they never
can come in conflict. The Christian religion originally was
nothing else but the religious experience of Christ, who was
not God but a man; in the course of time it has undergone
changes which are reflected in the shaping of Christian dogma.
Holy Scripture is, similarly, the expression of the religious experience of its human authors; the Sacraments are symbols,
arousing religious sentiments; the Church is not founded by
God, and only has the task of regulating the development of
Christianity, and of sanctioning at any time whatever religious
experiences the changeable spirit of progressive civilization may
produce.

This is Modernism, as represented chiefly in France, Italy,
and to an extent also in England; in Germany it did not appear
as a system, but even there its spirit became quite apparent.
Thus, Modernism is nothing else but the systematic arrangement
of those ideas which we have hitherto met, in various places, as
the fundamental principles of modern religious thought opposed to Christianity. It is subjectivism with its autonomy
of the human subject, its agnosticism, its relativism of truth,
sailing under the name of " historical method of thought " and
" progress," and, finally, with its freedom of thought and conscience which rejects all authority. It is *Kant* in the robe of
a Catholic theologian. Ultimately it is nothing else but the
shocking negation of everything supernatural, hence complete
apostasy. " The salient point is recognized," says *Troeltsch,*
" the enemy is the modern historical method of thought, the

concept of evolution, the theory of inner experience and relativism as applied to religion, the negation of supernaturalism as taught by the old Church " (l. c. 22). Hence, was it not manifest that the Church had to take measures against this positive denial of Christianity as a whole, the more so as the uneducated could be easily deceived by it? Every organism will throw off excrescences, the more energetically the stronger it is. Any religion lacking this strength is doomed. That the Papal declaration aroused such opposition must not be wondered at; it hit once more the central idea of the anti-Christian view of the world. The judgment was not passed against modern intellectual life, but only against the grave errors inherent in it; the Church did not condemn progress, nor the increase and deepening of knowledge of the truth; not the enrichment of the life of the mind, of feeling, and the will, but only pretended progress; she did not condemn the historical method nor the idea of evolution, but their false application, which dissolved anything and everything in growth, purely natural growth at that, without acknowledging a revelation of absolute truths.

Orthodox Protestants have openly praised this bold deed of the Pope as highly meritorious for the preservation of the Christian faith. Thus the South African Church Quarterly Review (Episcopal) of January, 1908, said: " The Syllabus and Encyclical of *Pius X.* against Modernism are deserving of the respectful consideration of all Christians. . . . At the present stage of history the opposing factors are driving with great speed towards a fierce and resolute struggle between Christ and anti-Christ. All who sincerely love Christ, our Lord, must rally under one flag. . . . Narrow-minded hostility towards the Pope must give way to the desire to be united with the great community which is fighting so valiantly for the old faith of our fathers. . . . One must be blind, to misjudge the tremendous influence exerted by the last deed of the Pope in favour of the faith."

Even the Evangelical " Kirchenzeitung " admitted that the encyclical is " directed chiefly against the more or less unchristian modern views of the world . . . which we must combat. . . . Undoubtedly it is not only the Pope's right to lay bare the unchristian tendency of these ideas and their incompatibility with the Christian faith, but it is also his duty and his merit " (November 29, 1908, n. 48).

Puny men, entangled in the ideas of their time and surroundings, are easily led to take for their standard the thoughts and actions of their age. They often imagine that

they possess not a little strength and independence, when they
are intellectually entirely dependent and unable to rise above
their time. " It is the fashion, others think that way, therefore I must think so, too "; these are often the principles of
their wisdom, and they ask the Church to do likewise. The
Church, however, looks back upon a long history, and numerous
ideas and opinions she has seen arise and vanish. And whoever
can look back upon a great experience, and moreover carries in
himself the call to lead the times, feels no restless impulse to
be carried away by changing doctrines.

THE INDEX

Whenever the subject of Rome's enmity to science and
progress of culture is discussed, there invariably appears on the
scene, beside Syllabus and *Galileo,* also the Index. The latter
is held by many to be Rome's permanent means of hindering
the progress of humanity in general, and the free scientific
activity of the Catholic in particular, and to annihilate the
freedom of teaching and learning (*Hoensbroech,* Die Kath.
theol. Fakultaeten, 1907, 40 *seq.*). They say " the Congregation of the Index has no pity nor consideration for the
classical works of literature, and condemns in the name of religion the most admirable products of the human intellect "
(Grande Dict. univ. du XIX. siècle, IX, 640, apud *J. Hilgers,*
Der Index der Verb. Buecher, 1904, 166; much of what we
shall say on this topic is taken from this work by *Hilgers*).

This statement again reminds that the accusations against the
Catholic Church and her institutions are to be considered with caution,
because of the ignorance of her opponents in Catholic things. This is
especially true of the Index. Thus the above assertion is false. *Dante's*
" Divina Commedia " (the work referred to) is neither forbidden nor
needs approval nor correction; of the classical literature of the world
little or nothing is forbidden; even morally offensive books, that are
considered classical, may without ecclesiastical permission be read for
the sake of their elegant diction, whenever their reading is required
by one's work or duty of teaching.

A few examples of the INCREDIBLE IGNORANCE alluded to will suffice.
In the " Grande Dictionnaire Universel du XIX. Siècle " it is actually
stated that the works of *Albert the Great* were condemned by a decree
of April 10, 1666. What does the Index really forbid? It states: " *Al-*

berto Magno, diviso in tre libri, nel primo si tratta della virtu delle herbe, nel secondo della virtu delle pietre, e nel terzo della virtu di alcuni animali. — Albert the Great, in three parts: the first treats of the virtue of plants; the second, of the virtue of stones; and the third, of the virtue of some animals." It is the title of a little superstitious book, attributed to "Albert the Great" by an unknown author.

The first edition of the Index of *Leo XIII.* in 1900 was sold out in less than a year; a second edition followed in 1901, and, like the first, could be had at all booksellers, at a very moderate price. In December, 1901, there appeared in the Anglo-American weekly, "The Roman World," an article which says that it is difficult to obtain this list of notorious books forbidden to Catholics, unless one be a Church official, since only a few copies are printed and even these are not handled by general book-dealers; hence that no details could be given about the purchase of the copy referred to; but it was quite evident that it had commanded a good price. "The copy in question, a model of fine printing, might be worth about $40 to $50, but owing to its rareness, it had undoubtedly cost $400. The history of this famous Index is interesting. The one who first hit upon the idea was *Charles V.* of Spain, about 1550. The first compilation of the book-list was made by the university of Louvain in 1564, Pope *Paul IV.* assuming the direction of the edition. It remained for 357 years in the hands of the Pope." Every one of these statements is false. And just as false is the statement that the "Syllabus condemns not only a book written by a Pope, but by Pope *Leo XIII.* himself." Still it could not surprise us, since even David's psalter is on the Index! When the Index of *Leo XIII.* was published, Dr. *Max Claar* wrote from Rome to the "Neue Freie Presse" of Vienna: "On the old Index we find among other things the Psalms of King David and the Divina Commedia of *Dante.*" We have already stated that the latter was never on the Index. But how in the world could this man find Holy Scripture condemned on the Index? Perhaps he found this passage: "Il salmista secondo la biblia" and "Salmi (sessanta) di David." The first is a superstitious booklet, the second is a translation of sixty Psalms of David by the heretic, *Giovanni Diodati.* The learned doctor in all seriousness mistook them for the Psalms of David (*Hilgers,* 167, *seq.*).

What then is the Index, and how is it to be judged?

Ever since the Apostle of the Nations had at Ephesus the superstitious books burned under his eyes, the Holy Fathers, Bishops, and Councils since the first centuries of Christianity have been careful to keep from the faithful writings hurtful to faith and morals. Thus even in the olden time we find several catalogues of forbidden books, then followed the Indices of the Middle Ages. In the year 1571 a special Congregation of Cardinals was formed, the "Congregation of the Index," which has ever since had charge of the ecclesiastical book-laws.

The last edition of the Index, obligatory for the whole Church, emanated from *Leo XIII*. The title of the work now in force reads, "The Index of Forbidden Books, revised and published by order of and in the name of Leo XIII. 1900." It is divided into two parts. The first and shorter part contains the general book regulations, giving in short paragraphs the rules on various classes of forbidden books, the permission required for reading them, the examination to be made previous to the publication of certain books. The second part enumerates the writings forbidden by special decree — the Index in the particular sense, and the part most often considered. But it is second in importance to the first, because by far not all books dangerous to faith and morals are named in it. Most such books are forbidden by the general laws contained in the first part, without mentioning the many which are forbidden by mere common sense.

Ecclesiastical legislation on books is composed of two factors: first, the previous censorship — certain books must be examined by ecclesiastical authority before their publication. Second, the prohibition of books already published.

The previous scrutiny in general is delegated to the Bishop; all books dealing with morals and theology must be submitted. The license to print the book is to be given if the book is in accord with the teaching of the Church, in so far as determined by ecclesiastical authority, the decision based on it rests solely with the censor; if the author of the book should fail to see that the passages objected to need revision he may try to clear himself by stating his reasons; however, he is also free to submit his work to another Bishop and to look for a printer in the latter's diocese. If one looks over the numerous books bearing the ecclesiastical imprimatur, he will readily notice how much freedom is given, if the author keeps within the doctrine of the Church.

The CONDEMNATION of a book never strikes at the person of the author, nor at what he has intended to express by the passages objected to; judgment is passed only upon what is actually expressed in them. Hence it is not necessary to give to the author himself a hearing, or a chance to explain.

The reason is that the judgment is rendered on the sense of the passages, not on the meaning of the author. In general those books and periodicals are forbidden which are likely to do serious damage to faith and morals. The isolated cases of indicting the works of Catholic authors in the nineteenth century — we may mention *Lamennais, Hermes, Guenther, Loisy,* and *Schell* — show that the Church proceeds but slowly and with consideration against the author involved.

To appreciate the Index properly, one must try to grasp without prejudice the PURPOSE the Church has in view. This purpose is to protect the faithful from error and from moral contagion, and to preserve the faith intact. " What is more precious than souls, what more precious than the faith? But both suffer damage from such reading." Such was the judgment of the Council of Ephesus when it drew up its book-decrees; such was the judgment of an *Augustine,* of *Leo the Great,* and of the Holy Fathers; such is still the judgment of the Church. Books and writings that offend against morals are a menace to her faithful. They become infected with wrong ideas; they are as a rule not in a position to distinguish by themselves the false from the true, and for the most part they are not morally strong enough to resist the allurements of error. It may also happen that certain thoughts are true in the abstract, yet for the time being would be a danger for many. Now, it is the right and duty of any social authority, beginning with the head of the family and up to the government, to protect with strong hand the precious possessions of its subjects.

The state keeps under control the sale of poison and dynamite, keeps out contagious diseases from its boundaries — it protects the possessions of its subjects. European states have for centuries claimed the right to censure books, and have used it much more rigorously than the Church ever did, to say nothing of the censures of the Protestant Church of former times (see abundant proof apud *Hilgers,* 206–402). The modern state also, despite the great freedom granted to the press, cannot entirely forego its sense of responsibility. It restricts the freedom of the press by censorship, and by preventive measures often not less drastic than the censure itself, and it always regards the confiscation of particularly dangerous writings to be a matter of course. It puts under censure school-books, political posters, and theatrical plays, and does not tolerate any socialistic literature in the soldiers' barracks. And do we not take it as a matter of course if a father forbids his child to associate with dangerous playmates, and takes bad books from its hands? We cannot find fault with the Church if she seeks to protect her children, if she represses the promiscuous dissemination of false ideas and doctrines, and if she takes dangerous books under her control. " Feed my lambs, feed my sheep," was the command given to the Church.

The objection should therefore not be made that " such precaution is proper when dealing with children but not with men; especially since the thinking elements among the Catholics of the Germanic tongue or origin are too profound and firm in their faith to warrant a fear of the effects of unrestricted free research " (from the petition of the so-called " Index-league " of Muenster). This perusal may become dangerous even for highly educated men, else how could Modernism break so forcefully into the Church? Manifestly only because learned theologians did not possess that firmness of Catholic faith and Catholic knowledge which would prevent them from being deceived by the misleading ideas of modern philosophy, and of the new Protestant theology. Moreover, all forbidden books may be read upon obtaining the necessary permission.

" Preserve the deposit of faith," the Church has been told. She cannot look on silently when her doctrines are being falsified and denied, when the most venerable sphere of theology is made the stamping ground for immature minds and a laboratory for all kinds of experiments. When *Zola's* novel, " Rome," had been put on the Index, the atheistic literary critic, *Sarcey,* made the following comment: " If my own criticisms of literature are regarded by many people as highest decisions, why should a positive criticism be looked upon as monstrous just because it comes from the Pope? It is my aim to guard good taste in literature, and it is the aim of the Pope to guard the true faith " (Allgemeine Rundschau, 1908, 828). Every social authority must interfere when its foundations are attacked.

A church that tolerates false doctrines cannot be the teacher that Christ sent to the nations. As a matter of fact the Index has from the first helped in no small degree to keep the Catholic doctrine pure, to induce caution in reading certain authors, and to keep awake in the faithful that aversion against immoral and irreligious writings which is the characteristic of Catholics, and which has rescued the faith for thousands.

To judge the Index fairly one must be convinced that the preservation of true Christian doctrine is its highest aim. Then the zeal of the Catholic Church will be intelligible. Of course, he who thinks that the true weal of mankind consists in the speedy emancipation from all Christian dogma, he who holds the task of science to be the establishment of a new " scientific view of the world," he who no longer knows faith, will see in the Index nothing but restraint. But, whoever is of a different view will not take offence at the restriction of the freedom of writing and reading when it is productive of higher good. Freedom of science cannot be unrestricted, especially in regard to teaching; the welfare of humanity must be considered. Moreover, the Index concerns almost exclusively theology and some branches of philosophy, the rest of the profane sciences but little or not at all; the scientific works prohibited, however, are not removed from scientific perusal : only permission is necessary, and this is granted without difficulty and without cost.

It is true, an error on the part of the Church authorities is not impossible. We know of such a case, putting on the Index the writings of *Copernicus,* in 1616. But just the circumstance that history knows of but one such case of importance is a clear testimony to the Holy Ghost's direction of the teaching office even when it is rendering non-infallible decisions. Besides, the damage that might result from a few mistakes would not be so great as the damage resulting if everything were allowed to be written and read.

The Catholic scientist who appreciates the supernatural mission of his Church will YIELD TO HER GUIDANCE IN HUMBLE CONFIDENCE, he will practise this submission to the Church by requesting permission for reading forbidden books, and by this spirit he will obtain God's blessing on his work.

In doing so he may recall to mind the edifying words of *St. Francis of Sales,* in the preface to his treatise on the errors of the Lutherans and Calvinists, where he gives the assurance of having conscientiously asked for and received permission to read their writings. "We fervently request our Catholic readers," writes the Saint, "not to let an evil suspicion against us arise, as if we had read the forbidden books in spite of the prohibition of holy Church. We are able to assure them in all truth of having done nothing forbidden to a good Christian, and of having taken every precaution due in a matter of so vast importance, so as not to incur in any way the very just censures of the Church, nor in any manner to violate the profound reverence we owe to her." The permission granted him, dated July 16, 1608, is still extant; likewise one asked by *St. Charles Borromeo.*

The Catholic scientist also will readily ask the ecclesiastical Imprimatur for certain of his works. If a careful author before publishing a work submits the proofs to a friend of his profession, taking his comment for a guide, why should we deem it intellectual bondage if the Catholic scientist, in matters of faith and morals, submits his work to the formal approval of his Church, which to him is a higher authority than any other? and does this willingly, as in consistency with his Catholic conviction? [1]

Via stulti recta in oculis ejus, qui autem sapiens est audit consilia, says the Wise Man. It is characteristic of the fool to be wise in his own eyes, and stubbornly to cling to his own judgment; but the prudent man seeks advice, and suffers his attention to be called to his mistakes.

The believing scientist, too, will submit to correction; should the rare case fall to his lot to have the Church condemn his work, he will know how to be generously obedient. Splendid examples are blazing the way for him. "Were we to draw up a list of the scientists, who, in a similar critical position as *Fénelon,*

---

[1] At a certain Austrian university, where the custom obtains that a member of a faculty of the university, in the regular order of the faculties, publishes during the year a book on some study in its particular branch, the turn came to the theological faculty. One of its members then issued a work on moral theology, of course with the ecclesiastical Imprimatur. Upon this being discovered the senate resolved not to acknowledge the book as a university publication, nor to issue it as such, as is usually the custom. They believed they saw in the Imprimatur a degradation of science and a violation of its freedom — a procedure entirely in accord with the traditional narrow-mindedness and intolerance of liberalism.

found strength in the virtue of obedience, and on the other hand a list of all those whose subjective scientific views did not allow them to submit, then we should perceive at a glance that their proud persistence in their own opinion has been injurious to true wisdom in the same degree as humble submission proved a benefit to science " (*Hilgers*, 412). Finally, he who is convinced that the Christian faith is the greatest heritance of truth from the past, which must be preserved in him, he will take no offence if the Church is not impressed even by names like *Kant, Spinoza, Schopenhauer, Strauss,* men much featured as the captains of modern science and philosophy. In the eyes of the Church nothing is genuine and true science that is contrary to the testimony of God, and errors are errors even then when their perpetrator is receiving cheers and applause. Just as the state prohibits the physician from designedly assisting any one to commit suicide, even though the physician be a noted scientist, just so the Church opposes any one who assaults God's truth, be he journalist or philosopher.

Frequently the GREAT NUMBER OF FORBIDDEN BOOKS MENTIONED BY THE INDEX is pointed out. The Index of 1900 contains about 5,000 titles belonging to the last three centuries; of these about 1,300 belong to the nineteenth century. Quite a small number, considering the immense literature of the world. Yet it will look even smaller when compared, for instance, with the censure of books by the PRUSSIAN STATE.

In the year 1845 there appeared the following catalogue: " Index librorum prohibitorum, Catalogue of the books forbidden in Germany during 1844–1845, first volume." The second volume was issued in 1846. The list is not complete: it does not contain, for instance, the names of prohibited newspapers and periodicals. Yet it contains 437 writings, forbidden by 570 decrees, *i. e.*, two or three times as many as the entire number of German books of the nineteenth century enumerated by name in the Roman Index. The " Historisch-Politischen Blaetter " of 1840 contain an article beginning thus: " *Veritas odium parit.* In Prussia there are now prohibited nearly all Catholic journals and periodicals, and in order to begin the matter *ab ovo* they have grasped a welcome opportunity to throw interdicts at wholesale against works not yet published, or to render their circulation difficult to a degree amounting to prohibition."

How the Prussian censorship proceeded in those days may be illustrated by another example. " At the time of the Vatican Council a publisher, *Joseph Bachem*, came to Dr. *Westhoff*, rector of the Seminary of Cologne, a man of venerable years, and told him of his misgivings about the dogma of the infallibility. In his youth he had been taught the maxim that that is Catholic which has been taught always, every-

where, and by everybody; yet he had until recently never found the doctrine of Papal Infallibility taught, neither in schools nor in text-books.
Then the reverend old rector took the visitor by the hand and led him
into the library of the seminary, where he showed him not less than six-
teen catechisms that had been in use in the Archdiocese of Cologne during the eighteenth century, and which stated without exception, clearly
and convincingly, the doctrine of Papal Infallibility in matters of faith
and morals. The publisher in utter astonishment then asked how it was
that this doctrine was not taught in later editions. Dr. *Westhoff* referred him to the Prussian censure, enforced until 1848, which had ex-
punged this doctrine from all Catholic catechisms. From that moment
Bachem no longer wavered in his opinions" (Koelnische Volkszeitung,
September 7, 1893).

One may also remember *Bismarck's* press-campaign during the
Kulturkampf. Professor *Friedberg*, Prussian court canonist, insti-
gated this campaign, and in many ways devised the plan of attack.
This much-praised liberalism — how tyrannically it proceeded against
the Catholic press! The Frankfurter Zeitung in those days took a
census of convictions due to the press law. According to the census,
which "does not by far claim to be complete," there were of newspaper
editors sentenced in 1875 — 21 in January, 35 in February, 29 in
March, 24 in April; in four months 137 newspaper writers were either
fined or sent to jail. During the same period 30 newspapers were con-
fiscated (Staatslexikon, IV, 550). This is not all. "We could mention
at least three instances," says *P. Majunke* in his History of the Kulturkampf, "where agents of the Berlin secret police have succeeded in obtaining a position on the editorial staff of Catholic papers, staying for a
year or more. Besides serving as spies these fellows had to perform the
task of *agents provocateurs*, viz., to incite the editors of Catholic papers
to extreme utterances, similar to the denunciations suggested to cor-
respondents of foreign Catholic organs for their papers." This happened in a civilized state, despite its constitutional freedom of the press,
by order of the same liberalism which always pretends to be full of
righteous indignation when the Church prohibits books and puts them
on the Index.

Towards the end of the last century, again with the aid of liberalism,
laws against the socialists were drawn up. After they had been passed
war was waged against socialistic literature. In the year 1886 there
appeared a real Index Librorum Prohibitorum, its title read, "Social
Democratic publications and societies prohibited by the imperial law
against the dangerous designs of Social Democracy," which law had
then been in force eight years. A supplementary list was published two
years later, in 1888. *Hilgers* makes this comment on it: "How many
additional pamphlets have been condemned in the time from March 28,
1888, to September 30, 1890, we cannot state. According to the foregoing official statement the average is 130 a year. Hence we assume
that the printed matter prohibited during the twelve years that the
law was in force amounted to between 15,000 and 16,000. This number
of social democratic pamphlets forbidden within twelve years exceeds by
far the number of all books prohibited by the Roman Index in the course

of the entire nineteenth century — books that are the products of all countries in the world and dealing with all branches; the number of these German prohibitions is ten times that of Roman prohibitions. Indeed, in the course of a year and a half the new German Empire prohibited more writings of Germans than Rome had prohibited during the entire past century. We may mention here *Goethe*. In the atheism dispute, at the end of the eighteenth century, decision was rendered upon *Goethe's* advice against the philosopher *Fichte; Fichte* was discharged in spite of petitions and mediations in his favour. The liberal Grand Duke *Karl August of Saxony Weimar* granted in 1816, after the French conqueror had been overthrown, freedom of the press. Professor *Oken* of Jena availed himself of this privilege, and printed in his " Isis " contributions complaining about the government. *Goethe* had to advise what should be done against it. He thought that the paper should have been suppressed by the police at its very first announcement; " the measure neglected at the beginning is to be taken immediately and the paper is to be prohibited. By prohibiting the ' Isis ' the trouble will be stopped at once " (Briefwechsel des Grossh. *Karl August v. Sax.-Weimar-Eisenach* mit *Goethe*, II, 1863, 90). And this was done, in spite of the freedom granted the press.

Frederick II. is called the Royal Free-thinker; and yet the general introduction of the book censure into Prussia occurred precisely during his reign. The first general censure edict was issued in 1749 and remained in force till the death of the king. All books, even those printed in foreign tongues, were subject to the censure. Even all episcopal and Papal proclamations were subjected to the royal censure. That the leaders in the Reformation and their successors were not prevented by their avowal of the principle of free research from exercising rigorous, often tyrannical, censure, not only against the Catholics but also against their fellow reformers, is well known.

M. Lehmann writes in the Preuss. Jahrb. 1902: " It claims to be infallible, this Papal Church, it wants to be to the faithful everything, in science and even in nationality. It offends every nation. The Index in the shape given it in 1900 by the present Pope proscribes the ' Oeuvres du Philosophe de Sanssouci,' *Kant's* ' Critique of Pure Reason,' *Ranke's* ' History of the Popes,' the greatest German king, the greatest German philosopher, and the greatest German historian " (1902, no. 8).

As to *Frederick II.*, his own works appeared only after his death in 1788, and even then only in part; later on there were other editions. None of these is put on the Index. On this list we find since 1760 the " Oeuvres du Philosophe de Sanssouci." Under this title appeared at first three volumes, in but a few copies, intended for the most intimate friends of the king. The first volume he soon withdrew and had it burned of his own accord; it contained the " Palladion " an imitation of Voltaire's " Pucelle," a salacious work throughout. In 1762 a new edition was issued. It also contains a philosophical treatise denying the immortality of the soul; this treatise was also published separately and specially prohibited in 1767. A third work put on the Index is a spurious attack on the Popes published by order of King *Frederick II.*, with a preface by him. Its author is said to have been the French abbé *Jean Martin De Prades*, reader to the king. These are the indicted works of *Frederick II.*, all written in French and in substance French Voltairianism. Thus came the greatest German king on the Index!

Ranke's "Roemische Paepste" is on the Index, because the book belittles the constitutions and doctrines of the Catholic Church: not because of the true things the author says about Popes. *Von Pastor's* "History of the Popes" is not on the Index, notwithstanding the bitter truths he writes about Popes *Alexander VI.* and *Leo X.*

He who knows even the fundamental ideas of *Kant's* "Kritik der reinen Vernunft" will see that not only the Catholic Church, but every Christian denomination, might forfeit its existence if it showed itself indifferent towards it. Heresies are especially dangerous to the uneducated when they bear the names of authors of scientific repute. But the Church willingly grants the permission to read them when there is reason for it. Moreover, it was not Rome alone that took steps against *Kant*. This was done by the Prussian king *Frederick II.* also. One may recall his cabinet order, under minister *Woellner*, against Kant's "Religion innerhalb der Grenzen der blossen Vernunft." Similarly the works of *Spinoza* were proceeded against, whereas his indictment by Rome now calls forth protest because he has since been assigned a prominent place among philosophers. *Freudenthal* registers a list of 500 sharp prohibitions issued against *Spinoza's* works during the years 1556–1580; they were condemned by the states of Holland, by the court, by synods and magistrates. Those judgments were passed during a period when the competent authorities had views different from those of to-day; when the state deemed it its duty to oppose the undermining of Christianity. The state's judgment has changed in many ways, Rome's judgment has remained the same. But the works of *Kant* and *Spinoza* likewise have remained the same, and so is Christianity, against which they occupy an irreconcilable position, still the same.

"In the moral world nothing can support that cannot also resist" is a truthful saying of *Treitschke:* it is also the principle of the Catholic Church. Without ever surrendering to the unchristian tendency of a time, she opposes error with unsubdued courage. If this be intolerance, it is not intolerance towards erring men but towards their errors, it is the intolerance that the gardener shows in uprooting harmful weeds, it is the intolerance of the physician towards disease. Obedience to the Index makes high moral demands upon the Catholic. But it has been characteristic of the Christian religion and of its faithful children never to shrink before any moral action where it appeared demanded. And if the preservation of moral purity exacts conscientious discipline, this is also true of the preservation of the pure faith, especially at a time when a neo-paganism in league with an uncontrolled mania for reading is threatening in many forms.

GALILEO, AND OTHER TOPICS

Galileo Galilei — but few names have achieved equal fame. Men like *Alexander* and *Cæsar,* like *Homer* and *Dante,* have scarcely succeeded in writing their names with a sharper pencil on the tablet of history than the astronomer of Pisa. His grand discoveries in natural science have done little to crown his temples with the wreath of immortality — it was the fate of his life that did it. And one may add: if this fate had been caused by the French government, or by a Protestant General Assembly, he would never have obtained his position in history; but since this lot came to him by the human limitation of a Roman Church authority, his name is not only entered on the calendar of the anti-Roman journalist, it also stands surrounded with the halo of a Martyr in the esteem of serious scientists, who see in *Galileo* and in the consequent condemnation of the Copernican system the proof that dogma and science cannot agree, that the Catholic Church assumes a hostile attitude toward science. Whenever this theme is mentioned, *Galileo's* ghost is paraded. For this reason we cannot pass by this fact of history. To a son of the Church they are unpleasant recollections, but this shall not keep us from looking history firmly in the eye.

There are some other charges brought forth from history, but the *Galileo* case overshadows them all. We shall touch upon them but briefly, and then return to *Galileo.*

Attention is called to the Church's condemnation of the DOCTRINE OF ANTIPODES. The Priest *Vigilius* was accused in Rome, in 747, of having taught that there exists another world under the earth, and other people also, or another sun and moon (*quod alius mundus et alii homines sub terra sint seu sol et luna*). Such was his doctrine as stated by Pope *Zacharias* in his reply to *Boniface,* the Apostle of Germany, in which he said that he had cited *Vigilius* to Rome in order that his doctrine be thoroughly investigated; if it should turn out that this had really been taught by him, he would be condemned. Further particulars of his teaching are unknown, because it is mentioned only in the above passage. The assertion ascribed to him is that there is another world besides this one, with other inhabitants and with another sun and moon — an assertion scientifically absurd and dogmatically inadmissible, as this might call in question the common descent of mankind from one pair of parents. The anxiety and rebuke of the Pope is directed solely against the latter point. The condemnation of *Vigilius* has never taken place, for he remained in his office, won great respect, was elevated to the bishopric of Salzburg, and later canonized by *Gregory IX.* Had a condemnation of his particular doctrine taken place, this would not have involved the condemnation of the antipodean theory, in the sense that the side of the globe opposite to us is also inhabited by human beings, a proposition which does not conflict with any doctrine of faith. The doctrine described above has another tendency. The entire case is hidden in obscurity (*Hefele,* Conc. Gesch., 2d ed., III, 557 *seq.*).

Furthermore, it has been said that at the time when the universities were in close union with the Church, medical science could not advance because the Church had prohibited human ANATOMY (Prof. *J. H. van't Hoff,* Neue Freie Presse, December 29, 1907). In amplification it was said: "*Boniface VIII.* had forbidden every anatomical dissection of a body" (*O. Zoeckler,* Theologie und Naturwissenschaft, 1877, I, 342). What is true of this assertion?

In the first place, *Boniface VIII.* did not forbid anatomy. He merely prohibited in 1299 and 1300 the hideous custom then prevailing regarding the bodies of noblemen who had died away from home: they were disembowelled, dissected, and boiled, for the purpose of removing the flesh from the bones so that the latter could be transported the more easily. This process had nothing to do with anatomy. The wish to possess the bones of the dead did not seem to the Pope a sufficient reason for treating the human body in such a way (Cfr. *Michael,* Gesch. des deutschen Volkes III, 1903, 433). Nor does history know of any other prohibition of anatomy by the Church. It tells us, however, that *Frederick II.* in his excellent rules for the benefit of his Sicilian kingdom in the regulation of medical science among other things emphasizes the study of surgery: he ordered that no one be allowed to practise surgery who could not show by attestation of his professors that he had studied surgery for at least one year, especially that he had learned at school how to dissect bodies; a physician must be perfect in anatomy, else he may not undertake operations (*Michael*, l. c. 430). This was done and practised under the eyes of the Church. The accusers also seem ignorant of the fact that bodies of those executed were given to universities for dissection. In the year 1336 the medical students of Montpellier, the famous medical school under the immediate direction of the Church (see above, page 154) were granted the privilege of obtaining once a year an executed criminal's body for dissection. The same privilege was extended to the medical students of Lerida by King *Juan I.* on June 3, 1391, who decreed that the delinquent should be drowned *pro speriencia seu anatomia fienda* (*Denifle*, Die Universitaeten des Mittelalters, I, 1885, 507).

The story is also circulated that the fourth Lateran Council in 1215 prohibited monks from studying natural sciences and medicine (Deutschoester. Lehrerzeitung 15th Dec., 1909). It will suffice to quote this particular decree of the Lateran Council: " No clergyman is allowed to pronounce capital sentence, nor to execute it, nor to be present at its execution. No clergyman is allowed to draw up a document concerning a death sentence: at the courts this should be done by laymen. No clergyman is allowed to assume command of Rotarians (freebooters), of archers or any others who shed human blood; no subdeacon, deacon, or priest is allowed to practise that part of surgery by which cutting and burning is done, nor must any one pronounce a benediction at an ordeal " (*Hefele*, Koncil. Gesch., 2d ed., V, 1887, 887). This will thoroughly dispose of that charge.

Just as briefly may we settle the story of COLUMBUS having been excommunicated because of his intention to discover new lands. It is said that the " Spanish clergy denounced his plans as against the faith, and that the Council of Salamanca excommunicated him " (*W. Draper*, ibid. 163). This is a fairy tale. The truth is, that King *Ferdinand* and Queen *Isabella* referred the plans of the bold Genoese to a council of scientists and ecclesiastical dignitaries, which was held in the Dominican Monastery of Salamanca, *Columbus* being present. There never was a Council of Salamanca. *Weiss* writes in his " History of the World ": " Much has been surmised concerning the objections and their refutation. It is only certain that the majority rejected the plan as impossible of execution, and that *Columbus* won over a minority of them, especially the priests, among whom the learned Dominican *Deza* deserves mention " (Weltgesch. VII, 187). *Denthofen*, in his biography of *Columbus*, says: " The Dominican Fathers supported him during the long time the conference lasted, and even defrayed the expenses of his journey. Father *Diego de Deza*, chief professor of theology, was convinced by the reasons of *Columbus*, and in turn convinced the more learned of his confrères. The majority, however, thought the idea but a phantom, while others deemed it impracticable. The conference adjourned without coming to any definite decision " (Christof Columbus, Eine biographische Skizze . . . , 1878, 21). *Columbus* found his warmest friend in the learned Father *Juan Perez*, Guardian of the

Franciscan Monastery of St. Maria de la Rabida. Within the quiet
walls of this cloister *Columbus'* plans were disclosed for the first time
in Spain, and admired and resolved upon. *Perez* spoke untiringly to
Isabella in favour of the plan, and even aided *Columbus* in gathering
men for his crew. This is the fact about the anathema the Church is
said to have pronounced on *Columbus.*

But let us return to GALILEO.[1]

GALILEO GALILEI, the great Italian physicist, was born in
1564, at Pisa. At first he was professor in his native town,
then at Padua, where he taught the doctrine of *Ptolemy,*
although at that time there was no obstacle to accepting the
Copernican system. In 1611 he became mathematician at the
court of *Cosimo II.* at Florence. His talents and happy discoveries soon won fame. In general he was more of a physicist
than an astronomer; his astronomical discoveries were, almost
without exception, of a kind that did not presuppose a thorough
astronomical training. As is known, he was not the original
inventor of the telescope, though with its aid he achieved some
of the most important of his discoveries; for instance, that of
the satellites of Jupiter. The telescope was invented in Holland.

When he went to Rome, in 1611, he was received with great
honour. In one of his letters from there he wrote: "I have
received marked favours from many Cardinals and prelates
here, and from several princes. They wanted to hear of my
inventions, and were all well pleased." The Jesuits gave a special reception in his honour at the Roman College. This
shows in what esteem science was then held at Rome. But

---

[1] A clear understanding of the case of *Galileo* has been made
possible only since the year 1877, when the papers of the trial were
published by two men of opposite religious views, — the Catholic-minded
historian, *de l'Epinois,* and the liberal author, *K. Gebler,* who in 1876 had
already published a work on " Galileo Galilei and the Roman Curia,"
in the spirit of the anti-clerical tendency of the times. Yet, in spite of
his attitude, he was given free permission to copy the papers — a mag-
nanimity by which the Holy See has earned the gratitude and admiration
of every fair-minded lover of history. In more recent times, *A. Favaro*
published, in 1890–1907, a work of twenty volumes containing all the
papers relating to the trial of *Galileo,* " Opere di Galileo Galilei,
Edizione Nazionale." He, too, had access to the ecclesiastical archives,
which he acknowledges with thanks. It may be said now that the *Galileo*
case has been settled by documentary evidence.

five years later *Galileo* returned to the Eternal City under quite different circumstances. What had happened? In 1612 he had issued a treatise on "The History and Explanation of the Sun-spots," in which he declared unreservedly for the Copernican system. And this caused the change. True, *Copernicus* himself was a Catholic Priest, and had dedicated his principal work to Pope *Paul III*. But it was generally supposed that he had brought forward the doctrine only as an hypothesis, only to illustrate and facilitate calculations, not claiming for it absolute certainty. This assumption was based on the preface of the first edition of his book, containing assurance to that effect. That preface, however, was not the work of *Copernicus*, but had been smuggled into the book by the Protestant publisher *Osiander*, without the author's knowledge, because *Osiander* feared HIS OWN church authorities.

Galileo spoke in quite another tone. He defended the doctrine as true. He soon aroused opposition. Men standing for the geocentric theory were opposed by others, siding with *Galileo* for the solar system, such as the learned Benedictine, *Castelli*. *Galileo's* great bitterness and sarcasm in dealing with his opponents aggravated the quarrel with the "partisans of *Aristotle*." Extreme irritability and love of praise were prominent traits of *Galileo's* character.

It was the custom of that time to bring Scripture into controversies about nature. This was done also in *Galileo's* case. Passages were quoted against him, referring to the "rising and setting sun," to the "earth that never moves," of *Joshua's* "commanding the sun to stand still." This prompted *Galileo* to cross over into the field of theology himself. In a letter to *Castelli* in 1613 he says: "Holy Writ can never lie nor err; on the contrary, its sayings are absolute and incontestable truth; but its interpreters are liable to err in various ways, and it is a fatal and very common mistake to stop always at the literal sense" (*Kepler*, even prior to *Galileo*, had interpreted the respective passages of the Scriptures properly and with surprising skill; especially in his introduction to his "Astronomia nova." Cfr. *Anschuetz*, Johannes Kepler als Exeget. Zeitschrift für katholische Theologie, XI, 1887, 1–24).

Correct as these arguments were, it was nevertheless imprudent for the court mathematician to trespass upon grounds regarded by theologians as their own, instead of furnishing natural scientific proofs. Thus the matter was brought to Rome before the Congregation of the Inquisition. *Galileo,* worrying about his case, went voluntarily to Rome, in 1615. He failed to assuage the opposition against his theory, though he says he was received favourably by the princes of the Church. Moreover, heedless of the admonition of his friends, he pursued the matter with indiscreet zeal, with vehemence and impetuosity, practically provoking a decision. Cardinal *Bellarmin* opposed the haste with which the matter was being pressed; the Jesuit *Grienberger* thought that *Galileo* should first set forth his proofs, and then speak about the Scriptures. Had scientific proofs been brought forth, theological difficulties would have been easily cleared away; but scientific proof was lacking, and what there perhaps was of it, *Galileo* failed to offer.

The right of the Congregation to take up the matter can hardly be denied, for although the matter was one of natural sciences, yet, by introducing theology and Scripture, it had assumed the character of theology and exegesis. *Galileo* personally was dealt with very leniently. During the discussions of 1616 he was never cited before the bar of the Inquisition, nor was his exterior freedom in any way restricted. Only one thing was done: he was cautioned by Cardinal *Bellarmin,* " by order of the Holy Congregation," not to adhere to, nor teach any longer, the Copernican theory. The documents of the case say that " *Galileo* submitted to this order and promised to obey." The Congregation of the Index prohibited, March 5, 1616, all books defending the Copernican theory, declaring the doctrine to be against Holy Scripture. Even the work of *Copernicus* was prohibited *donec corrigatur* — until it be corrected. A decision of the year 1620 declared which passages should be corrected. They are those in which the author speaks of his theory not as an hypothesis but as of an established truth: *non ex hypothesi, sed asserando.* The Protestant *Kepler,* upon hearing this, wrote: " By their imprudent acts some have caused the work of *Copernicus* to be condemned, after it had been left unmolested for nearly eighty years; and the prohibition will last at least till the corrections are made. I have been assured, however, by competent authority, both ecclesiastical and civil, that the decree was not intended to put any hindrance in the way of astronomical research " (*A. Mueller, J.* Kepler, 1903, 105). The reproach of imprudence was intended for *Galileo.*

To teach the doctrine as an hypothesis was permitted even to *Galileo,* and this left the way clear for the development of the hypothesis, because whatever showed the usefulness of the hypothesis was sure to increase its value as a truth, but *Galileo* would not keep within these limits. Instead of showing in a Christian spirit a submission to Providence, which even an erring authority may demand, he openly violated his promise and disobeyed the command he had received. In the spring of 1632 there appeared at Florence his " DIALOGUE ON THE TWO MOST IMPORTANT SYSTEMS OF THE WORLD." It contained an open, though by no means victorious, defence of the Copernican system — seeking to hide under a confidence-inspiring mask. It contained many passages of caustic sarcasm, with the evident intention of arousing public opinion against the attitude of the Roman Congregations. It was a flagrant VIOLATION OF THE COMMAND GIVEN HIM PERSONALLY.

The Pope under whom the proceedings against *Galileo* took place was *Urban VIII.,* who, when a Cardinal, had followed *Galileo's* discoveries with enthusiasm, though never partial to the system of *Copernicus,* and, in accord with the custom of the age, he had written an ode to *Galileo.*

Cited to Rome, *Galileo* came only after repeated urging, on February 14, 1633. The story of his having been imprisoned and tortured on this second visit to Rome is false. *Galileo* wrote on April 16 of that year: " I live in an apartment of three rooms, belonging to the Fiscal of the Inquisition, and am free to move in many rooms. My health is good." This stay in the apartment belonging to the Inquisition lasted but twenty-two days; after that *Galileo* was allowed to live in the palace of the Ambassador of Tuscany. During his whole life *Galileo* was never even for an hour in a real prison.

Galileo's demeanour before the Inquisition bespeaks little

truthfulness and manliness. It makes a painful impression.
Many other events in his life cast dark shades of insincerity
upon his character, especially his relations with *Kepler*. While
in his dialogue he openly defended the truth of the Copernican system, while he had written, time and again, that the
theory had been demonstrated by "forceful, convincing arguments," whereas nothing but insignificant reasons could be
pleaded for the contrary, he now assumes the attitude before
the Inquisition of denying that he had championed that theory,
at least not consciously; that he had never taught that doctrine otherwise than hypothetically. And this he asserts although he had taken the oath to say nothing but the truth. We
even hear him declare that he considers the doctrine to be false,
and that he was ready to refute it at once.

The judges were convinced of the untruthfulness of the defendant. In those times, in order to obtain further confessions,
especially when the accused had been previously convicted of
guilt, torture was resorted to. This regrettable practice was
then in vogue at every European court; the Inquisition, too,
had adopted it, but strict rules were laid down to guard against
abuses. Very old persons were exempt from the rack; they were
only threatened with it. This happened also in *Galileo's* case,
he was never actually put on the rack. Moreover, one can
safely presume that this threat did not terrify him much. His
reading must have enlightened him on this point, and even
without it he must have known the practice by his active intercourse with those theologians of the Curia who were friendly to
him. In fact, he clung obstinately to his denial, to the very end
of the hearing, although it must be surmised that he would not
have aggravated his case by confession. The commissioner of
Inquisition, *Macolano,* at the first stages of the trial had expressed his hope that in this event "it would be possible to show
indulgence to the guilty, and whatever the result might be, he
would realize the benefit received, apart from all other consequences to be expected from a desired mutual satisfaction"
(Letter to Cardinal *Fr. Barberini,* April 28, 1633).

On June 22 THE FINAL VERDICT was rendered: it told the
defendant: "Thou art convicted by the Holy Congregation

of being suspected of heresy, to wit, to have held for true, and believed in, a false theory, contrary to Holy Writ — which makes the sun the centre of the orbit of the earth, without moving from east to west, and which lets the earth, on the other hand, move outside the centre of the world, and to have believed that an opinion may be considered probable and be defended, though it had been expressly declared to be contrary to the Scripture." *Galileo* was declared suspect of heresy, because, in the opinion of the judges, he had assumed that a doctrine in contradiction to the Scriptures might be defended. *Galileo* retracted by oath. That upon retraction he arose and exclaimed, stamping with his foot, "*Pur si muove!*" ("and yet it does move!") is a fable. He was sentenced to be jailed in the Holy Office. But already the next day he was allowed to go to the palace of the Grand Duke of Tuscany and to consider that palace his prison. Soon after he departed for Siena, "in the best of health," according to the report of the Tuscan ambassador, *Niccolini,* and there took up his abode with his friend the Archbishop *Piccolomini.* After a lapse of five months he was allowed to return to his villa at Arcetri, near Florence, where he remained, with the exception of occasional visits to Florence, till his death. Two of his daughters were nuns in the nearby cloister of S. Matteo. His literary activity was not suppressed by the surveillance of the Inquisition. His lively and fertile mind, cut off from polemics, turned to the completion of his researches in other directions. His lively intercourse with friends and disciples, of whom many belonged to various Orders, proved beneficial to him. In the year 1638 he published his " Dialogue on the New Sciences," which he rightly pronounced to be his best effort, and by which he became the founder of dynamics. His productiveness continued until he became blind.

We may say without fear of contradiction that, apart from their theoretical error, the Roman Congregations had shown the greatest indulgence towards one guilty of having broken his pledge, and doubtless they would have been still more lenient had *Galileo,* confirmed by flattering friends in his anger at the supposed intrigues of his enemies, not himself made this impossible; if he had not continued to propagate secretly his views, verbally and in writing, which was bound to be discovered. Considering all this, Rome's proceeding in the case appears to be quite indulgent. Here the position was taken that the spread of the doctrine would mean an imminent danger to the purity of the faith. The unfortunate scientist died on January 8, 1642, at the age of seventy-eight years, fortified by the holy Sacraments. *Urban VIII.* sent him his blessing. Undoubtedly *Galileo* had nothing in common with the champions of that unbelieving freedom of science, which now tries to lift him upon its shield; notwithstanding his later bitterness he remained to his death steadfast in his Catholic faith.

Comments on the Galileo Case

The above is a brief history of *Galileo's* conviction, and of the occurrences leading to it. An event regrettable to all, a stumbling-block for not a few; for others a welcome event to make the Church appear in the light of an enemy of science. Let us now give more particulars of the merits of the case.

We have before us two decisions of Roman Tribunals: the Index decree of 1616, announcing the rejection of the Copernican doctrine and prohibiting books maintaining it, and the conviction of *Galileo* in 1633 by the Congregation of the Inquisition. It is freely admitted that these Roman Tribunals committed an ERROR in advocating an interpretation of the Bible which was false in itself, and is to-day recognized as false.

Well, DOES THIS CONFUTE THE INFALLIBILITY OF THE CHURCH? It does not. The matter in point is merely an error of the Congregations, of bodies of Cardinals, who were responsible for the transactions and decisions. The Congregations, however, are not infallible organs. There is no Bull or Papal decree designating the Copernican doctrine as false, much less is there extant a decision ex cathedra. Neither in 1616 nor in 1633, nor at any other time, has the Holy See ever manifested its intention of declaring, by a peremptory, dogmatic decision, the new system to be against Scripture.

It was thus the general understanding of that age that in the present case there was no irrevocable dogmatic decision given. For instance, the Jesuit *Riccioli*, wrote not long after the decision: " Inasmuch as no dogmatic decision was rendered in this case, neither on the part of the Pope nor on the part of a Council ruled by the Pope and acknowledged by him, it is not made, by virtue of that decree of the Congregation, a doctrine of faith that the sun is moving and the earth standing still, but at most it is a doctrine for those who by reason of Holy Writ seem to be morally certain that God has so revealed it. Yet every Catholic is bound by virtue of obedience to conform to the decree of the Congregation, or at least not to teach what is directly opposed to it " (Almagestum novum, 1651, 162). *Descartes, Gassendi,* and others of that time expressed themselves similarly (*Grisar,* 165, *seq.*). There is an interesting letter of the Protestant philosopher *Leibnitz,* written to the Landgrave *Ernest of Hessia,* 1688, begging him to work for the repeal of the condemnation of the Copernican theory, because of the growing verification of this theory: " If the Congregation would change its censure, or mitigate it, as one issued hastily at a time when the proofs for the correctness of the Copernican theory were not yet clear enough, this step could not detract from the authority of the Congregation, much less of the Church, because the Pope had no part in it. There is no judicial authority which has not at times reformed its own decisions."

But have we here not at least a WILFUL ATTACK ON SCIENCE? or a manifestation of the Congregation's narrow-mindedness and ignorance, which are bound to deprive it of all respect and confidence of sober-minded people?

This harsh judgment overlooks two points. In the first place, the error of the judges was quite PARDONABLE. Could the liberal critics of to-day, who so harshly denounce the Cardinals of the Congregation, be suddenly changed into ecclesiastical prelates, and transferred back to the years of 1616–1633, and placed in the chairs of the tribunal which had to decide those delicate questions, it may be feared that, did they carry into the decision but a part of the animosity they now show, they would disgrace themselves and compromise the Church even more than the judges of *Galileo* did. It is true that were we to judge the handling of the question by the knowledge of to-day, we might be astonished at the narrow-mindedness of the judges, trying to uphold their untenable views against the established results of scientific research. But it would be altogether unhistorical to look at the matter in that way. When

the Copernican theory entered upon the battlefield, it was BY
NO MEANS CERTAIN AND DEMONSTRATED.

The real arguments for the rotation of the earth were not then
known. There were no direct proofs for the progressive revolution
of the earth around the sun. *Galileo* advanced three main arguments
for his theory. First, he advanced the argument from the phenomenon
of the tides, which, he said, could not be accounted for but by the
rotation of the earth: an argument rejected as futile even at that
time. Next he argued from certain observations of the spots on the
sun: another worthless argument, which others, like *Scheiner*, looked
upon as proof of the older theory. The third argument was that the new
theory simplified the explanation of certain celestial phenomena; but
the scope of this argument, valid though it was in the abstract, could
not be expressed or grasped at the time, especially since the corrections
of *Tycho de Brahe* had removed the greatest objections to the Ptolemaic
system. The Copernican theory could not be considered certain till
the end of the seventeenth century, after *Newton's* work on gravitation.

Then there were difficulties, the greatest of which was probably the
old idea of inertia, which at that time meant only that all bodies
tend to a state of rest; hence it seemed impossible that the earth
could ceaselessly execute two movements at the same time, around the
sun and around its own axis. This notion of inertia had not been
doubted in 1616; even *Kepler* adhered to it. Later on *Galileo* came
very near to the new idea of inertia: that bodies tended to retain
their state of repose or motion. But this new notion, like everything
else new, gained ground but slowly. Then it was only with great
difficulty that he could dispose of the objection that were the earth
to speed through space, as the new theory claimed, the atmosphere
would take a stormlike motion. Lastly, the philosophical objection had
to be met: the sun and other celestial bodies, as far as we can know
by observation, are moving; if they do not move, then we must admit
that we can know nothing by observation.

Thus the new doctrine was not at all proven at that time, as could
be easily shown by its opponents; although it cannot be denied that
they did not always enter into the discussion with impartiality. The
astronomer, *Secchi*, testifies that "none of the real arguments for the
rotary motion of the earth was known at *Galileo's* time, also direct
proofs for the progressive movement of the earth around the sun
were lacking at that time" (*Grisar*, 30). Another famous astronomer,
Schiaparelli, writes: "In the sixteenth and seventeenth centuries the
Ptolemaic as well as the Copernican system could serve for the description of phenomena; geometrically they were equivalent to each other
and to *Tycho's* eclectic system" (*Schiaparelli*, Die Vorläufer des Copernicus im Altertum (German, 1876), 86).

Hence no direct evidence could be pleaded against the decision of
the Congregation, not even *Galileo* had that evidence. At any rate
no judge who observed his demeanour at the trial could have suspected
Galileo of coming in conflict with his conscience by swearing off the
theory.

For this reason it would be wrong to call *Galileo* a martyr for science, because he did not suffer any martyrdom. He has seen neither rack nor prison. But he was not a martyr chiefly for the reason that he could not have had any scientific conviction, apart from the fact that he did not claim any such conviction, even denied it expressly.

No wonder, then, that the heliocentric system had considerable opponents at that time; no wonder the opposite view was even the prevalent one. *A. Tanner* wrote in 1626: "*Ita habet communis ac certa omnium theologorum ac philosophorum naturalium sentia*" (Theol. Schol. I, disp. 6, q. 4., dub. 3). Had valid argument been brought forth there never would have been a *Galileo* case. In this respect a passage from a letter of *Bellarmin* deserves attention: "If it could be really demonstrated that the sun be in the centre of the world . . . then we would have to proceed quite cautiously in explaining the apparently opposite passages in the Scriptures, we would rather have to say that we do not understand them, than to say of things demonstrated that they are false" (to *Foscarini,* April 12, 1615). The Cardinals of that time could not be expected to anticipate the knowledge of a later period. They had to consult the judgment of their contemporaneous savants. When seeing the majority of them sharply rejecting the new theory and refuting the arguments of their opponents, it is little wonder that the Cardinals could not overcome their theological scruples.

The scruples arose from the opinion, then prevalent, that the Holy Scripture taught that the earth stood still and the sun moved; that the words of the Scripture must be taken literally till the contrary is demonstrated. The unanimous explanation of the Christian centuries was also cited. As a matter of fact, however, the Christian past had not taught this to be the only true sense of the words, but at that time the words were understood that way, because no one could arrive at any other sense in those days.

Under these circumstances, an error was hardly avoidable, if a decision was required. And a decision seemed to be urgent, and this is the second point we must not overlook, if we wish to judge fairly. It was a time eager for innovations, full of anti-religious ideas. A renaissance, sidling off into false humanism, was combating religious convictions, false notions were invading philosophy; in addition, Protestantism was trying to invade Italy. All this caused suspicion of any innovation apt to endanger the faith; interpretations of the Scriptures deviating from the accustomed sense were particularly distrusted. The *Galileo* quarrel happened at an inopportune time. Indeed a sudden spread of the Copernican theory might have been accompanied by great religious dangers. Even now, after nearly three hundred years, the leaders of the anti-Christian propaganda are still pointing out that the progress of natural science has proved Holy Scripture to be erroneous, and many are impressed by the argument; many thousands would have been confused in those days by the sudden collapse of old astronomical views that were connected with unclarified religious ideas — dreading that victorious science might shatter all religious traditions. Now, if one is convinced that the damage to religion is to be estimated greater than any other, then one may also have the conviction that it was better for the nations of the new era to have their scientific progress a little delayed, than to have their most sacred possession endangered. Of course considerations of this kind will have no weight with representatives of the naturalistic view of the world. Then it can only be emphasized that a science that has no appreciation of the supernatural character of the Catholic Church cannot be in a position to render a fair judgment on many facts in the history of that Church.

What we have said shows sufficiently that the condemnation of *Galileo* was not due to any hostility to science.

The idea that the Church's attitude towards *Galileo* and the Copernican theory was a result of her antipathy to science is entirely in contradiction with the character of that strenuous period. In Catholic countries, especially in Italy, intellectual life was zealously promoted by the Popes and their influence. It was developing and flourishing even in the natural sciences. "When reading the correspondence of *Galileo* one must be surprised to see how popular astronomical, physical, and mathematical studies were in the educated circles of the period. These studies belonged to the curriculum of a general philosophical education, and it was a matter of honour

for many ecclesiastical dignitaries to remain philosophers in that
sense, notwithstanding their official duties.   We recall to mind the
scientific discussion carried on with *Galileo* in Rome in 1611 and 1616,
by Cardinals *Del Monte, Farnese, Bonzi, Bemerio, Orsini,* and *Maffeo
Baberini,* and by clergymen like *Agucchi, Dini,* and *Campioli.*   Similarly
in France we meet with names like *Mersenne, Gassendi,* and *Descartes.*
And in Italy, after *Galileo* and at his time, we meet with a long list of
eminent naturalists like *Toricelli, Cassini, Riccioli,* and others.   In
1667 *Gemiani Montanari* could write that in Italy there were continually forming new societies of scientists.   The advance in knowledge of truth was made on safe grounds;   at Naples, Rome, and
elsewhere science was enriched by a great variety of new experiences, inasmuch as the scientists were making progress in the observation and
the investigation of nature.   *Targioni-Tozzetti* writes: "Astronomy
with us, about the middle of the sixteenth century, was a very diligently
cultivated branch of science" (Galileistudien (1882) 338 f.).   The
Church was by no means hostile to this newly awakened life, not even
holding aloof from it; on the contrary, it flourished especially in ecclesiastical circles; a proof that narrow-minded disappreciation of natural
science did not prevail, and that there was a different explanation for
the *Galileo* case.

COPERNICUS ON THE INDEX TILL 1835

And what of the fact that *Copernicus* remained on the Index
until the nineteenth century?   Does it not show a rigid adherence to old, traditional method and opposition to progress?
The fact is true: The work of *Copernicus,* and other Copernican writings, remained on the Index until 1835.   But it is also
true that a great deal connected with this fact is not generally
known or ignored. Let us mention here some of these facts.

To begin with, it must not be forgotten that we owe the new world
system, and with it the turning-point in astronomy, first of all to
representatives of the Catholic clergy.   After the learned Bishop
Nicholas Oresme had expressed with fullest certainty the most important point of the Copernican system as early as 1377 (in a manu-
script hitherto unknown, discovered a short time ago by *Pierre
Duhem* in the National Library at Paris.   Cfr. Liter. Zentralblatt
(1909), page 1618), and after the learned Cardinal *Nicholaus von
Kues* (d. 1474) adopted a rotary motion of the earth in his cosmic
system, it was *Copernicus,* a canon of the diocese of Ermland, who
became the father of the new theory, in his work "De evolutionibus
orbium coelestium."   He published it at the urgent request of Cardinal *Nikolaus Schoenberg.*   But the most zealous promoter of his
work was Bishop *Tiedemann Giese* of Kulm.   Enthusiastic over the
novel idea, he incessantly urged his friend to publish his work, took
care of its publication, and sent a copy to Pope *Paul III.,* who ac-

cepted its dedication. Again, it was a prince of the Church, Bishop *Martin Kromer*, who, in 1851, dedicated a tablet in the cathedral at Frauenberg to "The Great Astronomer and Innovator of Astronomical Science." All these men knew that *Copernicus* defended his work not as an hypothesis or as fiction, but as true. Before *Copernicus* issued his great work, *Clement VIII.* showed a lively interest in his system and had it explained to him by the learned *Johann Widmannstadt* in the Vatican Gardens (*Pastor*, Gesch. der Päpste, IV, 2 (1907) 550).

The first attack against the new system, as being contrary to Holy Writ, came not from Catholic but from Protestant circles. Among the latter the opposition against *Copernicus* was being agitated, while peaceful calm reigned among the former. Twelve Popes succeeded *Paul III.*, and not one interfered with this doctrine. *Luther*, even in *Copernicus'* time, hurled his anathema against the " Frauenberg Fool," and six years after the publication of *Copernicus'* chief work, *Melanchthon* declared it a sin and a scandal to publish such nonsensical opinions, contrary to the divine testimony of the Scriptures. In fear of his religious community the Protestant publisher *Osiander* smuggled in the spurious preface already mentioned, " On the hypothesis of this work." The Protestant *Rheticus*, a friend and pupil of *Copernicus*, got into disfavour with *Melanchthon* and had to discontinue his lectures at Wittenberg. The genial *Kepler*, finally, was prosecuted by his own congregation, because of his defence of the theory. And when on the Catholic side the Index decree of 1616 was already beginning to be regarded as obsolete, Protestant theology still held to the old view even up to the nineteenth century: a long list of names could be adduced in proof.

Certainly no fair-minded person can see wilful hostility against astronomy in this procedure. Likewise there should not be imputed dishonourable intentions to Catholics, if in the course of history they rendered tribute to human limitation.

But did not the decrees of 1616 and 1633 do GREAT HARM TO RESEARCH? Not at all. That this was hardly the case with *Galileo* himself we have shown above. Soon after we find in Italy a goodly number of distinguished scientists; the Church in no way opposed the newly awakened life, nor even held aloof from it. *Galileo* himself was honoured in ecclesiastical circles. Soon after *Galileo's* conviction the Jesuit *Grimaldi* named a mountain on the moon after him.

Nor was there any considerable harm done to the development of the Copernican theory. Although after *Galileo* the occasions were not lacking, still no further advocate of his theory was ever up for trial. Nor was any other book on the subject prohibited. Freedom was quietly granted more and more. In the edi-

tion of the Index of 1758, the general prohibition of 1616 of
Copernican writings was withdrawn; it was an official with-
drawal from the old position. But not until 1822 were the
special prohibitions repealed, although they had long since lost
their binding force. The occasion was given by an accidental
occurrence. The Magister S. Palatii of the time intended to
deny the Imprimatur to a book on the Copernican theory, on
account of the obsolete prohibition. An appeal was made, which
brought about the formal repeal of the prohibition. Of course
there had been no hurry to revoke a decision once given. But
according to the astronomer *Lalande's* report of his interview
with the Cardinal Prefect of the Congregation of the Index, in
1765, the removal from the Index of *Galileo's* Dialogue had been
postponed only on account of extraneous difficulties. *Leibnitz,*
while in Rome, worked for a repeal of the decree. According to
Eméry, there are extant statements of *Leibnitz* vouching for the
fact that he very nearly succeeded (*Eméry,* Pensées de Leibnitz,
I, 275). The name of *Copernicus,* too, was omitted in the next
edition of the Index, which appeared in 1835.

But even while the prohibition was still in force, the works
of *Galileo* and *Copernicus* were read everywhere. As early as
1619 *John Remus* wrote from Vienna to *Kepler* that the Copernican writings may be read by scientific men who had received
special permission, and that this was done in all Italy and in
Rome itself. Besides, it was allowed at any time to make use of
the doctrine as an hypothesis. Thus it advanced continually
nearer and nearer to the position of an established truth.

Soon after the publication of the decree, according to the
report of *Kepler,* it was the general conviction in ecclesiastical
and civil circles of Austria " that the censure was no obstacle to the freedom of science in the investigation of God's
work." In 1685 we are assured by the Jesuit *Kochansky,* that
any Catholic was free to " look for an irrefutable, mathematical,
and physical demonstration of the movement of the earth." It
was also known that the condemnation of the theory had been
aided by the supposition that there were no valid arguments
in support of the new theory. Hence the Congregation's decree
had in the eighteenth century for the most part lost its force.

The Jesuit *Boscovich,* a celebrated physicist and astronomer, wrote in 1755: " In consequence of the extraordinary arguments offered by the consideration of *Kepler's* laws, astronomers no longer look upon his theory as a mere hypothesis, but as an established truth " (Grisar, 347, 350).

Thus in the light of history the condemnation of the Copernican theory appears quite differently from the picture presented by the superficial accusation that Rome up to the nineteenth century condemned this theory. There is no trace of callousness and oppression, but only submission to legitimate authority, in so far and as long as one deemed himself obliged. It was a science enlightened by Christianity, which, in questions not yet clearly decided, laid down upon the altar of the Giver of all wisdom the tribute of humble submission, for the sake of higher interests.

We shall have to class with *St. Augustine* the uncertainty of human judgments and tribunals among the " troubles of human life," and say with him: " It is also a misery that the judge is subject to the necessity of not knowing many things, but to the wise man it is not a fault " (De Civ. Dei, IX, 6). May we therefore infer that the teaching authority is an evil? Were that true, we should have to abolish the authority of the state and of parents, because they also make mistakes. We should have to conclude that there had better be no authority at all on earth. Where men live and rule, mistakes will certainly be made. The physician makes mistakes in his important office, yet patients return to him with confidence. Every pedagogue, every professor, has made mistakes, yet they still command respect. The state government is subject to mistakes, yet none but the anarchist will say that it must therefore be abolished. " That the judge is subject to the necessity of not knowing many things, is a misery, but to the wise man not a fault."

CHAPTER V

THE "WITNESSES OF THE INCOMPATIBILITY OF SCIENCE AND FAITH"

THE OBJECTION

WE shall not go wrong in presuming that the reader, who has patiently followed our deductions, has had for some time in his mind the question: How about the representatives of scientific research themselves? Do not a large majority of them, perhaps virtually all, stand alien and repellant to Christian faith and its fundamental truths? We do not refer to our modern philosophers, for of them it might be said that their researches yield questionable speculations of individualistic stamp, rather than exact results. But there are the representatives of the more exact sciences, especially of the most exact of all, natural science. They may be considered the legitimate representatives of modern science, since their results are the most accurate, their methods the most strictly scientific; and are they not, every one of them, opposed to Christian faith, especially to its fundamental dogma? Is not *Haeckel* right when he states in the final summary of his " Welträtsel," in which he so strongly insists on the incompatibility of religion and natural science: " I am supported by the accord of nearly all modern naturalists who have the courage to express their convictions "? Is it not true that *A. von Humboldt* is considered the prince of German naturalists? and yet in his voluminous " Kosmos " he not once mentions the name of God? Have not, with few exceptions, German naturalists, under *Humboldt's* influence, turned against Christianity? (*W. Menzel,* Die letzten hundertzwanzig Jahre der Weltgeschichte, VI, 1860, p. 70; cfr. *Pohle,* P. Angelo Secchi, 1904, p. 6). Here indeed the antagonism between true scientific spirit and the faith seems to take shape in tangible reality, and to invalidate every argument to the contrary.

Thus runs the speech that is ever recurring in the literature of the day, in newspapers and magazines no less than in books. And this speech makes an impression on its hearers. Indeed, why should it not? After describing how these heroes of science in recent times marched on triumphantly from victory to victory, how they renewed the face of the earth, and became the pioneers of human progress, how can they fail to make a deep impression if in the same breath they state that these discoverers of truth have, almost to a man, broken with the ancient teachings of the Christian religion?

Without doubt the suggestive effect of such speculation must be very considerable with those who lack sufficient historical knowledge. The case is different with those better acquainted with the history of the natural sciences. They know that it is not true to state that the leading natural scientists, for the most part, or even unanimously, have rejected and denied Christian religion, that it is a *lie* and a falsification of history.

Let us illustrate it briefly. We do not, of course, mean to say, that *if* it were true that all the leading naturalists were infidels, the inference would necessarily follow that Christianity is untenable, and incompatible with science. Not at all. First of all, natural scientists who oppose Christianity could hardly ever come forward in the capacity of experts in this matter. For by venturing the assertion that world-matter and world-force are eternal and uncreated, that they develop by force of natural causality, by unending evolution, and not by the power and direction of an intelligent cause, they leave their own province and trespass on the domain of philosophy. These and similar questions are not solved by natural science research, by experiment, observation, or calculation, but are the subjects of philosophical speculation. Atheism, materialism, the denial of the soul's immortality or of eternal destination, all these are philosophical matters, and a natural science theory of the world is a misconception about as absurd as a Swiss England or a Bavarian Spain.

As it is impossible to review here all scientists of the past centuries, to probe their bent of mind, we shall restrict ourselves in the following to scientists of the first rank, for to them the assertion above mentioned must chiefly refer. First of all, they were possessed of that spirit of scientific research claimed to be incompatible with the faith; and they, more than others, should have been conscious of this contradiction. It is plain that if they did not know anything of the claimed antagonism between the theories of evolution and of creation, between physical facts and spirituality of soul, between natural law and miracles; if it be shown that many of them were actually orthodox Christians, believing in the supernatural and yet enthusiastic friends of science, fathoming the laws of nature and yet unshaken in their faith, then the fact that inferior minds talk of a contradiction unknown to these great ones can no longer make much of an impression.

Therefore let us look over the long list of great scholars of the last centuries, those great men to whom we owe knowledge and discoveries that are our joy to this very day. Among them we shall find many who, in their life and thought, have plainly confessed themselves faithful Christians; we shall find that others were at least the opponents of atheism and materialism, that they clung to the fundamental truths of the Christian faith, and that is a matter of moment when the antagonism between natural science and faith is under discussion.

We shall not go back to the ancient representatives of natural science, men like *Pythagoras, Aristotle, Archimedes, Albert the Great, Roger Bacon,* and others of past ages, partly because there is no doubt about the religious views of those men, partly because research at their time was imperfect. We begin at the rise of modern natural science.

The Old Masters

At the threshold of modern natural science there stands the man who solved the riddle that had puzzled centuries before him, the father of modern astronomy, *Nikolaus Copernicus.* He had studied at the universities of Cracow, Bologna, Ferrara, and Padua, and while he was one of the foremost historians of his time, it was astronomy that had engaged his enthusiastic devotion from his youth. He was a Catholic priest, a Canon of Frauenberg. "If recent representatives of the Roman Church," so writes the Protestant theologian, *O. Zoeckler,* "praise this Frauenberg Canon as a faithful son of their Church, this fact must be granted by Protestants, despite the frankness with which he opposed the Aristotelian and Ptolemaic theories taught by the scholastics, and despite his friendship with the Protestant *Rheticus"* (Gottes Zeugen im Reiche der Natur, 1906, p. 82). *George Joachim,* a native of Feldkirch, surnamed *Rheticus,* and a Protestant professor at Wittenberg, came to *Copernicus* at Frauenberg, and was cordially received. His praise for "his teacher" is unreserved. He speaks in the same admiring terms of *Tiedemann Giese,* in those days Bishop of Kulm.

For nearly forty years *Copernicus* sat in the modest observatory which he had erected at Frauenberg, studying and collecting the material for his book. Even after all this time this deliberate scholar, despite the urging of his friends, especially Bishop *Tiedemann Giese* and Cardinal *Schoenberg,* Archbishop of Capua, hesitated for ten years longer before publishing his discoveries. The work was entitled *De revolutionibus orbium caelestium, libri VI,* and was dedicated to Pope *Paul III.* The author himself could enjoy his achievement but very little. The first copy sent by the printer reached *Copernicus* on his deathbed, and a few hours later he breathed his last, on May 24, 1543.

In the introduction to his work this devout Christian scientist wrote: "Who would not be urged by the intimate intercourse with the work of His hands to the contemplation of the Most High, and to the admiration for the Omnipotent Architect of the universe, in whom is the highest happiness, and in whom is the perfection of all that is good?"

Without *Copernicus* there could have been no *Kepler,* without *Kepler* no *Newton.* These three men, in the words of a recent astronomer, belong inseparably together, they support and supplement one another. It might be fittingly asked, after which of these three the celestial system should be named; and were it possible to ask these three men for their opinion in this matter, they would probably all give the answer that has been ascribed to one or the other of them: Not my system, but God's Order. Like *Copernicus,* so *Kepler* and *Newton* were profoundly religious men.

Johann Kepler, born of Protestant parents in Württemberg in 1571, was raised a Lutheran. In 1594 he was appointed professor of mathematics at a school in Graz, and after that he dwelt for the most time in Austria, which country became his second home. From Graz he was called to Prague to be mathematician at the imperial court, and from there to Linz to be professor at the college there. His last years were passed at Sagan and Ratisbon, where he died in 1630. Even after having left Austria he gratefully remembered the *clementia austriaca* and the *favor archiducalis. Kepler's* astronomical achievements are known to everybody, especially his laws of the planets. With an untiring spirit of research he combined beautiful traits of character, cheerfulness, kindness, and modesty, but chiefly a profoundly religious mind. However, he was in difficult circumstances as far as his religious life was concerned. Quite early he came in conflict with the religious authorities of his confession, particularly for the reason that they considered *Kepler's* Copernican views as against the Bible, a fact which the learned astronomer could not see. There were also other differences. The conflict became more and more aggravated. It cannot be denied that the Lutheran Church-authorities proceeded against *Kepler* with a lack of consideration never shown by Rome against men like *Galileo. Kepler* was expelled from the Lutheran Church, and despite his efforts to be reinstated the ban was never lifted.

Like *Kepler,* so was his predecessor at the Catholic court of Prague, the Danish astronomer *Tycho Brahe* (died 1601), a devout Protestant, but the trials of *Kepler* were spared him. His erroneous idea that the Copernican system conflicted with Holy Writ kept him from subscribing to it; it led him to devise a system midway between *Copernicus* and *Ptolemy.* His religious sentiment is evidenced by a passage from a letter of his, written at his father's death, "Although there are many consolations for me, of a religious nature based on Holy Writ, and of a philosophical kind drawn from the contemplation of the fate of all men and of the inconstancy of everything under the moon, it is a special comfort for me that my father departed so sweetly and piously from this valley of misery to the heavenly eternal home, where, according to *St. Paul,* we shall find a lasting abode."

But let us return to *Kepler*. There is evidence that at various times in his life he wavered between his Lutheran confession and the Catholic faith, but that is as far as he went. He was of the opinion that the fundamental truths of both were in accord, and he would not presume to judge of the differences; he had taken a view-point of his own, from which he could not be made to recede. On the other hand, he was shocked when his fellow-Lutherans in Styria were on two occasions severely dealt with, although he personally had been treated with especial consideration. Otherwise his opinions on Catholic matters and the " wisdom " of the Catholic Church were eminently fair; he censured his co-religionists for their invidious attacks on Rome, and for their hesitancy in adopting the Gregorian reform of the calendar. He had friendly relation with many a Catholic scientist, was in correspondence with many Jesuits, was even frequently their guest, receiving stimulus, commendation, and scientific communications from them.

To *Kepler* the study of astronomy became largely a prayer; the finest of his scientific works he was wont to conclude with the doxology of the Psalmist, " Great is our Lord, and great is His power, and of His wisdom there is no number: praise Him ye Heavens; praise ye Him, O Sun, and Moon, ye Stars and light, and praise Him in your language. Thou, too, praise Him, O soul of mine, thy Lord, thy Creator, as long as it is granted to thee " (*Harmonices Mundi*, v. 9). His name and work is commemorated in the Keplerbund in Germany, which aims at the promotion of scientific knowledge in the sense of *Kepler,* in opposition to the misuse of natural science for purposes of materialism and atheism.

The work, begun so happily by *Copernicus* and *Kepler,* was completed by the great Englishman, *Newton* (died 1727). It was he who in his immortal work, *Philosophiae naturalis principia mathematica,* laid bare the law of the universe, which compels the heavenly bodies to revolve about one another. Therewith the laws of *Kepler,* and consequently the Copernican hypothesis, became established. When, in 1727, this scientist, at the age of eighty-five, died, his mortal remains were entombed in Westminster Abbey, the Pantheon of the British nation. Lofty science and the reverent worship of his Creator were combined in the noble mind of this great Briton. In an appendix to his master-work, referred to above, he cited his proofs for the existence of God, and stated that " the entire order, as to space and time of all things existing, must have necessarily proceeded from the conception and will of an existing Being," that " the admirable arrangement of sun, planets, and comets could only emanate from the decree and the design of an All-wise and Omnipotent Being," that " we admire Him for His perfections, we adore and worship Him as the ruler of the world, we, the servants of the great Sovereign of the Universe." According to *Voltaire,* it was stated by *Newton's* disciple, *Clarke,* that his master invariably pronounced the name of God with reverent attitude and expression.

Inseparably connected with the history of the Copernican system there is the name, which recalls harsh accusations and painful memories, the name of *Galileo.* That he had nothing in common with the aims of those who have broken with faith and Christianity, nor with that hostility against his Church for which his name is so often misused, has been made evident by what we have said on another page (see page 189). Not only during his early life was his religious turn of mind evidenced, but also later on and up to the end of his life he continued to observe faithfully the duties of his religion.

One of the greatest physicists of recent times was *Christian Huygens,* who died in 1695 at his native city, The Hague. To him we owe the epoch-making discovery of the undulation of light, while *Newton* had held light to be a matter of emission. But while *Huygens* advanced over *Newton* in this respect, he paid tribute to human limitation by remaining prejudiced against *Newton's* theory of gravitation, which he rejected. *Huygens* was a believing Christian.

In his philosophic dissertation " Kosmotheoros," a posthumous work, he says in regard to the possibility of the celestial bodies being inhabited: " How could the investigator look up to God, the Creator of all these great worlds, otherwise but in the spirit of deepest reverence? Here it will be possible for us to find manifold proofs to demonstrate His providence and wonderful wisdom; likewise will our contemplation contend against those who are spreading false opinions, such as attributing the origin of the earth to the accidental union of atoms, or of the earth being without a beginning and without a creator."

Religious fervour is still more pronounced in *Huygens'* contemporary, *Robert Boyle* (died 1692), a son of Ireland. While he had made considerable achievements in physics, his chief fame lies in chemistry: he inaugurated the period in which chemistry became gradually an independent science. Although working in a different field of research, he is similar to *Newton* in many respects: like *Newton* and *Huygens*, his love of scientific studies induced him to remain unmarried, like *Newton* he found his last resting place in Westminster Abbey, but chiefly he is like *Newton* because of his pious, religious mind. He was much occupied with theological studies, and in them the demonstration from nature of the existence of God, and the author's reverence for the Scriptures are most conspicuous: "In relation to the Bible," he writes, "all the books of men, even the most learned, are like the planets that receive their light and brightness from the sun." On his deathbed he made a foundation for apologetic lectures: the Boyle-lectures are held to this very day.

We shall have to pass by others. We might point to the English philosopher and statesman, *Francis Bacon* of Verulam (died 1626), who won his place in the history of natural science by his urging of the empiric method; we might point to *W. Harvey* (died 1658), the discoverer of the blood-circulation, a man of earnest and simple piety; we might mention the pious *Albrecht von Haller* (died 1777), *J. Bernouilli* (died 1728) the co-inventor of integral calculus, the man of whom his great disciple *Euler* relates that this *Bernouilli*, co-inventor of the most difficult of all calculations, this great mathematician, expressed regret in his old age that he had devoted so many years to science, and only few hours to religion, and that on his deathbed he admonished those around him to adhere to the Word of God because that alone is the word of life.

We shall name but one more, a son of northern Sweden, the famous botanist, *Karl Linné* (died 1778). He, too, found God in the living nature which he studied so diligently.

In commenting on his *Systema naturae* he writes: "Man, know thyself; in theological aspect, that thou art created with an immortal soul, after the image of God; in moral aspect, that thou alone art blessed with a rational soul for the praise of thy sublime Creator. I ask, why did God put man equipped thus in sense and spirit on this earth, where he perceives this wonderfully ordered nature? For what, but to praise and admire the invisible Master-builder for His magnificent work."

These are the great masters and reformers of recent natural science, the men who opened up the paths which natural science of the present day is still pursuing; most of these savants were of a Christian mind, many of them even pious. There were but few indifferent or irreligious, such as *E. Halley* (died 1742), who computed the cycle of the comet since named after him, and *G. de Buffon* (died 1788): but they are a small minority. The period of highest achievement in modern natural science bears the stamp of religion; indeed, to a great extent it bears the halo of devotion and fervour. An incompatibility of research and faith, a solidarity of science and anti-Christian tendency, was never known to the mind of these great masters.

"Any one who has grasped even the elements of natural science, the unity of natural forces and their rigid conformity to laws, becomes a monist if he has the faculty for clear reasoning, and as to the others, there is no help for them anyway" (*L. Plate,* Ultramontane Weltanschauung und moderne Lebenskunde, 1907, 11). This sort of argument is shouted at us in manifold variations. How does that statement look in the light of history? Men like *Copernicus, Kepler, Newton, Linné, Boyle,* thus knew nothing of the elements of natural science, nothing of the conformity to laws of natural forces: because they were neither monists nor atheists, but worshippers of the Creator of heaven and earth! A more painful contrast cannot be imagined than to see these great masters and pioneers rated as lesser minds, ignorant of real natural science, by those who trail far behind them and who are seeking their footsteps. The religious conviction of the natural scientists of a past age is sufficient proof that, not the research in natural science, but other causes lead minds to infidelity.

Modern Times

We turn to the nineteenth century. Does the picture perhaps change essentially in the century that has shown its children so much progress, that has disclosed so many secrets of nature, but has also taught irreligion to thousands of men? Does it become true now that natural science and Christian fundamental truths are opposed to each other in hostile attitude? Claims to this effect are not lacking. In fact, the number of those who refuse assent to the Christian religion is increasing. But even at this time we do not find such to be the majority of eminent scientists, and our inquiry is about eminent scientists, those who make the science of a period, not those who can hardly expect to have their names known by posterity. A considerable number, indeed the majority, of the master minds of natural science, even in the nineteenth century, reject materialism and atheism, and not infrequently they are pious Christians; another proof that just upon the deeper and more serious minds religion exercises a stronger power of attraction.

Let us commence with the astronomers.

"The sciences and their true representatives," so states the renowned *Mädler* of Dorpat, "do not deserve the reproaches and imputations heaped upon them from a certain side, that they would estrange man from God, even turn him into an atheist . . . we hope to show of astronomy especially that just the contrary is taking place" (Reden und Abhandlungen über Gegenstände der Himmelskunde, 1870, 326).

The greatest astronomer of the nineteenth century, and one of the greatest discoverers of all ages, was undoubtedly *William Herschel* (died 1822). His son *John Herschel* (died 1871) became his "worthy successor, almost his peer, who won a fame nearly equal to that of the inherited name" (*R. Wolf*, Geschichte der Astronomie, 1877, 505). While not hostile to religion, the father had been so engrossed in his restless research, that religion received little attention, but religious thought and sentiment played a prominent part in the son. Time and again he opposed with zeal the materialistic-atheistic explanation of the universe. "Nothing is more unfounded than the objection made by some well-meaning but undiscerning persons, that the study of natural science induces a doubt of religion and of the immortality of the soul. Be assured that its logical effect upon any well-ordered mind must be just the opposite" (Preliminary Discourse on the Study of Natural Philosophy, 1830, 7).

It was *Leverrier* (died 1877), Director of the Paris Observatory, who by calculations ascertained the existence and exact position of the remotest planet Neptune even before it was discovered. When eventually *Galle* of Berlin really found the planet in the position indicated, *Leverrier's* name became famous. But greater still were the achievements of this indefatigable investigator in respect to the known planets. When he presented to the French Academy the final part of his great work, the calculations of Jupiter and Saturnus, he said: " During our long labours, which it took us thirty-five years to complete, we needed the support obtained by the contemplation of one of the grandest works of creation, and by the thought that it strengthened in us the imperishable truths of a spiritualistic (*i. e.,* non-materialistic) philosophy." He was an orthodox Catholic, known as a Clerical. A newspaper complained of him that " Under the empire he was a clerical Senator, concerned with the interests of the altar no less than with those of the throne " (*Kneller,* Das Christenthum und die Vertreter der neueren Naturwissenschaft, 1904, 96. In the following pages we have made frequent use of the material gathered in this sterling work. See also *James J. Walsh,* Makers of Modern Medicine (1907) ; and the same author's Catholic Churchmen in Science, I (1909), II (1910)).

One year after the death of *Leverrier* another scientist of the first rank died. It was *A. Secchi* (died 1878). Member of nearly all the scientific academies of the world, he was not only a faithful Christian, but also a priest: for forty-five years, and until his death, he wore the garb of the Society of Jesus. As an astronomer he has been named, not without good cause, the father of astrophysics: he ascertained the chemical composition of about 4,000 stars and classified them into what is known as *Secchi's* four types of stars. As a physicist he wrote an important work on The Unity of Natural Forces. He was also an eminent meteorologist.

At the second International Exposition at Paris his meteorograph was quite a feature. The *Kölnische Zeitung* wrote, on March 2, 1878: " Visitors of the Italian Exhibition, at the second World's Fair in Paris, could see the marvellous instrument which does the work of ten observers and surpasses them in accuracy. At the same time they could obtain all needed information about details and scope of the meteorograph from the exhibitor himself; for *Secchi* was there daily, devoting several hours to answering questions in any of the civilized languages of Europe. It is peculiarly interesting to observe the silent movement of the hands working day and night like registrars of the natural forces, and recording for every quarter of an hour with the utmost accuracy all changes in temperature, in humidity, every variance of the wind, any movement of the mercury in the barometer. Even the force of the wind and the time of rain is registered by this wonderful instrument." The inventor, out of 40,000 art exhibitors, was awarded the great golden medal. He also received the insignia of an officer of the French Legion of Honor, while the Emperor of Brazil appointed him an officer of the " Golden Rose."

The French scientist *Moigno* writes of *Secchi:* " *Secchi* was very pious, and as a worker he knew no limits. He was ever ready to evolve new scientific plans, to enter into new and long campaigns of observation. The mere list of his 800 works reveals him as one of the most intrepid workers of our century. And let this be considered: every one of these writings, no matter how brief, was the result of subtle and difficult researches and observations. And after devoting the day to arduous writing, he passed the night searching the skies " (*Pohle*, P. Angelo Secchi, 1904, 191).

In the nineteenth century, too, astronomy has not failed in its mission of leading to God. A long list could be named of believing astronomers of great achievements. For instance, the Roman astronomer *Respighi* (died 1889), a resolute Catholic. And *Lamont,* Director of the Observatory of Munich, whose Catholic orthodoxy was generally known. *Heis* (died 1877) likewise was a zealous Catholic: when he had finished his map of the sky, after 27 years of hard work, he sent one of the first copies to *Pius IX.* The astronomers *Bessel* and *Olbers* speak in their letters of God, of the hereafter and Providence, in a way that has nothing in common with materialism.

Secchi was not the only priest and monk among the astronomers of the nineteenth century. The very first day of the century was made notable by the astronomical achievement of a monk. *Joseph Piazzi,* a member of the Theatine order (died 1826), discovered on that day the first asteroid, Ceres. The great mathematician *Gauss* named his first born son Joseph, in *Piazzi's* honor.

It is, indeed, a remarkable fact, testifying strongly against the incompatibility of natural science and faith, that just the Catholic clergy, the prominent representatives of religion and faith, have contributed a large contingent to the number of natural scientists. *Poggendorf's* Biographical Dictionary of the Exact Sciences contains, down to 1863, according to preface and recapitulation, the names and biographical sketches of 8,847 natural scientists. Of these, 862 are Catholic priests, amounting to 9.8 per cent. To appreciate these 10 per cent it must be taken into account that most of them were not connected with natural science by their position, but only through their personal interest, and most of them were engaged in other duties.

Mathematics, although not natural science proper, is inseparably connected with it. For this reason we may extend our consideration to mathematicians. We only point to the three greatest, *Euler, Gauss,* and *Cauchy,* and all three were religious men. *Euler* (died 1783 at Petersburg) has no peer in the recent history of science in prolific activity: ten times he was awarded the prize by the Paris Academy of Sciences. *Cantor* says of him: " Like most great mathematicians, *Euler* was profoundly religious, though without bigotry. He personally conducted every evening the private devotions at his home, and one of the few polemical books he wrote was a defence of revelation against the objections of free-thinkers." Its publication at Berlin in 1747, in close proximity of the court of *Frederick the Great,* presupposed a certain moral courage. In this book he refers to the difficulties found in all sciences, even in geometry, adding: " By what right then can the free-thinkers demand of us to reject at once Holy Writ in its entirety, because of some difficulties which frequently are not even so important as those complained of in geometry? " *Gauss* (died 1855) is perhaps the greatest mathematician of all times. It sounds incredible, yet it is well attested, that as a child of three years, when in the workshop of his father, a plain mechanic, he was able to correct the father if he made a mistake in figuring out the wages paid to his journeymen. His biographer, *Waltershausen,* says of him: " The conviction of a personal existence after death, the firm belief in an ultimate Ruler of things, in an eternal, just, all-wise and all-powerful God, formed the foundation of his religious life, which, with his unsurpassed scientific researches, resolved itself into a perfect harmony." *Cauchy* (died 1857) was a man of most extraordinary genius, whose creative genius knew how to discover new paths everywhere, and almost at every weekly meeting of the Paris Academy *Cauchy* had something new to offer. In addition he was a dutiful Catholic, and a member of St. Vincent's Society. When, shortly before the February revolution, an onslaught upon the Jesuit schools was made, he defended them in two pamphlets.

One of them contains the following confession of faith: " I am a Christian, that is, I believe in the divinity of Jesus Christ, with *Tycho*

Brahe, Copernicus, Descartes, Newton, Fermat, Leibnitz, Pascal, Grimaldi, Euler, Guldin, Boscovich, Gerdil; with all great astronomers, all great physicists, all great mathematicians of past centuries. I am also a Catholic, with the majority of them, and if asked for my reasons, I would enumerate them readily. By them it would be made clear that my conviction is not the result of inherited prejudices, but of profound inquiry. I am a sincere Catholic, as *Corneille, Racine, La Bruyère, Bossuet, Bourdaloue, Fénelon* were, and such as were and still are a large portion of the most eminent men of our times, among them those who have achieved most in the exact sciences, in philosophy and literature, and who have most prominently adorned our Academy" (*Valson,* Vie de Cauchy, I, 173). When near death, and told that the priest would bring the Holy Sacrament, he ordered the finest flowers of his garden used in the reception of the Lord.

We now come to the physicists. To begin with the most prominent representatives of the science of optics, which was developed especially during the first half of the century, there are to be named chiefly *Fresnel, Frauenhofer, Fizeau, Foucault.* *A. Fresnel* (died 1827), the originator of the modern theory of light, clung to his conviction of the spirituality and immortality of the soul. *Frauenhofer* (died 1826) showed himself to be a man of refinement and of kindness, which only occasionally was disturbed by natural irritability: he was much devoted to his religion, so that even his guests while at his house had to observe the abstinence prescribed by the Church; this was quite significant, considering the indifference of his times in this respect. *Fizeau* (died 1896), too, was a staunch Catholic, who fearlessly testified to his belief, even before the Paris Academy. Though his work was of the first rank, France's chief marks of honour passed him by, and little notice was even given to his death. A significant fact. "These circumstances," so writes *Kneller,* "induced us to inquire for particulars; and through the services of friends we obtained information in Paris from most reliable source that *Fizeau* was a faithful Christian, who fulfilled his religious duties. For this very reason his name had been stricken, at the Centenary of the Academy, from the list of candidates for the cross of the legion of honor, notwithstanding the fact that, on the strength of his scientific achievement, he should long have been Commander and even Grand Officer of this order." *Cornu* was the only one to protest against this slight. *Foucault* (died 1868) had, in the time of his restless scientific work, taken an unsympathetic attitude towards the Catholic religion. In his last illness he returned, step by step, to his Creator and Redeemer, in whom he found his comfort, and he breathed his last in peace with God and the Church.

Foucault's great countryman, *Ampère* (died 1836), the celebrated investigator in the fields of electricity, was also estranged from the Christian religion, but, after passing through torturing doubts, he regained undisturbed possession of his Catholic faith, and was a pious Christian at the time of his brilliant discoveries. He had frequent intercourse with *A. F. Ozanam,* and the discussion almost without exception turned to God. Then *Ampère* would cover his forehead with his hands, exclaiming: "How great God is! Ozanam! how great God is, and our knowledge is as nothing." "This venerable head," *Ozanam* relates of his friend, "covered with honours and full of knowledge, bowed down before the mysteries of the faith; he knelt at the same altars where before him *Descartes* and *Pascal* worshipped humbly, beside the poor widow and the small child, who perhaps were less humble than he" (*A. F. Ozanam,* Oeuvres Completes, X, 37, and VIII, 89). As he was dying, and *M. Deschamps,* director of the college of Marseille, began to read aloud some passages from the "Imitation of Christ," the dying man remarked that he knew the book by heart.

Another great discoverer in the domain of electricity, who had preceded *Ampère,* was *Volta* (died 1827). Like his great fellow countryman, *Galvani* (died 1798), who did not disdain to be a member of the third order of St. Francis, *Volta* was a staunch Catholic; every day he recited the rosary.

At Como, his home, he was daily seen to go to holy Mass and, on holidays, to the Sacraments. Those who passed his house on Saturdays saw a small lamp burning before the picture of the Blessed Virgin Mary over his door. If the servant forgot to light the lamp, *Volta* did it himself. On Feast days, when visiting the parish church, the great electrician could be seen among the children, explaining the catechism to them.

A friend of *Volta*, the Canon *Giacomo Ciceri,* once was endeavoring to convert a dying man, who, however, refused to hear him, on the ground that whereas religion might be good for the common people, scientists did not need it, and he reckoned himself among them. *Ciceri* thereupon reminded him of *Volta*. This made an impression upon the dying man, who declared that if *Volta* be seriously religious, and not only as a matter of convention, he would consent to receive the Sacraments. The Canon then requested *Volta* to write a few lines. *Volta* replied as follows: " I do not understand how anybody can doubt my sincerity and constancy in the religion which I profess, and which is that of Catholic, Apostolic, Roman Church, wherein I was born and raised, and which I have professed all my life, inwardly and outwardly. . . . Should any misdemeanor on my part have prompted any one to suspect me of unbelief, then I will declare, for the purpose of making reparation . . . that I always have believed this Holy Catholic religion to be the only true and infallible one, and that I still think so, and I thank our dear Lord incessantly for having given me this belief, in which to live and to die is my resolution, in the firm hope of gaining the eternal life. It is true, I acknowledge this belief to be a gift of God, a supernatural belief; yet, I have not neglected human means to fortify myself in this belief, and to drive away all doubts that may arise to tempt me. For this reason, I have studied the faith diligently in its foundations, by reading apologetic and controversial writings, weighing the reasons for and against; a way, which supplies the strongest proof, and makes it most credible for the human reason to such a degree, that any noble mind, not perverted by sins and passions, cannot help embracing and loving it. I wish this profession, for which I was asked and which I willingly make, written and signed by my own hand, to be shown at will to any one, because I am not ashamed of the Gospel. May my writing bear good fruit.

Alexander Volta.

MILAN, January 6th, 1815.
(*C. Grandi*, Alessandro Volta, 1899, 575.)"

He who, for the first time, is made aware of the religious confession of the greatest natural scientists may perhaps be astonished. Hitherto, he had heard little of the Christian mind of these men, but a great deal about their alleged indifference for religion, and about their materialism and atheism. Now, suddenly, he sees a large number of them to be the enemies of atheism, many, indeed, to be zealous Christians.

This is due to the biographers: they dwell largely on the scientific achievement of a man, likewise on his human qualities, but his religion is often not mentioned at all. When, in 1888, a monument was erected to *Ampère* in his native city, Lyons, not a word in the speeches referred to the fact that he was a faithful Catholic. Nay, more; on one of the books seen on his monument is chiselled in bold letters the word " Encyclopédie."

Those unaware of the facts would infer that *Ampère* had been one of the Encyclopædists. His actual relation to this infamous work was that he had read it in his youth, but abhorred it in his later age.

The English physicist, *Faraday* (died 1867), according to *Tyndall* and *Du Bois-Reymond* the greatest experimentist of all times, was, like *Volta* and *Ampère,* of religious mind.

In a letter to a lady he wrote: "I belong to a small and despised Christian sect, known by the name of Sandemanians. Our hope is based upon the belief which is in Christ." In 1847, he concluded his lectures at the Royal Institution with the following words: "In teaching us those things, our science should prompt us to think of Him whose works they are." At a later lecture, he declared: "I have never encountered anything to cause a contradiction between things within the scope of man, and the higher things, relating to his future and unconceivable to (unaided) human mind" (*Jones*, The Life and Letters of Faraday).

Of the same bent of mind was *Faraday's* fellow countryman, *Maxwell* (died 1879), known to every one who has studied the development of the theories of electricity. This ingenious theoretician of electrics, professor of experimental physics at Cambridge, was deeply religious. Every evening he led in the family prayer; he regularly attended divine service, and partook of the monthly communion of his denomination. Those more intimately acquainted with *Maxwell* agree, that he was one of the worthiest men they ever met.

Nothing could better illustrate his religious sentiment than the splendid prayer found among his posthumous papers: "Almighty God, Thou who hast created man after Thy image and hast given him a living soul, that he should search Thee and rule over Thy creatures, teach us to study the works by Thy hands that we may subject the earth for our use, and strengthen our reason for Thy service, and let us receive Thy holy word thus, that we may believe in Him whom Thou hast sent us to give us the knowledge of salvation and the forgiving of our sins, all of which we pray for in the name of the same Jesus Christ, our Lord" (*Campbell-Garnett*, The Life of J. C. Maxwell).

Maxwell's devout mind is especially significant here, because, like *Ampère* and *Volta,* he occupied himself much with philosophical and theological questions. Every Sunday upon return from church he is said to have buried himself in his theological books.

Many others might be mentioned of English physicists of the past century, who combined religious belief with great knowledge. The peculiar trait of the English character to respect and preserve with piety the inherited institutions of the past, as against radicalism and the craze for innovation, manifests itself also in the absence of the immature and frivolous juggling with the great truths of the Christian past, not infrequently met with elsewhere. Let us mention but one more of England's great men who have died in recent years. In December, 1907, the papers reported the death of *William Thomson,* latterly better known as *Lord Kelvin.* He lived to the age of 83 years, up to his death incessantly busy with scientific work. As early as 1855, *Helmholtz* described him as "one of the foremost mathematical physicists of Europe.[1]" The Berlin Academy of Science expressed high praise and admiration in its address felicitating *Thomson* on his Golden Jubilee. Undoubtedly, he merited this admiration also by stoutly defending from the viewpoint of science the necessity of a Divine Creator.

"We do not know," he wrote, "at what moment a creation of matter or of energy fixed a beginning beyond which no speculation based on mechanical laws is able to lead us. In exact mechanics, if we were ever inclined to forget this barrier, we necessarily would be reminded of it by the consideration that reasoning, resting exclusively upon the law of mechanics, points to a time when the earth must have been

---

[1] After visiting *Thomson* at Kreuznach, *Helmholtz* wrote: "He surpasses all great scientists I have personally met, in acumen, clearness and activity of spirit, so that I felt somewhat dull beside him." *Helmholtz* himself (died 1894) has never expressed himself about religion. Absorbed by his scientific work, he seemed to have been indifferent to religion, but according to his biographer his father was a decided theist, and his philosophical views were held in great esteem, and partly subscribed to, by the son. According to *Dennert, Helmholtz* attended church now and then, and even partook of holy communion. Of decided religious bent of mind was *Helmholtz's* fellow-countryman, and co-discoverer of the law of energy, *Robert Mayer.* At the Congress of scientists at Innsbruck, in 1869, *Mayer* ended his address with the significant words: "Let me in conclusion declare from the bottom of my heart that true philosophy cannot and must not be anything else but propædeutics of the Christian religion." His letters breathe piety. For a time he had the intention of joining the Catholic Church.

uninhabited, and it also teaches us that our own bodies, like those of all living plants and animals, and fossils, are organized forms of matter for which science can give no other explanation than the will of a Creator, a truth, in support of which geological history offers rich evidence" (On Mechanical Antecedent of Motion, Heat and Light, 1884). "The only contribution of dynamics to theoretical biology consists in the absolute negation of an automatic beginning and automatic continuance of life" (Addresses and Speeches).

On May 1, 1902, the Rev. Prof. *G. Henslow*, according to the *London Times*, spoke at University College, before a big audience with the President of the University as chairman, on the subject "The Rationalism of To-day, an Examination of Darwinism." On conclusion of the speech the venerable octogenarian, *Lord Kelvin*, arose and proposed a resolution of thanks to the speaker. While fully subscribing to the fundamental ideas of Prof. *Henslow's* lecture, *Lord Kelvin* said, he could not assent to the proposition that natural science neither affirms nor denies the origin of life by a creative force. He stated that natural science *does*, positively, assert a creative force. Science forces every one to recognize a miracle within himself. That we are living, and moving, and existing, is not due to dead matter, but to a creating and directing force, and science forces us to accept this assumption as a tenet of faith. *Lord Kelvin* subsequently amplified these remarks in an article that appeared in the *Nineteenth Century*, of June, 1903. It concludes with the admonition, not to be afraid to think independently. "If you reason sharply, you will be forced by science to believe in God, who is the basis of all religion. You will find science to be, not an opponent of religion, but a support" (*Times*, May 8 and 15, 1903).

Such were the views of those to whom, in the first place, the establishment of natural science and its progress are due. It is not science and strong reasoning that. lead away from God, but the lack of true science. *Bacon* said: *Leviores gustus in philosophia movere fortasse animum ad atheismum, sed pleniores haustus ad Deum reducere.* Another thing must be observed. Among those earnest men, earnest in the investigation of nature, and earnest in the consideration of questions of a supernatural life, there are many who made the religious question the subject of mature study, and who were well acquainted with the objections against religion and Christianity. But they cling to their religious persuasion only the more firmly. We may be reminded of men like *Volta, Cauchy, Ampère,* and *Maxwell*.

To speak of authorities, what comparison is there between these great scientists and discoverers, and those who are satisfied with the general assurance that " any one who has grasped the elements of natural sciences must become a monist," and "that the supernatural exists only in the brain of the visionary and ignorant," that, "in the same measure in which the victorious progress of modern knowledge of nature surpasses the scientific achievements of former centuries, the untenableness of all mystical views of life that tend to harness the reason in the yoke of so-called revelation has been made clear" (*Haeckel*), and who in such assurance find perfect intellectual gratification. They recall an incident at the Congress of English natural scientists, held at Belfast in 1874, when *Tyndall* delivered from the platform a materialistic lecture, and among the audience sat *Maxwell*, his superior in scientific research, who put down the lecture in doggerel rhyme, in a humorous vein, of course, but not without deserved sarcasm.

We proceed on our way, trying to make haste, and omitting many names that might be mentioned, limiting ourselves to the most prominent ones.

Among the chemists we name *Lavoisier*. A martyr to his science, he died under the guillotine of the Revolution in 1794; he had remained true to his Christian faith. The Swede, *J. Berzelius* (died 1848), openly professed his belief in God. *Thénard* (died 1859), the discoverer of boron, of a blue dye named after him, and of many other chemicals, was a staunch Catholic. The pastor of St. Sulpice could testify at his funeral as follows: "He attended church every Sunday, eyes and heart fixed on his prayer-book, and on solemn Feast days he received Holy Communion. . . . With *Baron Thénard* one of the greatest benefactors of my poor people is gone" (*Kneller*).

Dumas (died 1884), who is esteemed by his pupil *Pasteur* as the peer of *Lavoisier,* was also a practical Catholic, as was his compatriot *Chevreul* (died 1889). This great man had the rare good fortune to be present at his own centenary in 1886. At this great celebration he received an address by the Berlin Academy, stating that his name had a prominent place on the list of the great scientists who had carried the scientific repute of France to all quarters of the globe. When, in view of the mundane character of the celebration, the liberal press endeavoured to rank him among the representatives of unbelieving science, and this question being discussed in public, *Chevreul* felt himself constrained to proclaim his religious persuasion openly in a letter to *Count de Montravel,* in which he said: " I am simply a scientist, but those who know me, know also that I was born a Catholic, that I lead a Catholic life, and that I want to die a Catholic " (Civilta Cattolica, 1891, 292).

Two Germans may conclude the list of chemists, *Schoenbein* (died 1868) and *J. Liebig* (died 1873).

In his diary, "Menschen und Dinge," 1885 (page 29), *Schoenbein* writes: "There are still people who fancy in their limited mind that, the deeper the human intellect penetrates the secrets of nature, the more extensive its knowledge, the wider its conception of the exterior world, the more it must forget the cause of all things. Many have gone even so far as to assert that natural science must lead to the denial of God. This view is without all foundation. He, who contemplates with open eyes, daily and hourly, the doings and workings of nature, will not only believe, but will actually perceive, and be firmly convinced, that there is not the smallest place in space where the divine does not reveal itself in the most magnificent and admirable way." And in a similar strain *Liebig* writes: "Indeed, the greatness and infinite wisdom of the Creator of the world can be realized only by him who endeavours to understand His ideas as laid down in that immense book, — nature, in comparison to which everything that men otherwise know and tell of Him, appears like empty talk " (Die Chemie in ihrer Anwendung).

Now let us turn to the geographers. We merely mention *Ritter* (died 1859), the man who raised geography to the dignity of a science; he was a faithful Protestant, while biassed against the Catholic Church. In spite of this, a Catholic historian, *J. Janssen,* has sketched his life, in which we read: " Firm in his belief in the living God, and in the Incarnate Son of God, His Redeemer, he furnishes a clear and convincing proof that this faith, far from being a contradiction to natural science . . . alone enables man to acquire an extensive and deep knowledge of nature." We give only passing notice to the founder of scientific crystallography, *R. Hauy* (died 1822), who was a dutiful Catholic priest. The geologists now will get a hearing.

Among them we meet, in the first place, the noted geologist and zoölogist, *Cuvier* (died 1832), a faithful Protestant: also the foremost French geologist of his time, *L. De Beaumont* (died 1874), " a Christian in all things and a steadfast Christian . . . which he remained through his whole life; so *Dumas* testifies of him in his obituary (Comptes Rendus, 1874). Then there is *J. Barrande*, the untiring explorer of the antediluvian strata of Bohemia. He came in 1830 to Bohemia with the banished royal family, as *Chambord's* teacher, and died 1883 at Frohsdorf near Vienna. He was a pious Catholic. The volumes of his works are nearly all dated on Catholic feasts. The recently deceased French geologist, *A. De Lapparent*, was a practical Catholic, and such were the two Belgian geologists, *J. d'Omalius* (died 1875), and *A. Dumont* (died 1857), to both of whom Belgium owes it geological exploration. The English geologists, *Buckland* (died 1856), *Hitchcock* (died 1864), and *A. Sedgwick* (died 1872), were ministers of the English Church. *J. Dwight Dana* (died 1895), the foremost geologist of North America, begins his celebrated text-book of geology with a homage to his Creator, and concludes it by paying tribute to Holy Writ. *W. Dawson* (died 1899) the worthy geological explorer of his native land, Canada, published several apologetic dissertations on the Bible and Nature. A kindred sentiment animated the German scientists, *Bischof* (died 1870), *Quenstedt* (died 1898), the geologist of Suabia *Pfaff* (died 1886), *Schafhœutl* (died 1890), and the equally pious as learned Swiss geologist *O. Heer* (died 1883). They all have much to say about the greatness of their Creator, but not a word of any insolvable contradictions between the Bible and geologic research.

As a last division of an imposing phalanx, there are now the biologists and physiologists. Modern biology, as the science of life, has in the eyes of many accomplished the bold deed of demonstrating the superfluity of a soul distinct from matter. Claim is made that it has sufficiently explained the sensitive and mental life by the sole agency of physical and chemical forces, and thus to have removed the boundary between live and dead matter. It is said, further, that biology in conjunction with zoölogy and botany has furnished proof that the wonderful organic forms of life may be explained by purely natural causes, without having to assume as an ultimate cause the act of a higher intelligence; that a never ceasing evolution is the sole ultimate cause, — creation is made superfluous by evolution. Biology is thus claimed to have refuted the old dualism of soul and matter, of world and God, and to have awarded the palm to monism.

Are the eminent representatives of this science really the materialists and monists they would have to be, if all this were true? The foremost physiologist of the nineteenth century was *J. Müller* (died 1858), buried in the Catholic cemetery at

Berlin. He was a decided opponent of materialism; he not only contended for the existence of a spiritual soul, but also for an immaterial vital force in plants. *Th. Schwann* (died 1882) is the founder of the cellular theory. In the year 1839 he accepted a call to take the chair of anatomy at the Catholic University of Louvain. One of the most prominent physiologists of the nineteenth century was *A. Volkmann* (died 1877). He was a stout champion of the spirituality and immortality of the soul, of purposive cause in animated beings, and an opponent of *Darwin's* theory. *G. J. Mendel* (died 1884) became by his work on *Experimenting with Hybrid Plants* the pioneer of the modern theory of hereditary transmission, adopted by modern biology; and scientists like *H. de Vries, Correns, Tschermak,* and *Bateson* followed his lead. " His important laws of hereditary transmission are the best so far offered by the research in this field " (*Muckermann,* Grundriss der Biologie). He was a Catholic priest, and the abbot of the Augustinian Monastery at Old-Brünn. *Karl von Vierordt* (died 1884) is well known by his " Manual of Physiology," still in demand as a reference book in the libraries of universities. In 1865 he delivered a speech at the Tübingen University on the unity of science, concluding with this appeal to the students: " Until your religious notions become clear by a mature insight, trust in the well-meant assurance that the belief in the divinity of the religion of Jesus has not been put falsely into your heart. True piety is equally remote from narrow pietism as from freethinking indifference; it leaves to reason its full rights, but it also assures to us the faculty to be aware, in joyful confidence in Almighty Providence, of an immaterial and for us eternal destiny." *Ch. Ehrenberg* (died 1876) is the explorer of the world of little things: of infusoria and protozoa. He did not countenance *Haeckel's* materialism nor *Darwin's* denial of teleology: to him they were fantastic theories and romances. A friend of his, and of the same mind, was *K. von Martius,* who admired God's wisdom in the wonders of the world of vegetation. Long before his death he ordered his burial dress to be made of white cloth embroidered with a green cross, — " a cross because I am a Christian, and green in honour of botany."

Another renowned name may be mentioned, that of the Austrian anatomist *J. Hyrtl* (died 1894).

In the years when materialism was flourishing, *Hyrtl* was painfully grieved to see science fall into disrepute through the fault of individuals. He gave vent to his indignation on the occasion of the fifth centenary of the Vienna University (1864), when, having been elected Rector, and being considered the greatest celebrity at that college, he delivered his inaugural speech on the materialistic tendency of our times. Summing up he said: "I am at a loss how to explain what scientific grounds there are to defend and fortify a revival of the old materialistic views of an *Epicurus* and a *Lucretius,* and to endeavour to insure to it a permanent rule. . . . Its success is due to the boldness of its assertion and to the prevailing spirit of the time, which popularizes teachings of this sort the more willingly, the more danger they seem to entail for the existing order of things." It was the same protest made some years later by another famous scientist against "the dangerous opinion that there were dogmas of natural science in inimical opposition to the highest ideals of the human mind." He stated that "it would be a desirable reward for the efforts of our foremost naturalists to erect with the aid of anthropology a barrier to this error which is so demoralizing for the people" (*J. Ranke,* Der Mensch, 1894).

Hyrtl's speech at once aroused a storm of indignation in the liberal press of Vienna, and the great scientist, until then honoured and extolled, became the object of denunciation and sneer. Thus was the freedom of science understood in those circles.

Haeckel was much vexed by two fellow scientists, *M. von Baer* (died 1876) and *G. J. Romanes* (died 1894). *Baer* was prominent in the science of evolution. He was led to theism by his studies. *Romanes,* a friend of *Darwin,* had been an adherent of materialism, but through serious study he returned to the belief in God and Christianity. His posthumous work, "Thoughts on Religion, a scientist's religious evolution from Atheism to Christianity," furnishes a brilliant voucher thereof. *Romanes's* conversion was a sad blow for *Haeckel.* However, he constructed an explanation to give himself comfort. "When the news of this conversion," he wrote, "was first circulated by a friend of *Romanes,* a zealous English Churchman, the assumption suggested itself to me that it was all a mystification and invention, for it is known that the fanatical champions of ecclesiastical superstition have never hesitated to pervert the truth to save their dogma. Later on, however, it was found that it was really an instance (analogous to the case of old *Baer*) of one of those interesting psychological metamorphoses with which I have dealt in Chapter 6 of my book. *Romanes* was in his last years a sick man. It was pathological debility. The first condition, however, of an unbiassed, pure conception of reason is the normal condition of its organ. His phronema was not in a normal condition." *Haeckel* will have to rank among those whose phronema is not in a normal condition a good many other natural scientists; indeed, most of those of higher standing.

Every one knows the celebrated name of *Louis Pasteur* (died 1895), the discoverer of various bacteria, of whom *Huxley* says that his manifold inventions have repaid to French industry the five billion francs indemnity which France had to pay to Germany after the war. It is equally well known that *Pasteur* was to his death a staunch Catholic. " As his soul departed, he held in his hands a small cross of brass, and his last words were the confession of faith and hope " (La Science Catholique, X, 1896, 182). The story is told that one of his pupils asked him how he could be so religious after all his thinking and studying. *Pasteur* replied: " Just because I have thought and studied, I remained religious like a man of Brittany, and had I thought and studied still more, I would be as religious as a woman of Brittany " (Revue des Questions Scientifiques, 1896, 385).

In the year 1859 great commotion was caused in the world of thought by the appearance of *Darwin's* book on the " Origin of Species." It stated that the various species had gradually evolved from most simple, primordial forms, and this by natural selection; not, therefore, in the sense that the Creator had put the laws of evolution into nature, but that in the struggle for existence the survival of the fittest was the result of natural selection. Soon it was claimed that man, too, in his rational life, was the result of an evolution from animal stages; indeed, the whole universe had arisen by the survival of the accidentally fittest. Evolution was to be substituted for creation. In Germany, *E. Haeckel* was the man who considered it the task of his life to spread those ideas as the established result of science. In our own time a belated high tide is sweeping over the intellectual lowlands.

Darwin himself was an agnostic; to begin with, he lacked all religious training; his mother had died early, his father was a freethinker, and his education at school was rationalistic. The doubt of all higher truths, and finally, according to his own confession, the doubt respecting the power of reason, were his companions through life. Yet he confesses: ". . . I never was an atheist in the sense that I would deny the existence of God. I think, in general (and more so the older I grow), but not at all times, agnostic would be a more accurate description of my state of mind " (*F. Darwin*, The Life and Letters of Charles Darwin, I, 304). Remarkable, however, is the following passage at the end of *Darwin's* chief work: " It is a great belief, indeed, of the Creator having breathed the embryo of all life surrounding us into a few forms, or in but one single form, and an endless row of most beautiful, most wonderful forms having evolved and are still evolving from such a simple beginning, while our planet, following the laws of gravitation, has steadily revolved in its circle."

What *Darwin* was lacking in a high degree was a philosophical training of the mind.

In itself the THEORY OF EVOLUTION, which asserts the variability of species of animals and plants, is by no means opposed to religious truths. It neither includes a necessity of assuming the origin of the human soul from the essentially lower animal soul, nor is it an atheistic theory. On the contrary, such an evolution would most clearly certify to God's wisdom in laying such a wonderful basis for the progress of nature, provided this theory could be proved by scientific facts; indeed, for an evolution within narrow limits, circumstantial evidence is not lacking. That there is no contradiction between the theory of evolution and the fundamental tenets of Christian Creed is sufficiently shown by the representatives of the theory. *Lamarck* (died 1829) and *Saint-Hilaire* (died 1844), both of them representatives of the theory of evolution long before *Darwin*, believed in God. There were, prior to *Darwin*, two celebrated Catholic scientists, to wit, *Ampère* and *d'Omalius*, who had decidedly taken the part of *Saint-Hilaire* in his controversy with *Cuvier*. And also after *Darwin*, a number of Christian and Catholic scientists have contended for the idea of evolution, as, for instance, the pious Swiss geologist, *Heer;* also *Quenstedt*, *Volkmann*, and the American geologist, *Ch. Lyell*. More recently Catholic scientists have expressed themselves in favour of the theory of evolution; for instance, the noted zoölogist, *E. Wasmann*, and the geologists *Lossen* and *W. Waagen*, both of whom had to bring bitter sacrifices in their career on account of their Catholic faith.

MATURE SCIENCE RESPECTS FAITH

There have now passed in review the great natural scientists of the past, those living at the present time we shall leave to the judgment of the future. Is it true, then, that the foremost representatives of natural science had the conviction that science and faith are incompatible? No! On the contrary, most of them, and the greatest of them, have professed the fundamental truths of religion, or have even been devout Christians themselves.

" Theism in natural science, or, if you prefer, in natural philosophy," so says a modern scientist, " rests upon the basis of a fundamental view which an old formula has clothed in words as simple as they are sublime: ' I believe in God, the Almighty Creator of Heaven and of Earth.' This confession does not cling to theistic scientists like an egg-shell from the time of unsophisticated childhood faith; it is the result of their entire scientific thought and judgment. This conviction has been professed by the most discerning natural scientists of all ages " (*J. Reinke*, Naturwissenschaft und Religion).

Still it cannot be denied that some of the great scientists were of different mind, men like *R. von Virchow, Tyndall, A. von Humboldt, Du Bois-Reymond*. Nor shall it be disputed that, at the present time, a large number of men of average learning are on the side of unbelief. However, it must not be forgotten that unbelief is more frequently pretended to the outside world for appearance's sake than it really dwells in the heart. This is, to a great extent, due to human respect, to public opinion, and the prevailing tendency of science. Then again, it must be remembered, that religiously minded scientists are often crowded out from the schools of science, with the natural result that the others predominate. Another point to be borne in mind is that the atheistic representatives of science are doing more to get themselves talked about; they are seeking more diligently the attention of public opinion. Men like *Tyndall, Vogt, Moleschott, Haeckel,* are known in larger circles than men like *Faraday, Maxwell, Ampère, Volta, Pasteur,* who, engaged in serious work, gave no time to making propaganda, as the others did by lecturing and popular writing for materialistic and monistic views in the name of science; they had no desire for the limelight of attention, and for posing as personified science.

All this does not change the fact that a very large number, indeed the largest number, of natural scientists of first rank were believers in God, or of pious, Christian mind. And that is of the greater importance. To do pioneer work in the field of science, to give impetus, to make progress, requires a penetrating and, at the same time, an independent mind, one that can rise above conventional commonplace. The fact that such men have largely been very religious, that they never belittled religion, weighs much more in the balance than the disparagement of inferior minds.

These, then, are the often-cited witnesses for the incompatibility of science and faith. While only taken from the province of natural science, they may in our case be deemed representative of science in general. For natural science is generally regarded the most exact of all, and as the one which, more than any other, has the scientific spirit said to be incompatible with faith, and which, by many, is believed to have brought about in the modern world of thought the irreconcilable conflict between faith and science. This is not so! Such antagonism does *not* exist. It cannot exist, because it is certain from the outset that both faith and science unfold the truth. Truth, however, can never be in conflict with truth. Nor has that antagonism ever existed historically in any of the great representatives of science. This antagonism is fictitious, it is false in its very essence. It is fabricated, either by distorting faith into a blind belief of absurd things, or else by distorting the human faculty of conception into infallible omniscience, or, the other extreme, by denying its faculty for a higher perception.

Faith has nothing to fear from a mature science that has arrived at the conviction of its cognitions, nor has it anything to fear from the great intellects who reason profoundly and seriously. But it has to fear mock-science and ignorance, and those small and superficial minds that aim at stretching their pseudo-knowledge to a gigantic infallibility.

THIRD SECTION

The Liberal Freedom of Research

THE LIBERAL FREEDOM OF RESEARCH

THE YOKE OF THE SUN

THE gifted Danish writer and convert, *J. Jörgensen,* tells
a parable which is pregnant with thought. "In the
midst of a large rye-field," he relates, "there stood a tall
poplar, with other trees standing nearby. One day the poplar turned to the other trees and plants, and thus began
to speak: 'Sisters and brothers! To us, the glorious tribe
of plants, belongs the earth, and everything upon it is dependent on us. We fertilize and feed ourselves, while beasts
and men are fed and clothed by us. Indeed, the earth itself
feeds upon our decaying leaves, upon our boughs and branches.
There is only one power in the world our existence and growth
is said to depend on; I refer to the Sun. I purposely used the
words, "is said," because I am sure that we do not depend
on the Sun. This doctrine of sunlight being a necessity and
a benefit to our plant life is nothing but a superstition, which
at last ought to give way to enlightenment.' Here the poplar
paused. From some old oaks and elms in the neighbouring
grove there came signs of disapproval, but the inconstant rye-
field muttered assent. Thus encouraged and raising its voice
the poplar continued: 'I know well that there is a musty faction
amongst us which clings obstinately to obsolete views. However,
I have confidence in the independence of the younger generation
of plants. They will realize the baseness of continuing to do
homage to an absurd superstition. Our freeborn heads shall
never bow to a yoke, not even to the yoke of the Sun. Down,
therefore, with that yoke! And free from restraint there will
arise a free and beautiful generation that will astonish the
world.' The poplar paused for the second time, and now the
applause was long and loud, the fields cheered and the groves
gave boisterous applause, so that the disapproval of a few old

trees could not be heard. The following days looked upon an odd spectacle. At daybreak, when the Sun ascended and cast its first rays over the landscape, the flowers closed their cups and denied admission, as if asleep; the leaves no longer turned toward the Sun. But when the dispenser of warmth and light had gone down behind the hills, the gayly coloured flowers opened in the dim starlight, as if now the time had come for them to grow and blossom.

"Alas, how sad was the fate of these poor rebels! The rye soon began to languish till it lay prone on the ground; green leaves turned yellow, the flowers drooped, faded and withered. Then the plants began to grumble at the poplar. There it stood, its leaves a seared yellow. 'What simpletons you are, brothers and sisters!' it said. 'Can't you see that now you are much more like yourselves than under the rule of the Sun? Now you are refined, independent beings, well rid of the sluggish health of yore.' There were some who still believed what the poplar said. 'We are independent, we are unfettered,' they clamoured, till the last spark of life was gone. Not long after the poplar, too, stood there with its branches bared, — it had died. The farmers, however, complained about the failing of the crop, and consoled themselves by hoping for better success the next year."

A parable of deep meaning! It may serve as an illustration for the facts stated, and for those yet to be dealt with.

According to the Christian view, man is dependent on his Creator, from whom he receives life and light, and, in the same way, his mind depends on truth, by which it lives as the plants live, by the light and the warmth of the sun. To many generations this was self-evident, and withal they felt themselves free, because they looked for the freedom only of the dependent creature. And, keeping within these bounds, they had a cheerful existence in the happy possession of their faith, contented and serene in the possession of truth; their higher spiritual life throve and flourished, promoted by the Eternal Giver of light and warmth, who held out to them the prospect of completing their mental life in the contemplation of His eternal truth.

What the fathers deemed self-evident has now become a problem to their sons. What to their fathers was lofty and revered, the things to which they ascribed their ennoblement, have become to the sons an obstacle to free development. They have forgotten what they are. They demand independence and freest realization of their own individuality, in which they see the sole source of greatness and progress. In every dependence they perceive a hampering of their natural development.

We have in previous chapters become acquainted with this *liberal freedom,* particularly in reasoning and in scientific research, the child of the philosophy of humanitarianism and subjectivism, the philosophy that emancipates man from God's rule, from the immutable religious truths, and which sees in this emancipation perfect freedom. We have listened to the arguments in behalf of this position, especially arguments against the duty to believe. All that we have set forth hitherto was to prove that such a freedom is not required. In the faithful adherence to God's revelation and to His Church there is no degradation of reason, an exaltation rather; because to join in the eternal reason of its Creator is not bondage but a privilege.

We proceed. We shall demonstrate that this freedom is not only not required, but that it is entirely untenable and ruinous; that it is especially so because it is urged and demanded in the name of truth and proper order, in the name of uplift of human intellectual life, and of progress towards real enlightenment. We shall see that this freedom is not a liberation from mean fetters, but simply a revolt against the natural order, an apostasy from God and the supernatural which one shuns. Hence, not the natural and orderly development of the human individual, but a principle of negation under the garb of freedom, the severance of man from the sources of his greatness and strength, the perversion of true science; not the only admissible scientific method, but an altogether unscientific method. We shall show that it becomes thereby the principle of mental pauperization and decay, a principle of mental decadence, which in the sphere of idealism will reduce mankind to beggary.

Thereby public testimony is given that in the midst of mankind there is needed an intelligent force that preserves, with conscientious earnestness and unyielding firmness, the intellectual inheritance of mankind, the ideal treasures of truth and of morality.

CHAPTER I

FREE FROM THE YOKE OF THE SUPERNATURAL

IGNORAMUS, WE IGNORE

THE liberal principle of research rests on the basis of the humanitarian view of the world, which makes man autonomous, and causes him to turn his eyes from above and downward, and to fix them upon his earthly existence. To remain true to its own idea, this liberal science will feel the necessity to sever itself gradually from the restraining powers of the world beyond, and to shun the thought of God and of His divine influence and supremacy over the world and human life. It must resent such truths as a burdensome yoke that oppresses human freedom.

And to this thought it remains faithful, if not in all its representatives, then at any rate in a good many of them. With unremitting persistency it enforces in all its domains the demand: SCIENCE MUST NOT RECKON WITH SUPERNATURAL FACTORS. Ignoramus is its watchword, " we do not know it " in the sense of its usual agnosticism, but " we ignore it " in the spirit of the impulse which dreads the loss of its freedom through higher powers. Creation and miracles, divine revelation and the God-imposed duty of belief, it does not know. A moral law, as given by God, does not exist for this science. It wants nothing to do with a religion that worships a personal God, much less with a supernatural religion, with mysteries, miracles, and grace. It praises all the higher that modern religion of sentiment, without dogmas and religious duties, which sovereign man creates for himself, a poetical adornment of his individuality, a religion he need not ask what he owes it, but rather what it offers him. All connection with the world beyond is cut off. Man is now free in his own house. We shall show this in detail, by the testimony chiefly of men generally accepted as foremost representatives of modern science. We do not assert, however, that all representatives of modern science belong here. Far be it from us to sit in judgment as to the good intentions of the champions of liberal science. We know very well that an education indifferent to religion, early habitual association with the ideas of a sceptical, naturalistic philosophy, the acquisition of prejudices and unsolved difficulties, a continuous stay in an intellectual atmosphere foreign and inimical to religious belief — all this, we well understand, will gradually rob the mind of all inclination and unbiassed judgment for religious truth, and thus make for apostasy from religion. Nor do we assert that the idea of God and Christianity are extinct in the hearts of the representatives of liberal science, but we do assert that their SCIENCE no longer wants to know God and His true religion, that only too often it is in the grip of a Theophobia, which slinks past God and His works, with its eyes designedly averted.

At the same time the UNPREPOSSESSION OF THIS SCIENCE will be made clear. " A feeling of degradation pervades the German university circles," so the learned *Mommsen* expressed himself some years ago when Strassburg was to get a Catholic chair of history; therefore a Catholic who takes his Catholic view of the world as his guide cannot be unprepossessed, hence cannot be a true scientist. We have become used to this reproach; nevertheless it is very painful to a Catholic, especially when he devotes his life to scientific work. The other side claims very emphatically to have a monopoly on unprepossession and truthfulness; it gives most solemn assurances of not desiring anything but the truth, of serving the truth alone, with persevering unselfishness, unaffected by disposition and party interest, and that it has its unbiassed spiritual eye turned only to the chaste sunlight of truth. Hence, we may be permitted to inquire whether these assurances square with the facts. As they demand belief, we may also demand proofs; and if those assurances are accompanied by sharp accusations, the accused will have even a greater right to examine the deeds and records of this assertive science.

What about the unprepossession of liberal science, especially in the province of philosophy and religion? It cannot be our intention to explore the whole territory in every direction. We shall keep to the central and main road, the road to which chiefly lead all other roads of life, we mean the attitude of this school of research towards the world beyond. We find this attitude to be one of persistent ignoring! Science cannot acknowledge the supernatural; this presumption, unproved and impossible of proof, it never loses sight of, it is even made a scientific principle, which is called:

The Principle of Exclusive Natural Causation

This principle demands that everything belonging to nature in its widest sense, consequently all objects and events of irrational nature and of human life, must be explained by natural causes only; supernatural factors must not be brought in. To assume an interposition by God, in the form of creation, miracle, or revelation, is unscientific; he who does so is not a true scientist. A presumption, a mandate of truly stupendous enormity! How can it be proved that there is no God, that creation, miracles, the supernatural origin of religion, are impossible things? And if they are possible, why should it be forbidden to make use of them in explaining facts which cannot otherwise be explained?

However, it is readily admitted that the principle is merely a postulate, an UNPROVED presumption.

"The postulate of exclusive natural causation tells us that natural events can have their causes only in other natural events, and not in conditions lying outside of the continuity of natural causality"; so *W. Wundt.* This is a "postulate, accepted by modern natural science partly tacitly, partly by open profession." "Even where an exact deduction is not possible, natural science nevertheless acts under this supposition. It never will consider a natural event to be casually explained, if it is attempted to derive that event from other conditions than preceding natural events."

Professor *Jodl* protests against alliance with the Catholic Church, for the reason that the latter does not acknowledge the fundamental presumption of all scientific research, namely, the uninterrupted natural causation, and because the Church is essentially founded on supernatural presumptions. Prof. *A. Messer* thinks he has proved sufficiently the untenableness of the Catholic faith by the simple appeal to this presumption: " Natural sciences rest upon the presumption that every-thing is causally determined. This means, that the same causes must be followed by the same effects, and all natural events take their course according to invariable laws. It is against this presumption that the Church exacts a belief in miracles, in immediate divine mani-festations, not explainable by natural causes. God is not a causal factor in the eyes of natural science, because everything, and for that very reason, nothing, could be explained through Him." We see that the principle is expressly admitted to be a mere presumption. " I concede readily," says *Paulsen,* " that the law of natural causation is not a proven fact, but a demand or presumption with which reason approaches the task of explaining natural phenomena. But this postulate . . . is the hard-fought victory of long scientific effort. . . . Gradually there were eliminated from the course of nature demoniacal influence and the miraculous intervention of God, and in their stead the idea of natural causation was installed."

It is merely another expression for the same thing if one calls, with *Paulsen,* the unbroken causal connection " the fun-damental presumption of all our natural research "; or con-cludes, with *A. Drews,* that the assumption of a transcendental God, beyond the visible, and in causal relation to the world, destroys the universal conformity to laws in the world, the self-evident presumption of all scientific knowledge; or one may say, with *F. Steudel,* " The theory of unbroken causal con-nection has become the fundamental presupposition of all philo-sophical explanation of world happenings. This finally disposes of a transcendental God, together with his empiric correlative, the miracle, as a philosophical explanation of the world." The same result is achieved by declaring evolution from natural factors as the universal world-law.

" I Know not God the Father, Almighty Creator of Heaven and of Earth "

With inexorable persistency this principle is now applied wherever science meets with God and the world beyond. Hence, let us proceed on our way and halt at some points to watch this science at work.

The unbiassed reasoning of the mind shows that this world, limited and finite, in all its phenomena accidental and perishable, cannot have in itself the cause of its existence, hence, that it demands a supernatural creative cause. This solution of the question is by no means demonstrated by liberal science as untenable, it is simply declined.

" Natural science, once for all, has not the least occasion to assume a supernatural act of creation "; this we are told by the famous historian of materialism, *F. A. Lange.* " To fall back upon explanations of this sort amounts always to straying from scientific grounds, which not only is not permissible in a scientific investigation, but should never enter into consideration." And *L. Plate* states: " A creation of matter we cannot assume, nor would such an assumption be any explanation at all; at most, it would be tantamount to exchanging one question mark for another. We natural scientists are modest enough, as matters now stand, to forego a further solution of the question." They will subscribe to *Du Bois-Reymond's* " ignoramus " rather than assume the only solution of the question, an act of creation. This scientist, asking himself the question, from where the world-matter received its first impulse, argues: " Let us try to imagine a primordial condition, where matter had not yet been influenced by any cause, and we arrive at the conclusion that matter an infinite time ago was inactive, and equally distributed in infinite space. Since a supernatural impulse does not fit into our theory of the universe, an adequate cause for the first action is lacking."

Thus they frankly violate the scientific method that demands acceptance of the explanation demonstrated as necessary, and violate it only for the reason to dodge the acknowledgment of a Creator. This is not science, but politics.

But let us ask, Why should it be against science to reckon with supernatural factors? Is it because we cannot disclose with certainty the other world? Are they not aware that such a principle is opposed by the conviction of all mankind, that always held these conceptions to be the highest, and therefore not to be considered illusions? Do they not see, moreover, how they involve themselves in flagrant contradictions? Does not science by means of its laws of reasoning, especially on the principle of causality, constantly infer invisible causes from visible facts? From physical-chemical facts ether and physical atoms, which no man has ever seen, are deduced: from falling stones and the movement of astral bodies is inferred a universal gravitation, undemonstrable by experience; from an anonymous letter is deduced an author. The astronomer deduces from certain facts that fixed stars must have dark com-

panions, visible to no one; from disturbances in the movements of Uranus *Leverrier* found by calculation the existence
and location of Neptune, then not as yet discovered. Hence,
what does it mean: " to fall back upon explanations of this
sort always amounts to straying away from scientific ground "?
Let us imagine a noble vessel on the high seas to have become
the victim of a catastrophe. It lies now at the bottom of the
sea. Fishes come from all sides and stop musingly before the
strange visitor. Whence did this come? Was it made out of
water? Impossible! Did it creep up from the bottom of the
sea? No! At last a fish reasons: " What we see here has
undoubtedly come down to us from a higher world, far above
us, and invisible to us." The speech meets with approval. But
another fish objects: " Nonsense! To fall back upon explanations of this sort always amounts to straying away from the
scientific grounds on which we fish must stand. We cannot
assume such a world to exist, because this would offend against
the first principle of our science, the principle of the exclusive
natural causation of sea and water." With these words the
speaker departs, wagging his tail, his speech having been received
with stupefaction rather than with understanding.

To this philosophy may be applied the word of the Apostle:
" Beware lest any man cheat you by philosophy and vain deceit " (Col. ii. 8). No, it is not the spirit of true science
that opposes the belief in supernatural factors, but it is the
desertion of the traditions and the spirit of a better science.
To the representatives of paganism, to *Plato* and others, the
highest goal of human quest of truth was to find God and
to worship Him. For the great leaders in recent natural science,
Copernicus, Kepler, Newton, Linné, Boyle, Volta, Faraday, and
Maxwell, the highest achievement was to point to God's wisdom in the wonderful works of nature; their science ended
in prayer. A principle of unbroken natural causation, as a
boycott of the Deity, was to them not a postulate of science
but an abomination. They were carried by a conviction expressed by a later scientist, *W. Thomson,* in the following words:
" Fear not to be independent thinkers! If you think vigorously
enough, you will be forced by science to believe in a God, Who

is the basis of all religion"; and expressed by *R. Mayer* in the following words: " True philosophy must not and cannot be anything else but the propædeutics of the Christian religion."

But let us proceed. We have before us an astonishing ORDER, we behold uncounted wonders of well-designed purpose in the world. The question suggests itself: Whence this Order? The watch originates from the intelligence of a maker, an accident could not have produced it; hence also the great world-machine must have had an intelligent maker. This is the logic of unbiassed reason. But the principles of liberal research object to the acceptance of this explanation. What is theirs?

There have been some scientists endeavouring to discover the purposeless in nature, and they have gleaned various things. *Haeckel* invented for them the name Dysteleologists; and this is now the name they go by. Why the destruction of so many living embryos? What is the purpose of pain, of the vermiform appendix? " To what purpose is the immense belt of desert extending through both large continents of the Old World? Could the Sahara not have been avoided? . . . Indeed, numerous forms of life we cannot look at but with repugnance and horror; for instance, the parasitical beings." . . . (*F. Paulsen*). Hence the order claimed for the world does not exist, on the contrary, " it is beyond doubt that the most essential means of nature is of a kind which can only be put on a level with the blindest accident" (*F. A. Lange*). But they do not feel satisfied with this. They feel that even if all these things were actually purposeless, they would amount only to a few drops in the immense ocean of order which still has to be explained. At most, they would form but a few typographical errors in an otherwise ingenious book, — errors that evidently are no proof that the whole book is a mass of nonsense and not dictated by reason.

There appears to them, like a rescuing plank in a shipwreck, *Darwin's* Natural Selection. The artistic forms in the kingdom of plants and animals arose, says *Darwin,* by the fact that, among numerous seemingly tentative formations, there were some useful organs or their rudiments which survived in the struggle for existence and became hereditary in the offspring, while others disappeared. It was seen very soon, and it is even better understood to-day, that this enormous feat of " natural selection " is contrary to the facts, and would be, above all, an incredible accident. Nevertheless *Darwin* has become the rescuing knight for many who became alarmed about the threatening Supernaturalism.

Du Bois-Reymond speaks very frankly: "Albeit, in holding to this theory we may feel like a man kept from drowning only by holding firmly to a plank just strong enough to keep him afloat. But when we have to choose between a plank and death, the preference will decidedly be with the plank." The same idea is expressed somewhat more gracefully by *W. Ostwald:* "That the quite complicated problem concerning the purposiveness of organism loses its character of a riddle, at least in principle, and assumes the aspect of a scientific task, all by virtue of this simple thought . . . is a gain that cannot be sufficiently appreciated." With vehement plainness *H. Spitzer* maintains: "Purposiveness in nature, which was feared by positive research like a ghost, because it really seemed only to be due to the intervention of ghosts in the course of the world, has now been traced by *Darwin* to its origin from natural causes, and he thereby made it a fit object for the science that is at home only in the sphere of natural causes." "To the height of this point of view," *D. F. Strauss* boasts, "we have been led by modern natural research in *Darwin.*" [1]

At any rate one thing is settled: "The theological explanation must be rejected," as *Plate* puts it. "It sees in adaptation the proof for the love and kindness of a Creator, who has ordered all organisms most conformable to their purpose. Natural Science cannot accept such an explanation."

Is this the boasted spirit of truthfulness, which desires only the truth, — but is evading it persistently? Is this that unbiassed eye that seeks only the truth? Truly, it seems to be unsound, since it cannot bear the rays of truth. Let us go to another workshop of liberal science. It is known now that our earth has once been a ball of glowing fluid, with a temperature in which no living being could exist. Consequently the latter must have appeared at a later stage of evolution. As a fact, palæontology does not show any remnants of organisms in the lower strata of the earth. Now again a question suggests itself to the scientist, WHENCE DID THE FIRST LIFE COME FROM? We have the choice of only two explanations: either it has risen by itself, out of unorganic, dead matter, or it was produced by

[1] Others take refuge in the fantastic theory of an "All-Animation." According to it all organisms, including trees, shrubs, grasses, are possessed of a soulful sensation and feeling for the purposes they serve, and for the elaborate actions they undertake: this is the reason for their efficacy, not because a wise Creator had arranged them thus. *R. H. Francé* exclaims triumphantly: "When the powers that be should ask in their dissatisfaction: 'Where has God a place in your system?' we can answer calmly: 'We do not need the hypothesis of a personal God.'" God is superfluous — this is the precious gain which this unscientific explanation is to yield.

the hand of a Creator: either by *generatio aequivoca* or the act of creation. Now there has never been observed a *generatio aequivoca,* as is testified to by natural science itself, and never has it been accomplished in the laboratory. Therefore, inasmuch as the natural laws of olden times cannot have been any different from those of the present, there has never been a primordial genesis. Do they perhaps give the Creator his due here, where the case is so obvious? Let us see.

The noted zoölogist, *R. Hertwig,* writes: "Inasmuch as there has doubtless been a time when the prevailing temperature of our globe made any life impossible, there must have been a time when life on it arose either by an act of creation or by primordial genesis. If, conformable to the spirit of natural sciences, we are relying only on natural forces for an explanation of natural phenomena, then we are necessarily led to the hypothesis of primordial genesis," although it contradicts all experience. But the deduction is only brought forth as a " logical postulate": there "must" be such genesis after creation is eliminated. " We natural scientists say," states *Plate,* "that all living beings must have originated some time in former geological periods . . . from dead, unorganic matter; to assume a creation would be no explanation at all, exactly as it would be no explanation to assume the creation of matter." Which philosophy teaches that it is not an explanation of a fact to assume for it the only reasonable cause? But just this cause they do not want. *Virchow* says in this respect: "If I do not wish to assume a creative act, if I desire to explain the matter in my way, then it is clear that I must resort to *generatio aequivoca. Tertium non datur.* There is nothing else left, if one once has said: ' I do not accept creation, but I want an explanation of it.' If this is the first thesis, the second thesis is, ergo, I accept the *generatio aequivoca. But we have no actual proof of it.*" Hence *Haeckel* only follows the lead of others when he writes: "We admit that this process (*primordial genesis*) must remain a pure hypothesis, as long as it is not directly observed or duplicated by experiment. But I repeat that this hypothesis is indispensable for the entire coherence of the history of natural creation. Unless you accept the hypothesis of primordial genesis at this one point in the theory of evolution, you must take refuge in the miracle of a supernatural creation."

Is this science, or is it not rather Theophobia? Does the freedom of science consist, first of all, in the privilege of emancipating one's self from truth, whenever truth is not to one's taste? True, liberal science will then be free from distasteful truths, but all the more shackled by its irreligious prejudices.

In modern times, the THEORY OF EVOLUTION is in high favour.

On earth we do not only see life, but life in a great variety
of forms, from plant to man. The question, whence this
variety, admits in its turn only of the alternative: either it
was immediately created by God's hand, or it is the result of
a slow evolution from common original forms. Whether there
has been an evolution within the vegetable and animal kingdom is a problem for natural science. But it is a philosophical
question, whether the essentially superior human soul, endowed
with spirituality and reason, could have evolved from the inferior animal soul. Philosophy must answer: No, just as impossible as to evolve ten from two, or a whole book from a
single proofsheet. Faith says the human soul is created by
God. We do not intend to discuss the problem here any further,
but shall only point out how science here, too, expressly or tacitly, is determined very energetically by the presumption of the
exclusive natural causation; this is applied to the entire theory
of evolution, but especially in regard to man.

"The notion of the evolution of the living world on earth," thus
states *Weismann* quite significantly, "extends far beyond the provinces of individual sciences, and it influences our entire range of
thoughts. This notion means nothing less than the elimination of
miracle from our knowledge of nature, and the classification of the
phenomena of life on an equal footing with the rest of natural events."
The guiding motive is plainly in evidence.

The aim to eliminate the "miracle of creation" is manifested even more conspicuously in the question about the origin
of man: man with his entire equipment, intellectual as well
as cultural, must have evolved upward from the most imperfect
rudiments; this is regarded as a self-evident proposition.

M. Hoernes, for instance, writes: "The Cosmogonies, *i.e.*, the
theories of creation, of all nations ascribe the origin of man to a
supernatural act of creation, whereby the Creator is imagined as a
human being, because at the intellectual stage corresponding to these
notions something created could only be conceived as something formed,
something constructed." Thus the theory of creation, and the Christian doctrine of the genesis of man, is disposed of as a notion of the
lower intellect. "On the contrary, we are taught by science to look
upon the highest mammals as our nearest blood-relatives." This "we
are taught by science," although it is confessed: "We know the fact of
the existence of the man of the fourth, or glacial, period, but we have

not a solitary fact that would throw light upon his origin and his previous existence."

"The theory of miracles can be given up only when we shall cease to contemplate man as a creature apart from the rest of creation, and look upon him as a being developed within creation to what he is now. Then, however, reason and language, as well as man himself, are the products of a continuous evolution," says *Wundt* in his "Psychology of Nations." *Fr. Müller*, in a text-book on the science of language, argues: "According to *Darwin* and to modern natural science, man was not created but has evolved from a lower organism during a process of thousands and thousands of years. . . . For this reason, we must (?) assume that the first language of primitive man could not have ranked above the speech by which animals living in families communicate with each other."

On the basis of this truly dogmatical presumption, that the "miracle theory" of creation must not be accepted, they proceed then to construe one hypothesis upon another, of the origin of language, of thought, of conscience, of religion, according to the method of *Darwin* and *Spencer*, hypotheses of utmost arbitrariness, and frequently most fantastic. "Ethnographical researches," so we are told by *E. Lehmann*, "made by travellers, representatives of science and of practical life, in all parts of the globe, . . . are starting to-day, almost without exception, from the tacit presumption that the civilization of peoples living in the primitive state represent an early and low stage in a historical chain of evolution."

All these are suitable commentaries upon the trite proposition that natural science, or more generally science, is incompatible with religious belief. Of course research, like that described above, does not agree with Faith. But the fault lies in its unscientific method, rather than in its scientific character, in its latent atheistic presumption which prevents an unbiassed conception of truth.

In February, 1907, the well-known biologist and priest of the Jesuit order, *E. Wasmann*, gave three lectures in Berlin on the theory of evolution, before a large audience; they were followed on the fourth evening by a discussion, in the course of which eleven opponents voiced for nearly three hours their objections and attacks, to which *Wasmann* replied briefly at midnight, but little time having been allotted to him for this purpose. *Wasmann*, as well as his chief opponent, Prof. *Plate* of Berlin, have published the arguments on both sides with notes, comments, and supplements. The report of Prof. *Plate* lays stress upon the assertion, which had also formed the refrain of all opposing speeches, viz., "the discussion has shown, in the first place, that true research in natural science is impossible for those taking the position of the Roman Catholic Church; secondly, the glaring and irreconcilable opposition of the scientific theory of the world to the Orthodox-Christian view was sharply manifested." In examining how this was demonstrated by this particular natural science, one meets with a painful surprise.

Even the facts concerning the arrangements for the discussion make an unpleasant impression. It is true, *Plate* accused *Wasmann* of calumny on account of the latter's complaint. However, upon comparing closely the statements of both, the following facts remain undisputed. *Wasmann* notified *Plate* that he desired to speak twice during the discussion, and that the entire discussion should not last much over two hours. *Plate* promised to arrange matters accordingly. But on the forenoon of February 18th, the opponents held a meeting, *Plate* presiding, and they resolved, without the least notification to *Wasmann*, that there should be eleven speakers against *Wasmann*, and that the latter should reply but once, at the end. Only just before the beginning of the discussion, the same evening, *Plate* informed *Wasmann* of the arrangement, making it practically impossible for the latter to change the situation. Furthermore, upon *Plate's* proposal, an intermission of five minutes before the appearance of the tenth speaker was decided upon, " in order to give those in the audience, who might find the session too exhausting, a chance to leave." Thus the audience was to be subjected for three long hours to the influence of heated attacks on Theism, Christianity, and the Church, and without hearing the reply unless they held out from half-past eight in the evening to half-past twelve in the morning.

Plate's Monism rejects principally everything metaphysical: " Monism is the short term for the natural science view of the world, that rejects all preternatural and supernatural ideas." Solutions, not given by the natural sciences, simply do not exist for him; for him the sun sets on the horizon of his natural science. " Natural laws comprise all that we are able to fathom: what is behind them, or what is living in them and operates in them, is the ultimate question for philosophy, and there one thinks this way, another that way " (*Plate*). Nevertheless, he knows that " Out of nothing can come nothing: hence matter is eternal," and he is certain that there is no personal God, no angel nor devil, no beyond nor immortality. Whoever fails to think the same way is no scientist, he is not even a man of sound reason: because " he who has grasped even the elements of natural science, the unity and strict conformity to law of the natural forces, and has a head for sound reasoning, will become a monist all by himself, while the rest are past help, anyhow."

" The Polytheism of the orthodox Church," he says further, referring to the mystery of the Trinity, " is irrational "; for " Common Sense says that 3 is not equal to 1, nor 1 to 3," and this is sufficient for *Plate*. " Trinity, the Incarnation of the Son of God, Christ's Ascension and His descent into hell, Original Sin, Redemption from sin by Christ's sacrifice, Angels and Devils, the Immaculate Conception, the Infallibility of the Pope, all these and many other doctrines of the orthodox Church are thrown to the winds by anybody convinced of the permanence and imperviousness of the natural laws." This again is sufficient for him. "The question whether God is personal or impersonal," says he, in another place, "should never be raised: it is just as preposterous as the question whether God has eyes or not." Another of his arguments reads: "If the body after death can become dust by natural means, then there must have been conditions under which the dust became by natural means a body." An analogous argument would be: "If a book can of itself finally wear away into withered and loosened leaves, then there must be conditions under which the perfect book could originate all by itself, and without Prof. *Plate*, out of withered, loose leaves."

Plate assures us: "I do not know anything about metaphysics." We do not want to dispute that. It is regrettable that so many scientists of our times are betraying a pitiable lack of philosophical training, a lack which becomes a social danger if they, nevertheless, yield to the temptation to invade the domain of Philosophy. Even the Protestant scientist *G. Wobbermin* in referring to the above-mentioned discussion remarked: "*Wasmann's* opponents on that evening have betrayed without exception a really amazing lack of philosophical training." In glaring contrast with this ignorance stands their intolerance for any different theory of the world. Because he thinks as a Christian, *Wasmann* is peremptorily expelled from the ranks of natural scientists. "*Father Wasmann* is not a true natural scientist, he is not a true scholar." With this crushing verdict Prof. *Plate* concluded his speech. He repeats this finding on the last page of his book in conspicuous type: "*Father Wasmann,* S. J., no true natural scientist, no true scholar." That his opponent, in answer to questions that go beyond mere natural science, is giving philosophical replies, in accord with the doctrine of Christianity, is explained by "his voluntary or involuntary submission to the Church," "natural science bows to Theology." He therefore lacks "the freedom of thought and of deduction." Sophistical stunts in the service of intolerance! But let us proceed on our way.

The compulsory dogma of the inadmissibility of a supernatural order of the world, and of its operation in the visible world, becomes most manifest when liberal science comes in contact with the miracle. Forsooth, it shirks this contact. But time and again, now and in the past, it is confronted by clearly attested facts and it cannot avoid noticing them. However, it is determined from the outset that miracles are impossible. Of course, this cannot be proved except by the presumption that there is no supermundane God. Even the agnostic *Stuart Mill* admits that if the existence of God is conceded, an effect produced by His will, which in every instance owes its origin to its creator, appears no longer as a purely arbitrary hypothesis, but must be considered a serious possibility (Essays, 1874).

Generally, however, liberal science does not try hard to demonstrate in a scientific way the impossibility.

"It is my unyielding conviction," so speaks *A. Harnack*, and his is perhaps the most telling expression of this dogmatic mood, "that anything that happens within time and space is subject to the laws of motion. Hence, that in this sense, *i.e.*, of interrupting the natural connection, there cannot be any miracles." One simply does not believe such things. "That a tempest at sea," thus *Harnack* again, "could have been stilled by a word we do not believe, nor shall we ever again believe it." Similarly reads *Baumgarten's* declaration regarding the resurrection of Christ: "Even if all the reports had been written on the third day, and had been transmitted to us as a certainty . . . nevertheless modern consciousness could not accept the story." And *W. Foerster* writes: "The supposition that such interferences do not occur, and that everything in the world is advancing steadily and in accordance with fixed laws, forms the indispensable presumption of scientific research." And *H. von Sybel* holds "An absolute concord with the laws of evolution, a common level in the existence of things terrestrial, forms the presumption of all knowledge: it stands and falls with it."

This is the presumption, from which is drawn the most extravagant conclusion, which, though so manifestly improper, is made the basis for rejecting the entire supernatural religion of Christianity. Because God's Incarnate Son, in a small town of Palestine, once turned water into wine, will the Christian housewife lose her confidence in the stability of water? When it was suddenly discovered that the orbit of the planet Uranus was not a perfect ellipsis, as required by the law of *Kepler,* was it thought that these deviations are impossible because there must not be any exception to the law of perfect elliptical movements? Happily, this law continued to be accepted without deeming an irregularity impossible, and shortly afterwards Neptune was discovered and found to be the cause of the disturbance. But anything miraculous, no matter how well proven, must be considered unacceptable by reason of such unsound presumption. Philosophical a-priorism is superior to facts.

Thus *St. Augustine* tells in his work "De civitate Dei" (l. xxii. c. 8) of a number of miracles happening in his time, of which he had knowledge either as eye-witness or by authentical reports from eye-witnesses. *E. Zeller* renders judgment on the historical value of the statement as follows: "The narrator is a contemporary, and partly even an eye-witness, of the events reported: by virtue of his episcopal office he is particularly commissioned to closely investigate them; we know him as a man overtowering his contemporaries in intellect and knowledge, second to none in religious zeal, strong faith, and moral earnestness. The wonderful events happened to well-known persons, sometimes in the presence of big crowds of people; they were attested and recorded by official order." Hence the statement must be accepted without objection. But must it not also be believed? is the query of an unbiassed listener. Not in the judgment of one who is in the tyrannical yoke of his presumptions. "What are we to say about it?" continues *Zeller*, and finds that "in this unparalleled aggregation of miracles we can after all see nothing else but a proof of the credulity of that age." The report is incontestable, but it must not be believed!

In our times LOURDES has become the scene of events which are founded on facts, and the miraculous character has been proven at least of some of them. *Bertrin*, in his "Histoire critique des événements de Lourdes," deals with the attitude of the physicians toward the miracles. The believing physician can enter upon his investigation without prejudice: not so the unbelieving physician and scientist, who is shackled by his prejudice against the possibility of miracles. Of this a few examples:

"How did you get cured?" was the question put by a physician to a young woman who, after having suffered for four years from a suppurating inflammation of the hip joints, complicated by caries, had a few days previously suddenly regained her full health. Pains and sores had disappeared. "By whom was I cured? By the Blessed Virgin!" "Never mind the Blessed Virgin," replied the physician. "Young woman, why don't you admit that you had been assured in advance that you would get well. You were told that, once in Lourdes, you would suddenly rise from the box wherein you were lying. That sort of thing happens — we call it suggestion." The girl replied, unhesitatingly, that it did not happen this way at all. Finally the physician offered her money if she would admit having really been cured by suggestion. The girl declined the offer. — Another girl arrived in Lourdes, with a physician's attestation that she was a consumptive. She is cured after the first bath. At the bureau of verification her lungs were found to be no longer diseased. Her physician's statement having been very brief, a telegram was sent to him as a matter of precaution, asking him for another statement without, however, informing him of the cure. The physician immediately wired back: "She is a consumptive." This was also the opinion of other physicians who had treated the girl. The girl joyfully returns home, and hurries to her physician, requesting him to certify to her cure. He does so quite reluctantly. Upon reading his certificate, she discovers that it said she had been cured, but only of a COUGH. The case of consumption of his original testimonial had changed into a cough. His dread of a miracle had induced this physician to commit a falsehood.

A. Rambacher, as he relates in a pamphlet, sent the scientific treatise on Lourdes by Dr. *Boissarie* to Prof. *Haeckel*, with the request to read it, in order to gain a better notion of the existence of a supernatural world. After some urging he finally received the following reply, which speaks volumes for the attitude of the natural scientist towards facts: "With many thanks I hereby return the book by Dr. *Boissarie* on the Great Cures of Lourdes which you sent me. The perusal of the same has convinced me anew of the tremendous power of superstition (glorified as 'pious belief') of naïve credulity (without critical examination), and of contagious collective suggestion, as well as of the cunning of the clergy, exploiting them for their gain. . . . The physicians, said to testify in behalf of the 'miracles' and the supernatural phenomena, are either ignorant and undiscerning quacks, or positive frauds in collusion with the priests. The most accurate description of the gigantic swindle of Lourdes I know of, is that of *Zola* in his well-known novel. . . . With repeated thanks for your kindness . . . *Ernst Haeckel.*" Against all the facts in evidence this dogmatic scientist was safely intrenched behind the stone wall of his presumptions. He knew in advance that everything was superstition or the fraud of cunning priests, that all physicians who certified to cures were quacks and cheats. *Zola's* tendentious romance considered the best historical source! Mention should be made here how this celebrated novelist dealt with facts at Lourdes. In the year 1892, the time of the great pilgrimage, *Zola* went to Lourdes. He wanted to observe and then tell what he had seen. An historical novel it was to be; time and again he had proclaimed in the newspapers that he would tell the whole truth. At Lourdes all doors were opened to him; he had admittance anywhere; he could interview and obtain explanations at will. How he kept his promise to report the truth may be shown by a single instance: *Marie Lebranchu* came to Lourdes on August 20, 1892, suffering from incurable consumption. She was suddenly cured, and never had a relapse. One year after her cure she returned to the miraculous Grotto. The excellent condition of her lungs was again verified. Now, what does *Zola* make of this event? In his novel the cured girl suffers a terrible relapse upon her first return home, "a brutal return of the disease which remained victorious," we read in *Zola's* book. One day, the president of the Lourdes Bureau of Investigation introduced himself to *Zola* in Paris, and asked him "How dare you let *Marie Lebranchu* die in your novel; you know very well that she is alive and just as well as you and I." "What do I care," was *Zola's* reply, "I think I have the right to do as I please with the characters I create." If a romancer desires to avail himself of this privilege he certainly has not the right to proclaim his novels as truthful historical writings, much less may others see in such a novel the "most accurate description of the events at Lourdes."

Renan at one time said: "Oh, if we just once might have a miracle brought before professional scientists! But, alas! this will never happen!" He borrowed this saying from *Voltaire*, with the difference that the latter demanded God to perform a miracle before the Academy of Sciences, as if there were need for miracles in a physical or chemical laboratory. Those who desire in earnest to investigate miracles ought to go where they are performed. And even there, where the eyes can see them, it also takes good will to acknowledge them. In this respect an interview is instructive which *Zola* once had with an editor. The latter asked: "If you were witness to a miracle, that would occur under strictest conditions suggested by yourself, would you acknowledge the miracle? Would you then accept the teachings of the faith?" After a few moments of serious thought, *Zola* replied: "I do not know, but I do not believe I would" (*Bertrin*). On April 7, 1875, there came to the Belgian sanctuary, Oostacker, a Flemish labourer, by name *Peter de Rudder*, whose leg had eight years before been broken below the knee, and who was then suffering from two suppurating cancerous sores, that had formed at the place of the fracture and on the foot. He suddenly was entirely cured. The case was investigated in a most exact way. In 1900 a treatise concerning the case was published by three physicians. *E. Wasmann* had as early as 1900 published a short extract of it in the "Stimmen aus Maria Laach." In February, 1907, when, at Berlin, he delivered his lectures which were followed by a discussion, his opponents, headed by Prof. *Plate*, did not know of this article. When they learned of it, some time afterwards, he was put under the ban because he "had degraded himself to the position of a charlatan by vouching with his scientific repute for the happening of a miraculous cure"; and they said "they would fight him in the same way as they would fight every quack, but as a scientist he was discarded." *Plate* had on the evening of the discussion asked of the assembled scientists the question: "Have we ever observed anything like a suspension of the natural laws? The reply to it is an unconditional 'we have not'; consequently Theism becomes inadmissible to the natural scientist." Here, in the *de Rudder* case, is found the required instance. But *Plate* knows, in advance of any investigation, that it is a fairy tale, believed without critical examination. And Prof. *Hansemann*, another opposing speaker of that evening, subsequently sent word to *Wasmann* that: "One can pretty well judge what to think of a natural scientist who publishes such stuff. For this reason I now declare that I shall never in future, no matter how or where, enter into discussion of matters of natural science with Mr. *Wasmann*." When on a certain occasion *Hegel* was advised that some facts did not agree with his philosophical notions, he replied: "The more pity for the facts."

The English natural scientist, *W. Thomson,* once said before the British Society at Edinburgh: "Science is bound by eternal honour to face fearlessly every problem that can be clearly laid before it." The equally famous *Faraday,* in the name of empirical research, demands of its adherents the determination to stand or to fall with the results of a direct appeal to the facts in the first place, and with the strict logical deductions therefrom in the second. In general these principles are adhered to so long as religious notions are not encountered.

But as soon as these are sighted, the engine is reversed, and all scientific principles are forgotten.

A science led by this spirit will set out to emancipate man's moral conduct of life from God and religion. Indeed, the first postulate of modern ethics directs that MORALITY must be INDEPENDENT OF RELIGION. That God and eternal salvation is the end of man, the ultimate norm of his moral life, that God's Command is the ultimate reason of the moral obligation, and divine sanction its strongest support, it does not want to acknowledge. Here, too, we find the principle of natural causality in operation. " As in physics God's will must not be made to serve as an explanation, so likewise in the theory of moral phenomena. Both the natural and the moral world, as they exist, may point beyond themselves to something transcendental. But we cannot admit the transcendental . . . a scientific explanation will have to be wholly immanent, and anthropological " (*Paulsen*). According to this approved principle of ignoration, the supreme aim and law of a morality without religion is MAN, his earthly happiness, and his culture.

Its aims, according to Prof. *Jodl*, one of its noted champions, are: " Promotion of moral life, fostering of a refined humanity, development of a true fellow-feeling, without the religious and metaphysical notions upon which mankind hitherto has mostly built its ethical ideals." *Kant* was the pioneer here: " In so far as morality is based on the conception of man as a free being, it requires neither the idea of a superior being to make him cognizant of his duties, nor any motive but the law itself in order to observe it . . . hence morality for its own sake does not by any means need religion." This is the viewpoint of the autonomous man, who is his own law. " From the viewpoint of authority," so tells us *E. von Hartmann*, " autonomy does not mean anything else but that in ethical matters I am for myself the highest court without appeal. . . . The God, Who in the beginning spoke to His children from a fiery cloud . . . has descended into our bosom, and, transformed into our own being, speaks out of us as a moral autonomy." *Diis extinctis successit humanitas.*

" Although an individual representative of science may be a believer in God in his private life," so argues the English philosopher, *W. James,* " at any rate the times have passed when it could be said that the heavens announce to science the glory of God, and that the heaven shows the works of His hands."

The flight from divinity, atheism open or disguised, is the psychological effect of the liberal principle. Free thought aims to free man of all authority, it aims at severing from religion his entire existence, marriage, state, schools, and likewise science. " It is undeniable," we hear from the lips of champions of modern man, standing on the pinnacle of religious liberalism, " that there is a certain forsakenness in this existence of man, as compared to a life brightened by the idea of a God," but that forsakenness is not purchased too dearly, for " it is the solitude of autonomy, a possession so precious that no price for it could be too high " (*Carneri*).

Indeed, these modern men use even plainer language : science is applauded for having at last freed man from God. With *Kant's* principle that we cannot know anything of the supernatural, we are told, there " were thrown overboard the cosmogonic notions of the Semitic races, notions that have so severely oppressed our science and religion, and are still oppressing them. . . . By this insight an idol is smashed. In a previous chapter I called the Israelites the worshippers of abstract idols ; now, I believe, I shall be fully understood." Indeed, we understand. It means : Away with God. " This German metaphysics frees us from idolatry and reveals to us the living divinity in our own bosom " (*Chamberlain*).

This is the manner in which this free thought, within science and without, is fulfilling the earnest admonition of the Psalmist : " Seek ye the Lord and be strengthened : seek His face evermore " (Ps. civ. 4), and it turns into irony the words : " This is the generation of them that seek Him, of them that seek the face of the God of Jacob " (Ps. xxiii. 6).

" I Know not Jesus Christ, His Only Begotten Son, Our Lord "

Where the thought of independence and of this world enslaves the minds, and holds them captive in harsh aversion to the supernatural, an objective judgment on the nature and history of the Christian religion, to say nothing of the Catholic Church, can hardly be hoped for. What may be expected is that

we will also meet here with a science which, with its hands
held before the eye that fears the light, wards off and combats
everything that is specifically Christian. It is to be feared only
that it will turn light into darkness regarding the view of
life, as also the doctrine and history, of the Christian religion.

Regarding the Christian view of life we need only read the
superficial and yet so arrogant discussions of Christian philosophy, as found in *Paulsen, Wundt,* or *E. von Hartmann.*
From this judicial bench the wisdom of Him, of Whom it is
said " And we saw His glory, full of grace and truth," we see
condemned, if not even treated with subtle ridicule.

Let us for instance take *Paulsen's* presentment of the " View
of Life under Christianity." Whoever reads it, and believes it,
to him the teaching of Jesus Christ can only be, what the Apostle
said it was to the heathens, foolishness. No longer can he have
adoration for its Founder, but rather the pity that one has for
an enthusiastic visionary devoid of any knowledge of the world
and men. The wisdom taught by Christ is distorted into a
sombre grimace, while side by side with it the conception of
life of Hellenic paganism is transfigured into a beautiful ideal.

We are told there: " While classical antiquity saw as the task
of life the perfect development of the natural powers and talents of
man, . . . Christianity with clear consciousness makes the contrary
the goal of life." " The cultivation and exercise of intellectual faculties
was of great importance to the Greeks. . . . Primitive Christianity
looks upon reason and natural cognition with indifference, even with
suspicion and contempt . . . indeed, natural reason and knowledge are
an obstacle for the kingdom of God. Christianity at first was indifferent, even inimical, not only to philosophy and science, but also to art and
poetry. It cuts off not only sensual but also æsthetical gratification,"
because *St. John* condemned the gratification of the eyes (which means
something quite different from æsthetical gratification) Christianity
is said to reject " the arts of the Muses and athletics: they belong to
that sowing of the flesh of which the harvest is perdition." " What the
Christians valued highly was not erudition and eloquence, but silence.
Silence is the first thing recommended by *Ambrose* " (and he the great and
renowned representative of early Christian eloquence!). There is more:
" In the primitive view the first virtue was valour, especially valour in
war; indeed, in Greek and Latin speech the word ' virtue' meant
valour; the Christian's virtue, however, is patience and endurance. He
does not draw the sword; to him are expressly forbidden not only anger,
hatred, and private revenge, but even litigation."

In this tendentious strain *Paulsen* continues, with exaggerations and misrepresentations that have nothing in common with science. According to the Greek view, he says, high-mindedness was a great virtue, but, naturally, the Christian is not allowed to have it; "the virtue of the Christian is humility," *i. e.*, in *Paulsen's* sense low-mindedness; this is "the starting point of Christianity." True, the author assures us that Christianity of to-day is no longer the one he is describing; it has adapted itself more to the world. But it is sad to have this gloomy, visionary fanaticism described to us as the one which was taught by the words of Jesus Himself.

The adherent of this Christianity looks upon governments and their aims as something essentially foreign to it, even to be an official "would doubtless have been felt as a contradiction"; but a sudden change is said to have taken place under *Constantine*. Earthly joys and benefits, the holy ties of the family, those that Jesus in person blessed at Cana, they were, according to *St. Paul*, so we are told, in the spirit of Christ things to avoid and condemn.

And how are these theological discoveries proven, what sources are quoted in substantiation? By some arbitrarily selected passages of the Scriptures, that one must hate father and mother, wife and child, brother and sister; that the poor in spirit are blessed, that the lust of the eye is sinful, that evil should not be resisted; and in quoting these passages all scientific interpretation is carefully avoided, all the writers who have amply explained them are ignored. And what the scriptural passages fail to prove must be demonstrated by some extreme statement borrowed from *Tertullian*, who is generally prone to exaggeration. As a matter of course, gloomy Christianity then seems inferior to the brilliancy of Greek paganism; Christianity is directly a danger to civilization; it may be good enough for those tired of life. "The objection has been made that the fulfilment of this command would destroy our entire civilization. Most probably this would be the case. But where is it written (in Holy Writ) that our civilization must be preserved?" We have here the picture formed of the doctrine of Christ by the world, whereof the Lord has predicted: the world will hate you. *Paulsen* admits frankly: "Whence this hatred? Because the Christian despises that which to the world is the highest good. There can be no better reason for hating any one. . . ."

It is easy to understand that one who has for a long time mentally abandoned his Christian faith, cannot carry in mind its picture as undistorted as he did in his better days, and as would conform to reality. But it is reprehensible to exhibit in public this picture, without having previously and conscientiously examined the main lines, to see whether they are not caricatures. And they are caricatures, traced by a hand that is led by the mood of a secret anti-Christianity.

A treatment identical with that of its view of life is accorded to the DOCTRINE AND HISTORY OF THE CHRISTIAN RELIGION. Not science and uncorrupted truthfulness, but antipathy, presumption, harsh denial of everything divine, only too often point

the way. Let us listen again to the author named above, since
he knows to express modern thought with a clearness and pre-
cision almost unequalled by any one else.

It made a painful impression to find in the Christmas number, 1908,
of the liberal-theological " Christliche Welt " a posthumous article
by *Fr. Paulsen:* " What think you of Christ: Whose Son is He? " The
article was without doubt one of the last he had written. It contains the program of modern liberal science. " With the seventeenth
century," we read there, " begins the reorganization of the theory of the
universe by science. Its general tendency may be described by the formula: Elimination of the supernatural from the natural and historical
world." " Consequently, no miracles in history, no supernatural birth,
no resurrection, no revelation, in fact no interference by the Eternal in
temporal events." Hence, the man who " thinks scientifically IN THIS
WISE can have no doubt that the old ecclesiastical dogma cannot be reconciled with scientific thought." This, of course, amounts to a complete
renunciation of positive Christianity.

This scientific thought, in the words of *Baumgarten,* " rejects any
projection of the supernatural into tangible reality "; especially is " the
metaphysical genesis and nature of the Saviour highly offensive to our
ethical consciousness," even " absolutely unbearable." The Christian
religion can no longer be permitted to overtower other religions by its
supernaturalness. " The distinction between a revealed and a natural
religion becomes an impossibility," says *W. Bousset.* And *Wundt* declares: " Christianity, as an ' absolute ' or a ' revealed ' religion, would
stand opposed to all other religious development, as an incommensurable
magnitude. This point of view, evidently, cannot be competent for our
speculations."

Having become the ruling mode of thought, these presumptions determine from the outset the results to be obtained
by " research," and they force it to violate its own method, so
that it may be dragged along the by-ways and false ways of
a mistaken, philosophical a-priorism, thereby making freedom
of science a mockery. From the abundant material at our dis-
posal let us take only one example, viz., the MODERN CRITICISM
OF THE GOSPELS.

The Gospels contain many records of facts of a supernatural
character, of miracles and prophecies. That these records are
necessarily false is the first principle of the historical, or
critical, method, as it is called. " As a miracle of itself is unthinkable, so the miracles in the history of Christianity, and
in the Christianity of the New Testament, are likewise un-

thinkable. Hence, when miracles are nevertheless narrated, these narratives must be false, in as far as they report miracles: that is, either the relation did not happen at all, or, if it did, there was a sufficient natural explanation"; "the historian must under all circumstances answer, 'No,' to the question whether the report of a miracle is worthy of belief" (*T. Zeller*). Thus instructed, "unprejudiced" research proceeds to construct its results of the investigation of the genuineness, time and date, of the writing of the Gospels and of the Acts, as well as of their credibility. Let us see how this is done.

The tradition of the early Church, as well as intrinsic evidence, testify that the first Gospel was really written by the Apostle *Matthew,* and this certainly before the destruction of Jerusalem. Liberal-Protestant criticism, however, assigns its origin to a time after the year 70, chiefly for two reasons: First, the striking prophecy of the destruction of Jerusalem, conforming so accurately to the actual event, could have been written only after the year 70; otherwise it would have amounted to a real prophecy subsequently fulfilled, a conclusion that cannot be accepted. The second reason is this: The contents of *St. Matthew's* Gospel is already wholly Catholic, hence it must have been written during a later, Catholic, period. For as there can be no influences from above, and as everything is evolved in a natural way, the principle must govern: that the more supernatural and the more dogmas, so much later the period in question; at first there could have been only a religion of sentiment without dogma, which gradually developed into Catholic dogmatism. Similar are the presumptions which direct modern research in respect to the genuineness of the other Gospels and the Acts. A few proofs:

Prof. *Jülicher* thinks that, "While we cannot go prior to the beginning of the second century, because of external testimony, we cannot on the other hand maintain a later date. The most probable time for our Gospel is the one shortly before the year 100. . . ." Why? "Because the ill-fitting feature in the parable of the wedding feast, that the king in his wrath, because his invitation had been made light of, sent forth his armies and destroyed those murderers and burned up their city, could hardly have been invented before the conflagration of Jerusalem"—a prophecy, namely, of the coming destruction of Jerusalem cannot be admitted. "But to my mind, the decisive point is found in the religious position of *Matthew*. Despite his conservative treatment of tradition, he already stands quite removed from its spirit; he has written a Catholic Gospel. . . . To *Matthew* the congregation, the Church, forms the highest court of discipline, being the administrator of all heavenly goods of salvation; his Gospel determines who is to rule, who to give laws: in its essential features the early Catholicism is completed."

Jülicher arrives at a similar conclusion in his research on *St. Luke's* Gospel: "That *Luke's* Gospel was written sometime after the destruction of Jerusalem in 70 A.D., is proven beyond any doubt, by xxi. 22–24, where the terrible events of the Jewish war are 'foretold.' . . . All arguments in favor of a later date of writing concerning *Matthew* hold good also of *Luke*." Even more unreserved is *O. Pfleiderer*, until recently a prominent representative of liberal-Protestant theology at Berlin: "In this Gospel we find the elements of dogma, morals, the constitution of the developing Catholic Church. Catholic is its trinitarian formula of christening, this embryo of the Creed and of the apostolic symbol. Catholic is its teaching of Christ . . . Catholic, the doctrine of Salvation . . . Catholic are the morals . . . Catholic, finally, is the importance attached to *Peter* as the foundation of the Church and as the bearer of the power of the key." In regard to this latter point *Pfleiderer* remarks expressly: "In spite of all attempts of Protestants to mitigate this passage (Matt. xvi. 17–20) there is no doubt that it contains the solemn proclamation of *Peter's* Primacy." The unsophisticated reader thereupon would be likely to deduct: If the oldest Gospel is already Catholic, then it must be admitted that earliest Christianity was already Catholic. In so reasoning he might have rightly concluded, but he would have shown himself little acquainted with the method of liberal science. This infers contrariwise: early Christianity must not be Catholic, hence the Catholic Gospel cannot be so old, it must be the fraudulent concoction of a later time; "hence the origin of the Gospel of *Matthew* is to be put down not before the time of *Hadrian;* in the fourth century rather than in the third."

A. Harnack fixes the date of the Gospel at shortly after 70, because "*Matthew*, as well as *Luke*, are presupposing the destruction of Jerusalem. This follows with the greatest probability from Matt. xxii. 7 (the parable of the marriage feast)." This is to be held also of *Luke's* Gospel. "This much can be concluded without hesitation: that, as now admitted by almost all critics, *Luke's* Gospel presupposes the destruction of Jerusalem."

Remarkable is *Harnack's* latest attitude towards the Acts; it shows again that the results of modern biblical criticism are less the results of historical research than of philosophical presumptions. In his "Acts of the Apostles" *Harnack* admits: "Very weighty observations indicate that the Acts (hence also the Gospels) were already written at the beginning of the sixties." In substantiation he cites not less than six reasons which evidently prove it: they are based upon the principles of sound historical criticism. "These are opposed solely by the observation that the prophecy about the catastrophe of Jerusalem in some striking points comes near to the actual event, and that the reports about the Apparition and the legend of the Ascension would be hard to understand prior to the destruction of Jerusalem. It is hard to decide. . . . But it is not difficult to judge on which side the weightier arguments are " (viz., on the part of the contention for an earlier date). Yet *Harnack* is loath to accept the better scientific reasons: they must suffer correction by presumptions. He formulates his final decision in the following way: " *Luke* wrote at the time of *Titus,* or during the earlier time of *Domitian* (?), but perhaps (only *perhaps,* in spite of decisive arguments) already at the beginning of the sixties." (Recently *Harnack* recedes to the time before the destruction of Jerusalem without, however, acknowledging a divine prophecy of this catastrophe.)   Similar is this theologian's proof that the fourth Gospel could not have been written by *John,* the son of *Zebedee;* because xxi. 20–23 (I will that he tarry till I come) cannot be a prophecy, but must have been written down after the death of the favourite disciple. " The section xx. 20–23 obviously presupposes the death of the beloved disciple; on the other hand he cannot be left out of the 21st Chapter. This 21st Chapter, however, shows no other pen than that which had written Chapters 1–20. This proves that the author of Chapter 21, hence the author of Chapters 1–20, could not have been the son of *Zebedee,* whose death is there presupposed." The whole argument again rests upon the refusal to hold possible a prophecy from the lips of Jesus.

The main reason, however, for disputing the genuineness of the fourth Gospel, although external tradition and internal criterions testify to it as the writing of *St. John,* is, because it teaches so clearly the DIVINITY OF CHRIST: and this must be denied. Significant are, for instance, the words in which *Weizsäcker* sums up his objections to this gospel: " That the Apostle, the favorite disciple according to the Gospel, who sat at the table beside Christ, should have looked upon and represented everything that he once experienced, as the living together with the incarnate divine Logos, is rather a puzzle. No power of faith and no philosophy can be imagined big enough to extinguish the memory of real life and to replace it by this miraculous image of a divine being . . . of one of the original Apostles, it is unthinkable. Upon this the decision of this point will always hinge. Anything else that may be added from the contents of the Gospel is subordinate." This means, Christ cannot be admitted to be a Divine Being — impossible. An eye-witness could not take Him for it: therefore, this " miraculous picture of a Divine Being " cannot have been the work of an eye-witness.

Like the GENUINENESS of the Gospels, so is also their CREDIBILITY beyond a doubt. Two of them are written by Apostles, the two others by Disciples of the Apostles: they also have all the marks peculiar to writings of eye or ear witnesses, or of persons who have heard the narratives directly from the lips of eye-witnesses. Nor would any one doubt their credibility if they did not report supernatural facts. But, this being the case, infidel research is bound to arrive at the opposite result.

The writers were frauds — this was long ago the hypothesis of the superficial Hamburg Professor, *Samuel Reimarus,* whose " Fragments " were published by *Lessing.* But even to a *D. F. Strauss* " such a suspicion was repulsive." The Heidelberg Professor, *H. E. Paulus,* sought his salvation in trying to reduce the reports of miracles to a natural sense, by doing painful violence to the text: for instance, the Lord did not walk UPON the sea, but only ALONG the sea; the miracle of the wine at Cana was only a wedding joke. Then came *D. F. Strauss* (died 1874), and he tried it in a different way. " If the Gospels are really historical documents, then the miracle cannot be removed from the life of Jesus." Hence, it is to remain? Indeed not! The Gospels must not be accepted as historical sources. They are products of purposeless poetic legends, the miracles are garlands of religious myths, gradually twined around the picture of Jesus. Myths, however, need time for their formation, hence *Strauss* fixes the date of the Gospels within the second century. He openly admits that his hypothesis would fall to the ground if but a single Gospel has been written in the first century. As a fact, more recent rationalistic criticism has found itself constrained to drop this hypothesis. *F. Ch. Baur* (died 1860) fell back upon the fraud-hypothesis of a *Reimarus.* It, too, has been laid among the dead. Thus they have exhausted themselves in the attempt to shake off the burdensome yoke of truth.

Influenced by *Strauss, Baur,* and other German critics, *E. Renan* (died 1892) wrote his " Life of Jesus," a frivolous romance. Quite frank are the words he wrote down in the preface to the thirteenth edition of his " Vie de Jésus " (1883) : " If miracle has any reality, then my book is nothing but a tissue of errors. . . . If the miracle and the inspiration of certain books are real things, then our method is abominable." But he silences all doubts by the phrase: " To admit the supernatural is alone sufficient to place one's self outside of science."

The newer " historical-critical " school, while having disposed

of many contentions of the old schools, is nevertheless in its research bound just as energetically by the postulate of conformity
to natural laws. The fourth Gospel is pushed aside: in the
others all miraculous occurrences are expounded away, till the
" historically credible core " is reached.

The books of the Old Testament fare even worse, if possible.

" Does Genesis relate history or a legend? " asks Prof. *Gunkel*, and
continues: " this is no longer a question to the historian." Well, a
legend, then. But how does the historian know this? From his own
pantheistic philosophy, which recognizes no God differing from this
world: " The narratives of Genesis being mostly of a religious nature,
they continuously speak of God. The way, however, in which narratives speak of God is one of the most reliable standards to judge
whether they are meant historically or poetically. Here, too, the
historian cannot do without a world philosophy. We believe that
God acts in the world as the latent, hidden motive of all things . . .
but He never appears to us as an acting factor *jointly with others*
(the italics are the author's), but always as the ultimate cause of all
things. Quite different in many narratives of Genesis. We are able to
understand these narratives of miracles and apparitions as the art-
lessness of primitive people, but we refuse to believe them."

Analogous to Bible-criticism is the research in other branches
of theology. The ORIGIN OF CHRISTIANITY, this wonderful
power which so suddenly made its appearance in history and
speedily vanquished a whole world, must of course not be a
work of Heaven. Hence its origin must be explained at any
cost in a natural way, or " historically," as they put it. The
religious notions of Christianity must not be conceded a supernatural certainty over all other religions; and " to understand
an event historically means: to conceive it by its causal connection with the conditions of a given place and at a certain
time of the human life. Hence science cannot consider such a
thing as the appearance of a supernatural being upon the
earth " (*Pfleiderer*).

And then they proceed to show that Christianity is a natural,
evolutionary product of the Israelite religion, of Greek philosophy, of Oriental myths, and Roman customs. That it is far
superior to all these, and that it is the opposite to them in
various ways, is carefully hushed up. The inadequacy and impossibility of such an explanation is adroitly concealed. Nor

could the Israelite religion of the Old Covenant, according to the naturalistic principle of liberal theology, have had its origin in revelation and the prophets; hence it comes from Babylon, as the product of natural evolution from Oriental myths and customs. Any old and new analogies, hypotheses, and fancies are good enough then to demonstrate this as "historical."

THE TRUTH IS NOT IN THEM

We pause here. We might thus continue for a long time; but it is enough. The patient reader, who has accompanied us on the tedious way to this point, may begin to feel tired. May he excuse the detailed recital for the reason that we had to do some extensive reconnoitring, through the precincts of modern philosophical-religious research, to avoid the reproach that we were making accusations without furnishing proofs. Our contention was, that liberal science is trying to shake off the yoke of religious truth, and to explain it away by its self-made presumptions. We believe that we have proved our contention.

We are confronted by a science that boasts of monopolizing the spirit of truthfulness; as a matter of fact, we see that it uses all scientific devices to shirk the truth and to disguise its effort. In loquacious protests it rejects the " rigid dogmatism," the " fixed views," of the Christian faith, and it proclaims experience and reason as the sole criterions of scientific cognition; yet it always stands upon the platform of rigid presumptions, that are derived from no experience, and which no reason can prove. It clamours for research free from presumption, and, without winking an eye, substitutes its own presumption, secretly or openly. It is DISHONEST.

It promises to preserve for man the highest ideals and blessings for which his mind is yearning, yet it has no religion and no God. It recalls to mind the words spoken by *St. Augustine* of the philosophers whom he had followed in the false ways of his youth: " They said: truth, and always truth, and talked much of truth, but it was not in them. . . . Oh, truth, truth, how deeply my inmost spirit sighed after thee, while they filled my ears incessantly with thy bare name and with the palaver of their bulky volumes."

Free it wants to be, this science. One of its disciples boasted: " It has taught its disciples to look down without dizziness from the airy heights of sovereign scepticism. How easy and free one breathes up there!" Aye, it has made itself free, — from the yoke of unpalatable truth. So much more firmly is it fettered, not with the holy bonds of belief in God, but by the more burdensome mental yoke of a disbelief that weakens and blinds the eyes against the cognition of the higher truth: — and bound by the chains of public opinion, which threatens anathema to every one who fails to stop at the border of the natural. Truly free is only the science that enjoys a clear and free perception for the truth. Unfree is a science that restrains the mental eye with the blinkers of theophoby. Our age seeks for the lost happiness of the soul, it seeks longingly God and the supernatural that have been removed from its sight. But science, so often its leader, loathingly dodges God, and refuses to fold the hands and pray. As long as our age does not break with a science that refuses to know a God and a Saviour, so long will it hopelessly grope about without result, and look in vain for an escape from the wretched labyrinth of doubt.

CHAPTER II

THE UNSCIENTIFIC METHOD

THE efforts of liberal science, to remove more and more from its scope the supernatural powers, show clearly that man may feel the truth to be a yoke, and that he may attempt to free himself from this yoke by opposing the truth and by substituting postulates for knowledge. Sceptical, autonomous subjectivism, the philosophy of liberal free thought, has changed the nature of human reasoning, and its relation to truth, and perverted it to its very opposite. No longer is the human mind the vassal of Queen Truth, as *Plutarch* put it, but the autocratic ruler who degrades truth to the position of a servant. Thus liberal freedom of thought becomes the principle of an unscientific method, because it loses, by false reasoning and false truth, the first condition of solid and scientific research; furthermore, by treating the highest questions with consequent levity, it betrays a lack of earnestness which again renders it unfit for scientific research in serious matters.

FALSE REASONING

" The philosophical thinkers of to-day," says an admirer of *Kant, A. Sabatier,* " may be divided into two classes, the pre-Kantian and those who have received their initiation and their philosophical baptism from *Kant's* Critic."

The Christian philosophy of a *St. Thomas,* which is, as even representatives of modern philosophy are constrained to admit, " a system carried out with clear perception and great sagacity " (*Paulsen*), contains many a principle, the intrinsic merit of which will be fully appreciated only when contrasted with the experiments of modern philosophy. An instance is the principle of the old school, that cognition is the likeness of that which is cognized. Apart from the cognition by sense, we are given here the only correct principle, coinciding with the general conviction that reasoning is the mental reproduction of an objective order of existence, independent of us, even in our conception of the metaphysical world. Thinking does not create its object, but is a reproduction of it; it is not a producer, but a painter, who copies the world with his mental brush within himself, sometimes only in the indistinct outlines of indefinite conception, often, however, in the sharp lines of clear cognition.

If, according to its nature, thinking is subject to standards and laws given it by an objective world, then subjective arbitrariness, a method of thought which, while pretending to be a free producer of truth, yet determines it according to necessity or desire; and, even more so, a method of thought which feels itself justified to hold an opinion upon the same question in one way to-day, and another and entirely opposite one to-morrow, is wholly incomprehensible: just as incomprehensible as if a draughtsman, attempting to draw a true picture of St. Peter's Church, would not follow the reality but prefer to draw the picture at random, according to his fancy and mood.

We have stated these fundamental principles already at the beginning of our book, we have also set forth how greatly liberal freedom of thought is lacking the first presumption of any proper science, namely, the clear perception that there is an objective truth in philosophical-religious questions, to which we must submit, there, in fact, most of all.

No! We also want autonomy of thought, especially in questions of metaphysics, where, anyway, there can only be postulates! so shouted *Kant* to the modern world on the threshold of the nineteenth century. There are no stable truths, everything is relative and changing, adds the modern theory of evolution. At last there is freedom for thought and research, freedom from the yoke of absolute truth! Behold the aberrations of an unbridled rush for freedom which moves the world of to-day. This unruly hankering for a freer existence than allowed by their nature and position, makes unbearable to many modern children of man the idea of iron laws of truth and marked boundaries of thought. Revelling in the consciousness of their sovereign personality, they want to measure all things by their individuality, even religion, philosophy, truth, and ethics. Only that what is created and experienced by them within the sanctuary of their personality, only what is made important and legitimate by their sentiment, is truth and of value to them. AUTONOMISM thus changes unnoticeably into INDIVIDUALISM; the own individuality, in its peculiar inclinations, moods, and humours, its exigencies and egotistical aims, its infirmities and diseases — they have, under the name of INDIVIDUAL REASON, become the law of thinking and reasoning.

WITHOUT KNOWLEDGE OF THE HUMAN NATURE

" Varied, according to character, are the demands made by heart and mind," assures us a representative of modern philosophy, " corresponding to them is the image of the world to which the individual turns by inner necessity. He may waver hither and thither, uncertain as to himself; at last, however, his innermost tendency of life will prevail and press him into the view of the world corresponding to his individuality. Upon its further development worldly and local influences will play a very important part. But the deciding factor in giving the direction is personality." "And," continues Prof. *Adickes,* " the sharper and more one-sided a character type is brought to expression, the more it will be urged into a certain metaphysical or religious tendency, and this man will find no rest, nor feel himself at home in the world, until he has found the view of life that fits him. Nor does man assemble his metaphysics with discrimination on the grounds of logical necessity, choosing here, rejecting there, but it grows within himself by that inner compulsion identical with true freedom." Hence, not unselfish yielding to truth, no, the inclinations of heart and mind, the " personality " must form the view of the world. Let every type of character therefore develop itself sharply and one-sidedly, let every one get the view of the world corresponding to himself, without regard to objective truth and logical necessity. This precisely is the " true freedom." " For when is a man more free, than when he chooses and does — without any

compulsion, even resisting compulsion — what his innermost
soul is urging him to choose and do? How could he be more
true to himself, more like himself? " With such a freedom
" the outer compulsion " of an absolute truth, to say nothing of
the duty to believe, will not agree. " The core of one's very
being," so *Harnack* informs us, " should be grasped in its depths,
and the soul should only know its own needs and the way indicated by it to gratify them." " According to my character,"
says *Adickes* again, " is the world reflected within myself by
intrinsic necessity just as my creed represents it, and no opponent is able to shake my position by arguments of reason or
by empirical facts."

Hence it is not only true, as has been known from the beginning, that the inclinations of the heart are trying to prevail
upon reason to urge their desires, and to oppose what displeases
them, and that reason must beware of the heart — no, inclination and character are now directly called upon to shape our
religion and view of the world. Every type of man, every period,
may construct its own philosophical system, or, if this is beyond it, at least its own ideas; it may also shape its own
Christianity, according to its experience. As the individual
chooses his clothes, and puts his individuality into them, in like
manner may the individual put on the view of life that fits him.

These principles represent the apostasy from objective truth,
and, at the same time, the apostasy from the PRINCIPLES OF TRUE
SCIENCE: their first demand, the proper understanding of truth,
is perverted into its very opposite. A necessary quality of scientific research is exactness; exactness, however, demands most
conscientious cleaving to truth; scale and measure are its instruments. The reverse of exactness is to cast away scale and
measure, to turn eye and ear, not toward reality, but toward
one's self, so as to observe personal wishes and inclinations, and
then shape the results of the " research " accordingly. This may
be a method of freedom, but it cannot be the method of science.
The very thing that true research would eliminate in the first
place, viz., to have the decision influenced by hobbies and moods,
is most important in the method of individualism; objectiveness,
deemed by true science the highest requirement, is to that method

the least one: what true science first of all insists on, namely, to prove that which is claimed, this method knows but little of. It recalls the method of the gourmet who selects that which gratifies his taste: it may be likened to the dandy picking frock-coat and trousers that suit his whim. True research, with a firm hand at the helm, aims to direct its craft so as to discover new coasts, or at least a new island; the exploring done by liberal research is like casting off the rudder to be tossed by the waves, for its task is only to hold to the course which the waving billows of individual life give to it. True science, finally, seeks for serious results, able to withstand criticism: the research by individualism produces results which, as individualism itself confesses, must not be taken seriously. They are the subjective achievements of amateurs, creations of fashion, cut to the pattern of the ruling principle: *nihil nisi quod modernum est*. A science that professes such a method is beyond a doubt unfit to play a beneficial part in the endeavour of mankind.

Do not say: but it is not claimed that religion and view of life are matters of scientific research: on the contrary, they are always distinguished from science. It is true, this is not infrequently claimed. But it is also known how energetically just these matters are appropriated by science. Is it not exactly this sphere in which free research is to be active? Is it not its aim to construct a "scientific view of the world," as opposed to the Christian belief? Is there not the conviction that science has already carried much light and enlightenment into this very sphere, that it has upset the old tenets of faith?

And what an amount of IGNORANCE OF HUMAN NATURE underlies these principles! It is the same complete misconception that has always characterized liberalism, and which it has also manifested in economical matters. There, too, it demanded boundless freedom for all economic sources, ignoring man's disordered inclinations that will work disorder and destruction if not restrained by laws. In a similar manner they dream that man, if left to the unrestrained influence of his personality, will soar without fail to the heights of the pure truth. They know no longer the maxim once engraved by the wisdom of the ancient world upon Delphi's sanctuary: "Know thyself"! They no longer know the beguiling and benumbing influence exerted upon reason by inclination, how it fetters the mind. *Amor premit oculos,* says Quintilian. The thing we like, we desire to establish as true; favourable arguments are decisive, counter arguments are ignored or belittled, inclinations guide the observation, determine the books and sources drawn from. If we meet with something unsympathetic, something that interferes with the liberties we have grown fond of, it takes a rare degree of unselfishness to love the painful truth more than one's self. It is easy to leave cool reason in control in mathematical speculations: they seldom affect the heart; quite different, however, in questions of philosophy and religion that often have vexatious consequences.

We have to concede that *D. F. Strauss* was right when he wrote: " He who writes about the Rulers of Nineveh or the Pharaohs of Egypt, may pursue a purely historical interest: but Christianity is a power so alive, and the question of what occurred at its origin is involved in such vast consequences for the immediate present, that the inquirer would have to be dull-witted to be interested only in a purely historical way in the solution of these questions." But we must also regret that this personal interest has misled him, for one, into pernicious ways.

In view of the frequent assurances of the noted historian, *Th. Mommsen,* that he hates the sight of old Christian inscriptions [1] we may perhaps welcome it in the interest of history that he refrained from writing the fourth volume of his Roman history, wherein the Origin of Christianity was to be treated. One of his biographers asserts that the downfall of paganism through Christianity was a fact not to *Mommsen's* liking, that " a description of the decomposition of all things ancient, and the substitution therefor of the Nazarene spirit would not have been a labour of love." [2] And again, when we see the well-known historian of philosophy, *F. Ueberweg,* in a letter to *F. A. Lange,* denouncing from the bitterness of his heart " the miserable beggar-principle of Christianity," and the " surrendering of independence and of personal honour in favour of a servile submission to the master,

---

[1] Compare Corpus Inscriptionum Latinarum XI (1883, vii.).

[2] *L. M. Hartmann,* Theodor Mommsen (1908), 81. The author of the biography is a Jew. There is a much-circulated story, alleged to come from *F. X. Kraus. Mommsen* is said to have told *Kraus,* inasmuch as neither the origin, nor nature, nor the spread of Christianity can be explained by natural causes, and since he, in his capacity of historian, could never acknowledge anything supernatural, therefore the fourth volume will remain unwritten.

who is made a Messiah, nay, even the incarnate Son of God," then we may well dread the historical objectivity of a man of such notions in writing about the religion of Jesus Christ.

With reference to the chief subject of psychology, the noted psychologist, W. James, writes with utmost frankness: "The soul is an entity, and truly one of the worst kind, a scholastic one, and something said to be destined for salvation or perdition. As far as I am concerned, I must frankly admit that the antipathy against the particular soul I find myself burdened with, is an old hardness of heart, which I cannot account for, not even to myself. I will admit that the formal disposition of the question in dispute would come to an end, if the existence of souls could be used for an explanatory principle. I admit the soul would be a means of unification, whereas the working of the brain, or ideas, show no harmonizing efficacy, no matter how thoroughly synchronical they be. Yet, despite these admissions, I never resort in my psychologizing to the soul."

If we read such statement, if, in addition, we remember the popular-philosophical science of men like *Haeckel,* particularly perhaps the literature which he recommends for information about Christianity, and of which he himself makes use; if we have read *Schopenhauer, Nietzsche,* or the "Philosophy of Races" of a *Chamberlain,* — we can no longer be at a loss what to think of the "rule of reason" and of the "search for pure truth." Observe, also, the restless haste of those who, having turned their back upon the Catholic Church, now proceed to attack her, observe their agitated work and incitement, how they rummage and ransack the nooks and corners of the history of the Church in quest of refuse and filth, and if the find is not sufficient how they even help it along by forgery, all this to demonstrate to the world that the grandest fact in history is really absurdity and filth; — then one will understand what instincts may be found there to guide "reason and science." How even sexual impulses are trying to shape their own ethics we shall not examine here. *F. W. Foerster* relates: "I once heard a moral pervert expound his ethical and religious notions; they were nothing but the reflection of his perverse impulses. But he thought them to be the result of his reasoning." Is there not known in these days the inherited disorder of the human heart as characterized by the Apostle in the words: "But I see another law in my members, fighting against the law of my mind, and captivating me in the law of sin (Rom. vii. 23)"? The Ancients knew it. The wisdom of *Plato* knew it, who speaks of the "pricks of sin, sunk into man, coming from an old, unexpiated offence, giving birth to wickedness." The wise *Cicero* knew of it: "Nature has bestowed upon us but a few sparks of knowledge, which, corrupted by bad habits and errors, we soon extinguish, with the result that the light of nature does nowhere appear in its clearness and brightness." Truth is often disagreeable to nature. And if not subdued and ruled by strong discipline, nature proceeds to oppose the truth. Only to lofty self-discipline and purity of morals is reserved the privilege of facing the highest truths with a calm eye. "Blessed are the pure in heart, for they shall see God."

MENTAL BONDAGE

Of this wisdom the admirer of liberal freedom knows little. Instead of distinguishing the good from the evil in man, of unfolding his inner kernel, the pure spirit, and making it rule; instead of demanding, like *Pythagoras,* discipline as a preparatory school for wisdom, he has learned from *Rousseau,* the master of modern Liberalism, that everything in man is good. Depravity of nature, original sin, are unsympathetic things to his ear. Even *Goethe* wrote to *Herder,* when *Kant* had in his religious philosophy found a radical Evil in man: "After it has taken *Kant* a lifetime to clean his philosophical gown of many filthy prejudices, he now outrageously slabbers it with the stain of the radical Evil, so that Christians, too, may be enticed to come and kiss the seam." Instead of exhorting for a redemption from internal fetters, as the sages of all ages did, the principle of wisdom now proposed is to quietly let individuality develop, with all its inclinations. They call this freedom. Is it not the freedom whereof the slave of sensuality avails himself to form his theory of life? It, too, "grows up in man with that inner compulsion which is identical with true freedom" (*Adickes*).

Freedom this may be. But ONLY EXTERNAL FREEDOM, the only freedom they often know. They are unaware that they forfeit thereby the real, the inner freedom. "Thou aimest at free heights," admonishes even the most impetuous herald of freedom, "thy soul is athirst for stars. But also thy wicked impulses are athirst for freedom. Thy wild hounds want to be free, they bark joyfully in their kennel when thy spirit essays to throw open all dungeons." [1] They think to be free and speak of the self-assurance of individual reason, and they cannot see that the mind is in the fetters of bondage.

Else how is it that the atheistic free science, considered in general, arrives with infallible regularity at results that obviously tend to a morally loose conduct of life? How is it, that it tries throughout to shirk the acceptance of a personal God, and is at home only in open or disguised atheism? that it so persistently avoids the acceptance of anything supernatural? Why does it in its researches never arrive at theism, which has as much foundation at least as pantheism and atheism? Why does it, nearly without exception, deny or ignore the personal immortality of the soul and a Beyond; why does it never reach the opposite result which, in intrinsic evidence, ranks at least on a par with it? Why is it not admitted, that the will is free and strictly responsible for its acts, although this fact is borne out by the obvious experience and testimony of mankind? Why does it so regularly arrive at the conclusion that the Christian religion has become untenable, and needs development; that its ethics, too, must be reformed, more especially in sexual matters? Why does it not defend the duty to believe, but reject it persistently? A striking fact! The matters in question here concern truths that impose sacrifices upon man, whereas their opposites have connections of intimate friendship with unpurged impulses. It may be noted also that this same science, that announces to the world these results of research, meets with the boisterous applause from the elements that belong to the morally inferior part of mankind.

St. Augustine prays: "Redeem me, O God, from the throng of thoughts, which I feel so painfully within my soul, which feels lowly in Thy presence, which is fleeing to Thy mercy. Grant me that I may not give my assent to them; that I may disapprove of them, even if they seek to delight me, and that I may not stay with them in sleepiness. May they not have the power to insinuate themselves into

---

[1] *Nietzsche*, "Thus spoke Zarathustra."

my works; may I be protected from them in my resolution, may my conscience be protected by Thy keeping." It is the realization of the want of freedom of the human reason, the only way to the liberation from the fetters of our own imperfection. He, who has seriously begun to take up the struggle with his inner disorders, will, by his own experience, pray as *St. Augustine* prayed.

Recognizing this fact, man will try to rise above himself, to cleave to a superior Power and Wisdom, who, in purer heights, untouched by human passions, holds aloft the truth, in order to rise thereby above his own bondage; he will understand the necessity of an authority clothed with divine power and dignity, so that it may hold in unvanquished hands the ideal against all onslaughts of human passions. He will without difficulty find this power in the religion of Jesus Christ and in His Church: in Him, who could not be accused of sin, who by His Cross has achieved the highest triumph over flesh and sin, who has surrounded His Church with the bright throng of saints. And if he sees this religion and Church an object of persecution, he will behold in it the signature of its truth. For truth is a yoke despised by sensualism and pride, and the spiritual power that contends for purity and truth will be hated.

WITHOUT EARNESTNESS

The regrettable conception of truth proper to the modern freedom of thought, leads to that flippancy with which our time is prone to treat the highest questions. Why conscientiousness and anxious care? All that is needed is to form one's personal views; there is no certain, generally valid, truth in religious matters. Hence there is often in this sphere of scientific research a method wholly different from that in use anywhere else. In history, philology, natural science, there is a striving for exactness, but in these matters exact reasoning is replaced only too often by discretionary reasoning, by loose forming of ideas; in the very domain which has ever preeminently been called the province of the wisdom of life, there is now in vogue the method of flippancy.

True wisdom is convinced that reason has not been given

to man to grope in the dark in respect to the most momentous questions of life; that reason, though limited and liable to err, is given him to find the truth. True wisdom knows its difficulties when the matter in quest is metaphysical truth: it knows how, in this case, more than in any other, reason is exposed to the influence of inclinations from within, and to the power of error and of public opinion from without; that in these matters, least of all, reason is not in the habit of taking the truth by assault. True, there are intuitions, and inspiration by genius — they have their rights, but they are the exceptions. The ordinary, and only safe, way is to advance cautiously, by discoursive thinking, from cognition to cognition, otherwise there is danger of a sudden fall from the steep path.

In the early Christian ages this insight led to careful cultivation and application of certain methodical means of thinking and terms of expressions, to definitions, distinctions, and forms of syllogism, with that "insulting lucidity," in the words of a modern philosopher, which gives to them the stamp of scrupulousness. The same insight into the cognitive weakness of reason leads to the noble union between science and modesty.

What, however, do we see in modern philosophic-religious thinking? Often unsolidity, with hardly a remnant of the principles of the serious pursuit of knowledge.

The autonomous freethinker of these days lacks chiefly humility and modesty. The ancient Sage of Samos once declined the name of "sage," saying that God alone is wise, while man must be content to be wisdom-loving (φιλόσοφος). Not always so the sages of modern times.

Kant believed of his system: "Critical philosophy must be convinced that there is not in store for it a change of opinions, no improvement nor possibly a differently formed system, but that the system of criticism, resting on a fully assured basis, will be established forever, indispensable for all coming ages to the highest aims of mankind." *Hegel*, in turn, was no less convinced of the indispensability of his doctrine. In the summer term of 1820 he began his lectures with the words: "I would say with Christ: I teach the truth, and I am the truth." Yet, to *Schopenhauer Hegel's* philosophy is nonsense, humbug, and worse. *Schopenhauer* knew better, and was convinced that he had lifted the veil of truth higher than any mortal before him; he claimed that he had written paragraphs "which may be taken to have been inspired by the Holy Ghost." Shortly before his death he wrote: " My curse upon any one, who in reprinting my works shall knowingly make a change; be it but a sentence, or a word, a syllable or a punctuation point." *Nietzsche* held: " I have given to the world the most profound book in its possession." To the eyes of this philosophy, modesty and humility are no longer virtues. *B. Spinoza,* a leader in later philosophy, states expressly: " Humility is no virtue; it does not spring from reason. It is a sadness, springing from the fact that man becomes aware of his impotence."

An arrogant mind is not capable of finding the higher truth with certainty; conscientious obedience to truth, unselfish abstention from asserting one's ego, and one's pet opinion, can dwell only in the humble mind. Here applies what *St. Augustine* said of the Neoplatonists: " To acquiesce in truth you need humility, which, however, is very difficult to instil into your minds." [1]

When God's authority steps before scientists and earnestly demands faith, they will talk excitedly about their human dignity that does not permit them to believe; about reason being their court of last resort that must not know of submission; and if the Church, in the name of God, steps before them, they become abusive.

Men who have scarcely outgrown their minority often feel it incumbent upon themselves to furnish humanity with new thought and to discard the old. *D. F. Strauss,* a young undermaster of twenty-seven years, writes his " Life of Jesus, critically analyzed " (1835) ; he tells the Christian world that everything it has hitherto held sacred is a delusion and a snare; he feels the vocation to " replace the old, obsolete, supernatural, method of contemplating the history of Jesus with a new one," which changes all divine deeds into myths. Hardly out of knickerbockers and kilts, they feel experienced enough to come forth with novel and unheard-of propositions on the highest problems. In business and office, as in public service, sobermindedness and maturity are demanded; but to work out the ultimate questions of humanity, inexperience and lack of the deeper knowledge of life do not disqualify in our time. If *Schiller's*

---

[1] " *Veritati ut possetis acquiescere, humilitate opus erat, quae civitati, vestrae difficillime persuaderi potest* " (De civit. Dei, X, 29).

complaint of the Kantians of his time was that, "What they have scarcely learned to-day, they want to teach to-morrow," what is to be said of those who teach even before they have learned? And what superficial thinking do we meet in the philosophy of the day! Lacking all solid training, they proceed to construct new systems, or at least fragments of them. As regards their competence, one is often tempted to quote the harsh words of a modern writer: " I believe *Schopenhauer* would have formed a better opinion of the human intellect, had he paid less attention to authors and newspaper-writers, and more to the common sense evinced by men in their work and business " (*Paulsen*).

It would be highly instructive to take a longer journey through the realm of modern philosophy, in so far as it touches upon questions concerning the theory of the world, or even liberal Protestant theology, so as to subject to a searching criticism the untenable notions and attempts at demonstration even of acknowledged representatives of this science, whereby they generally do away with God and miracles, the soul and immortality, freedom of the will, the divine moral laws, the Gospel, the divinity of Christ, and so much more, and show what they offer in place of all this. It would disclose an enormous lack of scientific method: instead of assured results they offer questionable, even untenable theories; in place of proofs, emphatical assertions, imperatives, catch phrases; or else arguments which under the simplest test will prove miscarriages of logic. These philosophers vault ditches and boundaries with ease, and derive full gratification from imperfect and warped ideas. Of course, exactness in philosophical thinking is not a fruit to be plucked while out taking a walk; it is the product of serious mental work, of sterling philosophical training, which, alas, is wanting to-day in large circles of scientists.

As an instance, we point to the method described in a previous chapter, by which all supernatural factors are rejected by the arbitrary postulate of " exclusively natural causation," without valid proofs, based only upon the arbitrary decision of so-called modern science — in the gravest matter an unscientific process that cannot be outdone.

Another instructive instance, of serious matters treated with levity, is furnished in the unscrupulous way in which the Catholic Church, her teaching, institutions, and history, are passed upon in judgment by those having neither knowledge nor fairness.

WITHOUT REVERENCE

True wisdom accepts advice and guidance. It feels reverence for sacred and venerable traditions, for the convictions of mankind on the great questions of life, and greater reverence still for an authority of faith that has received from God its warrant to be the teacher of mankind, and which has stood the test of time. True wisdom is convinced that continuity in human thinking and in knowledge is necessary. Life is short, and gives to the individual hardly time to attain mental maturity. Philosophy, and this is the matter before us at present, — philosophy can never be the work of a single person; it is the achievement of centuries; succeeding generations, with searching eye and careful hand, building further upon the achievement for which past ages have laid the foundations. By nailing together beams and boards the individual may erect a house good enough for a short time to serve his sports and pleasures; and if wrecked by the first storm, it may be replaced by another. But the building of massive and towering cathedrals that last for ages required the work of generations. And only skilful and experienced hands may do the work; haste is out of place here. The ancient sages of Greece, *Plato, Pythagoras,* and *Aristotle,* had this reverence for the philosophical and religious traditions of the past. These representatives of true wisdom did not consider philosophy and theology as the product of individual sagacity, they did not attempt to be free rulers in the realm of thought; on the contrary, they looked upon wisdom as the patrimony of the past, which it was their duty to preserve.

They pointed to their venerable traditions, however meagre they were. "Our forefathers," says *Plato,* "who were better than we are, and stood nearer to the gods than we, have handed down to us this revelation.[1] That the testimony of the great sages, to the effect

---
[1] *Plato,* Phil. 6 c. Similarly *Pythagoras, Aristotle,* and *Cicero.*

that the most essential elements of their philosophy had their origin in religious traditions, is based upon truth and not on fancy has been proven by O. *Willmann*, whose knowledge of ancient civilization was very extensive, in his monumental " History of Idealism." Delhi, the home of mysteries, the generations of priests in ancient Egypt, the doctrinal traditions of the Chaldeans, the Magi of Medes and Persians, and the wisdom of the Brahmins of ancient India are witnesses to the fact. " The Ancients were correct," says *Willmann*, " in tracing their philosophy to earliest traditions . . . they knew what they owed to their forefathers better than we do. They direct our astonished eyes to a very ancient reality, to a towering remoteness of living thought." This fact is very much against the taste of our times. . . . An inherited wisdom, springing from an original revelation, adapted to the nations, shining with renewed brightness in true philosophy, is quite the opposite to a philosophy that seeks the source of mental life only in isolated thinking; that thinks its success to be conditioned upon unprepossession; that holds the refutation of tradition to be the test of its strength.

Unfortunately this latter view is widespread in our time. Research is often directed, not by reverence for the wisdom inherited from many Christian centuries, but by the mania, unwise and fatal alike, of seeking new paths. " Love of truth," so we are told, " is what urges on the great leaders of humanity, the prophets and reformers, to seek new and untrodden paths of life. ' Plus ultra ' is the rallying-cry of these pathfinders of the future, who are clearing the way for the mental life of mankind. No authority can restrain them, no prejudice, however holy: they are following the light which has dawned upon their soul " (*Paulsen*).

And a multitude discover this light in their souls, and join the prophets and pathfinders! Everybody goes abroad looking for untrodden paths; from all directions comes the cry: Here and there, to the right, to the left, is the right way! Do we not only too often see self-willed and self-satisfied thinkers, whose shortsighted conceit gets within the four walls of their study puffed up against God and religion, offer us for holy truth the fanciful products of their narrow brains? Do we not see, only too often, champions of shallow reasoning, without discipline of thought and without ethical maturity, recommending their undigested efforts as the wisdom of the world? Youthful thinkers there are in numbers, each of whom claims that he at last has succeeded in solving the world riddle; they offer us new theories of the world, new ideas on ethics, on law and theology, for a few dollars per copy or less. The holy abode of truth has become the campus for saunterers, each eager to displace the other so that he may be sole proprietor, or at least a respected partner. Day by day new solutions of "problems," "vital questions," or at least "outlines" of them; new "views of the world"; new forms of religion and of Christianity for the "modern man"; "reforms" of marriage and of sexual ethics, and so on. Truth had not been discovered until the newcomer puts his pen to the paper. Every one is free to join in. Yea, more, he may not only join in, but lash those who do not applaud him. According to this notion, nothing has a right to exist, no "sacred prejudice" may be claimed once this self-appointed representative of science takes the field for "research." Behold the Christian truth, it has stood the test of centuries: but it cannot resist these scientific freebooters, they rush over it with banners flying.

Severe speech would here be in order. A painful spectacle, these doings of modern thought in the sacred precincts of truth. "Put off the shoes from thy feet; for the place whereon thou standest is holy ground," we imagine to hear; yet this sanctuary of truth has been made a profane place of bartering.

While still a pagan, but moved by his desire for truth, the philosopher *Justin* went to the schools of his day to seek the solution of his doubts and queries. First he turned to a Stoic, but as he taught nothing of God, *Justin* was unsatisfied. He next went to a Peripatetic teacher, then to a Pythagorean, but failed to find what he desired. The Platonist at last gave him something. Walking alone along the beach, and musing over *Plato's* principles, he met an old man who referred him to the truth of Christianity, to the Prophets and the Apostles: "They alone have seen the truth and proclaimed it unto man, they were afraid of no one, knew no fear; yielded to no opinion; filled with the Holy Ghost, they spoke only what they saw and heard. The Scriptures are still extant, and he who takes them up will find in them a treasure of information about principles and ultimate things, and all else the philosopher must know, if he believes them." [1] And *Justin* found truth and peace, and bowed to the yoke of the doctrine of Jesus Christ.

What a striking contrast between this serious love of truth in the days of passing heathendom, and the uncontrolled thinking of so many in our Christian age! To them truth is no longer a sacred treasure, a yoke to be assumed in reverence; it has become the plaything of their impressions and inclinations. Indeed, they consider it a burden to accept the old Christian truth, with which they meet on all their ways.

[1] Dial. c. Tryph. 2.

CHAPTER III

THE BITTER FRUIT

THE VOCATION OF SCIENCE

SCIENCE is, and ever was, an influential factor operating upon the thought, aims, and actions of man. Hence science must remain conscious of its vocation. First of all it is to hold aloft and preserve the SPIRITUAL POSSESSIONS OF MANKIND. True, science must also progress; but progress means growth, which presupposes the preservation of what has been received from of old. This applies pre-eminently to the philosophical-religious patrimony of the past; no error could be more fatal than to presume that each generation must start from the beginning, that the foundations, which have safely supported human life for centuries, must be obsolete because human nature is suddenly considered changed.

What are these foundations? They are the tested religious and moral convictions of mankind, and, for our nations particularly, the divine tenets of Christianity, that have been their highest ideals for centuries, and have produced serenity and a high standard of morality. If science aims to be the principle of conservation and not of destruction, it must look upon the safeguarding of those possessions of the nations as its sacred task. Indeed, it would perform this task but poorly were it to waste this patrimony piece by piece, or to shatter it with wicked fist, instead of respecting and honouring it, or to set fire to the sanctuary where mankind hitherto has dwelled in peace and happiness. A science of this kind would not only cease to be a bulwark for the mental life of mankind, but turn into a positive danger.

In as far as it follows the principles of liberal freedom of research, present-day science does present this danger. This cannot be denied, the facts speak too plainly. By its very nature it MUST become such danger. For it recognizes no belief, neither in God nor in the Church; no dogmas, no " prejudices," no traditions, however sacred, are to be respected; it is fundamental unbelief, the principle of opposition to the Christian religion. Its autonomous Subject emancipates himself from the yoke of objective truth which he cannot procreate free out of himself. It confesses the principle that there are neither truths nor values that endure; *plus ultra!* always new ideas! *Quieta movere,* hitherto the watchword of unwisdom, is this science's maxim. And liberal freedom of research is what its nature compels it to be. Can it do any more than it has done, to prove itself a principle of mental pauperism? We shall not demand a list of the things it has thrown aside and shattered. Let us rather ask, WHAT IT HAS LEFT WHOLE of the sacred institutions of truth, inherited from a Christian past. Alas, it has cast off and denied everything; it has lost not only the things a Christian age has treasured, but even those a higher paganism had revered. Let us examine this sad work of negation and annihilation. It is a more melancholy spectacle than any war of extermination that was ever waged against Europe's Christian civilization by a people bent on trampling down every flower of Christian culture, and on razing every castle to the ground.

Are We Still Christians?

This was the question proposed some scores of years ago by *D. Strauss* to himself, and to those of his mind. With this question we will begin. To our forefathers, especially of the German nation, nothing was more sacred than the Christian religion; no people like the German has absorbed it so fully, has been so permeated with it. But now, wherever liberal science — here especially modern Protestant theology that brings liberal freedom of research into full application — wherever it has made the Christian religion a subject of its study, one treasure after another has been lost; of the whole of Christendom nothing remains but an empty name and a formal homage, reminding of the courtesy paid to deposed rulers.

In the first place, there has been dropped the fundamental thesis of the DIVINITY OF CHRIST, whereupon rests the entire structure of Christianity. Man's modern emancipation from everything supernatural has been accomplished also with respect to the person of Christ: the man Christ is divested of His divinity and of everything miraculous; His birth by the virgin, His miracles and prophecies, His resurrection and ascension, once the subjects of exalting feasts, have fallen a victim to unbelieving science. It is true, they exert themselves to keep His person in view, they want the purely human Jesus to hold His old position of God and man in the believing consciousness, to conceal the mental pauperization. But this trick is failing more and more. The Son of God sees Himself gradually placed among the great men of history; we are becoming accustomed to find in the " Biographies of Celebrated Men," among " Religious Educators," side by side with *Confucius, Buddha, Augustine, Mohammed, Luther, Kant,* and *Goethe,* also the name of Jesus. The lustre of the past belief in His divinity is paling. In the eyes of unbelieving science He has ceased to be the infallible, all-surpassing Authority, and the basis of the faith. The teaching of Jesus has become the subject of an analyzing and eliminating criticism, and whenever deemed advisable His authority is simply ignored; He was human, affected by the views and errors of His age.

Thus they know, as does *H. Gunkel,* that " Jesus and the Apostles evidently have taken those narratives (the miracles of Genesis) to be reality and not poetry "; " the men of the New Testament on such questions take no particular attitude but share the (erroneous) opinions of their times." They also know " that in regard to persons possessed with demons Jesus shared the erroneous notions of his time " (*Braun*), and *Fr. Delitzsch* informs us that it was " particularly a Babylonian superstition," in consequence of which " the belief in demons and devils assumed such importance in the imagination of Jesus of Nazareth and of his Galilean disciples." Thus the word is fulfilled literally: " He is a sign which will be contradicted."

No one knows really WHO JESUS WAS. His person is the football of opinions. " If any one desiring reliable information, as to who Jesus Christ was, and what message He brought, should consult the literature of the day, he would find buzzing round

him contradictory voices. . . . Taken all in all, the impression
made by these contradicting opinions is depressing: the confusion seems past hope," admits Prof. *Harnack.*

Also *E. V. Hartmann* remarks: " Thus, according to some, Jesus
was a poet, to others a mystic visionary, a third sees in him the militant hero for freedom and human dignity, to a fourth he was the
organizer of a new Church and of an ecclesiastical system of ethics, to a
fifth the rationalistic reformer . . . to the eleventh a naturalistic pantheist like *Giordano Bruno*, to the twelfth a superman on the order of
Nietzsche's Zarathustra. . . ." A chaos of opinions agreeing only in the
one aim of rejecting His divinity. *A. Schweitzer*, himself a representative of liberal Protestant research, says, " Nothing is more negative
than the result of the research concerning the life of Jesus." And knowing Jesus's person no longer, they no longer know anything certain
about His teaching, as is clear from the above. According to *I. Well-
hausen*, from the " unsufficient fragments at hand we can get but a
scanty conception of the doctrine of Jesus." — The fathers were rich,
the children have grown poor. *Dissipaverunt substantiam suam!*

To many even the EXISTENCE OF JESUS has become doubtful; and this
not only to men of an irreligious propaganda, like Prof. *A. Drews*, who,
carried away by the corroding tendency of a radical age, journeyed
from town to town in order to proclaim, in the twentieth century of
Christian reckoning, the scientific discovery of the " Myth of Christ";
but even to others the existence of Jesus has become doubtful or at
least valueless. The task now is to do away entirely with the person of
Jesus, and to solve the problem of preserving a Christian faith without
a Christ. In this sense Prof. *M. Rade* writes: " Serious and gifted
men having asserted that Jesus never existed (or, what amounts to
the same, that, if He ever lived, nothing is known of Him; hence,
His existence is of no historical importance), we dogmatists almost
have to be grateful to them for having helped us to put a very concrete
question no longer in general terms: how does religious certainty face
historical criticism? but quite specifically: how does religious certainty (of the Christian) regard the historic-scientific possibility of the
non-existence of the historical Jesus?" They frankly assert that they
could entirely forego the person of Christ. Thus Prof. *P. W. Schmiedel*
declares: " My innermost religious conviction would not suffer injury
were I to be convinced to-day that Jesus never lived. . . . I would
know that I could not lose the measure of piety that has become my
property long since, even if I cannot derive it any longer from
Jesus." " Neither does my piety require me to see in Jesus an absolutely
perfect type, nor would it disturb me were I to find someone else actually surpassing Him, which undoubtedly is the case in some respects."
For him to whom Christ is no longer God but a man and capable of
error, His person and existence have necessarily lost their value.

Thus we have arrived at a CHRISTIANITY WITHOUT A CHRIST.
As yet the person of the Lord is usually surrounded by a halo;

it is the after-effect of a faithful past, the last rays of a setting sun. That this last glimmer, too, will pale and give way to darkness is but a question of time, when with more honesty expression will be given to the conclusion necessarily arrived at. If Christ is not what He claimed to be, God and Messiah, then the belief in His being the Son of God and the Messiah, in His right to abrogate the religion of the Old Testament and to found a new religion, commanding its acceptance under penalty of damnation — all this can be nothing but the result of religious fanaticism and mental derangement. And science is, in all seriousness, preparing to turn into this direction.

It is true, many are hesitating to draw these fearful conclusions and to utter them; arriving at this point, they cautiously stop: so *Harnack.* "How Jesus could arrive at the consciousness of His unique relation to God as His Son, how He became conscious of His power as well as of the obligation and task involved in this power, that is His secret, and no psychology will ever disclose it. . . . Here, all research must halt." It is the silence of embarrassment, but equally of unscientific method. Having arrived at untenable conclusions, when question upon question is impetuously suggested, they stop suddenly and have nothing to say but a vague word about inscrutableness.

But there are those who actually speak the word so horrible to a Christian heart: Jesus was demented, a subject for pathology. *Strauss* indicated this cautiously: "One who expects to return after his death in a manner in which no human being had ever returned, he is to us . . . not exactly a lunatic, but a great visionary." Others speak more plainly. *Holtzmann's* answer to the question: Was Jesus an Ecstatic, is an emphatic: "Yes, He was." *De Loosten* considers him insane. *E. Ramussen* thinks Him an epileptic, but grants to physicians the right to reckon him among paranoiacs or lunatics. To *A. Jülicher* Jesus is a visionary, "a mystic, not satisfied to dream of his ideals, but who lived with them, worked with them, even saw them tangibly before his eyes, deceiving himself and others." Thus the supernatural has become madness; Jesus Christ, for whose divinity the martyrs went to their death, wears now, before the forum of a false science, Herod's cloak of foolishness.

With the fall of this fundamental dogma there must necessarily fall all other specific truths of Christianity, and they have fallen. The Holy Writ, once the work of the Holy Ghost, has now become a book like the Indian Vedda, to some perhaps even more unreliable; original sin, Redemption and grace, the Sacrifice of the Mass and the Sacraments, have been dropped or changed into symbols, of which every one may think what he pleases. They have tried to make Christianity "acceptable to our times," to "bring it nearer to the modern idea." There is really nothing left to offend modern man, nothing that could get in conflict with any idea. The essence of Christianity is depreciated and emptied until it has become only a vague sentiment, without thought; a few names, without ideas. "Christianity as a Gospel," so teaches *Harnack*, "has but one aim: to find the living God, that every individual may find Him as his God, gaining strength and joy and peace. How it attains this aim through the centuries, whether with the Coefficient of the Jewish or the Greek, of flight from the world or of civilization, of Gnosticism or Agnosticism — this all is of secondary consideration." Of secondary consideration it is, then, whether one is convinced of the existence of God or whether he doubts with the agnostics, whether he believes in a personal God or not. To-day even the pantheist who does not acknowledge a Creator of Heaven and Earth may be a Christian; and so can he who no longer believes in personal immortality and in a hereafter; for, we are informed, "this religion is above the contrasts of here and the beyond, of life and death, of Reason and Ecstatics, of Judaism and Hellenism." (*Harnack*). Thus there is no thought which could not be made to agree with this despoiled Christianity. For, we are told further, "much less does the Gospel presuppose, or is joined to, a fixed theory of nature — not even in a negative sense could this be asserted" (*Harnack*). Materialism and Spiritualism, Theism and Pantheism, Belief or Negation of Creation, everything will harmonize with a Christianity thus degraded to a thing without character or principle.[1]

All that is left is a word of love, of a kind Father, of filiation to God, and union with God: words robbed of their true meaning; a shell without a kernel, ruins with the name "Christianity" still inscribed thereon, telling of a house that once

---

[1] "But for the retention of names and terms *Harnack* leaves nothing of the specific nature of Christianity," admits the Protestant Professor of Theology, *W. Walther*, in his book, "Harnack's Wesen des Christentums" (1901).

stood here, wherein the fathers dwelt, but long since vacated by their children. *Dissipaverunt substantiam suam!*

As to God and divine filiation, everybody is welcome to his own interpretation. He may form with *O. Pfleiderer* the "Neoprotestantism" which, "after breaking with all ecclesiastical dogmas, recalled to mind the truths of the Christian religion, hidden beneath the surface of these dogmas, in order to realize, more purely and more perfectly than ever before, the truth of God's incarnation in the new forms of autonomous thought and of the moral life of human society." Christianity and God — the symbols of autonomous man! Or he may follow *Bousset*, to whom nature is God, and in this way combines harmoniously Christianity and Atheism. "This is the forceful evolution of Christian religion," says he, "the notion of redemption, the Dogma of the divinity of Christ, the trinity, the idea of satisfaction and sacrifice, miracles, the old conception of revelation — all these we see carried off by this wave of progress." "What is left? Timid people may think: a wreck. But to our pleasant surprise we found stated at many points in our inquiry: what is left is the simple Gospel of Jesus." And what does this simplified Gospel contain? "Of course we cannot simply accept in full the Gospel of Jesus. . . . There is the internal and the external. The external and non-essential includes the judgment of the world, angels, miracles, inspiration, and other things. All this may be disregarded. "But even the essentials, the internal of the Gospel cannot be simply subscribed to. They must be interpreted." What, then, is this essential, this internal of the Gospel, and what is its interpretation? "The belief of the Gospel in the personal heavenly Father; to this we hold fast with all our strength. But we carry this belief in God into our modern thought." And what becomes then of "God"? "To us, God is no longer the kind Father above the starry skies. God is the Infinite, Omnipotent, who is active in the immense universe, in infiniteness of time and space, in infinitely small and in infinitely large things. He is the God whose garb is the iron law of nature which hides Him from the human eye by a compact, impenetrable veil." We see the belief of the Gospel has dwindled down to atheistic Monism.

As early as 1874 *Ed. von Hartmann*, in his book "Die Selbstzersetzung des Christentums," came to the conclusion that "liberal Protestantism has in no sense the right to claim a place within Christendom." In a later book his keen examination demonstrates how the speculation of liberal Protestantism has changed the Christian religion step by step into pantheism: "Not a single point in the doctrine of the Church is spared by this upheaval of principle, every dogma is formally turned into its very opposite, in order to make its religious idea conform to the tenet of divine immanence."

This is called the development of Christianity. It is this "religious progress," the same "free Christianity," that they are now trying to promote by international congresses. The invitation to the "World's Congress for free Christianity and religious progress" at Berlin, in 1910, was signed by more than 130 German professors, including 47 theologians. We have here the development of the dying into the lifeless corpse, the progress of the strong castle into a dilapidated ruin, the advance of the rich man to beggary.

We began our inquiry with the question proposed some years ago by *D. Strauss* to his brethren-in-spirit: Are we still Christians? We may now quote the answer, which he gives at the conclusion of his own investigation: " Now, I think, we are through. And the result? the reply to my question? — must I state it explicitly? Very well; my conviction is, that if we do not want to make excuses, if we do not want to shift and shuffle and quibble, if yes is to be yes, and no to remain no, in short, if we desire to speak like honest, sincere men, we must confess: we are no longer Christians."

This is the bitter fruit of autonomous freedom of thinking, which, declining any guidance by faith, recognizes no other judge of truth than individual reason, with all the license and the hidden inclinations that rule it. Protestantism has adopted this freedom of research as its principle; in consistently applying it, Protestantism has completely denatured the Christian religion. If anything can prove irrefutably the monstrosity and cultural incapacity of modern freedom of research, it is the fate of Protestantism. Any one capable of seriously judging serious things must realize here how pernicious this freedom is for the human mind.

REDUCED TO BEGGARY

But the loss is even greater. The better class of paganism still clung to the general notion of an existing personal God, of a future life, of a reward after death; it was convinced of the existence of an immortal soul and a future reward, of the necessity of religion, of immutable standards for morals and thought. Has liberal science at least been able to preserve this essential property of a higher paganism? Alas, no! It has lost nearly everything.

No longer has it a personal God. While belief in God may still survive in the hearts of many representatives of this science, it has vanished from science itself. It begs to be excused from accepting any solution of questions, if God is a factor in the solution. The opinion prevails that *Kant* has forever shattered all rational demonstrations of the existence of God. Yet *Kant* permits this existence as a " postulate," which, according to *Strauss,* " may be regarded as the attic room, where God who has been retired from His office may be decently sheltered and employed." But now He has been given notice to quit even this refuge. There must be nothing left of Him but His venerable name, which is appropriated by the new apostasy in the guise of pantheism or a. masked materialism. Monism is the joint name for it: this is the modern "belief in God." In days gone by it was frankly called " atheism."

This disappearance of the old belief in God is noted with satisfaction by modern science: " It is true," says *Paulsen,* " the belief in gods . . . is dying out, and will never be resurrected. Nor is there an essential difference whether many or only one of these beings are assumed. A monotheism which looks upon God as an individual being and lets him occasionally interfere in the world as in something separate from and foreign to him, such a monotheism is essentially not different from polytheism. If one should insist on such conception of theism, then, of course, it will be difficult to contradict those who maintain that science must lead to atheism."

Therefore God, as a personal being, is dead, and will never come to life again. While there is an enormous exaggeration in these words, they nevertheless glaringly characterize the ideas of the science of which *Paulsen* is the mouthpiece. It does not want directly to give up the name of God; it serves as a mask to conceal the uncanny features of pantheism and materialism.

" The universe," we hear often and in many variations, " is the expression of a uniform, original principle, which may be termed God, Nature, primitive force, or anything else, and which appears to man in manifold forms of energy, like matter, light, warmth, electricity, chemical energy, or psychical process. . . . These fundamental ideas of monism are by no means ' atheistic.' Many monists in spite of assertions to the contrary believe in a supreme divine principle, which penetrates the whole world, living and operating in everything. Of course, if God is taken to mean a being who exists outside of the world . . . then it is true we are atheists " (*Plate*). We have already seen that one can even be a Protestant theologian and yet be satisfied with a " God " of this description.

In the place of God has stepped MAN, with his advanced civilization, radiant in the divine aureole of the absolute as its highest incarnation. But what has liberal research done even to him? According to the Christian idea, man bears the stamp of God on his forehead: "after My image I have created thee"; in his breast he carries a spiritual soul, endowed with freedom and immortality — *gloria et honore coronasti eum*. Liberal science pretends to uplift and exalt man; but in reality it strips him of his adornments, one after the other. He is no longer a creature of God because this would contradict science. His birthplace and the home of his childhood are no longer in Paradise, but in the jungles of Africa, among the animals, whose descendent man is now said to be. Liberal science, almost without exception, denies the freedom of will which raises man high above the beast, and as a rule it calls such freedom an "illusion": of a substantial soul, of immortality, of an ultimate possession of God after death, it frequently, if not always, knows nothing.

Let us take up a handbook of modern *Psychology* of this kind, Wundt's, for instance. We see at a glance that it is a very learned work. The thirty lectures inform us in minute investigations of the various methods and resources of psychological research. The reader has reached the twentieth lecture, and he asks, how about the soul? The title of the book states that the chapters would treat of the human soul, but so far not a word has been said about it. But there are ten lectures more; he continues to turn over the leaves of the book. He finds beautiful things said about expression and emotions, about instincts in animal and man, about spontaneous actions and other things. At last, the third before the last page of the book, there arises the question, what about the soul, and what does the reader learn? "Our soul is nothing else, but the sum total of our perception, our feeling and our will." The conviction he held hitherto, that he possessed a substantial, immortal soul, which remains through changing conceptions and sentiments, he sees rejected as "fiction." The reader learns that, though he may still use the term "soul," he has no real soul, much less a spiritual soul, least of all an immortal soul. In its stead he is treated to some learned statements about muscular sensations and such things, by way of compensation. *Jodl*, too, speaks of the "illusions, based upon the old theories about the soul," and he rejects the dualistic psychology which "mistook an abstract thought, the soul, for a real being, for an immaterial substance"; and which defended this notion "with worthless reasons."

It is manifest that, together with the substantial soul, immortality is also disposed of. True, here too the word is cautiously retained; but by immortality is now understood perpetuation in the human race, in the ideas of posterity, in "objective spirit," in the "imperishable value of ethical possessions," for which the individual has laboured. Some fine words are said about it, as roses are used to cover a grave. Yet, it is only the immortality of the barrel of Regulus, or the Gordian knot in history, the immortality of which the printers' press may partake in the effect of the books it prints. To quote *Jodl* again: "The fact of the objective spirit, together with the organic connection of the generations to one another, form the scientific reality of what appears in popular, mythological tenets of faith as the idea of personal immortality . . . and which has been defended by the dualistic psychology with worthless, invalid arguments." The refutation of these arguments does not bother him. "A refutation of these scholastic arguments is as little needed as a refutation of the belief in the miracles and demons of former centuries is needed by a man standing on the ground of modern natural science." This reminds one of *Haeckel's* method. The latter nevertheless found it worth while in his "Weltraetsel" to dispose in thirteen lines of six such arguments, and then to assure the reader that "All these and similar arguments have fallen to the ground." That the matter in question is an idea that has been the foundation of Christian civilization and ethics for thousands of years, that has led millions to holiness; an idea, indeed, that has been the common property of all nations at all times — this seems to count for very little.

This technique of a superficial speculation, which, devoid of piety, casts everything overboard, finds no trouble in disposing of the entire SPIRITUAL WORLD. "No one is capable," says *Jodl* again, "of imagining a purely spiritual reality." This is disposed of. "Since the war between the Aristotle-scholastic and the mechanical method has been waged, spiritual powers have never played any other part in the explanation of the world than that of an unknown quantity in equations of a higher degree, which, unsolvable by methods hitherto prevalent, are only awaiting the superior master and a new technique (*sic*) in order to disappear" (p. 77 *seq.*).

With the denial of a personal God and of the immortality of the soul, true RELIGION is abandoned. Of course, there is much said and written about religion in our days; the scientific literature about it has grown to tremendous proportions — to say nothing of newspapers, novels, and plays. One might welcome this as a proof that this world will never entirely satisfy the human heart. But it is also a sign that religion is no longer a secure possession, but has become a problem — that it has been lost. Even on the part of free-thought it is not denied that " only unhappy times will permit the existence of religious problems; and that this problem is the utterance of mental discord." Yet they do not want to forego religion entirely, for they feel that irreligion is tantamount to degeneration. But what has become of religion? It has been degraded to a vague sentiment and longing, without religious truths and duties, a plaything for pastime.

For *Schleiermacher* religion is a feeling of simple dependence, though no one knows upon whom he is dependent; according to *Wundt* religion consists in " man serving infinite purposes, together with his finite purposes, the ultimate fulfilment whereof remains hidden to his eye," which probably means something, but I do not know what. *Haeckel* calls his materialism the religion of the true, good, and beautiful; *Jodl* even thinks, "As the realm of science is the real, and the realm of art the possible, so the realm of religion is the impossible." Religion having been degraded to such a level, it is no longer astonishing that religion is attributed even to animals, and in the words of *E. von Hartmann*, " we cannot help attributing a religious character, as far as the animal is concerned, to the relation between the intelligent domestic animals and their masters."

What, finally, has become of the old standard of MORALS? A modern philosopher may answer the question.

Fouillée writes: " In our day, far more so than thirty years ago, morality itself, its reality, its necessity and usefulness, is in the balance. . . . I have read with much concern how my contemporaries are at fundamental variance in this respect, and how they contradict one another. I have tried to form an opinion of all these different opinions. Shall I say it? I have found in the province of morals a confusion of ideas and sentiments to an extent that it seemed impossible to me to illustrate thoroughly what might be termed contemporaneous sophistry " (Le Moralisme de Kant, etc.).

Where is left now to liberal science a single remnant of those great truths on which mankind has hitherto lived, and which it needs for existence? There was a God — but He is gone. There was a life to come, and a supernatural world; they are lost. Man had a soul, endowed with freedom, spirituality, and immortality; he has it no longer. He had fixed principles of reasoning and laws of morals; they are gone. He possessed Christ, full of grace and truth, he possessed redemption and a Church; everything is lost. Burnt to the ground is the homestead. In the blank voids, that cheerful casements were, sits despair; man stands at the grave of all that fortune gave! The names alone have survived; now and then they speak of God and religion, of Christianity and faith, immortality and freedom; but the words are false, pretending a possession that is lost long since. They are patches from a grand dress, once worn by our ancestors; ruins of the ancestral house that the children have lost. They are still cherished as the memories of better times. People thus acknowledge the irreparable forfeit-ure which those names denote, without realizing how they pro-nounce their own condemnation by having destroyed these pos-sessions.[1] *Dissipaverunt substantiam suam.*

The son came to his father. In his heedless anxiety for freedom he would leave the father's house, to get away from restraining discipline and dependence. "Father, give me the portion of the goods that falleth to me." And he departed into a far country. Soon he had spent all and had nothing to ap-pease his hunger.

Despairing of Truth

These, then, are the achievements liberal research can boast of in the fields of philosophy and religion: Negations and again negations; temples and altars it has destroyed, sacred images it has broken, pillars it has knocked down. Free from Christi-anity, free from God, free from the life to come and the super-natural, free from authority and faith — it is rich in freedom and negation. But what does it offer in place of all the things it has destroyed? What spiritual goods does it show to the expectant eyes of its confiding followers? The most hopeless things imaginable, namely, despair of all higher truth, mental confusion, and decay. One other brief glance at the conse-

[1] *Uhlich*, founder of a community of free-thinkers, who died in 1873, thus describes his evolution from rationalism to atheism: "At the beginning I could say: We hold fast to Jesus, to Him who stood too high to be called a mere man. Ten years later I could say: God, virtue, immortality — these three are the eternal foundation of religion. And after ten more years I could issue a declaration wherein God was mentioned no more." Similar progress in spiritual disintegration has been shown by Liberalism in recent years: first it partially abandoned Christian dogma, without however quite breaking loose from it; in the eighteenth century rationalistic enlightenment tore loose from all revelation, adhering only to natural religion; to-day even this is lost.

quences and we shall be competent to judge of the fitness of liberal freedom of thought for the civilization of mankind.

As far as it is inspired by philosophy, modern science confesses the principle: "No objective truth can be positively known, at least not in metaphysics"; restless doubt is the lot of the searching intellect. We have amplified this elsewhere in these pages. This result of the modern doctrine of cognition is not infrequently boasted of. It was good enough, say they, for the ancients to live in the silly belief of possessing eternal truth; they were simple and unsuspecting; we know there is in store for man only doubt and everlasting struggle for truth.

"We confess that we do not know whether there are for mankind as a whole, and for the individual, tasks and goals that extend beyond this earthly existence" (*Jodl*). "There is no scientific philosophy of generally recognized standard, but only in the form of various experiments for the purpose of defining and expressing the harmony and the idea of the active principle; consequently there cannot be a final philosophy, it must be ready at all times to revise any point that previously seemed to have been established" (*Paulsen*). "Only to dogmatism," says another, "are the various theories of the world contradictory; to science they are hypotheses of equal value, which, as they are all limited, may exist side by side, the theistic as well as the atheistic, the dualistic, the monistic, and whatever their names may be. Man, who conceives these hypotheses, is master over them all and makes use of them, here of one, there of another, according to the kind of the problem he is occupied with at the time. Thus, he is independent of any view of the world" (*L. von Sybel*). Again we are told: "There has been formulated a free variety of metaphysical systems, none of them demonstrable. . . . Is it our task, perhaps, to select the true one? This would be an odd superstition; this metaphysical anarchy is teaching, as obviously as possible, the relativity of all metaphysical systems" (*W. Dilthey*). Therefore, nothing but impressions and opinions, and not the truth; indeed, for the cognition of transcendental, metaphysical truths, they often have only words of disdain.

"The fact should be emphasized," says *G. Spicker*, "that philosophy really is devoid of any higher ideal; that, through its doubt of the objective cognizability of things above us, outside and inside of us, it has fallen prey to scepticism, even if philosophers do not admit it and try to evade the issue with the phrase 'theory of cognition.'"

A science cannot sink to a lower level than by the admission that it has nothing to offer and nothing to accomplish. It is tantamount to bankruptcy. This science undertakes to nourish the human mind, but offers stones instead of bread; it wants to uplift and to instruct, and confesses that it has nothing to tell. *Amphora coepit institui, currente rota urceus exit.* In the beginning a proud consciousness and the promise to be everything to mankind; at the end mental pauperism and scepticism, a caricature of science.

This, then, is the terminal at which the free-thought of subjectivism has arrived: the loss of truth, without which man's mind wanders restlessly and without a goal. That is the penalty for gambling boldly with human perception, the retribution for rebelling against the rights of truth and for the vainglorious arrogance of the intellect, which would draw only from its own cisterns the water of life, while alone those lying deep in the Divine may offer him the eternal fountains of objective truth. Scepticism is gnawing at the mental life of the world. A scepticism cloaked with the names of criticism and research, and of positivism and empiric knowledge, but which, nevertheless, remains what it is, an ominous demon, liberated from the grave into which has been lowered the Christian spiritual life, the spirit of darkness now pervading the world.

In All Directions of the Compass

They have lost their way, puzzled by mazes and perplexed with error they are in hopeless confusion; a correlative of individualistic thinking. If the absolute subject and his experiences of life are the self-appointed court of last resort, the result must be anarchy and not accord. This is manifest; moreover, it is frankly admitted by the spokesmen of free-thought.

This anarchy is described in vivid words by Prof. *Paulsen*, recently the indefatigable champion of freest thought: "We no longer have a Protestant philosophy, in the sense of a standard system. *Hegel's* philosophy was the last to occupy such a position. Anarchy rules ever since. The attempted rally around the name of *Kant* failed to put an end to the prevalent anarchy, or to the division into small fractions and individualisms. Then there is the mental neurasthenia of our times, the absolute lack of ideas, especially noticeable among so-called educated people. . . . Billboard art has found a counterpart in billboard-philosophy. Here, there, and everywhere we meet the cry: here is the saviour, the secret ruler, the magic doctor, who cures all ills of our diseased age. . . . After a while, the mob has again dispersed and the thing is forgotten" ("Philosophia Militans").

"There is no uniform philosophic theory of the world, such as we, at least to a certain extent, used to have," says *Paulsen* elsewhere, "the latest ideas are diverging in all directions of the compass." When one buildeth up, and another pulleth down, what profit have they but the labour? (Ecclus. xxxiv. 28). "We have no metaphysics nowadays," says *R. Eucken* in the same strain, "and there are not a few who are proud of it. They only would have the right to be so if our philosophy were in excellent shape, if, even without metaphysics, firm convictions ruled our life and actions, if great aims held us together and lifted us above the smallness of the merely human. The fact is an unlimited discordance, a pitiful insecurity in all matters of principle, a defencelessness against the petty human, and soullessness accompanied by superabounding exterior manifestation of life."

This is the status of modern philosophy and also of liberal, Protestant, theology. Of views of the world, of notions and forms of Christianity, of ideas, essays and contributions to them, there is choice in abundance. Here, materialistic Monism is proclaimed, warranted to solve all riddles. There, spiritualistic Pantheism is retailed in endless varieties. Yonder, Agnosticism is strutting: no longer philosophy, but facts and reality, is its slogan. Then comes the long procession of ethical views of life: "Contemplations of life; theories of human existence surround us and court us in plenty; the coincidence of ample historical learning with active reflection induces manifold combinations, and makes it easy for the individual to draw pictures of this kind according to circumstance and mood; and so we see individual philosophies whirling about promiscuously, winning and losing the favour of the day, and shifting and transmuting themselves in kaleidoscopic change" (*Eucken*). *Hegel,* although he lectured with great assurance on his own system, lamented: "Every philosophy comes forth with the pretension to refute not only the preceding philosophy, but to remedy its defects, to have at last found the right thing." But past experience shows, that to this philosophy, too, the passage from Holy Writ is applicable: "Behold, the feet that will carry thee away are already at the threshold." Indeed, often it has come to pass that these philosophers themselves bury their ideas, preparatory to entering another camp. Consider the changes that men like

Kant, Fichte, Schelling, Strauss, Nietzsche, have essayed in the short course of a few decades, and we are justified in assuming that they would again have changed their last ideas had death not interfered.

Now and then such confusion of opinions is considered an advantage, the advantage of fertility. To be sure, it is fertility, — the fertility of fruitless attempts, of errors, and of fancies, the fertility of disorder and chaos. If this fertility be a cause of pride for science, then mathematics, physics, astronomy, and other exact sciences, are indeed to be pitied for having to forego this fertility of philosophy, and the privilege of being an arena for contradictory views.

WITHOUT PEACE AND WITHOUT JOY

After the hopeless shipwreck of the modern, godless thought, can we wonder at meeting frequently the despondency of PESSIMISM? Is not pessimism the first born of scepticism? At the close of the nineteenth century we read, again and again, in reviews of the past and forecasts of the future, how the modern world stands perplexed before the riddles of life, confessing in pessimistic mood that it is dissatisfied and unhappy to the depth of its soul. With proud self-consciousness, boasting of knowledge and power of intellect, they had entered the nineteenth century, praising themselves in the words: How great, O man, thou standest at the century's close, with palm of victory in thy hand, the fittest son of time! With heads bowed in shame these same representatives of modern thought make their exit from the same century.

Of the number that voiced this sentiment we quote but one, Prof. *R. Eucken,* who wrote: "The greatness of the work is beyond doubt. This work more and more opens up and conquers the world, unfolds our powers, enriches our life, it leads us in quick victorious marches from triumph to triumph. . . . Thus, it is true, our desired objects have been attained, but they disclosed other things than we expected: the more our powers and ideas are attracted by the work, the more we must realize the neglect of the inner man and of his unappeased, ardent longing for happiness. Doubts spring up concerning the entire work; we must ask whether the new civilization be not too much a development of bare force, and too little a cultivation of the being, whether because of our strenuous attention to surroundings, the problems of innermost man are not neglected. There is also noticeable a sad lack in moral power; we feel powerless against selfish interests and overwhelming passions; mankind is more and more dividing itself into hostile sects and parties. And such doubts arouse to renewed vigour the old, eternal problems, which faithfully accompany our evolution through all its stages. Former times did not finally solve them, (?) but they were, at least to a degree, mollified and quieted. But now they are here again unmitigated and unobscured. The enigmatical of human existence is impressed upon us with unchecked strength, the darkness concerning the Whence and Whither, the dismal power of blind necessity, accident and sorrow in our fate, the low and vulgar in the human soul, the difficult complications of the social body: all unite in the question: Has our existence any real sense or value? Is it not torn asunder to an extent that we shall be denied truth and peace for ever? . . . Hence it is readily understood why a gloomy pessimism is spreading more and more, why the depressed feeling of littleness and weakness is pervading mankind in the midst of its triumphs."

Similar, and profoundly true, are the words spoken some years ago by a noted critic in the " Literarische Zentralblatt " (1900) : " A painful lament and longing pervades our restless and peaceless time. The bulk of our knowledge is daily increasing, our technical ability hardly knows of difficulties it could not overcome . . . and yet we are not satisfied. More and more frequently we meet with the tired, disheartened question: What 's the use? We lack the one thing which would give support and impetus to our existence, a firm and assured view of the world. Or, to be more exact, we have found that we cannot live with the view of the world which in this century of enlightenment has stamped its imprint more and more upon our entire mental life. Materialism, in coarser or finer form, has penetrated deeply our habits of thought, even in those who would indignantly protest against being called materialists; the name seemed to imply scientific earnestness and liberal views. However, there was still left a considerable fund of old, idealistic values, and as long as we could draw upon them we saw in materialism only the power to clear up rooted prejudices, and to open the road for progress in every field. To the newer generation, however, little or nothing is left of this old fund, hence, having nothing else but materialism to depend upon, they are confronted by an appalling dreariness and emptiness of existence. And ever since the man on the street has absorbed the easy materialistic principles, and looks down from the height of his ' scientific ' view of life contemptuously upon all reactionaries, we have become aware of the danger that imperils everything implied by the collective word ' humanism.' This explains the plethora of literature which in these days deals with the questions of a world philosophy." Who is not reminded after reading this mournful confession of the words of *St. Augustine:* " Restless is our heart, till it finds rest in Thee "?

If it be true, then, that philosophical thought stands in closest connection with civilization, determining the latter in its loftier aspects, then the freedom of thought of modern subjectivism has proved its incompetence as a power for civilization; it can produce only a sham-civilization, it can incite the minds and keep them in nervous tension, until, tired of fruitless endeavour, they yield to pessimism. However painful it may be to admit it, this freedom of thought is and remains the principle of natural decadence of all the higher elements of a culture that is not determined by the number of guns, by steam-engines, and high-schools for girls, but which consists, chiefly, in a steadfast, ideal condition of reason and will, from which all else obtains significance and value. What further proof of intellectual and cultural incompetence can be demanded which this principle has not furnished already?

If this be the fact, then it follows in turn that in the life of higher culture, where the health of the soul and the marrow of mental life is at stake, there can rule but a single principle, the OBJECTIVISM OF CHRISTIAN THOUGHT, the principle of absolute submission, without variance and change, to a truth against which man has no rights. The submission of Christian thought to a religious, teaching authority, recognized as infallible in all matters pertaining to its domain, while not an exhaustive presentment of this principle, is its perceptive and concrete effect.

A ROCK IN THE WATERS

The history of human thought of all ages, but especially of the last centuries, proves how necessary a divine revelation is to man; viz., the clear exposition of the highest truths in the view of world and of life, emphasized by a divine authority, which links the human mind to the one immutable truth; not only in ignorant nations, not only in the man of the common people, but also, and more especially, in the educated man and in the scientist, he, namely, who, through the moderate studies of a small intellect, has collected a little sum of knowledge that is apt to confuse his limited understanding and to rob him of modesty. It is just as manifest that revelation alone does not suffice, that there is needed also the enduring forum of a teaching Church, which in the course of centuries gives expression to truth with infallible, binding authority.

The full truth of this is felt even by those unfavourably disposed toward this authority. A recent champion of autonomous freedom of thought, the Protestant theologian, *F. Troeltsch,* makes this concession in the words: " The immediate consequence of such autonomy is necessarily a steadily more intensified individualism of convictions, opinions, theories, and practical ends and aims. An absolute supra-individual union is effected only by an enormous power such as the belief in an immediate, supernatural, divine, revelation, as possessed by Catholicism, and organized in the Church as the extended· and continued incarnation of God. This tie gone, the necessary sequel will be a splitting up in all sorts of human opinions." [1]

This is to the Catholic a caution to appreciate the ministry of his Church ever more highly, and to cleave to it still closer. He will not agree with those who think that in our time the principle of Authority must retire. The more his eyes are opened by the present situation, the more clearly he realizes where thought emancipated from faith and authority has led, the more he will affirm his conscious belief in authority. His foothold upon the rock of the Church will be the firmer the more restless the billows of unsafe opinions rise and roll about him. The Catholic of mature, Catholic, conviction would consider it folly to abandon the rock for the restless and turbulent play of the waves. Many, indeed, who are looking for a safe place of truth, we see for this reason taking refuge in a

---

[1] Dr. *Spencer Jones,* an Episcopal clergyman, says in his book, " England and the Holy See ": " For the Episcopal Church the junction with Rome, with its sharply defined dogmas, its supreme ministry, and its firm leadership, is a question of life. More and more the supernatural belief is replaced by individual opinions, a condition which in itself causes faith to disappear. A condition like the present, making it possible that in one and the same congregation the most pronounced contrariety of opinions in respect to most essential tenets, as well as a general confusion of minds, is not only tolerated, but directly welcomed, such a condition cannot endure in the long run."

strong Church; many are impressed by the stability of Catholic authority.[1]

The present situation is similar socially to that of the ancient world at its close, and also in regard to the spiritual life. Then, as now, there was learning without idealism, corroded by scepticism, without harmony and cheer. Then, as now, there was but one power to offer rescue, Faith and Church. A longing for help is now also prevailing in the world. It feels its helplessness. If they only had the conviction of a *St. Augustine,* who prayed for deliverance from his errors: " When I often and forcefully realized the agility, sagacity, and acumen of the human mind, I could not believe that truth was hidden completely from us — rather only the way and manner how to discover it, and that we must accept these from a divine authority " (*De utilit. credendi,* 8).

It was a solemn hour, pregnant with profound significance, when at midnight at the beginning of this century all the churchbells of the Catholic globe were ringing, and, while everything around was silent, their blessed sound was resounding alone over the earth, over villages and cities, over countries and nations. Grandly there resounded into the whole world, over the heads of the children of men about to enter upon a new century of their history, that the Catholic Church is the Queen in the realm of mind, that she alone preserves infallibly the truths and ideals of which mankind is in quest, by which they are raised above earthly turmoil — those truths and

---

[1] A French author, *G. Goyau,* states with truth: " What makes the (Catholic) Church lovable in the eyes of thinking minds outside of the Church, is just her uncompromising attitude. They see a Church steadfast, permanent, imperturbable. The stumbling block of yore has become for them an isle of safety. They are thankful to Rome for holding before their eyes *the* Christianity, instead of giving them the choice of several kinds of Christianity, including kinds still unknown, which they undoubtedly themselves may discover, if so inclined. They welcome the Roman Church as the ' Teacher of Faith ' and ' Conqueror of Errors,' and, to quote more of the forcible language of the Protestant *de Pressensé:* ' they are disgusted with a Christianity for the lowest bidder, but are impressed by the rigid inflexibility of Catholicism. . . .' " (Autour du Catholicisme social, I, 1896).

ideals in which the heart and mind of earthly pilgrims find rest and peace on their long journey to the goal of time. Since she assumed the mission of Him who said, "I am the Way and the Truth," and, "I am with you all days, even unto the consummation of the world," the Church has travelled a long way through the centuries, has withstood hard times and fierce storms. And she has faithfully preserved for mankind the precious patrimony from God's hand. And now, at the dawn of new times, her bells proclaimed that she is still alive, holding the old truths in a strong hand. And after another century the bells of the globe will ring again, they will, so we hope — ring more loudly and more forcefully, over the nations. And these bells will also ring over the graves of this present generation, over fallen giants of the forest and over collapsed towers, over mouldy books, and the wreckage left by a culture that the emancipated, fallible human mind created, but which truth did not consecrate. And again the bells will proclaim to a new century that God, and the world's history, are thinking greater thoughts than the puny child of man is capable of thinking within the narrow compass of his years and of his surroundings.

FOURTH SECTION

FREEDOM OF TEACHING

FREEDOM OF TEACHING

Preliminary Conceptions and Distinctions

ACQUISITION and distribution, labour and communication of the fruits of labour, are the two factors that determine the progress of mankind. Thus the precious metal is mined and brought to the surface by the labourer, whence it speeds through the world; thus the faithful missionary journeys into remote countries, to disseminate there the mental treasures acquired by study and hard religious effort. And thus science desires to work, and should work, for the culture and progress of mankind, and this work is pre-eminently its task. To properly pursue this vocation science demands freedom, FREEDOM IN RESEARCH AND TEACHING. There is, as we have already pointed out, an important distinction between the two. Although research and teaching are mostly joined, the former only attaining its chief end in teaching, there is a real difference between the two elements; and not unfrequently they are separated. It makes quite a difference whether some one within the four walls of his room studies anarchy, or whether he proceeds to proclaim its principles to the world; it is quite different whether a man embraces atheism for his personal use only, or whether he makes propaganda for it from the pulpit; it makes also a world of difference whether a man is personally convinced that materialism is the sole truth, or whether he proclaims it as a science, and is able to affirm that of the German edition of "Welträtsel" 200,000 copies have been sold, of the English edition about as many, and that a dozen other translations have spread the fundamental notions of monism broadcast through the world (*E. Haeckel, Monismus u. Naturgesetz*). Teaching must be viewed from a different point. Research is a personal function, whereas Teaching is a social one. This fact, of itself, makes it evident that teaching cannot be allowed the same measure of freedom as research, hence that teaching must be confined within narrower limits.

But Freedom is demanded not only for research, but also for teaching, in most cases even an unlimited freedom. It is demanded as an inalienable right of the individual, it is demanded in the name of progress, which can be promoted only by new knowledge. Some countries grant this freedom in their constitutions. Before discussing this demand and its presumptions, we shall have to make clear some preliminary conceptions.

First, the meaning of FREEDOM OF TEACHING. How is it precisely to be understood? Freedom in teaching in general means, evidently, exemption from unwarranted restraint in teaching. Teaching, however, to use the words of a great thinker of the past, means *Causare in alio scientiam,* to impart knowledge to some one else (*Thomas Aquinas,* Quaest. disp. De verit. q. XI al.). Thus the pious mother teaches the child truths about God and Heaven, the school-teacher teaches elementary knowledge, the college-professor teaches science. Teaching is chiefly understood to be the instruction by professional teachers, from grammar school up to university. Hence freedom in teaching does not necessarily refer to scientific matters only; we may also speak of a freedom of teaching in the elementary school. As a rule, however, the term is used in the narrower sense of freedom in teaching science.

Here it may not be amiss to mention further distinctions. As we may distinguish in teaching three essentials, namely, the matter, the method, and the teacher, so there is a corresponding triple freedom of teaching. If we regard the matter, we meet with the demand, that no one be excluded in an unjust way from exercising his right to teach, that no single party should have the monopoly of teaching; the right to found free universities also belongs here. It is part of the freedom of teaching. As it has relation to the state, we shall return to this point later on. A second freedom, which might be called methodological, concerns the choice of the method. This is naturally subject to considerable restraint; not only because the academic teacher may frequently have to get along without desirable paraphernalia, but also because of the commission he receives with his appointment, wherein his field and scope are prescribed. This is necessary for the purpose of the university; the students are to acquire the varied knowledge needed later on in their vocations of clergyman, lawyer, teacher, or physician. There is frequent complaint that this freedom in method is abused to a certain extent, that the students are taught many fragments of science with thoroughness, but too little of that which they actually need later on; they are trained too much for theoretical work and not enough for the practical vocation. Thus there is limitation here, too. But this is not the freedom in teaching which occupies the centre of interest to-day.

The trophy for which the battle is waged is the freedom relating to the SUBJECT of teaching; we shall term it " doctrinal " freedom in teaching: Shall the representative of science be permitted to promulgate any view he has formed? Even if that view conflicts with general religious or moral convictions, with the social order? Or must this freedom be curbed? This is the question.[1]

Obviously, teaching need not always be done VERBALLY, it can be done also by WRITING. The professor lectures in the classrooms, but he may also expound his theories in books; this latter the private scholar may also do. In this way *Plato* and *Aristotle* and the Fathers are still teaching by their writings, though their lips have long been silent. True, this way of teaching has not the force of the spoken word, vibrating with personal conviction, but it reaches farther out, with telling effect upon masses and remote circles. Thus, freedom in teaching includes also the freedom to print and publish scientific theories, hence it includes part of the FREEDOM OF THE PRESS; in its full meaning, however, the freedom of the press relates also to unscientific periodicals, especially newspapers.

A counterpart to the freedom in teaching is presented by the FREEDOM IN LEARNING. It concerns the student, and may consist of the right granted to the "academic citizen" to choose at his discretion, but within the restrictions set by his studies, his university, his teachers, and his curriculum.

[1] " The Independent " (New York) of Feb. 2, 1914, reports under the head FREEDOM OF TEACHING the dismissal of a professor from the Presbyterian University at Easton, Pa. After quoting from the charter article VIII, which provides " that persons of every religious denomination shall be capable of being elected Trustees, nor shall any person, either as principal, professor, tutor or pupil be refused admittance into said college, or denied any of the privileges, immunities or advantages thereof, for or on account of his sentiments in matters of religion," the report goes on to say: " it appears however, from the investigations of the committee, that President *Warfield* insists that the instruction in philosophy and psychology has to be such, as, in his opinion, accords with the most conservative form of Presbyterian theology."

CHAPTER I

FREEDOM OF TEACHING AND ETHICS

NOW for a closer examination of the problem of freedom of teaching, from the point of GENERAL ETHICS, not of law. This is an important distinction, not seldom overlooked. The former point of view deals with freedom in teaching only in as far as regulated or circumscribed by ethical principles, by the moral principles of conscience, without regard to state-laws or other positive rules. The freedom in teaching as determined by governmental decrees may be called freedom of teaching by state-right. It may happen that the state does not prohibit the dissemination of doctrines which may be forbidden by reason and conscience, for instance, atheistical doctrine. There may be immoral products of art not prohibited by the state; yet ethics cannot grant license to pornography. The state grants the liberty of changing from one creed to another, or of declaring one's self an atheist; yet this does not justify the act before the conscience. The statutes do not forbid everything that is morally impermissible; their aim is directed only at offences against the good of the commonwealth. Moreover, even such offences may not be prohibited by statute, for the simple reason that the enactment of such laws may be impossible on account of the complexion of legislative bodies, or because of other conditions.

We will now take the ethical position and try to judge the freedom of teaching from this point of view. First of all, we shall have to explain the SOCIAL CHARACTER of teaching and the RESPONSIBILITY attached thereto. We start again with the meaning of freedom of teaching. It demands that the communication of scientific opinions should not be restrained in unwarranted manner. "In unwarranted manner"; because, manifestly, not all bars are to be removed; no one will assert that a man may teach things he knows to be false. Every activity, including scientific activity, must conform to truth and morals. Hence there is only the question to determine, when is freedom in teaching morally reprehensible, and when not; which are the bars that must not be transgressed, and which bars may be disregarded? Is it allowed or not to teach any opinion, if the teacher subjectively believes it to be true? Here the views differ. However, one thing at present is clear:

FREEDOM OF TEACHING IS NECESSARY

Also in respect to method. Even the teacher in public and grammar schools, though minutely guided by the plan of instruction, must be granted, by the demands of pedagogy, a certain liberty; he should be free to arrange and to try many things. Only where individual spontaneity is given play will love for work be aroused, which in turn stimulates devotion to the cause and makes for success. This applies with even greater force to the college-professor, in respect to method, course of instruction, subject, and the results of his research. He must be free to communicate them, without consideration for unwarranted prejudices, or for private and party interests.

If the scientist were condemned to do nothing but repeat the old things, without change and variance, without improvement and correction, without new additions and discoveries, all alertness and impulse would disappear; but his alacrity and ardour will increase, if allowed to contribute to progress, if assured beforehand of publicity for the new solutions he hopes to find, if allowed to promulgate new discoveries.

This freedom is demanded, even more imperatively, by the vocation of science to work for the progress of mankind, primarily for the intellectual and through this for the general progress. The demand in behalf of the individual is even more urgent in behalf of science at large: no standing still, ever onward to new knowledge and the enrichment of the mind, to moral uplift, to a beautifying of life — and ultimately to the glorification of God! For, verily, the purpose of the whole universe is the glory of the Creator. Glory is given to Him by the world of stars, as they speed through space, conforming to His laws; glory is given to Him by the dewdrop, as it reflects the rays of the morning sun; glory is given to Him by the butterfly, as it unfolds the brilliancy of colours received from His hand. The chief glory of all is given to Him by the reason-endowed human mind, developing its powers ever more fully, the crowning achievement of visible creation, wherein God's wisdom reflects brighter than the sun in the morning-dew. And for this is needed the freedom of scientific progress, which would be impossible without a freedom in teaching.

And this applies not only to fixed conclusions; it must also be per-mitted, within admissible bounds, to teach scientific HYPOTHESES. Science needs them for its progress; they are the buds that burst forth into blossoms. Had men like *Copernicus, Newton, Huygens*, not been free to propound their hypotheses, the sun would still revolve around the earth, we still would have *Ptolemy's* revolution of the spheres, and the results of optical science would be denied us.

A TWOFOLD FREEDOM OF TEACHING AND ITS PRESUMPTION

There cannot be any doubt that science must have freedom in teaching. But of what kind? One that is necessary and suitable. Yes, but what kind of freedom is that? Here is the crux of the question. Now we are again at the boundary line where we stood when defining the freedom of science in gen-eral, at the parting of the ways of two contrary conceptions of man.

One is the Christian idea, and also that of unbiassed rea-son. Man is a limited creature, depending on God, on truth and moral law, at the same time dependent on social life, hence also dependent on social order and authority; consequently he cannot claim independence, but only the freedom compatible with his position. Therefore the barriers demanded by truth and by the duty of belief are set to his research; hence his freedom in teaching can only be the one permitted by his social position; personal perception of truth AND consideration for the welfare of mankind will be the barriers of this freedom.

This view is opposed by another, claiming full independence for both research and teaching, a claim prompted by the modern philosophy of FREE HUMANITY, which sees in man an autonomous being, who needs only follow the immanent impulses of his own individuality; and this especially in that activity which is deemed the most perfect, the pursuit of science: this hypostatized collective-being of the highest human pursuit is also to be the supreme bearer of autonomism. As a matter of course this results in the claim for unlimited freedom in teaching, a freedom we shall term LIBERAL: in communicating his scientific view the scientist need merely be guided by his perception of truth, without any considerations for external authorities or interests, provided his communication is a scientific one, viz., observing the usual form of scientific teaching. This latter limitation is usually added, because this freedom is to apply to the teaching of SCIENCE only; to the popular presentation of scientific views, appealing directly to the masses, such a freedom is not always conceded.

"Research," we are told, "demands full freedom, with no other barrier but its own desire for truth, hence the academic teacher who teaches in the capacity of an investigator is likewise not to know any barriers but his inner truthfulness and propriety." "In this sense we demand to-day freedom in teaching for our universities. The freedom of the scientist and of the academic teacher must not be constrained by any patented truth, nor by faint-hearted consideration. We let the word of the Bible comfort us: 'if this doctrine is of God, it will endure; if not, it will pass away'" (*Kaufmann*). Whatever the academic teacher produces from his subjective veracity must be inviolable; he may proclaim it as truth, regardless of consequences. "The searching scientist," so says another, "must consider only the one question: What is truth? But inasmuch as there cannot be research without communication(?), we must go a step further: the teaching, too, must not be restricted. The scientific writer has to heed but one consideration: How can I present the things exactly as I perceive them, in the clearest and most precise manner?" (*Paulsen*). "Scientific research and the communication of its results must, conformable to its purpose, be independent of any consideration not innate in the scientific method itself, — hence independent of the traditions and prejudices of the masses, independent of authorities and social groups, independent of interested parties. That this independence is indispensable needs no demonstration." "Nor can any limitation of the freedom of research and teaching be deduced from the official position of the scientist or teacher" (*Von Amira*). Just as soon as he begins his research according to scientific method, *i.e.*, adapts his thoughts to scientific rules, customs, and postulates, he may question Christianity, God, everything; neither state nor Church must object, no matter if thousands are led astray.

This freedom is pre-eminently claimed for philosophical and religious thought, for ideas relating to views of the world and the foundations of social order; because only in this province is absolute freedom of teaching likely to be seriously refused. In mathematics and the natural sciences, in philology and kindred sciences, there is hardly occasion for it; there only petty disputes occur, differences among competitors, things that do not reach beyond the precinct of the learned fraternity. Whether one is for or against the theory of three-dimensional space, for or against the theory of ions and the like, all that touches very little on the vital questions of mankind; but the case is quite different when it comes to publicly advocating the abolition of private property, to the preaching of polygamy: it is here where great clashes threaten. Here, also, there enter into the plan the social powers, whose duty it is to shield the highest possessions of human society against wanton attack. Nevertheless the demand is for unlimited freedom in teaching. What, then, are the arguments used in giving to this exceptional claim the semblance of justification? This shall be the first question.

UNLIMITED FREEDOM IN TEACHING NOT DEMANDED

1. *Not by Veracity*

Veracity is appealed to first; it obligates the teacher, so it is said, to announce his own convictions unreservedly, for to " deny one's own convictions would offend against one of the most positive principles of morals "; hence the academic teacher could not grant to the state the right to set a barrier in this respect, " it would be a violation of the duty of veracity, which is innate to the teacher's office " (*Von Amira*).

Was it realized in making this claim what the duty of truthfulness really demands? This duty is complied with when one is not untruthful, that is to say, does not state something to be his opinion when secretly he believes the contrary to be true; to force him to do this would of course be instigating untruthfulness. Truthfulness, however, does not require any one to speak out publicly what he thinks; one may be silent. Or is cautious silence untruthfulness? It is oftentimes prudence, but not untruthfulness. There is a considerable difference between thinking and communicating thought, even to the scientist.

Or is the scientist OBLIGED, for instance, to proclaim publicly views he has formed contrary to the prevailing principles of morals, — views he calls the "results of his research," so that mankind at last may learn the truth? Was *Nietzsche* in duty bound to proclaim to the wide world his revolutionary ideas? Any sober-minded man might have told him he need not worry about this duty. Has the teacher of science this duty? How will he prove it? How are they going to prove that it is incumbent upon an atheistic college-professor to teach his atheism also to others? Or, must he teach that the fundamental principles of Christian marriage are untenable, if this has become his personal opinion? Is it, perhaps, impossible for him to refrain from such teaching in the lectures he is appointed to give? This view will mostly prove a delusion. A conscientious examination of his opinion would convince him that he, too, had better abandon it, since it is merely an aberration of his mind. But let us assume that he could neither correct his views nor refrain from proclaiming them, that he would declare: "I should lie if, in discussing the question in how far this or that public institution is morally sanctioned, I were to halt before certain institutions; for instance if, having the moral conviction that monarchy is a morally objectionable institution, I omitted to say so" (*Th. Lipps*).

Well, he has the option to change his branch of teaching, or to resign his office; he is not indispensable, no one forces him to retain his office. Indeed, he owes it to TRUTHFULNESS to leave his post the very instant he finds he is not able to occupy it in a beneficial way; he owes it to HONESTY to yield his position, if he has lost the proper relation to religion, state, and the people, to whom his position is to render service.

2. *Not the Duty of Science*

"Nevertheless," we are told, "the representatives of science have the duty of freely communicating their opinions; they are

called by people and state to find the truth for the great multitude, that is not itself in the position to pursue laborious
research. Where else could it get the truth but from science?" "The multitude participates in truth generally in
a receptive, passive manner; only a few pre-eminent minds are
destined by nature to be the dispensers and promoters of knowledge" (*Paulsen*), and with this vocation of science a restriction
of its freedom of speech would be incompatible.

The idea has something enticing about it. It also has its
justification, if the matter at issue concerns things outside of
the common scope of human knowledge, such as the more precise research of nature, of history, and so on. But the idea
is not warranted when applied to the higher questions of human
life. Here it is based on the false premise that man cannot
arrive at the certain possession of truth without scientific research. We have demonstrated previously how this notion in-
volves a total misconception of the nature of human thought.

There is, beside the scientific certainty, another true certainty,
a natural certainty, the only one we have in most matters, and a
safe guide to mankind especially in higher questions, nay, in general
much safer than science, which, as proved by history, goes easily astray
in such matters. Long before there was a science, mankind possessed
the truth about the principles of life; and it possesses this truth still,
through common sense and, even more, through divine revelation,
which offers enlightenment to every one regardless of science. Here
apply the words of the poet:

> " Das Wahre ist schon laengst gefunden
> Hat edle Geisterschaar verbunden
> Das alte Wahre, fasst es an! "

Nevertheless, it is claimed, science remains the sole guide to
truth and progress. Must not truth be searched for and struggled for always anew? There are no patented truths for all
times — each age must sketch its own image of the world, must
form new values. And it is for science to point out these
new roads. Therefore, full swing for its doctrines. "Science
knows not of statutes of limitations or prescription, hence of
no absolutely established possession. Consequently real, scientific, instruction can only mean absolutely free instruction"
(*Paulsen*). We may be brief. Every line bears the imprint of

that sceptical subjectivism which we have met so often as the philosophical presumption of modern freedom of science. It is the wisdom of ancient sophistry, which even Aristotle stigmatized as a " sham-science," " a running after something that invariably slips away." A freedom in teaching with such a theory of cognition can never be a factor of mental progress, least of all when it seeks to rise above a God-given, Christian truth to " higher " forms of religion. This, however, is often the very progress for which freedom in teaching is intended — the unhindered. propagation of an anti-Christian view of the world.

3. *No Innate Right*

Very well, we are told, leave aside the appeal to the province of science; but it cannot be denied that man has at least an innate right of communicating his thoughts in the freest manner. The first right of the human individual, a right which must not be curtailed in any way, is his right to free development according to his inner laws, provided the freedom of the fellow-man is not thereby injured. Hence every man has the right of freely uttering his opinion, in science especially, because the free right of others is thereby not infringed upon in any matter whatsoever.

This is the claim. It is again rooted in the autonomy of the human subject, the main idea of the liberal view of life, and, at the same time, the principal presumption of its freedom of science. It leads to the INDIVIDUALISTIC THEORY OF RIGHTS, which declares freedom to be man's self-sufficient object, viz., freedom in all things regardless of the weal and woe of others, no matter if the sequel be error, scandal, or seduction, if only the strict right to freedom be not violated.

" Act outwardly so," says the philosophic preceptor of autonomism, " that the free use of thy free will may be consistent with the liberty of others according to a general law." " This liberty," continues *Kant*, " is the sole, original right of every man by virtue of his humanity." And *Spencer* concurrently teaches: " Every one is free to do what he wants, as long as he does not infringe upon the liberty of others."

This is termed the " Maxim of Co-existence." Accordingly any one may say and write anything at will, no matter if people are led

astray by his errors. Even the government must in no way limit this
freedom, except where rights are violated; to defend religion and
morals against attacks, to guard innocence and inexperience against
seduction, is, according to this theory, not allowed to the state.
W. *von Humboldt* writes: " He who utters things or commits actions,
offending the conscience or the morals of other people, may act im-
morally; but unless he is guilty of obtrusiveness, he does not injure
any right." Hence the state must not interfere. " Even the assuredly
graver case, when the witnessing of an action, the listening to certain
reasoning, would mislead the virtue or the thought of others, even
this case would not permit restraint of freedom."

We are dealing here with that misconception of the social
nature of man which has always characterized liberalism. It
knows only of the right and liberty of the individual; of
his duties to society it knows nothing, not even that men should
not injure the possessions of others, but rather promote them;
nor does it know that men are placed in a society that requires
the free will of the individual to yield to the common weal of
the many. To liberal thought human society is only an accidental aggregation of individuals, not connected by social unity.
The autonomous spheres of the single individuals are rolling side
by side, each one for itself: wherever it pleases them to roll,
there they are carried by the autonomous centre of gravity,
whatever they upset in their career has no right to complain.
This principle of freedom was given free rein in the economical
legislation of the nineteenth century. Free enterprise, free
development of energy, was the rallying cry; the result was
devastation and wreckage.

UNRESTRICTED FREEDOM OF TEACHING INADMISSIBLE

Hence the claim for absolute freedom in teaching is not warranted; on the contrary, its chief arguments are borrowed from
a philosophy that is unacceptable to the Christian mind. Is it
even admissible? Though not warranted, is it permissible at
least from the viewpoint of ethics? It is not even this. The
claim is ethically inadmissible, because the RELIGIOUS, MORAL,
AND SOCIAL institutions, especially the CHRISTIAN FAITH and
the Christian morals of mankind, would be seriously injured.

In other words: The claim that it is permissible to proclaim scientific theories which are apt to do great DAMAGE to the foundations of religious, moral, and social life, especially to Christian conviction and morals, is ethically reprehensible.

A few remarks in explanation. We merely speak here of the freedom in teaching relating to the philosophical-religious foundations of life; that it cannot be the subject of serious objection in other matters we have previously mentioned. Nor do we yet inquire what social powers should fix the needed limitations, whether state or Church should regulate them; we are merely investigating, from the viewpoint of ethics, what barriers are set by the law of reason, and would have to be set even in the absence of state laws, because of the important influence exercised by scientific doctrine upon the social life — the social welfare of mankind is the consideration beside the truth that is decisive in considering freedom in teaching.

The teacher or writer may himself be of the opinion that his pernicious errors are not dangerous; he may fancy them even of utmost importance to the world; hence he thinks he has the right, even the duty, to communicate them to the world. And do we not hear them all assure us that they desire only the truth? We do not wish to sit in judgment on the good faith of them individually; we make no comment when a man like *D. F. Strauss,* looking back upon the forty years of his career as a writer, vouches for his unwavering and pure aim for truth; and when even *Haeckel* asserts this of himself. Every fallacy has made its appearance with this avowal.

But, by way of parenthesis, there is no reason to boast in a general way of the sincere aim at truth and the pure mind for the ideal, alleged to prevail in the modern literature of our times, especially in philosophical literature. He who stands upon Christian ground knows that the denial of a personal God, of immortality and other matters, are errors of gravest consequence. Furthermore, if one is convinced of the capability of man to recognize the truth, at least in the most important matters, and if one knows that God has made His Revelation the greatest manifestation in history, and proved it sufficiently by documents — indeed, had to prove it; that He will let all who are of good will come to the knowledge of the truth; then it remains incomprehensible how modern philosophy considered as a whole is said on the one hand to be guided by a sincere desire for truth, while on the other hand it clings with hopeless obstinacy to the most radical errors.

Such talk of general sincere searching for truth is apt to deceive the inexperienced. He who has obtained a deeper insight into modern philosophy, he who steadily watches it at work, will recall to mind only too often the word of the Holy Ghost: " For there shall be a time when they will not endure sound doctrine, but according to their own desires shall they heap to themselves teachers . . . and will indeed turn away their hearing from the truth and shall be turned unto fables " (2 Tim. iv. 3).

Even if the teacher is himself convinced of the truth and inoffensiveness of his theory, it does not follow by any means that society is obliged to receive it. Indeed not. The state prohibits cults dangerous to the common weal: it does not intend to suffer damage just because the adherents of such cults may be in good faith. And if some one thinks himself called to deliver a people from its legitimate ruler, let it be undecided whether his purpose is good or not, he will nevertheless be restrained by rather drastic means from proceeding according to his idea. This proves that the principle of " no barrier but one's own veracity " is not conceded in practical life. The teacher and author, this is the sense of our thesis, must ever be conscious of the grave responsibility of science, against whose power the unscientific are so often defenceless; his great duty will be to make use of this power with utmost compunction, to teach nothing whereof he is not fully convinced, nor to announce for truth anything he is still investigating.

As we turn to the demonstration of our proposition, a start from the DEFINITION OF SCIENTIFIC TEACHING suggests itself; manifestly this must be decisive for the measure of its freedom. No doubt, its purpose obviously is: to promote the weal of mankind by communicating the truth, by guarding men against errors, especially against those which would most harm them, by elevating and increasing the blessings of this life: for knowledge guides man in all his steps, it is the light on his way.

Science is not self-sufficient. It is an equally false and pernicious notion to make science a sovereign authority, throning above man, who must pay homage, and subordinate his interests to it, but which he must not ask to serve him for his own ends in life. There are such notions of science and also of art. Art, too, it is sometimes claimed, should serve its own ends only; the demand, that it should edify, or promote the ideals of society, is deemed a desertion of its purposes, " the furtherance of worldly or heavenly ideals may be eliminated from its task " (*E. von Hartmann*). These are the excrescences of unclarified cultural thoughts. Since man and his culture is more and more replacing the divine Ideal, this culture itself has grown to be the overshadowing ideal of the Deity, without whom evidently man cannot live. The Egyptians worshipped Sun and Moon; modern man often burns incense before the products of his own mind. It is a reversal of the right proportion. Science and its doctrine are activities of life, results of the human mind. Activities of life, however, have man for their end, they are to develop and perfect him: man does not exist for the clothes he wears — the clothes exist on account of man; the leaves exist for the sake of the tree that puts them forth, nor can grapes be of more importance than the vine that has produced them.

Hence, where science does not serve this end, where it in consequence becomes not a blessing, but an injury to man, where it tears down, instead of building up, there it forfeits the right to exist; it is no longer a fruitful bough on the tree of humanity, but a harmful outgrowth. Like every organism actively opposes its harmful growths, society, too, must not tolerate within its bosom any scientific tendencies which act as malign germs, perhaps attack its very marrow.

From the true object of science, as above stated, it follows that it is wrong to disseminate doctrines that are apt to injure mankind in the possession of the truth, which may even imperil the authenticated foundations of life. For nobody will deny that firm foundations are needed to uphold and support the highest ideals of life; they can no more withstand a constant jarring and shaking than can a house of frame and stone. Such foundations are, first of all, the moral and religious truths and convictions about the Whence and Whither of human life, about God and the hereafter, the social duties toward the fellowman, obedience to authority, and so on. If man is to perform

burdensome duties as husband and father, if, as a citizen, he
is to do justice to others and yield in obedience to authority, he
must have powerful motives; else his impulses will take the
helm, the sensible, moral being becomes a sensual being who
reverses the order and drives the ship of life towards the cata-
ract of ethical and social revolution. And these motives must
rest deeply in the mind, like the foundation that supports the
house; they must become identified with it, as the vital principle penetrates the tree, as the instinct of the animal is part
of its innermost being. If new notions are continually whizzing
without resistance through the minds, like the wind over the
fields, repose and permanence are impossible in human life.
To jolt the foundations invites collapse and ruin.

It is the duty of self-preservation, for which every being
strives, that society guard these foundations of order against
subversion and capricious experimentation. Of the Locrians it
is told that any one desiring to offer a resolution for changing
existing laws, was required to appear at the public meeting with
a rope around his neck. He was hanged with it if he failed to win
his fellow-citizens over to his view. This custom pictures the
necessity of erecting a powerful dam against the inundation by
illicit mental tidal waves, that endanger the stability of the
order of life. This, of course, does not oppose every new progress. In building a house, firm foundations do not prevent the
house from growing in size; but the foundations are a necessary preliminary to a suitable construction. Under no circumstances must a man be permitted, in his individualistic mania
for reform, to lay an impious hand at the fundamental principles of life; and the scientist must bear in mind the fact that
it is not the task and privilege of his individualistic reason
to put the seal of approval on these principles as if the truth
had never before been discovered.

To CHRISTIAN nations the immutable truths of Christianity
are these safe foundations. They are vouched for by divine
authority, they have stood all historical tests of fitness; they
sustain the institutions of family and of government, they
determine thought, education, the ideas of right and wrong —
a venerable patrimony of the nations. Shall every *Nietzsche,*

big or little, be free to attack them? Experiments may be made with rabbits, flowers, or drugs; but it would violate the first principle of prudence and justice to allow every Tom, Dick, and Harry, who may have the neological itch, to experiment on the highest institutions of mankind.

Primum non nocere is an old caution to the physician; for many medical practitioners and surgeons not an untimely admonition. It is asserted, and vouched for by proof, that patients are made the subjects of experiment for purposes of science; not, indeed, rich people, but the poor in hospitals and clinics (comp. *A. Moll,* Arztliche Ethik, 1902). Every conscientious physician will turn with moral abhorrence from such action. Indeed, man and his greatest possession, life, is not to be made the victim of scientific experiment. If this holds good as to the physical things of life, then how much more of the ideal things of mankind!

"Every One to Form His Own Judgment"?

But, then, cannot every one decide for himself as to the teachings of science, and reject whatever he thinks to be false? Then would be avoided all damage that might result from a freedom in teaching. Science does not force its opinion upon any one. With due respect for the discernment of its disciples, science lays its results before them, leaving it to them to judge and choose, whatever they think is good.

Such words voice the optimism of an inexperienced idealism. To be sure, were the devotee to science, be he a student at a university or a reader of scientific works, a clear-sighted diagnostician, who could at once perceive error, and, moreover, if he were a mathematical entity, without personal interest in the matter, the argument might be listened to. But any one past the immaturity of youth, he, especially, who has earnestly commenced to know himself, is aware that unfortunately the opposite is the case.

First the lack of ability to DISTINGUISH ERROR FROM TRUTH. Even when recognized, error is not without danger; it shares with truth the property to act suggestively, especially when it repeatedly and with assurance approaches the mind. And often error does pose with great assurance, as the result of science, as the conclusion of the superior mind of the teacher, perhaps of a famous teacher! It is taken for granted that whatever serious men assert in the name of science must be right; or, if not that, there is the overawing feeling that there must be some justification for the confidence of the assertion. Authority impresses even without argument, and impresses the more strongly, the less there is of intellectual independence. The latter is at lowest ebb at the youthful age. That which in hypnotic suggestion is intensified into the morbid: the effective psychical transfer of one's own thought into some one else, occurs in a lesser form through the influence of the morbid scepsis of our times; it is a poisonous atmosphere, affecting imperceptively the susceptible mind which remains long in it.

For this reason the religious savant, who has to do a great deal with infidel books, must be on his watch incessantly, even though he has the knowledge and the intellect to detect wrong conclusions. Thus we find that great scholars often display a striking fear of irreligious books. Of Cardinal *Mai* it is told: "He said — and this we can vouch for — 'I have the permission to read forbidden books; but I never make use of it nor do I intend to do so'" (*Hilger*, Der Index, 1905, 41).

The learned *L. A. Muratori* wrote a refutation of a heretic book. In the preface he thought it necessary to apologize for having read the book. He said: "The book got into my hands very late, and for a long time I could not get myself to read it. For why should one read the writings of innovators except to commit one's self to their folly? I seek and like books which confirm my faith, but not those which would lead me away from my religion. But when I heard that the book was circulated in Italy, I resolved to muster up my strength for the defence of truth and religion, and for the safety of my brethren."

Saint Francis of Sales, with touching simplicity, gives in his writings praise to God for having preserved him from losing his faith through the reading of heretical books. Of the learned Spanish philosopher *Balmes* is preserved a saying that he once addressed to two of his friends: "You know, the faith is deeply rooted in my heart. Nevertheless, I cannot read a fallacious book without feeling the necessity of regaining the right mood by reading Holy Writ, the Imitation of Christ, and the writings of blessed *Louis of Granada*."

What then must happen when the needed training is lacking? when one easily grasps the objections to the truth, but cannot find the answer? when one is not in a position to ascertain whether the asserted facts are based on truth, whether something important is kept back, whether there are stated positive facts, or mere hypotheses, or perhaps even idle suppositions? If one is not capable to recognize wrong conclusions, to note the ambiguities of words? Our present treatise cites proof of it. How many earnest men, who in good faith are the warm advocates of freedom of science, are aware how ambiguous that term is; how a whole theory of cognition and view of the world is hidden behind it? How many can at once see the ambiguity of phrases like " Difference between knowledge and faith," of " experiencing one's religion," of " evolution and progress " of " humanism," of " unfolding personality "? And of the self-conscious postulate that science cannot reckon with supernatural factors, how many perceive that it is nothing but an undemonstrated supposition? We are told that all great representatives of science reject the Christian view of the world; who knows at once that such assertion is untrue? We read that the Copernican theory was condemned by Rome, even prohibited up to 1835, and this cannot fail to make an impression; but the part omitted in the story, who will at once supplement or even suspect it?

Then there is the great WANT OF PHILOSOPHICAL TRAINING. Formerly a thorough philosophical education was the indispensable condition for maturity, and considered the indispensable foundation for higher studies. All this has changed; frequently there is not even the desire for philosophical training. Of course, modern philosophy in its present state does not promise much of benefit. " Students of medicine and law remain for the larger part without any philosophical education, and among those of the other two faculties but few students do better than come into a more or less superficial touch with philosophy " (*Paulsen*). The consequence is, they cannot scientifically get their bearings in respect to ultimate questions, and easily lose their faith, succumbing to errors and sophisms.

Imagine a young man, untrained; in books, in the lecture room, in his intercourse, everywhere, he is courted by a disbelieving science, with its theories, its objections, its doubts, — tension everywhere that is not relieved, accusations that are not explained; how is he to bring with a steady hand order in all this? To clinch it, he hears the obtrusive exhortation to form forthwith his own conviction by his own reasoning!

He is, moreover, likely to be informed as follows: "The university is a place for mental struggle, for incessant investigation of inherited opinions. For years and years the student was fed with prescribed matter which he had to swallow believingly, . . . at last the moment has arrived when he can choose and decide for himself. True, this freedom of mental choice — and it is the essence of academic freedom — has also its anguish. But how magnificent it is, on the other hand, when the gloomy walls of the classroom vanish, and the bright ether of research dawns into view with its wide horizon! He who cannot grasp and enjoy this moment in its grandeur and exquisiteness, he who prefers to the free life of the colt on the vast prairies the dull existence in a narrow fold . . . he has taken the wrong road when he came to the gates of the Alma Mater to study worldly science — he should have remained at the restful hearth of the pious, parental home, in the shadow of the old village-church " (*Jodl*).

What a lack of earnestness and of knowledge of man, what lack of the sense of responsibility! Of young men, without thorough philosophical and theological preparation, it is demanded to doubt at once their Christian religion, despite all compunctions of their conscience, and to argue the dangerous theses of an anti-Christian view of the world. They are expected, as if they were heirs to the wisdom of all centuries, to judge and correct forthwith that which their teachers call the result of their long studies — for they are not supposed to follow them blindly, they are expected to sit in judgment over theological tendencies and philosophical systems, and to struggle through doubts and aberrations, untouched by error, to display a mental independence which even the man of highest learning lacks. Such a knowledge of human nature might be left to itself, if the wrecks it causes were not so saddening.

"How terrible is the power of science! " a voice of authority warned a short time ago. "The unlearned are defenceless against the learned, those who know little against those that know much; the unlearned are incapable of independently judging the theories of the learned; error in the garb of knowledge impresses them with the force of truth, especially when it finds an ally in their evil lusts. No wielder of state-power can lay waste, can destroy, as much as an unconscientious, or even merely careless, wielder of the weapons of knowledge.

Exalted as is the pursuit of knowledge, and as knowledge itself is if guided by strong moral sentiment and earnest conscience, so degraded it becomes if it tears itself from the self-control of conscience. This fatal rupture will happen the instant science deviates but a hair's breadth from the truth it can vouch for upon conscientious examination. . . . Sacred is the freedom of science keeping within the bounds of the moral laws; but transgressing them it is no longer science, but a farce staged with scientific technique, a negation of the essence of science " (Count *A. Apponyi*, former Hungarian Minister of Education, officiating at a *Promotio sub auspiciis*, 1908).

In the year 1877, at the Fiftieth Congress of Natural Scientists in Munich, Prof. *R. Virchow*, founder and leader of the Progressive Party in Germany, sounded a warning to be conscientious in the use of the freedom in teaching, and in the first place, to announce as the result of science nothing but what has been demonstrated beyond doubt: " I am of the opinion that we are actually in danger of jeopardizing the future by making too much use of the freedom offered to us by present conditions, and I would caution not to continue in the arbitrary personal speculation, which spreads itself nowadays in many branches of natural science. We must make rigid distinction between that which we teach and that which is the object of research. The subjects of our research are problems. But a problem should not be made a subject of teaching. In teaching, we have to remain within the small, and yet large domain which we actually control. Any attempt to model our problems into doctrines, to introduce our conjectures as the foundation of education, must fail, especially the attempt to simply depose the Church and to replace its dogma without ceremony by evolutionary religion; indeed, gentlemen, this attempt must fail, but in failing it will carry with it the greatest dangers for science in general. . . . We must set ourselves the task, in the first place, to hand down the actual, the real knowledge, and, in going further, we must tell our students invariably: This, however, is not proved, it is MY opinion, MY notion, MY theory, MY speculation. . . . Gentlemen, I think we would misuse our power, and endanger our power, if in teaching we would not restrict ourselves to this legitimate province."

And is nothing known of the inclinations and passions, especially of the youthful heart, to which truth is so often a heavy yoke, constraining and oppressing them? Will they not try to use every means to relieve the tension? Will they not gravitate by themselves to a science that tells them the old religion with its oppressive dogmas, its unworldly morals, is a stage of evolution long since passed by, and that many other things, once called sin by obsolete prejudices, are the justified utterances of nature? Will they not worship this science as their liberator? He who once said " I am the truth," He was crucified; a sign for all ages. Base nature will at all times crucify the truth.

F. Coppée, a member of the French Academy, led back by severe sickness to the faith of his youth, relates the following in his confessions: " I was raised a Christian, and fulfilled the religious duties with zeal even for some years after my first Holy Communion. What made me deviate from my pious habits were, I confess it openly, the aberrations of youthful age and the loathing to make certain confessions. Quite many who are in the same position will admit, if they will be frank, that at the beginning they were estranged from their creed by the severe law which religion imposes on all in respect to sensuality, and only in later years they felt the want to extenuate and justify the transgressions of the moral law by a scientific system." " Having taken the first step on the downward road, I could not fail to read books, listen to words, see examples, which confirmed my notion that nothing can be more warranted but that man obey his pride and his sensuality; and soon I became totally indifferent in respect to religion. As will be seen, my case is an everyday case."

Only exalted moral purity can keep the mind free from being made captive and dragged down by the passions.

In a college town in southern Germany a Catholic Priest some time ago met a college girl who belonged to a club of monists. They started upon a discussion, and soon the college girl had no argument left. But as a last shot she exclaimed, " Well, you cannot prevent me from hating your God."

Prof. *G. Spicker* relates in his autobiography instructive reminiscences of his college years. Religiously trained in his youth, and in his early years for some time a Capuchin, he left this Order to go to the university. Previous to this he had been led to doubt by the perusal of modern philosophical writings, and at Munich he sank still more deeply into doubt. Prof. *Huber* advised him to hear the radical *Prantl.* In his dejection he went to a fellow-student in quest of comfort, and received the significant advice: " Indeed, *Huber* is right; you are not a bit of a philosopher; you still believe in sin, that is only a theological notion; go and hear *Prantl*, he 'll rid you of your fancies." Of the impression *Prantl's* lectures made upon the susceptible young students he relates: " They were especially overawed by his passionate enthusiasm, his trenchant criticism, his sarcastic treatment of everything mediocre and superficial, and, chiefly, by his self-conscious, authoritative, demeanor. Like a tornado he swept through hazy, obscure regions, whether in science, art, poetry, or religion. Even by only attending the lectures one became more conscious of one's knowledge and looked down with silent contempt upon semi-philosophers and theologians." In regard to himself he admits that a few weeks sufficed to destroy the last remnants of his former religious persuasion: " *Huber's* prophecy was completely fulfilled, the last stump of my dogmatic belief was smashed into a thousand splinters."

Vae mundo a scandalis! What a responsibility rests especially upon those who become the scandal for inexperienced youth!

In the upper classes of a largely Protestant college in northern Germany the professor of mathematics, some years ago, asked the question, who among the students had read *Haeckel's* "Weltraetsel." All except four or five rose to their feet. Upon his further question, who of them believed in what is said in the book, about half of the classroom rose. "The immature youth who read the 'Weltraetsel,'" so says *A. Hansen*, "unfortunately conclude: '*Haeckel* says there is no God, therefore we may boldly live as it suits our natural immorality. . . . Is *Haeckel* the strong mind to assume for a long future the responsibility for this conclusion?'"

One is frightened by the manner the highest ideals of mankind are often juggled with, what they dare offer with easy conscience to the tenderest youth. Prof. *Forel* is known by his widely spread book on "The Sexual Question," perhaps better known even by his lectures on the subject, which some cities prohibited in the interest of public morals. In the seventh edition of his book we find published as a testimonial, also as proof of the good reading the book makes for early youth, a letter of a young woman whose opinion of the book had been requested by the author. Her answer reads: "You ask me what impression your book made upon me. I should state that I am very young, but have read a great deal. My mother has given me a very liberal education, and so I have a right to count myself among the unprejudiced girls." She assures the author: "I never thought for a single moment that your book was immoral, hence I do not believe that you have corrupted me." And such books are offered to young girls as fit reading!

Some years ago a sensation was created when in Berlin a young author, twenty-two years of age, *George Scheufler* by name, killed himself. Though of a religious training, he began at an early age to read the writings of infidel natural scientists and philosophers. His belief became weaker and weaker, and he finally abandoned it entirely. Only a few years afterwards, the young man, who had become a writer of repute, put a revolver to his heart, nauseated by the world, tortured by religious doubts. An organ of modern infidelity commented upon the event in the cold words: "The truth is probably that the undoubtedly talented author had not nerves strong enough for the Berlin life, hence he dies. May his ashes rest in peace!" Heartless words on the misfortune of a poor victim of the modern propaganda of disbelief.

Heavy, indeed, is the responsibility courted by representatives of science when they sin against the holiest ideals of mankind, especially when they induce the maturing youth, with his susceptibilities and awakening impulses, to emancipate himself from the belief of his childhood, and to tear down the fortifications of innocence! If the teacher is high-minded, this cannot mitigate the perniciousness of his teaching, but only increase it, neither can the fact that his personal morals are without a flaw vindicate him. If a man by strewing poison does no harm to himself, this does not give him the right to injure others. If science demands the privilege of assuming the mental education of our people, then science assumes also the duty of administering these interests conscientiously, and the gravest responsibility will rest upon him in whose hand science spreads ruin.

"Knowledge does no Harm"?

"The increase and spread of knowledge" (this is a further objection) "can never harm society, only benefit its interests" (*Von Amira*). Hence, do not get alarmed: nothing is to be feared from science. The apostles of the enlightened eighteenth century tried to quiet their age with similar assertions. "It is not true," says *Lessing*, "that speculations about God and divine things have ever done harm to society; not the speculations did it — but the folly and tyranny to forbid them."

If this were amended to read TRUE knowledge can never do harm, then the mind might be set at rest, although even then it might become dangerous to teach the truth without discrimination or caution. Not all are ripe for every truth: truth can often be misunderstood, lead to false conclusions. Thus, it may become certain, perhaps, that a much-worshipped relic, a much-visited shrine, is not genuine: nevertheless in giving such explanation to simple, pious people one would have to display caution in order to keep them from doubting even the tenets of the creed.

But there is also false knowledge; can this "never do harm but only benefit?" Will all knowledge exert the same influence, whether the Christian tenets of love and mercy, or *Nietzsche's* moral for the wealthy, whether young people are given to read Christian books, or those of *Haeckel, Buechner,* and *Strauss?* The story is told of *Voltaire,* that he sent all servants out of the room when he had friends for guests and philosophical discussions started at the dining-table, because he did not wish to have his throat cut the next night. So this free-thinker, too, did not think that all knowledge is beneficial.

But, we are further assured, let science peacefully pursue its way; if it should err it will correct itself.

It is true, sciences of obvious subjects, that have no direct relation to moral conduct of life, do, sooner or later, correct their mistakes; recent physics has corrected the mistakes of the physics of past ages; historical errors, too, are disappearing with the times. Quite different is the matter when philosophical-religious questions are at issue. Pantheism, subjectivism, "scientific" rejection of faith, are errors, grave errors, yet it does not follow that they will fall of themselves into desuetude; they may prevail for a long time, may return with the regularity of certain diseases. Their error is not tangible, and the desires of the heart incline to them by the law of least resistance. From the earliest ages to this day the same philosophical errors have returned, in varied form.

But let us assume that this would be the case; that these errors, too, would disappear after some time, disappear for good. Is it demanded that the errors in the meanwhile ought to have free play? Shall the surgeon be allowed to perform risky experiments on the patient, because later on he will realize that his act was objectionable? Will the father hand to his son an improper book, consoling himself that truth must prevail in the end, even though defeated temporarily?

These are delusions of the abstract intellectualism of our times, which sees all salvation and human perfection merely in learning and knowledge, and forgets that knowledge signifies education and benefit for mankind only when attached to truth and moral order. Not knowledge, but knowledge of the truth, and moral dignity, make for civilization and perfection; knowledge no longer controlled by truth and ethics becomes the hireling of the low passions, and fights for their freedom.

"THE VEHICLE OF TRUTH"

Back of the urgent demands for unrestricted freedom in teaching stands invariably a thought that operates with palsying effect upon the minds: to wit, that science is the embodiment of truth, a genius carrying the unextinguishable beacon of light: to silence it would be to resist the truth.

Our first thought when we began our dissertation of the Freedom of Science was, that science is not the poetical being so often described: it is an individual activity, a product of the human mind, sharing its defects and weaknesses. For this reason science is not the infallible bearer of the truth; least of all in the higher questions of life, where its eyes are dimmed, and where inclinations of the heart still further obscure its strength of vision. And this is admitted, even to the point of despairing of the ability to find the truth on these questions, and if one is not ready to admit this, the fact is made apparent by a glance at the countless errors exhibited in the history of human thinking.

Is error to have the same right that truth has? If wholesome beverage may rightly be offered to anybody, can, with the same right, poison be given? May one follow his false sense of truth, calling it science, and teach anything he thinks right?

Moreover, is not this science, which, according to its exponents, need not regard anything but its own method, entirely a SPECIAL KIND OF SCIENCE? Indeed it is, as we have learned to know it. We have learned to know this free science, with its autonomous subjectivism, that shapes its changing views according to personal experience; this feeble but proud scepticism; we have learned of those ominous imperatives, that banish everything divine from the horizon of knowledge — a science with its torch turned upside down. And its aim — negation. The beautiful thought is frequently expressed that science, especially the science of our universities, is to act as the leader in the mental life of the nation, " a universal Parliament of science, which would represent the authoritative power so urgently needed by our discordant and sceptical age, an age that has lost faith in authority."

The idea is beautiful, it is sublime; it coincides with a conception of the divine Spirit, who has already realized it, though, it is true, in another manner. The divine Spirit has founded in the bosom of mankind such a centre of mental life; namely, the Church. She, and only she, bears all the marks of the universal teacher of truth. By virtue of divine aid the Church alone has the prerogative of infallibility, as necessary to the teacher of the nations; human philosophy is not infallible, least of all a science that despairs of the highest truth, nay, that often deals with it as the cat does with the mouse. A teacher of the nations must possess unity of doctrine. The Church has this unity, her view of the world stands before us in perfect concord; while discord reigns in the philosophy of a free mankind, one thought opposed to another. The Church is holy, holy in her moral laws, holy in her service of the truth; she never shirks truth, not even where truth is painful; the Church never surrenders the truth to human passions. The Church is Catholic, general, for the learned and the unlearned; she is apostolic, with faithful hand she preserves for all generations the spiritual patrimony of the forefathers. And the unbelieving science of liberalism, where is its holiness, when its eye cannot bear the sight of heaven? when it numbers among its admirers all the unholy elements of humanity? Where is its catholicity, its reverence for traditions, its historic sense, the indispensable requirement for the teacher of centuries? The ruins of overthrown truths, amongst which wanton thought holds its orgies, bear witness to the unfitness of infidel science to be the teacher of mankind.

Serious Charges

The science of our day must often listen to charges of the gravest nature. They are uttered not only by servants of the Church, but in public meetings, legislative bodies, and in numerous articles by the press: science, we are told, has become a danger to faith and morals, it has become the teacher of irreligion, a leader in the war against Christianity. The force of the accusation is felt and attempts are made to ward it off. And then we are assured that science is not the enemy of religion, nor of the precious possessions of society.

It is clear, without further proof, that science in itself cannot be a social danger; hence the charge cannot apply to science in general, but only to that special brand of science cultivated in an ANTI-CHRISTIAN spirit. The assurance from its champions, that their intentions are the best, may often be a proof that they do not realize the scope of their doctrines; nevertheless, it cannot be denied that this science has become, through its principles, as taught in lectures and in print, the greatest danger to the religious-moral possessions of our nations and to the foundations of public order, hence an unlimited freedom for the activities of this science means unlimited freedom for a destructive power that spells ruin to our mental culture.

Can the principles of this science be anything but a danger? Their sharp antagonism to the principle of authority, must it not undermine the respect for state authority, must it not strengthen the elements of social disorder? Its contempt of sacred traditions, must it not become a danger to everything existing? "If all mankind were of one opinion," it teaches, "and but one single man were of a different opinion, then mankind would have no more right to impose silence on him than he to silence all of mankind, if he could," must not such an individualism become the fertile soil of revolutionary ideas? Its ethics without religion tells every one that his own individuality is the court of last resort for his moral doings, that moral laws are subject to change, and must such views not become a danger to moral order? Finally, the separation of mankind from God and its eternal destiny, must it not necessarily lead the whole of life to materialism? and from the scullery it is not far to the sewer. Through its antagonism to Christian faith this science becomes the chief factor in dechristianizing the nations.

It is objected that this accusation is not true, because science addresses itself to PROFESSIONAL CIRCLES only; the people, of course, cannot digest these things, therefore religion is to be preserved for the people.

Why this distinction? The principles of liberal science of to-day are either true or they are not true. If not true, why profess them? If they are true, as is vehemently asserted, then why should the people be excluded from a true view of the world? Have the people not an equal right to the truth in important questions, equal right to light and happiness? Ah, the consequences of this doctrine of freedom are feared; it is feared the people's natural logic would take hold of these principles and draw from them its conclusions. And by that very fear these principles stand condemned of themselves. The truth can stand its consequences, as does the Christian view of the world; and the more zealously its consequences are pursued, the more blessed the fruits. It is otherwise with error. Therefore, if the principles of liberal science cannot stand their consequences, they must be erroneous. "Consider chiefly to be good that which enhances when communicated to others," is a wise maxim of the Pythagoreans. Anything spelling damage and ruin, when communicated to others, is not good, but evil.

Nor is it true that science confines itself to professional circles. Any one who does not lead the isolated existence of pedantry knows that this is not the case. What the professor of our day teaches in the lecture room, finds its way into the minds of his students, and from there into preparatory and public schools; ideas committed by the scientific writer to paper and print, go into all the world, and, transformed into popular speech, become the common property of the millions. The flood of books, pamphlets, and leaflets attacking and vilifying the Christian tenets of faith is ever swelling, and day by day tons of this literature are spread without hindrance over Christian countries. There is not a single book against the Christian truth, be its author named *Feuerbach, Strauss, Darwin, Haeckel, Carneri, Nietzsche,* or otherwise, that does not soon circulate in popular editions in every country, or at least has to lend its subject to pamphlets and booklets, which then carry these "results of science" to every nook and corner, to the remotest backwoods village. And the fruits? All those who in these days profess infidelity and radicalism, they all unanimously profess adherence to modern free science.

Tell Me with Whom Thou Goest

In stately array they come along nowadays, free-thinkers and freemasons, free-religionists and representatives of the free view of the world, monists, agitators for "free school" and socialists, all impetuously active in the service of anti-Christianity, bent on reviving and spreading ancient heathendom. All are avowed disciples of free science, all spread its doctrines, and all work for the popularizing of their ideas. There they press on, the living proof that modern science, as far as it is infidel, has become, voluntarily or involuntarily, the teacher of radicalism, of paganism, and the leader in the battle against religion and Christian morals.

And in its train is marching Free-thought in all its varieties. Its aim at destruction, its dismal designs against religion and state, have become manifest in its books and conventions; for instance, the international free-thinker conventions lately held at Rome and at Prague were plainly of anarchistical sentiment. In their midst we see men of science, academic teachers. Under their auspices are arranged "scientific lectures" to make known the "results of modern science," with the conviction that this will suffice for the overthrow of religion; they demand that "the instruction in public institutions be only a scientific one"; itinerant orators are sent to speak with preference on "Science and the Church," on the theocratic view of the world and free science. The doctrines of liberal science are adopted by freemasonry, its rallying-cry is "freedom from God, freedom of the human reason." And following the band-wagon of free science, we see a shouting and jeering multitude, its clenched fists threatening any one who would dare to attack this fine science, their liberator from the yoke of religion; they are the thousands of the common people, whose faith has been torn out of their hearts, and, with faith, also peace and good morals. We see marching there hundreds from the ranks of youth, who in the heedless impulse of their inexperience have cast off belief, and, with belief, frequently all moral discipline; they, too, look upon science as their liberator. The morally inferior part of mankind, which declares anything to be ethical that "promotes life"; which fights against "love-denying views" and against obsolete maxims of morals, it, too, follows in the tracks of free science. And wherever the issue is to fight Christian institutions, under the name of marriage-reform, free-school, or what not, there we are sure to see representatives of science and of universities, and to hear them hold forth for free science.

Where the purpose is to kindle the fires of revolt against religious authority, there we are certain to meet in the first rank the modern teachers of science.

Science and its representatives have an ideal vocation. They should be the hearth of the spiritual goods of the nations; new and wholesome forces should at all times emanate from the abodes of science, and the people should look up with confidence to these watch-towers of knowledge and truth. What a shocking contrast to this exalted ideal it is, to hear time and again the believing people and their leaders raise a complaining and indignant voice against a science that has become a most dangerous antagonist to their holiest goods! Is it not painful to see the devout mother apprehensively cautioning her son, who departs for the university, not to let his faith be taken from him by teaching and association? Is it not sad to observe that it has become the common saying: "He has lost his faith at the university"? Is it not regrettable to see that Catholic universities have become necessary to preserve the ideal goods of the Christian religion? It is unavoidable that such complaints are sometimes exaggerated. In their generality they include universities that have given small reason for them; honourable men and representatives of sciences who should not be reproached are being mixed up in these charges. But it is true, nevertheless, that many have given such occasion. Is it not true also that many remain silent instead of protesting in the name of true science? that they feel it incumbent upon themselves to protect such a procedure, for the sake of the freedom of science?

For a generation and longer, *Haeckel* misused science to make war upon religion, and went to the extreme in his scientific outrageousness, not even stopping at forgery. Professor *W. His* had already in 1875 expressed his opinion of *Haeckel* in relation to the false drawings of his embryonic illustrations in the words: "Others may respect *Haeckel* as an active and reckless leader: in my judgment he has on account of his methods forfeited the right to be considered an equal in the circle of serious investigators." When Dr. *Brass*, a member of the Kepler Bund, recently disclosed new forgeries of this kind, it should have been made the occasion for a protest in the interest of science and its freedom against such methods. Instead of that, however, forty-six professors of biology and zoölogy published a statement in defence of *Haeckel*, declaring that while not approving of *Haeckel's* method in some instances, they condemned in the interest of science and of freedom of teaching most strongly the war waged against *Haeckel* by *Brass* and the Kepler Bund. Is the freedom to use methods like *Haeckel's* included in the freedom of teaching, which they consider must be defended? Can it surprise any one that this freedom of teaching is viewed with concern?

Much excitement was caused a few years ago by a pamphlet of an Austrian professor. Another Austrian professor, of high rank in science, criticized the pamphlet as "A reckless and absolute negation of the foundation of the Christian dogma in the widest sense of the word, proclaimed as the verdict of science and of common sense. It is replete with blasphemous jokes, such as may usually be heard only in the most vulgar places."

A cry of indignation was raised by the Catholic people of the Tyrol against this base insult to their creed; it was shown that the author of this pamphlet had misused his lectures on Catholic Canon Law, to speak to his Catholic students disdainfully of the Divinity of Christ, of the Sacraments, of the Church, and the prime foundations of Christianity. Upon indictment by the public prosecutor, the pamphlet was condemned in Court as a libel upon the Christian religion.

It was expected that the representatives of science, in defence of the threatened honour of science, would repudiate all community of interest with a production that was merely the expression of an anti-Christian propaganda. That expectation was not fulfilled; on the contrary, those in authority at the Austrian universities, and numerous professors of other countries, joined in a protest against the violation of the rights of a professor, against the attacks on freedom of science. They demanded full immunity for the author of the libel. Even the state department of Religion and Education expressed the opinion that the accused "had only availed himself of the right of free research." Is this the freedom in teaching that is to be protected by the state? And yet there are those who indignantly deny that there is danger for religion in this freedom!

He who really has at heart the honour of science and of the universities, and is inspired by their ideals, should bear in mind that to realize these ideals the first thing necessary is public confidence; not the confidence of a revolutionizing minority, — a scrutiny of those elements that give them their plaudits ought to arouse reflection, — but the confidence of earnest, conservative circles of the uncorrupted people.

In academic circles the increasing lack of respect for the university and its teachers is complained of. Professor *Von Amira* writes: "Thirty years ago the academic teacher was reverenced by the highest society; his association was sought; he had no need of any other title than the one that told what he was. To-day we see a different picture, particularly as to the title 'professor.' To-day they smile at it. Nowadays, if a professor desires to impress, he must bear a title designating something else than what he really is. A literature has grown up that deals with the decline of the universities. The fact of a decline is taken for granted, only its causes and remedies are discussed. And this is not all. Invectives are bestowed upon the institutions, upon the teachers as a body, upon the individual teacher. And there is no one to take up

the cudgels in our defence! " A fact suggesting earnest self-examina-
tion, and the resolution not to forfeit still more this respect. It is not
sufficient to repudiate with indignation the complaints. Nor will it do
to pretend a respect for religion and Christianity, and a desire to see
both preserved, that are not really felt. What is needed is the admission
that the road taken is the wrong one.

THE RESPONSIBILITY BEFORE HISTORY

The distressing fact is realized that the worm of immorality
is devouring in our day the marrow of the most civilized
nations. It is also known that its wretched victims are in no
class so numerous as in the class of college men. Earnest-
minded men and women are raising a warning cry, and are
forming societies to stem the ruin of the nations. The alarm
bell is ringing through the lands.

Remarkable words on this subject are those written not long ago
by *Paulsen:* " It looks as if all the demons had been let loose at this
moment to devastate the basis of the people's life. Those who know
Germany through reading only, through its comic weeklies, its plays,
its novels, the windows of its bookshops, the lectures delivered and
attended by male and female, must arrive at the opinion that the para-
mount question to the German people just now is whether the restrictions put on the free play of the sexual impulse by custom and
law are evil and should be abolished?" *Paulsen* puts the responsibility
for it upon the sophistry on the sexual instinct and the present naturalism in the view of the world: "The prevailing naturalism in the view
of world and life is leading to astonishing aberrations of judgment, and
this is true also of men otherwise discerning. If man is nothing else but
a system of natural instincts, similar in this to the rest of living beings,
then, indeed, no one can tell what other purpose life could have than the
gratification of all instincts. . . . Reformation of ideas — this is the cry
heard in all streets; cast off a Christianity hostile to life, that is kill-
ing in embryo thousands of possibilities for happiness. True, even in
past ages young people were not spared temptation. But the barriers
were stronger; traditional, moral, religious sentiment, and sensible
views. Our time has pulled down these barriers; young people everywhere are advised by all the leading lights of the day: old morals and
religion are dead, slain by modern science; the old commandments
are the obsolete fetters of superstition. We know now their origin;
they are but auto-suggestions of common consciousness which mistakes
them for voices from another world, that has been deposed long since
by the scientific thought of to-day."

These are words of indignation of a well-meaning friend
of mankind. Do they not rebound upon the speaker himself

to become terrible self-accusations for him and others, who, while perhaps of similar well-meaning sentiment, are actually working for the annihilation of the moral-religious sentiment, as *Paulsen* himself has done by his books?

"The old religion is dead, slain by science," is proclaimed in innumerable passages of his books; the idea of another world has long been disposed of by the scientific reasoning of the present time, "hence a philosophy," he tells us, "which insists upon the thesis that certain natural processes make it necessary to assume a metaphysical principle, or a supernatural agency, will always have science for an irreconcilable opponent." "It will be difficult for a future age to understand," he writes elsewhere, "how our times so complacently could cling to a system of religious instruction originated many centuries ago under entirely different conditions of intellectual life, and which in many points forms the decided opposite to facts and notions which, outside of the school, are taken by our times for granted." In respect to morals, too, one can do without a supernatural law. "According to the view presented here, ethics as a science does not depend on belief. . . . Moral laws are the natural laws of the human-historical life of time and place. . . . Nor does it seem advisable in pedagogical-practical respect to make the force or the significance of ethical commands dependent on a matter so uncertain as the belief in a future life." We might cite many similar expressions from his writings.

It is significant that they have to condemn their own science in view of its sad consequences.

Paulsen loudly demands RESTRICTION FOR THE FREEDOM OF ART, for the industry of lewdness, for the literature of perversity.

He says: "The English people, admired by us because of their liberal principles and free institutions, are less afraid to show by the sternest means the door to salacious minds . . . the feeling of responsibility for preserving the roots of the strength of the people's life is in England far more wide awake than with us, who still feel in our bones the fear of censure and the policeman's club. . . . But what are the things committed by our nasty trades and the publications in their service other than so many assaults upon our liberty? Are they not primarily an assault upon the inner freedom of adolescent youth who are made slaves of their lowest instincts by the industries of these merchants? Therefore admonish the hangman not to be swerved by the plea of freedom."

No one will deny approval to these words. But do they not, again, become a severe condemnation of the reckless freedom in teaching, that claims the right to assault without hindrance the truths which are the foundation of our nation? If art must not become a danger, why may science? If the artist is asked to take into consideration the innocence and weal of young people, if he is cautioned not to follow solely " his sense for beauty," why should the teacher be allowed to follow his " sense for truth " without regard for anything else? If no statute of limitation and restriction exist for science, neither prescribed nor prohibited ideas for the academic teacher, why should there be any prohibited " æsthetic principles " for the artist? Manifestly, because here the absurdity of this freedom is more clearly perceptible, because it leads to shamelessness. At this juncture, therefore, they are constrained to concede the untenability and the senselessness of the unlimited human freedom, that is defended with so much volubility.

Paulsen points to an age in which, similarly to our times, progressive men arose and, in the name of science, discarded religion and morals; they called themselves men of science, sages, " sophists." " It is remarkable that the very same occurrence was observed more than 2,000 years ago, when *Plato* experienced it in his time with the young people of Athens, who became fascinated by similar sophistical speech."
The noble Sage of Greece had caustic words for *Protagoras*, the champion of sophistry, and his brethren in spirit: " If cobblers and tailors were to put in worse condition the shoes and clothes they receive for improving, this would soon be known and they would starve; not so *Protagoras*, who is corrupting quietly the whole of Hellas, and who has dismissed his disciples in a worse state than he received them, and this for more than forty years. . . . Not *Protagoras* alone, but many others did this before and after him. Did they knowingly deceive and poison the youth or did they not realize what they were doing? Are we to assume that these men, praised by many for their sagacity, have done so in ignorance? No, they were not blind to their acts, but blind were the young people who paid them for instruction, blind were their parents who confided them to these sophists, blindest were the communities that admitted them instead of turning them away."

What a responsibility to co-operate in the intellectual corruption of entire generations! And the corruption by dechristianizing is increasing in all circles, owing to the misuse of science. That the condition is not even worse is not the merit of this science, nor evidence of the harmlessness of its freedom; it is the merit of the after effect of a Christian past, which continues to influence, consciously or unconsciously, the thought and feeling even of those circles that seem to be long since estranged from Christianity.

Concerning the decline of morality in our age *Paulsen* observes: " *Foerster* rightly emphasizes the fact that the old Church rendered an imperishable service in moralizing and spiritualizing our life, by urging first of all the discipline of the will, and by raising heroes of self-denial in the persons of her Saints. That we still draw from this patrimony I, too, do not doubt. THAT WE WASTE IT CARELESSLY IS INDEED THE GREAT DANGER."

" It was a wonderfully balmy evening in the fall of 1905," relates Rev. *L. Ballet,* missionary in Japan, " and the sun had just set behind Mount Fiji. Unexpectedly a young Japanese appeared in front of me, desiring to talk to me. I noticed that he was a young student. I bade him enter, and we saluted each other with a low bow, as persons meeting for the first time. I asked him to take a seat opposite to me, and took advantage of the first moments of silence to take a good look at him. But imagine my astonishment when his first question was, ' Do you believe life is worth living?' asked in an earnest but calm manner. I confess this question from lips so young alarmed me and went to my heart like a thrust. ' Why, certainly,' was my reply, ' life is worth living, and living good. How do you come to ask a question that sounds so strange from the lips of a young man? You certainly do not desire to follow the example of your fellow-countryman *Fijimura Misao,* who jumped into the abyss from Mount Kegon?' — ' No, sir, at least not yet. I confess, however, that I feel my hesitation to be cowardice, for I have made this resolution for some time. In my opinion man is purely a thing of blind accident, a wretched, ephemeral fly without importance, without value. Why then prolong a life in which a little pleasure is added to so much sorrow, so much disappointment; a life that at any rate finally melts away into nothing? I am more and more convinced that this is the truth.' — ' And what brought you to such views?' — ' Well, science, philosophy, the books which I have read for pastime or study. If it were only the opinion of our few Japanese scientists one might hesitate; but the science, the philosophy, of Europe, translated and expounded by our writers, teach the same thing. God, soul, future life, all is idle delusion. Nothing is eternal but only matter. After twenty, thirty, sixty years, man dies, and there remains nothing of him but his body, which will decay in order to pass into other beings, matter like he was. This is what science teaches us; a hard doctrine, I confess; but what is there to be said against it, considering the positive results of scientific research?' "

Great responsibility is borne by a science that despoils mankind of its best, of all that gives it comfort and support in life! In faraway Japan there is not the spiritual power of Christianity to counteract the misuse of science; the poison does its work and there is no antidote.

That the Christian nations " carelessly waste their patrimony, that, indeed, is the great danger."

CHAPTER II

FREEDOM OF TEACHING AND THE STATE

CLOSE bonds of mutual dependence and solidarity interlink all created beings, especially men. Insufficient in himself, both physically and mentally, man finds in uniting with others everything he needs; thus do individuals and families join forces, generations join hands; what the fathers have earned is inherited and increased by new generations. Human life is essentially social life and co-operation — in the indefinite form social life within the great human society, in the definite form social life within the two great bodies, Church and state. Within both bodies human benefits are to be attained and protected against danger by common exertion — within the Church the spiritual benefits of eternal character, within the state the temporal benefits.

Hence both bodies, or societies, will have to take a position in relation to science and its doctrine. Indeed, in civilized nations there is hardly a public activity of mightier influence upon life than science. The contemplation of this position shall now be our task.

Science, as we have above set forth, addresses itself to mankind — a fallible science addressing itself to men easily deceived; therefore, an unrestricted freedom in teaching is ethically inadmissible. Hence it follows, as a matter of course, that the authorities of state and Church, who must guard the common benefits, have the duty of keeping the freedom in scientific teaching within its proper bounds, so far as this lies in their power. Hitherto we have left these social authorities out of consideration; the position taken was the general ethical one.

The case might be supposed that the Church had provided few restrictions of this kind, and the state none at all; nevertheless, an absolute freedom in teaching would still present a condition dangerous to the community at large, contrary to the demands of morality; we should then have an unrestricted freedom in teaching, permitted by law, but ethically inadmissible.

The distinction is important. Quite often freedom in teaching is spoken of as permitted by the state, as if it was identical with ethical permission. If freedom in teaching is permitted by the state, this evidently means only that the state permits teaching without interference on its part; it says, I do not stand in the way, I let things proceed. But this does not mean that it is right and proper. The burden of personal responsibility rests upon him who avails himself of a freedom which, though not hindered by the state, is in conflict with what is right. The state tolerates many things — it does not interfere against unkindness, nor against extravagance, nor deceit; nevertheless everybody is morally responsible for such doings.

If, then, we take up the question, what position social authority should take toward scientific teaching, whether it be in the higher schools, or outside of them, we are considering chiefly the state. It is the state that enters most into consideration when freedom in teaching nowadays is discussed; the state may interfere most effectively in the management of schools and universities, for these are state institutions in most countries.

Universities as State Institutions

They were not always state institutions. The universities of the Middle Ages were autonomous corporations, which constituted themselves, made their own statutes, had their own courts, but enjoyed at the same time legal rights. Conditions gradually changed after the Reformation. The power of princes began more and more to interfere in the management of the universities, until in the seventeenth century, and still more in the eighteenth, the universities became state institutions, subject to the reigning sovereign, the professors his salaried officials, and text-books, subject and form of instruction were prescribed by the minute, paternal directions of the sovereign, and with the mania for regulating that was a feature of the eighteenth century. The nineteenth century brought more liberty; it was demanded by the enlarged scope of universities, which no longer were only the training schools for the learned professions, but became the home of research, needing freedom of movement.

Nevertheless, universities are in many countries still state institutions. They are founded by the state, are given organization and laws by the state; the teachers are appointed and given their commissions by the state. They are state officials, though less under government supervision than other state officials. At the same time these universities are possessed of a certain measure of autonomy, a remainder of olden times. They elect their academic authorities, which have some autonomy and disciplinary jurisdiction. Likewise the separate faculties have their powers; they confer degrees, administer their benefices, and exert considerable influence in filling vacant chairs.

The state then considers it its duty to grant freedom in teaching. " Science and its teaching are free," says the law in some countries. No doubt a loosely drawn sentence; at any rate, it means that science should be granted the *proper* freedom. And this freedom it must have. We have become more sensitive of unjustified paternal government than were the people of the eighteenth century.

The Object of the State

What kind of a freedom in teaching, then, should be granted by the state? Unlimited freedom? This is, at any rate, not a necessary conclusion. The state must also grant freedom to the father for the education of his children, to the landowner for the culture of his fields, to the artist in the production of his works; but that freedom would not be understood to be an unlimited one, having no regard to the interests of society, but merely as the exclusion of unwarranted interference. Hence if the state, for reasons of the commonwealth, were to restrict freedom of teaching, the restraint could not be considered unjust. The purpose of the state must not suffer injury; to attain this purpose the state has the right to demand,

and must demand, all that is necessary to the purpose in view, even though it entails a restriction of somebody's freedom. Now for a definition of this purpose of the state.

Like any other society, the state seeks to attain a definite object, so much the more because the state is necessary to man, who otherwise would have to forego the things most needed in life; and but for the public co-operation of the many these could be attained not at all, or at least not sufficiently. To provide these things is the object of the state, viz., the public welfare of the citizens; it is to bring about public conditions which will enable the citizens to attain their temporal welfare. To this end the state must protect the rights of its subjects, and must protect and promote the public goods of economic life, but especially the spiritual benefits of morals and religion. The state, through its legislative, judicial, and executive functions, is to DIRECT effectively the community to this end; therefore it is incumbent upon the state to care for the preservation and promotion of both material and spiritual benefits, for the protection of private rights, and for the conditions necessary to its own existence, even against the arbitrary will of its subjects.

Protection for the Spiritual Foundations of Life

From this the conclusion naturally follows, that the state must not grant freedom to propound in public, by speech or writing, theories that will ENDANGER THE RELIGIOUS AND MORAL GOODS OF ITS CITIZENS AND THE FOUNDATION OF THE STATE.

We claim that the state neglects a solemn duty if it permits without hindrance — we will not say, the ridicule and disparagement of religion and morals: the less so, as freedom to ridicule and to slander has nothing to do with freedom in teaching — but the public promulgation of theories which are either irreligious, or against morals, or against the state. Even though they be done in scientific form, injuries to the common weal remain injuries, and they do not change into something else by being committed in scientific form. The state must seek to prevent such injuries by strictly enforced penalties and by the selection of conscientious teachers. The enforcement of the principle may not be possible under circumstances, legislatures may lack insight or good will, or the complexion of the state may not admit of it for the time being, or permanently. Then we would simply see a regrettable condition, a government incapable of ridding itself of the morbid matter which is poisoning its marrow. But if there is good will and energy, one thing may always be done to check injurious influences, and that is the awakening and employment of forces of opposition.

The University of Halle is said to have been the first one to enjoy modern freedom in teaching. What, at that time, however, was meant by freedom in teaching, is shown by the words of *Chr. Thomasius* in 1694: "Thank God that He has prompted His Anointed (the prince) not to introduce here the yoke under which many are now and then languishing, but gracefully to grant our teachers the freedom of doctrines THAT ARE NOT AGAINST GOD AND THE STATE." One hundred and fifty years later Minister *Eichhorn* advised the University of Koenigsberg that in natural sciences neither the individual freedom in teaching nor of research are limited, that the case is different, however, with philosophy as applied to life, with history, theology, and the science of laws. "The first requisite there," he said, "is a proper bent of mind, which, however, can find its basis and its lasting support only in religion. With the proper bent of mind there will be no desire to teach doctrines which attack the roots of the very life of one's own country."

Now, what considerations make it plain that the duty of the state is as stated? Two: consideration for its subjects, and consideration for the state itself. The state must protect the highest POSSESSIONS OF ITS CITIZENS. For that reason men are by nature itself prompted to found states, so as to protect better their common goods, by the strong hand of an authority, against foes from within and without, and to enable them to bequeath those goods inviolate to their sons and grandsons. Hence they must demand of state-power not to tolerate conditions which would greatly jeopardize those goods, and certainly not to allow attacks thereon by its own educational organs. The highest spiritual benefits of civilization, and at the same time the necessary foundations of a well-ordered life, are, first of all, morality and religion; not morality alone, but also religion, do not forget this. Man's first duty is the duty of worshipping God, of recognizing and worshipping his Creator, the ultimate end of all things. A profound truth was stated by *Aristotle,* when, coupling the duties to God with those to parents, he said that those merit punishment who question the duty of worshipping the gods and of loving one's parents. Hence the first thing to be preserved to the nations is religion; it is in many ways their most precious possession, too. Not only do all nations possess religion, not excepting the most uncivilized; but there is no power that influences life and stirs the heart more than religion. Consider the religious wars of history; while they were surely deplorable, they demonstrate what religion is to man. Even in individuals who to all appearance are irreligious, religion never fully dies out; it appears there in false forms, or is their great puzzle, maybe the incubus of their lives, giving them no rest. Only in conjunction with firm religious principle can morality stand fast. Nowadays they work for ethics without religion, for education and school without God. Theoreticians in their four walls, removed from all real life, are busily working out systems of this sort. This new ethics has not yet stood the test of life, or, if it did, it has succeeded in gaining for its adherents only those who are at odds with religion and morals. These theories must first be otherwise attested before they may replace the old, well-tried religious foundations.

The noted and justly esteemed pedagogue, *Fr. W. Foerster,* writes: "On the part of free-thinkers vigorous complaint has been made that my book so decidedly confesses the unparalleled pedagogic strength of the Christian religion. The author therefore repeats emphatically that this confession has not grown out of an arbitrary metaphysical mood, but directly out of his moral-pedagogic studies. For over ten years of a long period of instructing the youth in ethics, he has been engaged exclusively in studying psychologically the problem of character-forming, and the result of his studies is his conviction that all attempts at educating youth without religion are absolutely futile. And, in the judgment of the author, the only reason why the notion that religion is superfluous in education is prevalent in such large circles of modern pedagogues, is, that they have no extensive practical experience in character-training, nor made thorough and concentrated studies." "The fact is, that all education in which religion to all outward appearance is dispensed with, is still deeply influenced by the after-effect of religious sanction and religious earnestness. What education without religion really means will become more clearly known in the coming generation."

The state is zealous in protecting the property of its citizens, to which end a powerful police apparatus is constantly at work. If the state deems it its duty to interfere in this matter, must it not consider it a still higher duty to protect religion and morals, for the very reason that they are the property of its citizens, and even their most precious? *Pro aris et focis,* for home and altar, was what was fought for by the old Romans. Is it possible that a pagan government was more sterling and high-minded than the Christian state of the present? If it is to be the bearer of civilization, it ought to consider that man liveth not by bread alone. The only true mental civilization is the one which does not hamper but helps man in attaining his eternal goal.

Modern state power is being urged from all sides to take measures against the corruption of morals by the novel and the shop window, and not to look on apathetically when the consuming fire is spreading all about, in the name of art. Are the dangers to the spiritual health of society any less if reformers, in the name of science, shake at the foundations of matrimony, advocate polygamy, teach atheism? Because a so-called reformer has lost the fundamental truths of our moral-religious order, must all the rest submit to an attack upon the sacred possessions of themselves and their descendants?

That the rights of the teacher are not unrestricted was set forth by an American paper (" Science," No. 321) in its comment upon the removal of certain professors: " There are barriers set to them on the one hand by the rights of the students, and by the rights of the college where he teaches, on the other. The college must preserve its reputation and its good name, the student must be protected against palpable errors and waste of time. . . . If a professor of sociology should attack the institution of matrimony, and propound the gospel of polygamy and of free love, then neither the right to teach his views nor his honesty of purpose would save him from dismissal. This is of course a very extreme case, not likely to happen."

Is it so very extreme? Certainly not in regard to teaching by books. Listen: " From the foregoing it is self-evident that polygyny based upon the rivalry of men for women (analogous to the animal kingdom) presents the natural sexual practice of mankind. Whether there is to be preferred a simultaneous or a successive polygyny, or a combination of both, would depend on varying conditions. The ethical type of the sexual condition, viz., in general the desirable biological type, is the one that would best suit a polygyny based upon a selection of man." It is taught further: " The monogamic principle of marriage in general is only conditionally favorable to civilization, whereas it is destructive of it constitutionally, hence in need of reform." " Our contemporaneous sexual reform wave has not yet assumed the position of this knowledge; on the contrary, notwithstanding its revolutionary aspect in some particulars, it is still under the ban of the traditional ideal of marriage "; continence before marriage is an " absurd " proposition!

This new system of morals, fit for the barnyard, but for women the lowest degradation, is now to become the ideal of men, nay, even of women: " True motherly pride, true womanly dignity, are incompatible with the exclusiveness of the monogamic property principle. If our movement for sexual reform is to elevate us instead of plunging us into the mire, then this view must become part and parcel of our women." " The picture of the motherly woman, of the woman with the pride of sexual modesty, instead of with the exciting desire of possession . . . this picture must become the ideal of men, and sink down to the bottom of their soul and into the fibres of their nervous system; it must animate their fancy and awaken their sensual passions."[1] We stand right in the midst of the world of beasts!

This perilous moral teaching is allowed also in public lectures. On November 14, 1908, the " Allgemeine Rundschau " wrote: " Imagine a spacious concert-hall, brightly illuminated, every one of the many seats occupied, the boxes filled to the last place, the aisles crowded, by a most variegated audience: men and women, young maidens, youths with downy beard; gentlemen of high rank with their ladies, faces upon which are written a life of vast experience side by side with childish faces whose innocence is betrayed by their looks, and on the platform a university professor and physician, holding forth about the most intimate relations of sexual life: the unfitness of celibacy, the Catholic morals of matrimony, prostitution and prostitutes, the causes of adultery, " sterile marriage," onanism, and many kinds of perversities. The man is, moreover, speaking in a fashion that makes one forget the admonishments of conscience."

The city council of Lausanne, in its meeting of February 10, 1907, prohibited *Forel's* lecture as an attack upon decency and public morals, making reference in its resolution to *Forel's* ideas as laid down in his book. In protest, *Forel* made a public statement, saying among other things: " If the council desires to be logical it would have to prohibit also the sale of my book." We have no objection to make to his conclusion.

We stated that religion is man's first duty. This applies not only to the individual, but also — and this is forgotten too often — to the state. Man, by his nature, and hence in all

---

[1] Prof. *Chr. von Ehrenfels*, Sexualethik. Similar passages might be quoted from numerous other books by college-professors.

forms of his life, including his citizenship, is obliged to have religion. He remains in all conditions the creature which is dependent upon God. And does not the state, too, owe special duties of gratitude to God? It owes its origin to God: the impulse to found states has been put into the human nature by its Creator; the state owes to God the foundation of its authority: in a thousand difficulties the state is thrown upon His help. Therefore a public divine service is found with all peoples. Does the state comply with this duty by silently supporting a public atheism when it might do otherwise? by even becoming its patron, when, posing as science, it ascends to the lecturing desk to teach adolescing youth?

Of course, free-thought is of a different opinion, especially the one of to-day. Its principle is: the state need not trouble itself about God and Religion, that is the private matter of each individual. In the eyes of free-thought the state is an imaginary being, hovering over the heads of its citizens; though they may be religious, the state itself should have no Religion. What absurdity! It is nothing short of nonsense to demand of the members of a state, the overwhelming majority of whom hold Religion to be true and necessary, that as a political community they are to act as if their Religion were false and worthless, as if to deny and to destroy it were quite proper. What else is the state but an organized aggregation of its citizens? To make of religious citizens a state without Religion is just as absurd as a Catholic state composed wholly and entirely of Protestant citizens. This leads us to a further consideration. The state must protect its own foundations. Just as it must defend its existence against enemies from without, it must protect itself against those enemies from within, who, whether realizing the consequences or not, are by their actions actually shaking its foundations. These foundations consist of proper views on social and political principles, on morals and Religion. If the state does not intend to abolish itself, it must not permit doctrines to be disseminated which imperil these foundations and, consequently, the peaceful continuance of the state. In fact, no state power in its senses would permit a teacher, who directly attacks the validity of the state order, to continue; it would retire every professor of law who would dare to teach that regicide is permissible, or who would with the oratory of a Tolstoy preach the unnaturalness of a state possessing coercive power.

As a rule, open advocates of SOCIALISM are kept out of college-chairs. And rightly so. So long as the adherents of Socialism see in the state but the product of the egotism of the ruling classes, and an institute for subjugating the masses, and in the obtainment of political power the means of doing away with this state of affairs, so long will it be impossible for the state to trust the education of the future citizen to a Socialist, nor can the latter, as an honest man, accept a position of trust from the state, much less bind himself by the oath of office to co-operate in the work of the state. Prof. *C. Bornhak* makes the following comment: " The decisive point is not freedom in teaching, but the circumstance that the Socialist professor takes advantage of the respect connected with a state office, or of his position at a state institution, to undermine the state. A state that would stand for this would deserve nothing better than its abolition."

And *Paulsen* similarly writes: A state that would allow in the lecture rooms of its colleges Socialistic views to be taught as the results of science . . . such a state will be looked for in vain."

Hence it is certain the state cannot grant a freedom in teaching that would jeopardize the foundation of its existence. It must consequently recognize no freedom which, in lectures and publications, will seriously injure public morality and religion. Morality and religion are, first of all, the indispensable conditions for the continuance of the state.

Aristotle says the first duty of the state is to care for religion. *Plato* proposes heavy penalty for those who deny the existence of the gods; a well-ordered state, he claims, must care first of all for the fostering of religion. *Plutarch* calls religion the bond of every society and the foundation of the law. *Cicero* declares that there can be neither loyalty nor justice without regard for God. *Valerius Maximus* could say of Rome: " It has ever been the principle of our city to give preference to religion before any other matter, even before the highest and most glorious benefits." *Washington*, in his speech to Congress in 1789, declared religion and morality to be the most indispensable support of the commonweal. He stated that it would be in vain for one, who tries to wreck these two fundamental pillars of the social structure, to boast of his patriotism.

Without religion there can be no firm resistance by conscience against man's lower nature, no social virtues and sacrifices, there can only be egotism, the foe of all social order. No secure state-life can be built upon the principles that formed the basis of the French Revolution. So we see, generally and instinctively, the endeavour to prevent as much as possible anti-religious doctrines from being expounded directly to the broad masses of the people. This of itself is tantamount to the acknowledgment of their danger to the state. Yet, millions have tasted the fruit of an atheistic science, and the poison shows its effect; they have shaken off the yoke of religion; in its place dissatisfaction and bitterness are filling their breast, and fists are clenched against the existing order.

Bebel said in a speech in the German Reichstag, on September 16, 1878: " Gentlemen, you attack our views in respect to religion, because they are atheistic and materialistic. I acknowledge them to be so. . . . I firmly believe Socialism will ultimately lead to atheism. But these atheistic doctrines, that now are causing so much pain and trouble for you, by whom were they scientifically and philosophically demonstrated? Was it by Socialists? Men like *Edgar* and *Bruno, Bauer, Feuerbach, David Strauss, Ernst Renan,* were they Socialists? They were men of science. . . . What is allowed to the one — why should it be forbidden to the other?"

The notorious anarchist *Vaillant* said: " I have demonstrated to the physicians at Hotel-Dieu that my deed is the inexorable consequence of my philosophy, and of the philosophy of *Buechner, Darwin,* and *Herbert Spencer.*"

The youthful criminal *Emil Henry* read at his trial a memorandum wherein he said among other things: " I am an anarchist since 1891. Up to this time I was wont to esteem and even to idolize my country, the family, the state, and property. . . . Socialism is not able to change the present order. It upholds the principle of authority which, all affirmations of so-called free-thinkers notwithstanding, is an obsolete remnant of the belief in a higher power. I however was a materialist, atheist. My scientific researches taught me gradually the work of natural forces. I conceived that science had done away with the hypothesis of ' God,' which it needs no longer, hence that also the religious-authoritative doctrine of morals, built upon it, as upon a false foundation, had to disappear."

What political wisdom would it be to honor as science any doctrine that becomes a social danger the moment it is taken seriously; what logic to denounce those as dangerous who are putting into practice a science that is hailed as the bearer of civilization!

One may object: How is the state to determine whether scientific doctrines are warranted or not warranted? The state has the conviction that in its political offices it has no organs for the cognition of scientific truth, for this reason it leaves science to self-regulation. Only the scientist, it is said, is able to revise the scientist.

Nothing but scholarly conceit can engender such ideas. Then any one would have the right to pin upon himself the badge of the scientist and become thereby completely immune. Thus, the bearers of practical political wisdom are declared incompetent to recognize the chief foundation of their state-structure; to realize, what daily experience and the experience of centuries teaches, that disbelief in God, even if sailing under false colors, undermines authority, that communism and upheaval of moral conceptions are tantamount to social danger. They are directed to depend for their information in such matters upon the latest ideas of impractical scientists. The fact is, the matters at issue have, with hardly an exception, long been decided. And where the Christian faith is concerned, the Church and the Christian centuries tell us clearly enough, what has hitherto been understood by Christianity. If the objection here advanced were true, then the state would not have a right to decide in the matter of exhibiting immoral pictures in show windows, without having argued the matter previously with representatives of art. The state would not be allowed to pronounce a death sentence because some scientists denounce capital punishment; the state would have to expunge " guilt," " expiation," and " liberty " from its penal code, because many recent scientists, by rejecting the freedom of choice, have removed the dividing line between crime and insanity, between punishment and correction.

PROTECTION FOR CHRISTIANITY

Hitherto we have, in respect to religion, considered chiefly the rational truths, which are the foundations of every religion and also common to non-Christian creeds; the existence of a supermundane God and of a life after death are the most important of them. The revealed Christian religion contains, beside these truths, some others, which supplement them and surround them like a living garland, viz., original sin, redemption, resurrection, the divinity of Christ, grace and the Sacraments, the existence of a Church with its God-given rights, indissolubility of matrimony, etc. Should state-power protect the Christian and Catholic religion by warding off attacks against it, though such attacks are made in scientific form? This, too, in a state in which perhaps other confessions are enjoying the freedom of worship?

It would seem superfluous to propose this question specifically. If, according to the gist of our argument, religion is to be protected, what other religion can be meant than the Christian religion? That is the religion of our nations; none other is. While the stated distinction may have more of an academic than a practical interest, the discussion of this question will not be idle, if only for the reason that it will shed even more light upon our previous statements. Besides, there are manifest efforts to dislodge Christianity from the life of our people, and with it all true religion, under the pretext of opposing church-doctrines and dogmatism. The war against Christianity has not since the days of a *Celsus* been waged as it is to-day.

We premise a principle of a general nature. Of conflicting religions and views of the world, only one can be true; this is clear to every one who still believes in truth. It is equally clear that this one truth only can have the right to come forward and to enlist support in public life as a spiritual power; error has no right to prevail against truth. Hence it will not do to say simply: There are also the convictions of minorities in the state; some claim that none of the existing religions is the right one, others have dropped all belief in God; in our times we wish to concede to any conviction the right to enter into competition with others, provided mockery and abuse are barred. These remarks are quite true, in the sense that neither the individual nor the state may directly interfere with conscience or prescribe opinions; leaving entirely aside the question whether any one really could have a serious conviction of atheism. The foregoing is true also in the sense that public avowal of opinion must not be hindered by individuals. To interpret this to mean that the state must grant freedom to any expression of doctrine would be a grave misconception of the social influence which false ideas are liable to exercise. Does the state grant this freedom to any kind of medical practice, whether exercised skilfully or awkwardly, conscientiously or unscrupulously?

Moral-religious error may in public life expect only TOL-ERANCE — just as many other evils must be tolerated, because their prevention would cause greater evils to arise. This is the reason why the state may, and often must, grant freedom of worship even to false creeds, because its denial would give rise to greater harm to the public weal (*St. Thomas*, 2, 2 q. 10, 11). Freedom of teaching, likewise, must not be granted in the sense of acknowledging that false doctrines and truth have equal rights; this would amount to an assassination of truth. Freedom can be conceded to error for the one reason only, that by not granting it there would be engendered greater evils. Consequently, if a state-power, or the organs of its legislative part, are convinced that the Christian religion is the only true one, they cannot possibly concede to contrary doctrines the right to pose as the truth and thus deceive minds; they may be granted the same freedom in teaching only because restrictive laws can either not be enforced at all, or not without creating a disorder that would give rise to greater evils. Hence the lesser evil must be carefully ascertained.

With this general principle in mind, it is easily seen that a freedom large enough to include an open attack on the fundamental, rational, truths of religion and morals — this having been our subject hitherto — could be conceded only if disbelief and atheism had gained so much power as to make impossible its prohibition. In this case, however, the state should be conscious of the fact that it allows the undermining of its foundations. If, in another state, religious feeling were at so low an ebb, that the freedom of the Christian truth could not be obtained in any other way than by granting full freedom for everything, then even such unlimited freedom would be a good thing to be striven for; of itself a deplorable condition and contrary to God's intentions, but good as the lesser evil.

But let us return to the revealed religion. In the eyes of those who are convinced that the Christian religion, namely, the Catholic religion, is the only true religion, the ideal condition would be to have the entire population united in its faithful confession; then matters would simplify themselves in our case. But this ideal hardly exists anywhere. True, in many countries the population is almost wholly Christian; but the denominations are mixed, and many have separated at heart from Christianity. What standards, then, should rule in this case?

Looking at it specially, the demand of ethical reason is no doubt this: Nations and governments whose past was Christian, whose institutions and civilization are still Christian, and an overwhelming majority of whose members still think and believe in a Christian way, would fail in their gravest duties if they would expose or permit the Christian religion to remain unprotected against the attacks and the attempts at destruction by a false science, or by conceding to the adversaries of Christianity equal rights or even preference. The Christian religion will not be destroyed; but whole nations may lose it, and its loss will in great measure be the fault of those in whose hands their fate was laid. Here might be applied *Napoleon's* well-known saying: " The weakness of the highest authority is the greatest misfortune of the nations."

It remains an anomaly that a state, the members of which for the most part are Christians, should treat this religion with indifference, and tolerate that its tenets and traditions be represented as fairy-tales and fables, its moral law as a danger to civilization, and perhaps its divine Founder as a victim of religious frenzy. If the state is the expression and the REPRESENTATIVE OF ITS SUBJECTS, then such disharmony between public and private life is unnatural. Moreover, the Christian religion is held by the majority of its citizens to be the most precious legacy of their forefathers; they must demand from the state PROTECTION FOR THEIR GREATEST GOOD. And this may be claimed with even greater right by provinces where the population almost unanimously clings to the creed of their ancestors; at the colleges in these parts the faithful people will be entitled to protection more than elsewhere against dangers to its inherited religion. It would be unnatural in this case to apply the thoughtless principle of dealing uniformly with all provinces of the state. The state is not a heap of uniform pebbles, but an organism composed of different parts, each desiring to retain its own peculiar life.

Do not say this presumption does not admit of application to our conditions, the majority of the people of this age being long since estranged from Christianity. It is true, if we turn our eye only to the more conspicuous classes of society, the classes that control the newspapers and mould public opinion, this view might be admitted as to some countries. But if we look at the masses, those not infected by half-education, then this opinion is true no longer. And there are many who at heart are not so distant from faith as it would seem. In public life they pose as free-thinkers, but their domestic life bears frequently a Christian character. And often they approach more and more the faith, the older they grow. This is known to be the fact even of scientists. Instances are men like *Ampère, Foucault, Flourens, Hermite, Bion, Biran, Fechner, Lotze, Romanes, Littré*, and others. *Plato* claimed that no one who in his youth disputed the existence of the gods retained this view to his old age. " Christianity," observes *Savigny* rightly, " is not only to be acknowledged as a rule of life, it has actually transformed the world, so that all our thoughts are ruled and penetrated by it, no matter how foreign, even hostile, to Christianity they may appear."

It is a sign how deeply Christian religion has sunk its roots into the heart, that it remains THE religion even for those who have turned away from it. To be sure, for our nations Christianity is THE religion. For them the religion of a *Confucius* or *Zoroaster* does not enter into consideration; nor any of the products of modern religious foundations, which would replace Christianity with substitutions of all kinds of religious essences; they are on a level with the attempts at reconstructing sexual ethics: both are regrettable delusions. " Improvement " of Christian morality is tantamount to abandoning all morals, and desertion from the Christian religion, amongst our people, has always been apostasy from all religion. The Christian religion is so true, that no one can renounce it inwardly and then find peace in a self-made one. And all efforts aimed at displacing Christianity lead only to an abandonment of all religion.

Look at the number of people from whom slander and insinuation have torn their old religion to be replaced by another — a freer, higher religion; their moral decadence soon bears testimony of the religious consecration which has been given to them. Woe unto those authorities who, while able to oppose, are indifferent, and who lend a hand in causing Christian thought

to withdraw more and more from our mental atmosphere, to be
replaced by another spirit, a spirit that will gradually control the
decision of the judge, the practice of the physician, the instruction of the teacher, and thus more and more enter into the life
of the people.

It is not assured to those nations of Europe, whose public life is
feeding to-day upon the remnants of their Christian past, that they
will not relapse into a state of moral and religious barbarity. "Maybe
civilized mankind, or our nation at least, is really losing its hold more
and more upon definite moral standards," so complains a modern pedagogue; "possibly the emancipation of sensuality will increase without
end, perhaps we have passed forever the stage of true humanity and of
a live idealism, and we shall henceforth glide downward. . . . These are
no mere, feverish dreams; there is good reason for facing these possibilities with a determined eye, and no accidental or philosophical optimism
can ignore them" (*Münch*).

"It is quite possible," we are told by another, "that much will go
down in our old Europe during the next centuries; and the downfall will not be restricted by any means to Church and Christianity,
and in the crises that will come Europe will hardly get the needed
support from an æsthetic heathendom, from the Monists' Union, or
from the evidences of science" (*Troeltsch*).

If it does not come to it, it will not be the merit of authorities
who let the vessel of state drift rudderless toward the rocks of
dechristianization.

They do not realize that they greatly endanger thereby also
the foundations of the state. The foundations of our governments rest upon Christianity. The Christian faith created the state, created matrimony, family, and the education of
the youth; created the social virtues of loyalty and of obedience. What we have of religion is Christian, what we
have of the religious support of morality is equally Christian;
"Christianity, Christian faith, Christian formation of life penetrates all vital utterances of the Occidental world like an all-
pervading element" (*Paulsen*).

It is one of the first principles of political prudence not to
shake the foundations upon which the state rests. States
and nations are not ephemeral beings, existing from one day to
the other, they are historical structures measuring their lives
by centuries; past generations join hands with present generations, deeds and customs of the fathers live on in their sons.

States must remain on the historical tracks on which they have travelled to success, at least until the new track has stood the test of reliability. So far anti-Christian philosophy has terribly shaken governments; it has not yet proved itself a state-conserving principle.

It is a sad condition to see the guardians of states, devoid of historical appreciation, allow their people to tear themselves away from the soil wherein reposed the roots from which they drew life and strength. Sad, too, that complaints are made of college-professors who abuse freedom in teaching by constructing an unproved contradiction between knowledge and faith, by misrepresenting Christian tenets, by lowering the prestige of the Church, by distorting her historical picture. It would be regrettable for a Christian state, if the complaint were justified that for the most part our colleges have become places where religion is ignored; where the name of Jesus Christ, the Redeemer of mankind, is no longer mentioned; where the name of God never occurs in history, in natural and political science; where religion is considered the most unessential factor of mental life, a factor that has nothing to offer, that can answer no question — a treatment which, by the force of suggestion, must lead young men to think that religion is of no account. It is a banishment which in its effect is little different from an attack upon religion.

Sadder still would it be if the following view were to prevail at our colleges: "A right of the student to see protected and not destroyed any views and convictions, including those of a religious nature, which he may bring to the university from his home surroundings, from his preliminary education, as it is asserted time and again in the frequent complaints about the dechristianizing of youth at the universities — does not exist and cannot exist, because it would be in contradiction to the very essence of the university and its tasks" (*Jodl*).

Is not this the ethical principle of the bird of prey? Is it not allowed to guard the defenceless chick against the hawk? Christian people send their sons to the university, and demand that the education of the parental home be spared, that the inexperience of youth be not misused. The state must demand that the religious-moral education which it furthers in its public schools be not destroyed by the higher schools. Yet, all these rights must be silenced the moment the vision of the absolute freedom of teaching makes its appearance, since to refrain from dechristianizing the youth would be contrary to his tasks.

If such abuse in the management of the power of knowledge, within and without colleges, is not counteracted by all possible means, then none need be surprised when a science free from religion and Christianity is followed by an elementary school free from religion, when in public and preparatory schools the free-thinking teacher is telling the pupils that there is no creation but only evolution, and that the gospels and biblical history are poetical stories such as the Nibelungenlied and the Iliad and Odyssey.

We cannot be astonished to find the following rules advocated for the instruction in public schools: " Religious instruction in schools should not differ from the instruction in other subjects, namely, one of full freedom, bound only by recognized documents and personalities of religious literature and religious science. The school must teach that which is, it must present the tenets of all times and all nations in so far as this is possible within its modest compass. . . . But if the pupil should ask, What really is? What position should the teacher assume toward this question? In my opinion, he should speak in plain terms. He should say: There are people who believe all that is taught by the different systems of religion. . . . The child may further ask of the teacher whether he himself believes. No teacher who claims the confidence of the children should shirk the answer. He may confess his faith or disbelief, without need of worry. It cannot hurt his prestige in the eyes of the child, because, if for no other reason, either way he will find himself in an equally large and good company " (*Tews*).

But we hear much more radical utterances. For instance, the official organ of teachers in a Catholic country urges defection from the Church in the following words: " How long will Social-Democracy, now so formidable, remain inactive against clerical arrogance? How much longer will it shirk a duty that is clear to the dullest eye? If the millions of our Social-Democrats, including the women and children, would break away from Rome, the priestcraft in Austria is as good as defeated. A grave responsibility rests upon the Social-Democratic leaders. Should they miss the moment to act, they will be judged by history! " (Deutsch-oesterreichische Lehrerzeitung, June 1, 1909).

Another organ of teachers declares Christianity to be nothing else but VICTORIOUS HERESY, for which Christ had to lay down His life the same as *Giordano, Hus*, and countless others. " The subject of religion as taught in the preparatory schools is for the most part taken from ages whose customs and morals are — happily — no longer ours." We see radicalism rampant in large circles of public school teachers, demanding noisily, excitedly, and, of course, in the name of modern science and enlightenment, the abolition of the divine service, of prayer, and religious instruction in school, giving as reason that, " as to matters of mental freedom no difference should be made between a university and a village school." That our people will " carelessly waste their Christian patrimony, this is the great danger."

Our argument is not that only Catholics should be professors, nor even to limit the teaching office to Christians. But one thing must be demanded of the college-teacher, that he possess the pedagogic qualifications to render him competent of educating the hope of the Christian people. As a rule this demands a religious, Christian disposition. One thing the state must absolutely demand of the teacher, that he have appreciation for the foundations of the Christian state; he who has no understanding for the historical forms of the life of a nation, who even regards them with hostility, should remain away from this vocation.

In the United States the Jesuit Order has five free universities, founded and directed by the Order. Their professors are not all Catholics; there are professors of other creeds, even Jews. All work in harmony to the common end of the university.

Men who sincerely and conscientiously strive for the interests of science will everywhere show not only consideration, but even understanding and respect, for what is true in the ideas of others. " I gaze," so writes Prof. *Smolka*, " upon the likenesses of my venerable Protestant masters, under whom I studied at Göttingen. Thirty-seven years have passed since I went to them, in full confidence to find in their school the leaders who would be free from the influence of the Catholic view of the world. To their profound knowledge I owe, first of all, the emancipation from the prejudices I was raised in, from the views of an atmosphere devoted to Indifferentism in which I had passed my youth. Prof. *Waitz* opened my eyes to the grandeur of the Catholic Church in the course of the centuries, in the repeated prostration of the Papacy and its ever-following rise to unsuspected heights, a fact unparalleled in the history of human institutions. Prof. *Lotze* rebuked me at the very beginning of my studies at Göttingen for a slighting remark about scholastic philosophy; later he imbued me with profound respect for it and for the wealth of problems it embraces. These scientists, Protestants without exception and in exclusively Protestant surroundings, inoculated me with sincere love for scientific truth, regardless of the consequences it would lead to. They also introduced the youthful mind to the tried methods of scientific research, indicating the boundaries where the domain of research ends and the right of dogma, or arbitrary rule of subjective imagination, begins."

Restriction of Right

We need no further proof that the state is justified in restricting the freedom of teaching, whenever demanded by the business of the state as described above. Restriction of this kind can be considered unjustified only by a state theory of liberalism, which holds that the object of the state consists in merely protecting individual liberty, no matter if this liberty should lead to the gravest injuries so long as it does not affect the freedom of others; a theory which changes the state community from an integral organism into a conglomeration of autonomous individuals. *Lasalle* scornfully termed this theory the "nightwatchman idea" of the state. The state has the right and the duty to exert a necessary influence upon the pursuit of science, especially at the universities. Against it the pleading of AUTONOMY OF THE COLLEGE and its teacher will not hold. They have a certain autonomy, that was even greater in former times. An important part of it is the right to propose appointments for vacant chairs. It must be admitted that this method of appointment is proper; it vouches for the scientific fitness of the appointee, and will prove a protection against the exercise of undue political influence and ministerial absolutism, provided that this method is impartially exercised. But an autonomy that disputes the right of the state to protect its interests, where free science conflicts with it, that would demand, as has been asserted, that "no infringement of the freedom in teaching must be deduced from the official position as teacher," — such autonomy would be a palpable misconception of the dependency of the college-teacher and of the social service of science. The rules that apply to other, non-judicial, officers should apply to teachers appointed by the state, and offences in their office, or conduct injurious to the purpose and the dignity of their office, should be treated similarly as in the case of other public servants. Nor should members of the legislature be forbidden to defend the rightful interests of their constituents in regard to schools. They are elected by the people for this purpose, and the people have a claim on the schools, which are supported by their taxes and to which some of their greatest interests are attached.

It has been demanded to concede to college-teachers the independence and immunity of judges. This, however, would be overlooking the vast difference between professors and judges. The judge has to render legal decisions in concrete cases, according to existing laws; in order to lessen the danger of his being guided by outside considerations he is given a large measure of independence. But what questions has the college-professor to decide? Mathematical or physical questions? There his incorruptibility is not in such danger that he must be made independent of government. Religious and moral questions, questions of views of the world? These he is not compelled to decide. Neither state nor people have appointed him to question, time and again, the fundamental foundations of human life, and to render decisions which nobody requested.

It is not clear why science, pleading its independence, should oppose justified restrictions. As a matter of fact THIS INDEPENDENCE DOES NOT EXIST ANYWHERE. Numerous are the considerations, often unwarranted, it is actually tied to, yea, often tied to by its own hands. He who is familiar with scientific doings, especially academic doings, knows numbers of such ties — there is the professional opinion in scientific circles; woe unto him who in his scientific works dares to confess a supernatural view of the world! — ties of the predominance of certain leaders or schools, without or against whose favor it is difficult to attain recognition, approval, or position; the ties of parties and cliques in an academic career; the tie, too, of that insinuating power of the state that confers much-desired decorations and titles.

" Where is this freedom of science? " asks a modern academic teacher. " Some will say science and its teaching are free in our country. True, it is so written on paper. But those charged with keeping this principle inviolate are human. For instance the monists have the chief voice in appointments to zoölogical chairs. They will propose only scientists who are not opponents to the monistic faith. Far be it from me to assume any *mala fides*. They simply believe that only their faith is the proper one to promote science. But I ask again, where is the freedom of science? " (*Dahl*).

H. St. Chamberlain tells of an amusing incident in his life: " Many years ago, when I desired to devote myself to an academic career, a chemist said to me: ' My dear fellow, since you belong to the profession, I tell you as a friend that it is not enough for you to be proficient; you should try, first of all, to marry the daughter of one of the pro-

fessors, of a privy counsellor if possible.' 'This advice comes too late,'
I replied, 'I am already married.' My well-wisher was visibly shocked.
'What a pity! Too bad! You don't realize what an influence this has
here upon one's career.' What trouble I had to obtain even the *venia
docendi!* and then I stuck fast and could not budge despite all achievements until I undertook to marry the daughter of one of the 'head-
wirepullers'; then things were fixed within three months. I may have
looked at him in a peculiar way, for his wife was a veritable Xanthippe,
and, he added with a laugh: 'You know I am all day at the laboratory,
from morning until late at night.'" There is nothing new under the
sun. In the year of grace, 1720, *Johann Jacob Moser* started his lectures in Tuebingen, but could get no audience. "No wonder, even a
cleverer man than I would not have fared better at that time, when
everything depended on nepotism." The young man had crossed Chancellor *Pfaff* by rejecting a marriage arrangement (*Horn*).

One will find these things very human. Moreover, it would be unwarranted to assume that they happen always and everywhere. But
they prove that the pursuit of science rests also on general human
grounds, and does not always remain aloft, in the ethereal heights of
pure truth.

The Freedom of Teaching in History

When we said that it is the duty of the state to protect the
common benefits of life against injury by freedom in teaching,
and to stand guard over its Christian past, we stated nothing
but what has been the conviction of the Christian nations and
their rulers up into the nineteenth century. Absolute freedom
in teaching cannot plead the support of history, it is only of
yesterday. History shows it to be the natural child, not
of the first awakening of the consciousness of freedom, but
of THE DE-CHRISTIANIZING OF THE MODERN STATE. Its official entry coincides with the increasing de-christianizing of
public life during the nineteenth century, after the modern
state adopted more and more the principles of liberal thought.
A naturalistic view of the world, without faith, was struggling for supremacy; science had to proclaim it as higher enlightenment, and vehemently urged freedom in its behalf. The
state receded step by step, confused by the commanding note
in the new demands, by high-sounding words about the rights
of science; it allowed itself to be talked into the belief that it
must become the leader in the new course, and it took the banner
that was forced into its hands. It has always been so; claims

presented with impudence will intimidate, and assume in the
eyes of many the appearance of right.

In so far as it signifies the removal of the religious-moral bars in
teaching, the freedom in teaching developed first in Protestant Germany, together with the increasing change of universities into state
institutions. Reformation and the ensuing ENLIGHTENMENT had gradually prepared the way for it. Neither the rationalism nor the pietism of the eighteenth century could have an understanding for the
tenets of the faith. In addition there was the confusion engendered by
the multiplication of Protestant denominations, none supported by an
overtowering spiritual authority; it led more and more to the
parting between science and religious confession; political reasons,
too, made it desirable to disregard confessions. Thus the severance
of science from religion increased and the " freedom of teaching " in this
sense was finally adopted also by Catholic states as an achievement.

The enlightenment that had developed outside of the universities
made its entry into the halls of universities chiefly under the Prussian
Minister *von Zedlitz*, a champion of enlightenment and a friend of
the philosophers *Wolff* and *Kant*. That the universities at that
time were controlled by free-thinkers is illustrated by a saying of
Frederick II. On January 4, 1774, *von Zedlitz* asked of the king
whether *Steinhauss*, M.D., should be denied the appointment for professor extraordinary at Frankfort-on-the-Oder, for the reason that he
was a Catholic. The king decreed in his own handwriting that " This
does not matter if he is clever; besides, doctors know too much to have
belief " (*Bornhak*).

In the year of the Revolution, 1848, freedom of teaching became a
political catch-word. " The terms freedom of teaching and freedom of
learning, that became popular in 1848, when any phrase compounded
with freedom could not be often enough repeated, have been ever since
reminiscent of barricades, and men who have witnessed those times become nervous at their mere sound " (*Billroth*).

What was understood by freedom in teaching at the turning point
of the eighteenth century is shown by the demand of *Thomasius* for
" freedom of doctrines that are not against God and the state." The
first move was to break away from HUMAN authorities, *Aristotle* and
others. Thus the Kiel University, by its regulation of January 27, 1707,
ordered that " no faculty should enslave itself to certain principles or
opinions, in so far as they are dependent on a human authority "
(*Horn*).

In Göttingen and Halle freedom of teaching also became the maxim,
and " *Libertas sentiendi*," as *Münchhausen* declared, " was open to every
one and not restrained by statute, except that there should be taught
nothing UNGODLY and UNCHRISTIAN." In those days this restriction was looked upon as a matter of course. It is known that *Kant*
was disciplined by Minister *Woellner* in 1794, because of his treatise on
religion; at Koenigsberg this reproof was accepted with good grace,
and both the philosophical and the theological faculties pledged themselves not to lecture on *Kant's* religious philosophy. As recently as the

middle of the nineteenth century a restriction in this sense was ordered by the Prussian Minister *Eichhorn*, and the restriction was observed. The Materialist *Moleschott* was cautioned in 1845 by the Senate of Heidelberg University, and in reply he resigned his post; in the following year at Tübingen *Büchner's venia legendi* was cancelled, because, as he himself stated, " it was feared I would poison with my teaching the minds of my young students " (*Horn*).

In 1842, *Bruno Bauer*, the radical Bible-critic, was removed by the Prussian faculties from the academic chair because of his writings. *D. Strauss* lectured on philosophy at Tübingen, but was forced to resign when the first volume of his " Life of Jesus " appeared in 1835. Later on, when called by the authorities of Zurich to the chair for Church history and dogmatics, an emphatic protest of the people made the appointment impossible.

While showing a regrettable indifference for attacks against religion, the modern states, inoculated with the principles of Liberalism, have not entirely forgotten their traditions. Many sections in their penal codes still protect religion, not only against defamation, but, as is the case in Austria, also against public anti-Christian propaganda, and the " religious-moral education " in public schools is made compulsory by law. Of course there is a contradiction, between the conviction of the state that the principles of morals and religion must be preserved, and the grant of full freedom to an anti-religious misuse of science, whose effect upon the masses is unavoidable. It is a contradiction to tear down the dam at the river and then erect emergency levees against the onrushing flood. The amazing presumption, that holds inviolate and sacred everything that poses under the name of science, is the fault of it all.

Freedom of Teaching and Party Rule

In some countries the complaint is heard that a certain faction has obtained control of the universities, and so exercises its control that those who are not of its bent of mind are excluded from both teaching and taking part in the administration of its affairs, despite the fact that freedom in teaching and learning has been guaranteed by the state. It is the faction that professes free-thought and cultivates the freedom of science in this sense. This condition forces students faithful to their religion to study in a strange atmosphere, and they are looked upon as strangers. The parties so accused seek to disclaim these charges as unjust; for they feel that, if justified, it would disclose an unlawful condition of things. Nevertheless the facts are so notorious, that all protestations will be without avail.

These facts must be painful to the sense of justice, order, and good-fellowship; and to this sense it is not pleasing to deal further with matters which have often been the cause for indignant resentment, and to go into concrete details. We shall but briefly recall to mind how persistently candidates for academic positions are pushed aside when they are known to be of staunch Catholic mind. This is borne out by their trifling percentage among the large number of college-teachers; by the high pressure that is often needed to lift the embargo for a CATHOLIC; by assaults which not seldom resulted in physical violence. This small number is glaringly emphasized by the considerable, even disquieting, number of college lecturers of Jewish extraction. Furthermore, there is the improper usage that the theological faculty is passed over at the annual election of the rector, and likewise, that teachers even of lay-faculties are excluded from academic offices when they profess themselves openly as Catholics.

Catholic students have seen themselves treated as strangers at more than one university; they were not given the usual privileges, and were accorded rights only in the proportion that their number had to be reckoned with. Their corporate bodies were ignored, self-evident rights either denied or grossly violated.

As to the small number of religious-minded lecturers at colleges it is not to be denied that the number of those who combine fervent religious persuasion with high scientific efficacy is not considerable these days. Their long suppression furnishes a reason for it, but not the only one. A modern university professor rightly states: "While there never has been a want of courageous, determined confessors of the Catholic faith who have occupied a prominent, even leading, position in the progress of science, in the perfection of methods and means of scientific research, they were and still are the exception. They were men of SELF-RELIANCE AND INDEPENDENT judgment, who were able to exempt themselves from an humble submission to the powerful view of the world, which emanates from the hatred of Christianity and prevails in educated circles. The issue is still the same secular contrast between the two views of the world, which *St. Augustine* illustrated with unsurpassed mastery as long as fifteen hundred years ago. But the view of the world which has been in the ascendant in scientific circles long since, has certainly nothing in common with scientific research."

Our task, however, is not to examine the facts, but to prove that such conditions are unlawful, no matter where and when found. We do not wish to discuss further the fact that a university polity, exclusively in the spirit of a liberalism that gradually goes over into radicalism, would constitute a grave danger for Christian traditions. Indifference to the Christian and every other religion, or to an extent direct rejection, must make it appear more and more inferior and obsolete in the eyes of educated circles; this view will then easily find its way to the people. Nor do we intend to enlarge upon a second point, viz., the interest of science itself. The kernel of liberal research in the province of the spiritual is a frivolous agnosticism, with a rigid bondage to its naturalistic postulates, with which we have become sufficiently acquainted. Principles of this kind are poison for true science. For this reason alone it is necessary that a Christian philosophy be placed by the side of a philosophy in fear of metaphysics, one that never extends beyond puzzles and problems; that a history guided by Christian principles be placed alongside of one inspired by anti-ecclesiastical sentiment; in general that a spirit of veracity assert itself, which would give an example, from the home of highest culture, not of vain arrogance, but of that mental firmness which, conscious of the limits of human knowledge, is also ready to believe. How can our universities remain the seats of sterling mental life, if the highest power of truth that has ever been, the Christian religion, is ignored there, and even maligned; and if in its stead is cultivated a philosophical-religious research which leads only to the negation of everything that hitherto was our ideal, and which gives birth to a mental anarchy, which, before the forum of history, makes it a principle of pauperization.

One point to be particularly emphasized is the VIOLATION OF RIGHTS AND THE OPPRESSION OF MENTAL LIBERTY, resulting from a party-rule in the realm of higher education. Under a government of law every one, assuming he possesses the necessary qualification, has an equal right to teach: this is elemental to freedom of teaching. The state with its institutions exists for the benefit of all classes, not for one certain class that has formed the notion that it is the sole bearer of science. Enemies of the state should be excluded from teaching, but not good citizens. Nor can it be demanded, as a necessary preliminary for academic teaching, that one must subscribe to the catch-phrases of any particular party, and so discard one's religious belief. And there is the violation of the rights of faithful Christian people. Since their money in the form of taxes maintains to a large extent the schools and their teachers, they surely can demand a conscientious administration of their interests, and a representation of the Christian view of the world, in a way becoming its past and its dignity; Christian people can demand that their sons receive an education in consonance with their Christian convictions, and that the universities will train officials, physicians, and teachers, in whom they may have confidence. If there are no other but state universities in a country, and these are monopolized by a free-thought party, then a condition of mental bondage will arise for those of a different mind. They are compelled either to have their sons forego the learned profession, or else expose them to an atmosphere wherein they see danger of a religious and moral nature, in ideas, association, and example. No right is left to them, but the right to pay taxes toward the budget of education, and then to look on how an irreligious party is striving to turn the higher schools into training camps of obligatory liberalism, and to monopolize the entire mental life for this purpose. Now and then there is great indignation against state monopolies; it is said, shall the state determine what kind of cigars I should smoke, and what I am to pay for them! Now, then, where is freedom if the majority of the Christian population is to be forced into taking mental nourishment it does not desire and rejects, and pay for it besides? If we recall to mind the past, which gave birth to the most venerable universities of the present, a sorrowful feeling comes over us. We see how far our colleges have deviated from their original purpose, how our governments have lost their old traditions. Promotion of the Christian religion and of the fear of God, was the lofty aim which their founders had in mind.

In bestowing the charter upon Vienna University, Duke *Albrecht* stated that he beheld in the university an institution " whereby the glory of the Creator in heaven and His true faith on earth would be furthered, knowledge would be increased, the state benefited, and the light of justice and truth brightened." And when, in 1366, he donated property to the university, he declared the object of the donation to be "that the university may increase the prosperity of the entire Church."

When Leopold I, on April 26, 1677, signed the charter of Innsbruck University he declared that he founded this university pre-eminently for the protection and prosperity of the Catholic Religion, as a means for its preservation, and also that many of those who had lost the faith might be led back to religion, for the honour and the glory of the Tyrol.

In the charter of Tübingen University, *Eberhard* of Württemberg states: "I believe I can do no better work, none more helpful to gain salvation, none more pleasing to the eternal God, than to provide with special diligence and emulation for the instruction of good and zealous young men in the fine arts and sciences, to enable them to recognize God, to know, to honour, and to serve Him alone." "In those days there was no hesitation to assign to science the loftiest vocation and to declare . . . that, coming from God, science should also lead back to Him as its origin. . . . The school was charged to work for the spread and the defence of the true belief. Christian truth was once queen at these universities; now, she has only too often become a stranger, to be denounced at times if she attempts to knock at the portals of her old home" (*Probst*).

FREE UNIVERSITIES

Another manner, to provide proper freedom of teaching, is open to the modern state by incorporating free universities. Unlike the state institutions, they are not directly controlled by the state, but are independent of it in their internal affairs; they are founded and managed by private persons or societies. Universities of this kind are found in Belgium and in England, to some extent in France, but their home is chiefly in the United States. At the head of the free university of the United States is the president, with a governing body and a board of trustees elected from members of the university; they appoint teachers, prescribe schedules of study and examinations, and conduct its business. True, the state cannot relinquish its right to oppose a system of teaching dangerous to the common weal; it will also provide that those to be licensed to practice the professions possess the necessary education and training; but the state refrains from further interference in the management of free universities.

It is no doubt difficult to establish by private means univer-

sities equally efficient with those of the state; in the countries
of Middle Europe this undertaking is perhaps more difficult than
elsewhere, but the possibility is there, and it is even realized
in some places. This, however, is not a question to occupy us
here; we merely wish to declare, if similar foundations are
about to be undertaken, and the necessary conditions are
present, then the state must not prevent them, it must grant
freedom in teaching.

True, the state is obliged to assist its subjects in acquiring
material and spiritual goods, but only in so far as private means
are insufficient thereto; the state must only act in a supple-
mental way. If it does that which its citizens themselves are
able to do, then the state is needlessly abridging their free
right. This includes the establishment of schools and the teaching in them. Presuming fitness, everybody has a NATURAL
RIGHT to teach others; hence, also, to found schools, whether
by himself or jointly with others. Furthermore, instruction
is a part of education, even at the university; it could
hardly be said of the graduate of the preparatory school
that his education is completed. Education, however, is a
matter for the parents. Their rights would be infringed upon,
if needlessly forced by the state to intrust their sons exclusively to the state colleges and to their method of teaching.
How could the state's exclusive right to teach be proved?
Does the pursuit of science belong to its domain? No one will
care to claim this. If science were to be allotted to the jurisdiction of any one body, the Church would be the first to enter
into consideration, because of her international and spiritual
character. Or is this right to be conceded to the state because
it is to be the bearer of culture? The state is to promote culture, but not to prescribe a certain brand of it. The argument
that private universities cannot be founded and conducted in
the proper way is certainly not borne out by the facts.

Even if the state, owing to its superior facilities, could provide
better universities than private effort, it would not be entitled to the monopoly; the fact of being able to do something
better does not secure the sole privilege of doing it. Moreover,
in order to attract students, free universities will have to

emulate state universities. The right of the state to found universities will of course not be disputed; but this right must not deteriorate into a disguised monopoly, that would grant privileges to its own universities, and deny them to free universities in order to put them out of existence. At any rate, the state will always retain considerable influence over the studies at free universities. It may require certain standards in candidates for political and professional positions, for judges and lawyers, teachers at state schools, physicians; it may insist upon state examinations, or it may make its stipulations for recognizing the examinations and academic degrees of the free schools.

By free schools of higher learning, a greater degree of freedom in teaching and in learning would be assured, or, speaking generally, a greater freedom in the intellectual life. If these higher institutions of learning are exclusively in the hands of the state, it cannot fail that the higher intellectual life will be dangerously dependent upon the state, or fall into the control of a dominating clique. As an example might be cited the restrictions placed upon jurisprudence by Prussia in the eighteenth century; the long-continued control of Hegelian philosophy; the Université Impériale of Napoleon; the predominance of anti-Catholic thought in our own schools. Universities, founded upon a positive, Christian basis, would surely be a comfort for thousands.

No need to say that such foundations may also be undertaken by the Church. This right cannot be denied to the Church, just as little as to any other corporation. Nay, much less! Because of its intellectual and international character science is most closely related to the Church. The latter, furthermore, has an eminent, historical right; no one has done more for the foundation and promotion of the European universities than the Church.

A remarkable and at the same time CHARACTERISTIC ATTITUDE towards free, particularly Catholic, universities is assumed by Liberalism. The stereotyped objection to Catholic universities is known; it can be reduced to this formula: At a Catholic university there can be no freedom in research nor freedom in teaching; but without them there can be no science; consequently, a Catholic university is a contradiction. It is

the same old song: there is but one science, there is but one freedom
— the free-thought that rejects belief. If it is really so obvious that
a Catholic university is a contradiction to science, hence incapable to
foster it, why the excitement? Either such universities are incompetent, or they are not. Let the experiment go on; the result will tell.
If the result is certain, as is claimed, very well, one may serenely await
it. Liberalism shows itself again here in the shape of that nasty hybrid
of freedom and intolerance for which it is known. It is the head of
Janus with its two faces: the one showing the bright mien of freedom, the other the sinister scowl of an intolerant tyrant. They shout
for freedom, freedom they demand; Church and Revelation are put
under the ban, because they restrain freedom. The state is denounced
as soon as it wants to interfere. But if others attempt research free
and independently, though not just so as Liberalism would like, then
tyranny immediately takes the place of liberty, the herald of freedom
resorts to oppression, and those who just now proclaimed the independence of universities from the state, who protested against the interference of the state in science, turn about and loudly call for the help of
the state, avowing that science can thrive only under state control.

The Church and the Universities

In discussing the position of the social authorities toward
freedom of teaching, we have chiefly considered the state. Of
the Church we shall say but a brief word. It will suffice to
recall what has been said previously; what has been stated
about the relation of the Church to freedom of research, applies
in many respects equally to freedom of teaching. Little will
have to be added. The Church, and the Church alone, has
received from her divine Founder the command to preserve the
doctrine of revelation and to proclaim it to mankind. " Going,
therefore, teach ye all nations " — this is the commission of
the Lord.

For this reason the teaching of the revealed truth, Theology,
is the privilege of the Church. But the rest of the sciences
will not be exempt from the obligation to listen to the admonition of the God-appointed authority, in all cases where
religious grounds are invaded. To the Church is intrusted the
religious-moral guidance of her faithful; she cannot remain indifferent, when in the public teaching of science a system is
followed detrimental to the Christian principles of the faithful.
And whoever has entered the Church by baptism, remains subject to her authority in all matters within her sphere.

The state must acknowledge these rights of the Church, or else forfeit its claim to be a Christian state; these rights, belonging to the essence of the Christian religion, are guaranteed by God, and are independent of human sanction. Hence, in case of clashes in this respect, the state must listen to the grievances of the Church; this will chiefly concern Theology, rarely other sciences. Thus it would be partially correct to say that the theological faculties are subject to the Church, but those of the rest of the sciences to the power of the state. But only partially; spiritual interests cannot be marked out by faculties. Interests of faith may be also violated in other faculties; then cases may arise which lose their purely worldly character, and extend into the religious sphere of the Church. If a professor should lecture on a matter touching closely upon interests of faith, for instance, Catholic Canon law or philosophy, and should show bias against Church and Christianity, deny its authority, distort and attack its tenets — then this would constitute an evident wrong to the Church and a flagrant violation of the interests which to guard it is her duty, especially in a country overwhelmingly Catholic. In that case the Church would be entitled to make expostulation.

In rejecting the protests of the Church in such cases, as being the interference of a foreign power, the state would thereby prove that it misunderstands both, the religious vocation of the Church and the proper relation between state and Church. For the faithful, whom the state calls its subjects, are also the subjects of the Church, they are the lambs and sheep the Church is to feed, in obedience to divine command. Church and state having in common the same subjects, and being closely connected for so long a time that it has become historical, it would be unnatural if they were to treat each other as strangers, such as might be expected in a heathen country, Japan, for instance. The nature of the case and the weal of the people demand harmonious action in such matters. It cannot be denied, moreover, that the Church commonly meets the state government to the extreme limit of her ability. About the divine rights of the Church opinions differ, but those able to fully appreciate the precious benefits of religion and morality will regard it as one of the greatest boons to humanity, that there exists within its fold an organization which protects with fearless, awe-inspiring majesty these benefits against all attacks, even against the state and its all-devouring policy of utility, and in this way defends the mental dignity of the human individual against oppression by the reckless reality of external life.

Just to show how an avowed free-thinker appreciates the significance of a commanding spiritual force as against the state we will quote the French positivist *A. Comte*, who declares: "The absorption of the spiritual by the worldly power is a return to barbarity; the separation of the two powers, however, is the principle for mental uplift and moral dignity." "True," says he, "men struggle in blind aversion against spiritual power of any kind; yet it will even then prevail, though in a mistaken way. Professors, authors, and newspaper writers will then pose as the speculative leaders of mankind, although they lack all mental and moral qualification for it" (Cours de philosophie positive).

Short-sighted perception may upbraid the Catholic Church; but a far-sighted judgment will have to concede that mankind owes gratitude to the Church and the Papacy. A noted Protestant writer remarks: "But for the Papacy the Middle Ages would have fallen a prey to barbarity. Even in our day the liberty of nations would be threatened with greatest danger if there were no Papacy. It is the most effective counterpoise to an omnipotent power of the state. If it did not exist, it would have to be invented" (*Hübler*).

FIFTH SECTION

Theology

CHAPTER I

THEOLOGY AND SCIENCE

NOW one other, the concluding point. So far our discussion has dealt almost exclusively with the profane sciences, and while there were often under discussion general principles, applying also to theology, we did not refer to the latter expressly for the reason that it occupies a special position in regard to our question. Theology is the science of the faith, its subjects are truths established by divine or inspired authority; hence, in teaching, authority plays a larger part in this than in any other science. For this reason much fault is found with theology, and many consider that it forfeits thereby its claim to rank as a science. They say it lacks all liberty, the results are prescribed; it lacks possibility of progress; nothing but rigid dogmas, rejecting all development and improvement; its vocation is exhausted by the incessant transmitting of the immutable; hence it lacks all the essential conditions of a true science, it has no claim to a place at the university; if it nevertheless has established itself at the university, as is the case in some countries, it must be considered as an alien body, a remnant of an obsolete time.

A keen eye cannot fail to detect in these words the prompting voice of that view of the world which rejects everything supernatural, and declares that Christian dogmatics and morals, and ideas of sin, redemption, humility of faith, cross, and self-denial, do no longer correspond to modern man. At bottom is the struggle between the two views of the world — one the philosophy of modern, sovereign man, the other the contemplation of the world in the light of Christianity: a process of repulsion, psychologically easily understood, by which the one seeks to expel

the other from the position which it desires to occupy. A
closer examination of the matter will show this.

THEOLOGY AS A SCIENCE

Is theology a science in the proper sense? May it rightly
claim a place among the branches of human science? This
shall be the first question to be answered. Theology, meaning
the doctrine of God, is the science of the Revelation, or of the
faith; of the Revelation which began in the Old Testament
and reached its perfection in Christ, the Son of God, in whom
appeared the fulness of God, the image of the glory of God,
the perfection of all religion; the Revelation intrusted to the
Church to be preserved infallibly, so that by these truths, and
means of salvation, the Church might guide and enrich the
life of believing mankind. Hence, in the broad sense in which
it is understood now, theology is the science that gathers the
revealed truths from their sources, endeavours to grasp and to
defend them, and to deduce new truths from them; which also
studies these truths and the means given for salvation, in their
development and effect in the Christian life.

Thus it includes a wide range of subordinate branches, connected by a common object. The biblical sciences have for
their subject Holy Writ; the sciences of introduction to the
Bible deal with its external history, with historical criticism
playing an important part; exegesis is occupied with the
scientific interpretation of the text and uncovers the treasures
of truth in Holy Writ, assisted in this task by hermeneutics
and a number of philosophical-historical auxiliary sciences.
Ecclesiastical history and its branches of patrology, history
of dogma, ecclesiastical archæology, and art, and other auxiliary
sciences, describe the doctrine of Revelation in its historical
course through the centuries, and its development in the bosom
of the Church. Dogmatics (with apologetics) and morals have
the task to explain and defend the doctrine of faith and morals,
as drawn from the Scriptures and from tradition, to deduce new
truths from them and to unite them all in a system. Finally,
Canon law, and even to a greater degree the departments of

pastoral theology, homiletics, liturgy, show how the treasures of Revelation and Redemption find their realization in the practical life of the Church and of the Christian people.

Hence there cannot be any doubt but that theology is a science in the proper sense, unless a wrong definition of science is presumed. Of course, if we should identify science in general with empirical science, and scientific methods with the methods of natural sciences and mathematics, and refuse to recognize any results as scientific except those gained by observation and mathematical calculation, then, of course, theology would not be a science, nor would many other branches of knowledge come under this head; the fault, however, would lie with a narrow conception, that limits itself to the portion of human knowledge within its vision, ignoring everything that exists beyond its horizon.

What are we to understand by science? It is the systematic concentration of the knowledge and the research of things according to their causes; hence of our cognition of a subject that can be proved by careful demonstration to be certain or at least probable. This we find to be the case in theology. It is the sum total, systematically arranged, of knowledge and researches concerning the tenets of faith, considered in the abstract, in their history, and in their effects on the life of the Church. Applying the method of natural thought, theology first studies the presumptions and foundations of faith, examines the sources of revelation by the philosophical and historical-critical method, proves the doctrines of faith by these sources, endeavours to grasp these truths intellectually, by the methods of analytical and synthetical thinking, and to make clear their connection. We have here the same methods as applied in other sciences: ascertaining the facts, definition of terms, deduction, induction. In respect to the history of the Church and to Canon law their similarity with analogous profane sciences is at once obvious.

There is one DIFFERENCE: in the theological sciences there is active, not only rational research, but also the BELIEF in revealed truths. In some departments, like that of ecclesiastical history, this difference is less pronounced, they proceed by the method of critically establishing and connecting the facts; but they, too, are guided by the conviction that there is in the life of the Church not only natural causation, but also supernatural principle. Dogmatics takes faith to a greater degree as its point of support, in order to connect natural reason with the convictions of faith, and how richly natural reason may unfold itself is shown in the works of *St. Augustine* and *St. Thomas,* on the great mysteries of the faith. As regards faith itself, we must keep in mind that it has a scientific foundation: the credibility of revelation is proven, it is a reasoning faith. It may be likened to history. The historian, on the testimony of his sources, believes in the actuality of human events, having convinced himself of the credibility of his sources; this belief becomes then his starting point for further researches of a pragmatical nature: he penetrates more deeply into the facts, and connects them according to their causal relations. The difference is this: the historian rests upon human authority, the theologian upon divine.

Yet the objection is raised: theology is faith, or at least rests on faith. Faith, however, has nothing to do with science; faith is sentiment, whereas science is knowledge. That this view of faith is wrong, and the result of subjective agnosticism that denies to man any positive understanding of supernatural truths, we have shown repeatedly. Certainly, if faith were nothing but sentiment, no science could be built upon it; you cannot build stone houses upon water. But the Catholic faith is not simply sentiment, it is a conviction of reason, based upon God's testimony that the revealed doctrines are true. In the same way that the historian — to use the comparison once more — believes positively in his historical facts, on the strength of the authority of a *Livy* or *Tacitus*, or accepts as proved some events of ancient times, relying upon the testimony of Babylonian tablets of clay or upon the pyramids, and makes these events his starting point for further researches, without having to fear objections to his work on the ground that knowledge and belief are incompatible; just so the theologian believes in his religious truths because they are vouched for by God's testimony. This proves that the foundation for his further thought is not formed by uncontrollable, irrational sentiment, but by a conviction of reason.

Hence, if by knowledge is meant nothing but a conviction of reason — and in this sense faith and knowledge are usually contrasted by modern philosophical writers — then faith is knowledge in the proper sense and a contradiction does not exist. If, however, knowledge is taken to be the understanding gained by personal insight without reliance on external testimony, then, of course, there is a distinction, and theology would not be a science, in so far as it BELIEVES; just as little as history would be a science, in so far as it believes its sources. But theology is a science, in so far as it makes use of experience and reason, examines its sources, draws from them the facts of faith, and makes them the starting point for its investigations.

Theology also has mysteries among its subjects, namely, truths whose actuality is cognizable, but whose contents, while not indeed inconsistent, yet remain obscure and incomprehensible to us. But even this does not impair its scientific character. Other sciences share with it this lot of human limitation. Instances are plentiful in natural science where the existence of natural forces of one kind or another is proven; of which it is able to form some idea, but cannot fathom; they remain a puzzle to science, sometimes presenting the greatest difficulties. For instance, ether, gravitation, electricity, the nature of motion, and so on. The noted physicist *J. J. Thomson* says: "Gravitation is the secret of secrets. But the very same holds good of all molecular forces, of magnetism, electricity, etc. There are in animated nature even more things we cannot understand. We could say that of the processes of living organisms we understand practically nothing. Our knowledge of indigestion, of propagation, of instinct, is so small that we can almost say it is limited to the enumeration of them. What we do know and understand is not one thousandth part of what would be necessary for a knowledge in any degree complete. 'If we raise an arm,' says *Pasteur*, 'or put our teeth in action,' we do something that no one can explain.' "

THEOLOGY AND PROGRESS

With a very superficial conception of theology we might easily arrive at the opinion that it lacks a characteristic of science, which, in our time especially, is insisted upon, namely, progress. For it must adhere to dogmas and not go beyond them. Hence, seemingly, there is nothing to do for theology but to transmit unchangeable truths, perhaps in different aspects, but nevertheless the same truths.

It must be admitted that one kind of progress is barred in theology, as also in other sciences; to wit, the progress of incessant remodelling and reshaping, the continuous tearing down of the old facts, the eternal search after truth without ever gaining its possession.

This is often the progress demanded. " The new tuition," it is said, " starts from the premise that the truth is to be searched for " (*Paulsen*). " Science is not a perfected doctrine, but a research, ever to be revised " (*Harnack*). It is particularly demanded of theology that it procure a FURTHER DEVELOPMENT OF CHRISTIANITY, and substitute for it thoughts which modern age has adopted and which it calls scientific thinking. " There remains the task," they say, " of expressing faith and its objects so as to coincide with the conception formed by scientific thinking of the natural and historical reality " (*Paulsen*). Hence miracles, the divinity of Christ, and mysteries of any kind, must be eliminated; even the notion of a personal God will have to be changed to a pantheistic notion: " After the great revolution in our cosmic theories we can no longer think of God, the eternal holy Will that we revere as First Cause of all things, as the ' first mover ' throning outside and above the universe, as *Aristotle* and *Thomas* did " (*Paulsen*).

Such a progress is impossible in theology, at least in Catholic theology, and in any other that still aims to be the theology of the Christian, revealed religion. It cannot be expected from theology, nor from any other science, that it will degrade itself to a fashionable science, that takes for its level not truth but the variable imperatives and moods of the times, and, destitute of character, changes with each varying fashion. The science of faith cannot assume this position, so much the less as it must be aware that its truths often clash with the inclinations of the human heart, and that its vocation is to lift up mankind, not to let itself be dragged down. This kind of progress therefore is barred. This, indeed, is not progress, but a hopeless wavering from pillar to post, a building and tearing down, acquiring without permanent possession, searching without finding.

TRUE PROGRESS can be shown in theology as in any other science.

The POSSIBILITY of progress is manifest, particularly, in

Church-history, in the biblical and pastoral sciences: they are closely related to the profane-historical, philological, social, and juridical branches of science, hence theology shares in their progress. It would seem that dogmatics would have to forego progress. Its progress certainly cannot consist in changing the revealed doctrines, nor in interpreting differently in the course of times the formulas of creed; here the rule is, *veritas Domini manet in aeternum.* The development of dogmatic knowledge consists rather in the following: the revealed truths are in the course of the centuries more and more clearly perceived and more sharply circumscribed, more surely demonstrated, more and more extensively appreciated in their connections, relations, and deductions. The sources of Divine Revelation flow the richer the more they are drawn from; their truths are so substantial, so abundant in relation to knowledge and life, that, the more research advances, the less it reaches its limit. "No one gets nearer to the realization of truth than he who perceives that in divine things, no matter how far he progresses, there remains always something more to be examined" (*Leo the Great*).

Consider the progress in mathematics. No one will say the mathematician is doomed to stagnation because he cannot change the multiplication table or the geometrical propositions. The increasing mathematical literature, with its big volumes, contradicts this notion; but its growth of knowledge is not the zigzag progress of restless to and fro, it is the solid progress from the seed to the plant.

As early as the fifth century *St. Vincent* of Lerin described the progress in dogmatical knowledge: "Sed forsitan dicet aliquis: Nullusne ergo in Ecclesia Christi profectus habebitur religionis? Habeatur plane et maximus. Nam quis ille est tam invidus hominibus, tam exosus Deo, qui istud prohibere conetur? Sed ita tamen, ut vere profectus sit ille fidei, non permutatio. Siquidem ad profectum pertinet, ut in semetipsum quaeque res amplificetur; ad permutationem vero, ut aliquid ex alio in aliud transvertatur. Crescat igitur oportet et multum vehementerque proficiat tam singulorum quam omnium, tam unius hominis, quam totius Ecclesiae, aetatum ac saeculorum gradibus, intelligentia, scientia, sapientia, sed in suo duntaxat genere, in eodem scilicet dogmate, eodem sensu eademque sententia. . . . Quodcunque igitur in hac Ecclesiae Dei agricultura fide Patrum satum est, hoc idem filiorem industria decet excolatur et observetur, hoc idem floreat et maturescat, hoc idem proficiat et perficiatur. Fas est etenim, ut prisca illa coelestis philosophiae dogmata processu temporis excurentur, limentur, poliantur, sed nefas est, ut commutentur, nefas, ut detruncentur, ut mutilentur."

The PROOF FOR THE ACTUAL PROGRESS of theology is furnished by its history. It shows how theology has gradually grown from the first seed of the divine Word, placed by the hand of God's Son into the soil of humanity, until it became a great tree, rich in branches and leaves. The holiest men of the Christian centuries, equipped with the choicest mental forces, enlightened by the light of grace, have worked on its growth; toiling and praying, they filled libraries with their books.

It is not our intention to outline here a sketch of this development. A few hints may suffice. Hardly had the faith taken root in the civilized nations of the old times when researches were begun. A long list of Holy Fathers and ecclesiastical authors were the bearers of the first development. Drawing upon Greek philosophy in aid and to deepen their thought in the mental battle against the ancient pagan view of the world, against Judaism and heresy, they elucidated more and more the tenets of faith and morals, and endeavoured to draw ever more fully from their spiritual contents. We encounter among the shining host men like *Tertullian, Cyprian, Clement of Alexandria, Origines, Cyril of Jerusalem, Basil, Gregory of Nyssa*, and many others, up to the powerful dogmatist of the old time, *Augustine*, who treated scientifically and often extensively the great dogmas of faith. Truly a voluminous theological literature with a plethora of genius and truth. The great edition of the Greek and Latin Fathers by *Migne* numbers 382 volumes in quarto, each of 1,500 pages or more in close print. Comparing with these 382 volumes the modest book of the Bible, which had been their foremost source, the progress of these centuries becomes manifest.

Soon the way was broken for systematizing the tenets of the faith, especially by *St. John Damascene* (eighth century). Scholasticism completed the work: it created a systematical whole and connected theology and philosophy, especially the Aristotelian, into a harmonious union. Its pioneers were *St. Anselm* and still more *Petrus Lombard* (died 1160). Then, in the Middle Ages, when universities began to flourish, there followed the great theologians *Alexander of Hales, Bonaventure, Albert the Great, Scotus*, and chief of all *Thomas of Aquin* (died 1274), in whom scholasticism reached its perfection, and undeniably one of the greatest minds known in the history of science; distinguished by an astonishing prolificness, still more by a wealth and depth of thought combined with the greatest simplicity and lucidity in presenting truths, he will for ever remain unapproachable. The decline of scholasticism during the fourteenth and fifteenth centuries was followed by a new bloom, when the life of the Church, rejuvenated by the Council of Trent, gave birth to new forces in theology. The mighty tomes of men like *Suarez, Lugo, Gregory of Valencia, Ruiz, Bañez, Billuart*, and others joined the volumes of their predecessors and continued their work. At the same time the various departments of the science were branching off more and more, and became independent.

M. Canus created the theory of theological cognition as an introduction to dogmatics, *Bellarmin* and *Th. Stapleton* founded the newer controversial theology. Moral Theology became in the sixteenth century a separate science and was developed by men like *Lugo, Laymann, Busembaum, Alphons of Liguori*. Similarly a new period of research began in the biblical sciences. Not that the first foundations were laid at that time; there had been *Origines*, who had become the founder of biblical text criticism by his "Hexapla"; the Antioch school of exegetes, *Chrysostomus, Hilarius*, and especially *Jerome*. But it was fostered with renewed zeal. The great Antwerp and Paris polyglots furnished aids, men like *Maldonatus, Salmeron, Toletus, Cornelius, á Lapide*, wrote their exegetic works. To the seventeenth century belongs the creation of the propædeutics, by *Richard Simon* and *Bernard Lami*. The monumental work, "Cursus sacrae scripturae" (since 1885), containing so far thirty-six volumes, demonstrates, among other things, that there has been in recent years no standstill in the research in Holy Writ. In the province of ecclesiastical history, too, with its branches and auxiliary sciences, new life was awakened at that time. In the sixteenth century, when the defence of the creed by the witnesses of a former age became urgent, patristics and history of dogma enjoyed their first rise. *Petavius* was prominently connected with them. How these sciences have been fostered in the nineteenth century is indicated by the names of *Mai, De Rossi, Hergenroether, Hefele, Pastor*. There remains to be mentioned the gradual establishment of the science of Canon law, of the pastoral-theological departments which have attained an independent position since the close of the eighteenth century, and since then produced a voluminous literature. The fear of a standstill in theological research seems unwarranted in the light of its history. The errors of the present time will prevent a standstill. The more vehement the attacks by natural science and philosophy, by philology and archæology, the more they seek to shake the foundations of the Christian religion, the stronger theology must grow by the combat. The solid progress of our times in knowledge and methodics will not remain without influence; nor can the empirical, the historical-critical method, the theory of evolution, and so on, fail to exert their stimulating influence upon theology.

The progress that Catholic theology has made since the days of the Fathers, the vast amount of mental work it has performed, is perhaps made most clear by a glance at the "Nomenclator literarius theologiae catholicae," by *H. Hurter* (2d ed., 3 vols.; the 3d ed. is in 6 vols., 5 being ready). It gives in concise briefness the biographical data and the more important works of Catholic theologians of greater repute. Counting the names there presented, we find not less than 3,900 from 1109 to 1563; about 2,900 from 1564 to 1663; about 3,900 between 1664 and 1763; finally, from 1764 to 1894 about 4,000 theological authors; hence in the period from 1109 to 1894 nearly 14,700 theologians. That these 14,700 scientists — and their number is not exhausted by this figure — should have written their works without offering in them any new knowledge, would surely be a bold assertion! In addition consider the long rows of tomes which some of them wrote. Perhaps it would not be wholly amiss to refer to the restless zeal of many of them, as recorded by their biographers. *Baronius* (died 1607) could truthfully assert before his death, that for thirty years he had never had sufficient sleep; he usually slept only four or five hours. *Pierre Halloix* (died 1656) likewise was content with four or five hours of rest. *Dionysius Sanmarthanus* (died 1725) gave only four hours to sleep and devoted less than half an hour daily to recreation; likewise *Fr. Combéfis* (died 1679), during the last forty years of his life. *A. Fr. Orsi* (died 1761) contented himself with three or four hours of sleep; *Fr. Clement* (died 1793) and *H. Oberrauch* (died 1808) are said to have slept but two hours daily. *J. Caramuel de Lobkowicz* (died 1682) persevered for fourteen hours every day at his books; *Chr. Lupus* (died 1681) even for fifteen hours daily. The theologian *Lessius* is characterized by "*Parcissimus erat temporis, laboris pertinax*"; the same holds good of hundreds of others of these men.

A science, enumerating its disciples by so many thousands, with the greatest intellects among its workers, which has commanded so much zeal and work for centuries, should be safe from the reproach of having back of it a history of stagnation.

THEOLOGY AND FREEDOM OF SCIENCE

To many it seems obvious that theology lacks at least the other predicate of science, freedom; because it is bound to dogmas and ecclesiastical authorities, at least Catholic theology is.

Although this claim is pressed persistently and with confidence, we may dispose of it very briefly. The freedom missed in theology, and demanded in its behalf, is none other than the liberal freedom of science, the nature of which we have had sufficiently long under the searchlight, so that there remains nothing to be added. We have proved sufficiently that this freedom is not a freedom from unnatural fetters, but a dissolute subjectivism, that claims the right not to be bound to any unchangeable, religious truths. We admit that the Catholic theology does not possess THIS freedom. Convinced of the truth of the doctrines established by divine testimony, and by the infallible voice of the Church, theology sees not freedom but a sin against truth in the license to assert the contrary of what it has recognized as the truth.

There is but one freedom which science may claim: it is freedom from hindrance in reaching the truth in its legitimate domain. If this truth is transmitted to science infallibly, by the highest instance of wisdom — and of this every theologian is convinced — how can science be said to be hindered thereby in attaining the truth? Restrained it is, but only by truth: truth, however, can only be a barrier to license, but not to precious freedom. This restraint theology shares with the rest of the sciences. The physicist is tied to the facts brought forth by the experiments of his laboratory; the astronomer is tied to the results reported to him by the instruments of his observatory, the historian is tied to the events disclosed by his sources. Moreover, all sciences are tied to their methods. In this way, and in no other way, the theologian, too, is tied to the facts given him by Revelation, and to his method. Every science has its own method. The astronomer gains his facts by observation and calculation, the mathematician arrives at his facts by calculation and study; the historian, by human testimony; the theologian, however, by divine testimony, at least as to fundamental truths. That they are transmitted to him not by his personal study, but by external testimony, does not matter; the historian too draws from such sources. Nor can theological knowledge be less certain because vouched for by divine authority: it makes it the more certain. Or is there no divine authority, and can there be none? This is exactly the silent presumption, which is the basis of the charge against theology. But where is the proof for it? It can only be demonstrated by denying the existence of a supermundane God; for, if there is an Almighty God, there can be no doubt that He can give a Revelation and demand belief.

Perhaps it may be said further, the theologian is not permitted to doubt his doctrines, hence he is prohibited from examining them; he surely cannot be UNPREPOSSESSED.

We can refer to what we have previously said. Unprepossession demands but one thing, namely, not to assume something as true and certain that is false or unproved; it demands strong proofs for anything that needs proof. We may safely assert that there is no other science more exacting in this respect than Catholic theology, both of the present and of the past. It has not a single position that is not incessantly tested by attacks as to its tenability. Any one not unacquainted with theology, who knows the works of *St. Thomas* and of the later theologians, with their exact methods of thinking, who observes the conscientious work in Catholic biblical-exegetic, historical-critical field, must be convinced of the serious atmosphere of truth prevailing here. Unprepossession does not demand to doubt, time and again, that which has been positively proved, to rediscover it by new research. Positive facts are no longer a subject for research; in their case research has fully achieved its end. Methodical doubt, proper in scientific examination, is proper also in regard to religious truths.

Furthermore, the latitude of the theologian is much larger than presumed by those who derive their information solely from modern assertions about dogmatic bondage. One may safely assert that the freedom of movement of the mathematician is more limited by his principles, his train of thought more sharply prescribed, than is the case with the theologian. Of course the theologian is bound by everything he finds infallibly established directly by revelation and by the authority of the Church; or indirectly by the concurring teaching of the Fathers or the theologians; he is bound also by non-infallible decisions, especially those of congregations, though not absolutely and not irrevocably.

But this is only the smaller part of his province. In many departments, like the one of ecclesiastical history, there are almost no restrictions to his research, except those imposed by historical facts. Canon law and similar departments dealing with the laws of the Church, coincide in method and liberty of research with the profane science of law. Of all departments of theology, the dogmatical is the one most affected by the authority of faith. Yet even here a great deal is left to unhampered work. Many a void has to be filled, many a question solved, which the theology of the past has never taken up; even the defined truths still offer a large scope for personal work, in regard to demonstration, or to the philosophic-speculative penetration of the dogmas and their interpretation.

As a fact, the reader of theological literature, both old and new, will, in a multitude of cases, meet with unrestrained individuality.

ECCLESIASTICAL SUPERVISION OF TEACHING

The ENCYCLICA against Modernism (September 8, 1907) gave rise to fears that any free movement would henceforth be impossible for Catholic theology. These fears referred chiefly to the disciplinary measures, prescribed by the Encyclical for the purpose of supervising theological teaching in each diocese. Then came the papal Motu Proprio, of September 1, 1910, which, among other things, required the teacher of theology to confirm by oath his confession of the Creed and his intention to repudiate modernistic errors. Since then many a complaint has been heard about espionage and coercion. Similar complaint, about an imminent debasement of the Church, has been raised whenever important measures in the discipline of the Catholic Church were published, and they emanated primarily from the camp of the enemy.

It is not to be denied, however, that such an energetic call for watchfulness and action, issued from the highest ecclesiastical watchtower, like the one referred to, may lead in some cases to anxiety and false suspicions. This is no doubt regrettable; but it is an incident common to human legislation and will surprise no one who has any experience of life. A glance at these decrees will show that they are nothing more than an urgent injunction, and the exercise of that supervision of religious life and teaching which pertains to the authority of the Catholic Church, and which has been practised by her at all times. The language is urgent, it has a severity which is softened in the execution. Its explanation lies in the eminent danger of the modernistic movement to the continuance of Catholic life. Modernism, as described and condemned by the Encyclica, is nothing less than the absolute destruction of the Catholic faith, and of Christianity.

The Protestant theologian, Prof. *Tröltsch,* wrote after the publication of the Encyclica: " As viewed from the position of curialism and of the strict Catholic dogma, there existed a real danger. Catholicism had gotten into a state of inner fermentation, corresponding to the same condition caused by modern theology within the Protestant churches."

The danger of Modernism is often enhanced by a deceptive semblance of the right faith, and by the pretence to urge only the righteous interests of modern progress against obsolete forms of thought and life, now and then also by its secret propaganda. Hence this intervention by a firm hand, and this only after having waited a long time. They were measures of prevention, like those taken to stave off a serious danger; the tidal wave receding, their urgency disappears automatically.

The German bishops stated in their pastoral letter of December 10, 1907, that in some Catholic lay-circles there was uneasiness about the Encyclical, fearing that it might endanger scientific endeavour and independence in thought and research, and that the Church intended to prohibit or render impossible co-operation in solving the problems of civilization. "May they all recognize," they said, "how groundless such fears are! The Church desires to set bars only to one kind of freedom — the freedom to err." If the rules and precepts of the Church do sound harsh sometimes, it is because the Church adheres unconditionally to the principle: The truth above all. "The Church has at no time opposed the true progress of civilization, but only that which hinders its progress: heedlessness, haste, the mania for innovation, the morbid aversion against the truth that comes from God. But we Catholic Christians can join free and unhampered, with all our strength and talent, in the peaceful strife of noble, intellectual work and genuine mental education."

The fears of too great a pressure by the ecclesiastical authorities have been given trenchant expression in most recent times by a man who, while standing outside of the Catholic Church, has always shown himself well disposed towards it, namely, the noted pedagogue, *Fr. W. Förster* of Zurich. *Förster* has won merit and distinction by his manly and spirited defence of the Christian view in pedagogical science and mental culture. In the book referred to he again describes urgently the worthlessness and fatality of modern individualism, that knows a good deal about freedom but nothing of self-discipline, nor of authority or tradition, and which represents most superficial amateurism in the domain of religion and morals. Then he turns to criticize Church practice; and his criticism becomes a sharp accusation. His main charge is "fatal restraint of the spirit of universality." "Some groups in the Church," he asserts, "of mediocre learning, have established a clique rule, under which the others, the more creative and intensive souls, become the victims of intolerance, espionage, and false suspicion"; "universality, which unites the different mental tendencies, has given way to separation"; "everywhere a one-sided denunciatory information of the leading circles by accidentally ruling groups and factions; anxious intolerance for everything unusual, disciplinary austerity and unintelligent pedantry, individualistic and unchristian spirit of distrust and mutual espionage"; "levelling of the mental life"; "one is tired," we are told, "of the spirit of incessant disciplining"; "of the invariable cold and disdainful forbidding and repression." In the Middle Ages and earlier times it was different; then "universality was the ruling spirit, the working of the many into a unit full of life; this policy was changed for no other reason than because of the struggle of the Church against Protestantism." "The greatest harm that Catholicism suffered by the great rupture of the sixteenth century is most likely seen in the tendency of the Church to view thenceforth religious freedom within Catholic Christianity with an anxious, even hostile eye."

Readers of the literature of the day will recognize here views often met with during the last years, and the same excited note, which is quite in contrast to the even temper that ordinarily characterizes *Förster's* books. But what the reader will not find stated are the proofs for these enormous accusations.

Undeniably, things have happened in the wide range of ecclesiastical authority that cannot be approved. But where are the facts that would justify charges of such sweeping nature? A Protestant author can hardly be presumed to possess such a direct and positive insight into the ecclesiastical practice of the higher and the highest order, to give convincing strength to his bare assertion. Or is the number of dissatisfied voices that make these charges sufficient proof in itself? If the ecclesiastical authority be allowed, now and then, to emerge from its passiveness to take measures against dangerous doctrinal tendencies, is it not to be expected, as a matter of course, that some minds become disgruntled and complain about oppression and clique rule? Or must that right be denied the Church altogether? *Förster* says himself: "The spirit of dignity and responsibility has never ruled all parts of the hierarchy in the same measure as now, and rarely if ever were there found in its leading circles so many men leading an almost holy life as at present." And yet we are asked to believe that it was reserved exactly for this worthy hierarchy, and for these saintly men, to forget the traditions of the Church in the most irresponsible manner. One will have to say: "If *Förster* would examine without bias the situation and apply consistently in respect to authority the principles that he himself defends, he would be convinced that the Church could not have acted any differently than it did in regard to the regrettable events of the last years, and that it has ever been the aim of the Church, before the sixteenth century as after, to guard carefully the purity of traditions of faith against any attack" (Prof. *G. Reinhold* in a review of *Förster's* book).

The Church has never known a universality that did not oppose doctrinal errors. The Middle Ages did not know it; one need only read the many condemnations from Nicholas I. to Innocence VIII.; nor was such a universality known to the great Councils of ancient

Christianity up to the Nicæan, which hurled its anathema against numerous teachings that opposed no dogmas defined at that time; nor did the Holy Fathers know such a universality, nor the Apostles, with their strict admonitions of unity of faith. The reply is made, the "Church must not yield the least of its fundamental truths," that "its centralizing power ought to remain within the region of the most essential"; whereas she actually exercises it in the domain of the incidental. The ecclesiastical supervision of teaching has never limited itself to the most essential, nor would this practice ever accomplish the object to preserve pure the doctrine of faith. Furthermore, what is the "most essential" what is the "incidental"? *Förster's* book does not inform us about this most important question. The views against which the Church has made front in the last years, do they relate only to the incidental? Does this apply to the doctrines of a *Rosmini* and *Lamennais*, who are referred to in passing? No well-informed theologian will assert this.

We shall hardly be wrong in assuming that the charge of overstraining the ecclesiastical authority is based upon a presumption of a philosophical nature, which is in evidence in several other passages of the book — on the view, namely, that in religion the intellectual moment should recede before the mystical, before anticipation and inner experience. Hence the severe censure of "the narrow autocracy of the intellectual interpretation" against the "preponderance of the intellectual contemplation" in the Church, which is said to have become so prevalent as to exert unavoidably a paralyzing effect upon the entire religious life. Here we have the result of the notion that theory of life, religion, and faith, depend but little on rational knowledge. This notion is also in accord with the argument about the impossibility of an independent scientific ethics. We have discussed this elsewhere. We demonstrated that religion and faith relate to positive truths that can be realized, and that can therefore be accurately defined; they must be so defined. Of course this realization need not be a scientific one, it can be of the natural kind that is not clearly conscious of its reasons. *Förster*, too, touches upon this important distinction when quoting *Saitschick*: "The inner perception overtowers feeling and logical reason — here, too, lies the source of a light shining brighter, stronger, and incomparably more true than any light of reason"; and again, when his advice is, to foster to a greater extent the "inner perception." What is felt here vaguely has long since been expressed much more lucidly in Christian philosophy.

Certainly a view that fails to lay, first of all, absolute stress on the protection of the DOCTRINE of faith cannot understand the Catholic point of view; it will assume only too easily that the supervision relates to incidentals. It will also engender a criticism against which the Church may rightly protest, because it starts from presumptions that do not apply to the Church.

No one will be astonished to find a Protestant author lacking the clarified conception of the supernatural character of the Church that is possessed by the Catholic; to see him view the Church almost invariably in the light of a human organization, similar to the Protestant denominations which he may cite before the court of his individual reason and force to bow under the yoke of his criticism. The Catholic has a better understanding of the words: "I am with you all days, even unto the consummation of the world." There will be foreign to his mind the idea that the Church has since the days of Reformation, for now nearly four centuries, deviated from the right way, and degenerated more and more to a separatistic and insignificant community; a church able to forget its traditions to the extent of grossly misconceiving its proper sphere of authority, and fettering itself in a narrow spirit to incidentals, could not keep his confidence any longer.

The Oath Against Modernism

The Motu Proprio of September 1, 1910, decreed that teachers of theology, and also Catholic priests generally, had to bind themselves by oath to reject modernistic heresies, and to accept obediently the ecclesiastical precepts. Dispensed from this pledge were only the professors of theology at state institutions, to spare them difficulties with state authorities.

This anti-modernist oath at once became the signal for a storm of indignation, than which there has been hardly a greater one since the days of the Vatican Council. A cry was raised for freedom of science, for the exclusion of theological faculties, even for another "Kulturkampf." The General Convention of German college professors, held at Leipzig January 7, 1911, issued a declaration to the effect that "All those who have taken the anti-modernist oath have thereby expressed their renunciation of an independent recognition of truth and of the exercise of their scientific conviction, hence they have forfeited all claim to be considered independent scientists." Interpellations were made in legislative bodies, it was demanded that the option of taking the oath should be taken away from university professors, because "the dignity of the universities would be lowered if their members had the opportunity to bind themselves by such an oath."

Even threats were made by statesmen, hinting at reprisals by the state, because its interests were being jeopardized, while, on the other hand, there were those who declared: "If the Catholic Church thinks it necessary for her ecclesiastical and religious interests to put her servants under oath, it is her own business;

neither the state nor the Evangelical Church have a right to interfere " (Prime Minister *Bethmann-Hollweg,* in the Prussian Diet, on March 7, 1911).

The agitation of the minds will soon subside, as on former occasions of this kind; and, with calm restored, people will find, as *J. G. Fichte* told the impulsive *F. Nicolai,* one hundred and thirty years ago, that the fact has only just been discovered that the Catholics are Catholic.

Yes, indeed, the Catholics are Catholic, and desire to remain Catholic — this and nothing else is the gist of the anti-modernist oath. It does not oblige to anything else but what was believed and adhered to before. It obliges to accept the doctrines of faith; but they are the old truths of the Catholic Church, propounded and believed at all times, and the necessary inferences from them. Even the proposition that truths of faith can never be contradicted by the results of historical research, or by human science in general, is as old as faith itself. In addition, the oath avows obedient submission to Church precepts; but this has been demanded for centuries by the *professio fidei Tridentina,* a pledge by oath to which every professor of theology has been before obliged: *Apostolicas et ecclesiasticas traditiones reliquasque eiusdem Ecclesiae observationes et constitutiones firmissime admitto et amplector.* This was the opinion of all competent judges on this theological question. " We are convinced," declared correctly a prominent theological institution, " that there is not assumed by this oath any obligation new in subject, and no obligation not already existing. The oath is but the affirmation of a duty already imposed by conscience " (the professors of Theology of Paderborn, December 12, 1910). The Breslau faculty said, in the same sense: " The faculty does not see in the so-called anti-modernist oath any new obligation, nor one exceeding the rule of faith ever adhered to by the faculty." And this declaration was fully approved of by Rome.

Cardinal *Kopp,* at the session of the German Upper House on April 7, 1911, commented on these statements as follows: " Against the opinions of these circles (having a different opinion of the oath) I set the testimony and the statement of the most competent people, to wit, the professors of university faculties and also those at episcopal seminaries. Those who have taken the oath, as well as those who have refrained from it by the privilege granted them by the Holy See, they both declare positively that the oath does not contain any new obligations, nor does it impose new duties on them; hence that, on the contrary, they are not impeded in the pursuit of their tasks as teachers and of their scientific work of research. Now, gentlemen, I do not think it would be proper to insinuate that these earnest men, appointed by the Government, or at least in office by its consent, would make this declaration against their conviction and not in full sincerity."

No wonder, therefore, that of the hundreds of thousands of Catholic priests hardly a handful have refused the oath.

Nor is there anything new in the obligation to swear and subscribe in writing to a confession of creed. Very often in the course of the centuries decrees of creed and symbols had to be subscribed to in writing. In the days of Jansenism, when priests were required to swear to and sign a statement, many Jansenists tried to dodge this oath, and the Jansenist *Racine* complained that this demand was un-heard-of in the Church. Thereupon the learned theologian *Tournely* and others cited a number of examples of this kind from the history of the Church.

Therefore the anti-modernist oath has not created anything new. Consequently it has not changed anything in regard to the freedom of theological research. It is the same as before; nor has the oath changed anything in the quality of theological professors, they merely promise to be what they must be anyway; nor can, for instance, the oath induce the Catholic priest, in teaching profane history, to present the history of the Reformation in a different light than before, and thus render him unfit to teach history; the oath has created no new, confessional differences, hence has given no justified cause for excitement—provided one has the needed theological comprehension of the oath. If one has not this insight, and will not trust to information from a competent source, then it will be the act of prudence to leave the test to the future; and we can await this test serenely.

We referred above to the declaration of German college teachers, to the effect that all who have taken the oath have thereby expressed their renunciation of independent cognition of truth. These stereo-typed ideas we have so often heard, with the same haziness and inconsistency. "Because they have thereby expressed the renunciation of independent cognition of the truth," namely, by the acceptance of certain doctrines. But is not every one who clings to his Christian belief bound by this very fact to certain doctrines? Does every one who still prays his Credo express the renunciation of his independence? If the argument quoted is to mean anything at all, it means the full rejection of all Christian duty to believe; indeed, this is the real sense of this " independent recognition of truth," as we have already seen. But cannot some one, because of his conviction, renounce this independence and believe, and in this conviction accept the doctrines of the Church? If this conviction is his, and he affirms it by oath, how can any one see in this oath a want of freedom, nay, a renunciation of truth? If an atheist solemnly declared his intention to be and to remain an atheist, he would hardly be accused of lack of character by the advocates of modern freedom of thought. The judge, the military officer, the member of a legislature, the professor, who must all take the oath of allegiance, — all of these will have to be protected against the insinuation of disloyalty to truth. If a man affirms by oath his unalterable Catholic faith, he is without any hesitation accused of untruthfulness. The government has been urged to forbid this spontaneous exercise of Catholic sentiment. The inconsistency of modern catch-phrases can hardly be given more drastic expression. In order to guard the freedom of thought the government is to forbid one from pledging himself to his own principles; in order to remain an independent thinker a man must be forced by penal statute to confess unconditionally the brand of free science prescribed by a certain school and by no means have an opinion of his own; in order to be free in his research the teacher in theology must be tied to the catch-phrases of liberal philosophy. This is modern freedom, a hybrid of freedom and bondage, of sophistry and contradiction, of arrogance and barrenness of thought, which will exert its rule over the minds as long as they are guided by half-thinking.

Bonds of Love, not of Servitude

People to whose mind Catholic thinking is foreign will never be able to appreciate the energetic activity of the Church authority.

On close examination, however, they will not deny that, IF the Christian treasure of faith is to be preserved undiminished, IF in the hopeless confusion and the unsteady vacillation of opinions in our days there is to be left anywhere a safe place for truth and unity of faith, this cannot be accomplished otherwise than in the shape of a strong authority that has the assurance of the aid of God.

The Catholic theologian may be permitted to point in exemplifying this fact to the recent history of Protestantism and of its theology. Protestantism does not acknowledge a teaching authority; its theology demands complete freedom of research and teaching, making the most extensive use of both. The result is the demoralization of the Christian faith, which is speeding with frightfully accelerated steps to total annihilation. The very danger which Modernism threatened to carry into the Catholic Church has overwhelmed Protestant theology: the metaphysical ideas of a modern philosophy penetrated it without check, and killed its Christian substance. The measures against Modernism were sharply criticized by many Protestants who, at the same time, laid stress upon the fact that nothing of the sort could happen among themselves. Indeed it could not, at least not consistently with Protestant principle. But there is not a single fact in all history which demonstrates more clearly the necessity of the Catholic authority of faith, than just the condition of Protestantism at the present time. On the part of believing Protestants this is admitted, if not expressly, then at least in practice. To stem the destructive work of liberal theology they resort to authority; invoke Evangelical formulas of confession, the traditional doctrine, sometimes even the aid of the state; neological preachers are disciplined by censures, even by dismissal, against the loud protest of the liberals. Such action is easily understandable; one cannot hear without sadness the cry for help of pious Protestantism, a cry that grows more desperate every day; one cannot help regretting its forlorn situation in view of the millions of souls whose salvation is jeopardized, who are in danger of being despoiled of the last remains of their Christian faith. Yet it must be admitted that this cry for authority and obedience signifies the abandoning of the Protestant principle, and the involuntary imitation and therefore acknowledgment of the Catholic principle — for the Catholic an incentive to cleave the more closely to his Church.

Many to whom the Catholic way of thinking is foreign, look upon the duty of obedience which ties the Catholic to his Church as a sort of servitude; to the Catholic it is the tie of love, uniting free people to a sacred authority. Many look upon the Church of Rome as a tyrannical curia, where Umbrian prelates are cracking their whips over millions of servile and ignorant souls; to the Catholic the Church is the divinely appointed institution of truth, that possesses his fullest confidence. He knows that history has given the most magnificent justification to the Catholic principle of authority. Opinions have come and gone, systems were born and have died, thrones of learning rose and fell; only one towering mental structure remained standing upon the rock of God-founded authority in the vast field of ruins with its wrecks of human wisdom. And its ancient Credo, prayed by all nations, is the same Credo once prayed by the martyrs.

CHAPTER II

THEOLOGY AND UNIVERSITY

"HE is not for our turn, and he is contrary to our doings"; thus spoke in bygone ages the children of this world. "Let us therefore lie in wait for the just. . . . He boasteth that he hath the knowledge of God and calleth himself the Son of God" (Wisdom ii, 12 *seq.*). Centuries later the children of the world treated in the same manner God's Son and His doctrine. And in these days, when the science of the faith is to be driven from the rooms of the school, let us recall that in olden times the children of the world planned similarly.

In the days when the private and public life of Europe's nations was permeated with the Christian faith, and their ideas were still centred in God and eternity, then the science of the faith was held to be the highest among the sciences, not only by rank but in fact.

And when, in the budding desire for knowledge, they erected universities, the first and largest of them, Paris University, was to be the pre-eminent home of theology, and wherever theology joined with the other sciences it received first honours. Thus it was in the days of yore, and for a long time. The secular tendency of modern thought led to the gradual emancipation of science from religion; unavoidably, its aversion for a supernatural view of the world soon turned against, and demanded the removal of, the science representing that view. Reasons for the demand were soon found. Thus the removal of theology from the university has become part and parcel of the system of ideas of the unbelieving modern man; the liberal press exploits the idea whenever occasion offers. Resolutions to this effect are introduced in parliaments and diets, meetings of young students are echoing the ideas heard elsewhere. No wonder that the Portuguese revolution of 1910 had nothing more urgent to do than to close the theological faculty at Portugal's only university.

What are the REASONS advanced? Many are advanced; the main reason is usually disguised; we shall treat of it when concluding. In the first place we are again met by the old tune of free science, which has been in our ears so long; the rooms of the colleges, it is said, are destined for a research which seeks truth with an undimmed eye, and not for blindfolded science confined to a prescribed path.

No need to waste words on this. Just one more reference may be permitted us, namely, to the study of law. There is hardly another science with less latitude than the science of law. Its task is not to doubt the justification of state laws, but to look upon constitutions and statutes as established, to explain them, and by doing so to train efficient officials and administrators of the law. When explaining the civil code the teacher of law has small opportunity for pursuing " free search after truth "; neither will his pupil be tested at examinations in the maxims of a free research that accepts no tradition; he will have to prove his knowledge of the matter that had been given to him. Yet no one has ever objected to the teaching of jurisprudence at the university. Therefore the objection cannot be valid that theology is restricted to the established doctrines of its religion and has to transmit them without change to its future servants. It should be borne in mind that our universities are not intended for research only, but also, and chiefly, for training candidates for the professions.

This disposes at the same time of the objection that theology has to serve ecclesiastical purposes outside of and foreign to science. Religious science, like any other science, serves the desire that strives for truth. True, it serves also for the practical training of the clergyman for his vocation. But shall we eliminate from science the interests of practical life? Then medicine and legal science would also have to be excluded, and for these there would be planted only sterile theories, and the universities transformed into a place of abstract intellectualism.

Again it is argued that religion and faith are not really cognition and knowledge, but only the products of sentiment, and hence theology has no claim to a place among the sciences; that religion can only be a subject for psychology which lays bare its roots in the human heart, and a subject for the history of religion, to trace its historical forms and to study its laws of evolution — sciences which belong to the philosophical faculty.

Thus we come back to the principles of an erroneous theory of knowledge. No need to demonstrate again that the Christian belief is built upon the clear perception of reason, and that it is not a sentimental but a rational function.

But has not the Church her theological seminaries? Let theology seek refuge there! We answer the Church herself desires this; she does not like theological faculties, they are in her eyes a danger to the faith.

Now, IF the Church would be deprived of her authoritative influence upon the appointment of professors at theological faculties and upon the subject of their teachings, consequently, IF there would be jeopardized the purity of belief of the candidates for priesthood, and through them of the people, then, we admit, the Church would rather forego theological faculties at state-universities. This could not be done without considerable injury to the public prestige of the Church, to her contact with worldly sciences and their representatives and disciples, even to the scientific study of theology. In the latter particularly by the loss of the greater resources of the state, and by the absence of inducement to scientific aim, which is more urgent for theologians than for others at college. Neither would the state escape injury, because of the open slight and harm to religion, and of lessening its contact with the most influential body in Christian countries. But if the Church is assured of her proper influence on the faculties, she has no reason for an unfriendly attitude toward them. The object the Church seeks to achieve in her seminaries is the clerical education of her candidates, their ascetic training, the introduction into a life of recollection and prayer, into an order of life befitting priests; this cannot be sufficiently done in the free life at the university.

This is not a bar to scientific instruction by the theological faculty. Seminary and faculty supplement one another. We see very frequently, at Rome and outside of Rome, the theological school separated from the seminary with the approval of the Church. But all these objections do not give the real reason, the roots lie deeper.

When the Divine Founder of our Religion stood before the tribunal of Judea He said: "My kingdom is not of this world: if my kingdom were of this world, servants would strive for me." This was the whole explanation of why He stood there accused. The guardian of the doctrine of her Master may use these words to explain the fact that, in the eyes of many, she stands to-day accused and defamed. The mind of modern man has forsaken the world of the Divine and Eternal; no longer is he a servant of this kingdom. His ideals are not God and Heaven, but he himself and this world; not the service of God, but human rights and human dignity. This view of the world, which cannot grasp the wisdom of Jesus Christ, and which takes offence at the Cross, also takes offence at a science that confesses as the loftiest ideal *Jesum Christum, et hunc crucifixum.*

The real kernel of the question is: Does the Christian religion in its entirety still serve the purpose of to-day — or does it not? is it to remain with us, the religion wherein our fathers found the gratification of their highest mental aims, the religion that gave Europe its civilization and culture, that created its superior mental life, and still rules it to this hour? Or shall religion be expelled by a return to a heathendom which Christianity had overthrown? "We do not want Him to rule over us" — there is the real reason for the modern antipathy to Catholic theology. Else, whence the excited demand for its removal? Because it is superfluous? Even if this were the fact, there is many a category of officials, the little need of which can be demonstrated without difficulty, yet no one grows excited about it; many expenditures by the state are rather superfluous, yet there is no indignation. No, the matter at issue is not so much the scientific character of theology, nor misgivings about its progress or its freedom; the real question is this:

Do we Desire to Remain Christians?

For IF we still recognize the Christian religion as the standard for our thought, IF we are persuaded that it must remain the foundation of our life, then there can be no doubt that its facts, its truths, and standards of life require scientific presentation;

then it cannot be disputed that this science is entitled to a place alongside of the science of law, of chemistry, or Indology. Indeed, then it must assume the first place in the system of sciences.

Surely a science ranks the higher, the higher its object and its sources, the surer its results, and the greater its significance for the most exalted aim of mankind. The subject of theology is God and His works, the ultimate causes of all things in God's eternal plan of the universe, the "wisdom of God in a mystery, a wisdom which is hidden, which God ordained before the world, unto our glory" (1 Cor. ii. 7). Therefore it is wisdom; for "the science of things divine is science proper" (Augustinus, De Trinit. xii, 14). A science, having as its subject Greek architecture, geography, or physical law, may claim respect, yet it must step back before a science of Religion, that rises to the highest sphere of truth by a power of flight that participates in the omniscience of the Holy Ghost; for such is the faith. For this reason its results, in so far as they rest on faith, are more certain than the results of all other sciences.

Finally, the aims of life which theology serves are not physical health or advantages in the external life, but the knowledge of God, the spread of His kingdom on earth, and the eternal goal of all human life.

So long as the Christian religion is the valued possession of the people of a country, and the roots of their lives rest more in Christianity than in mathematics, astrophysics, or Egyptology, so long is the science of religion entitled to a seat at the hearth of the sciences; and the people, then, have the right to demand that the servants of religion get their education at the place where the other leading professions get their training. If the state considers it its duty to train teachers of history and physics for the benefit of its citizen, then it is still more its duty to help in the education of the servants of religion, who are called upon to care for more important interests of the people and state than all the rest of the professions. Let us consider the task of universities. As established in the countries of central Europe, they are destined to foster science in the widest sense, and to educate the leading professions; to be the hearth for the sum total of mental endeavour, this is their vocation; hence all things that contain truth and have educational value should join hands here. To eliminate the science of the highest sphere of knowledge would be tantamount to a mutilation of the university. Here all boughs and branches of human knowledge should be united into a large organism, of unity and community of work, of giving and taking. Theology needs for auxiliaries other sciences, such as profane history and philology, Assyriology and Egyptology, psychology and medicine. In turn it offers indispensable aid to history and other branches of science, it guards the ethical and ideal principles of every science, and crowns them by tendering to them the most exalted thoughts. Here is the place of education for the judge and official, for the physician and teacher; hence it should be the place also for the education of the servant of the chief spiritual power, religion.

The university should unite all active mental powers that lift man above the commonplace. But is there any stronger mental power than religion?

It is the oldest and mightiest factor in mental life; it is as natural to man as the flower is to the field; his mind gravitates to a religious resting place, whence he may view time and eternity, where he may rest. Therefore religion demands a science that inquires into its substance, its justification, its effect on thought and life. Man strives to give to himself an account of everything, but most of all of what is foremost in his mind. A system of sciences without theology would be like an uncompleted tower, like a body without a head.

The history of theology dates back to the very beginning of science and culture. If we trace the oldest philosophy we find as its starting point theological research and knowledge. *Orpheus* and *Hesiod*, who sang of the gods, and the sages of the oldest mysteries, were called theologians; *Plutarch* sees in the theologians of past ages the oldest philosophers, in the philosophers, however, the descendants of the theologians; *Plato* derives philosophy from the teachers of theology. Even more prominently was religious study and knowledge responsible for Hindoo, Chaldean, and Egyptian philosophy.

Was it reserved for our age to discard all the better traditions of mankind? Shall victory rest with the destructive elements in the mental education of Europe? Against this danger to our ideal goods, theology should stay at the universities, as a bulwark and permanent protest.

THEOLOGICAL FACULTY IN STATE AND CHURCH

For this reason the theological faculty has a birth-right at the university, whether state school or free university. Where it is joined to a state university, theology automatically becomes subordinate to the state, in a limited sense. More essential is its dependency upon the Church, because, being the science of the faith, theology is primarily subject to the authority and supervision of the Church. For the Church, and only the Church, is charged by its Divine Founder to teach His religion to all nations. Hence no one can exercise the office of a religious teacher, neither in the public school nor at college, if not authorized to do so by the Church. It is a participation in the ministry of the Church; and the latter alone can designate its organs. Whoever has not been given by the Church such license to teach, or he from whom she takes it away, does not possess it; no other power can grant it, not even the state. Nor can the state restore the license of teaching to a theologian from whom the Church has withdrawn it; this would be an act beyond state jurisdiction, hence invalid.

In granting the license to teach, the Church does so in the self-evident presumption that the one so licensed will teach his students the correct doctrine of the Church, as far as it has been established; and he binds himself to do so by voluntarily taking the office, and more explicitly by the profession of the creed. If he should deviate from the creed later on, it is the obvious right of the Church to cancel his license. In this the Church only draws the logical conclusion from the office of the teacher and from his voluntary obligation. He holds his office as an organ of the Church, destined to lecture on pure doctrine before future priests. Whether or not he has honestly searched for the truth when deviating therefrom, this he may settle with his conscience; but he is incapacitated to act still further as an organ of the Church, and it is only common honesty to resign his office if he cannot fulfil any longer the obligations he assumed. The professor of theology is therefore in the first place a deputy of his Church. Also he is teacher at a state institution and as such a state official; he is appointed by the state to be the teacher of students belonging to a certain denomination, he is paid by the state, and may be removed by the state from his position as official teacher. But withal the right must not be denied to the Church to watch over the correctness of the Christian doctrine, and to make appointment and continuance in the teaching office dependent upon it.

Indeed, this demand was urged by Prof. *Paulsen,* notwithstanding his entirely different position; he says: " The Catholic-theological faculties are in a certain sense a concession by the Church to the state; of course they are also a service of the state for the Church, and a valuable one, too; but they rest in the first place upon a concession made by the Church to the state, with a view to the historically established fact, and to peace. Naturally, this concession cannot be unconditional. The condition is: the professors appointed by the state must stand upon ecclesiastical ground, they must acknowledge the doctrine of the Church as the standard of their teaching, and they must receive from the Church the *missio canonica*. The Church cannot accept hostile scientists for teachers. Hence for the appointment an agreement must be reached with ecclesiastical authority. The universities are not merely workshops for research, they are at the same time educational institutions for important public professions; in fact, they were founded for this latter purpose: they are the outcome of the want for scientifically educated clergymen, teachers, physicans, judges, and other professionals. And this purpose necessitates restrictions: the professor of Evangelical theology cannot teach any arbitrary opinions any more than his Catholic fellow-professor can; the lawyer is also restricted by presumptions, for instance, that the civil code is not an accumulation of nonsense, but, on the whole, a pretty good order of life. Just as little as we should dispute the lawyer's standing as a scientist on this account, so little shall we be able to deny this standing to the Catholic theologian who stands with honest conviction on the platform of his Church." "We want the Catholic theological faculties to be preserved; of course, under the presumption of freedom of scientific research within the limits drawn by the creed of the Church."

In a similar sense the Bavarian minister of education, Dr. *V. Wehner,* said, on Feb. 11, 1908, in the course of a speech in the Bavarian Diet: " Thus the Catholic professor of theology is bound to the standards of creed and morals as established by the Church. The decision as to whether a Catholic professor of theology teaches the right doctrine of the Church is not for the state to give, but for the Church alone." " The business of the professors at theological faculties is to transmit the teachings of the Church to future candidates for the priesthood, and this is what they are employed for by the state. That the Church does not tolerate a doctrine to differ from her own is to me quite self-evident." Hence we may conclude, " The attacks directed here and there in recent times against the continuance of Catholic theological faculties need not worry us in any way. Nor are they likely to meet with response at the places where the decision rests. Times have changed. Even non-Catholic governments are no longer blind to the conviction that an educated clergy must be reckoned among the most eminent factors for conserving the state " (*Freiherr von Hertling*). Even during the heated debates on the anti-modernist oath in the Prussian Diet and upper house, the importance of the theological faculties was acknowledged by the speakers, none of whom demanded the removal of these faculties, though outspoken in their criticism of the oath. Prime minister *Bethmann-Hollweg* declared on March 7: " Catholic students will get their training at the Catholic faculties the same as hitherto, even after the anti-modernist oath is introduced. The state never will claim for itself the authority to determine in any way which, and in what, forms doctrines of faith shall be taught to Catholic students. This is no affair of the state. If, and this is my wish, the Catholic faculties will retain that value to teachers, students, and the total organism of the universities, which is the natural condition of their existence, then they will continue to exist for the profit of both, the Catholic population and the state. Should they lose this value, however, an event I do not wish to see, then they will die by themselves. But I do not see that it is demanded by the interest of the state to abolish without awaiting further development these faculties with one stroke, thereby harming our Catholic population, whose wants and needs deserve as much. consideration as those of any other part of the population."

There is no warrant for the view that theology is subject to a foreign power, and therefore it cannot claim a place in a state institution. In its external relations the theological faculty is subject also to the state, serving the public interests so much the better the more continually the priest by his activity influences the life of the people. By the way, why this urgent demand for state control in the pursuit of a science by a party that otherwise is striving zealously to put the university beyond the influence of the state? To be a state institution or not can only be an extrinsic matter to the university itself. Or has the science of medicine not enough intellectual substance and consistency to thrive at a free university? Is science as such a matter of state? Therefore, why find fault with theology because it will not be entirely subordinated to the state? Nor is it proper to call the Church a " foreign " power. It is certainly not a foreign power to theology; neither to the Christian state, that has developed in closest relation to the Church, which owes its civilization and culture to the Church, shares with her its subjects, and is based even to-day upon the doctrines and customs of the Church.

Against Christ there arose the Jewish scribes and denounced His wisdom as error; the scribes have passed away, we know them no longer. To the Neoplatonics Christianity was ignorance, even barbarity; Manicheans and Gnostics praised as the higher wisdom Oriental and Greek philosophy adorned with Christian ideas. They belong to history. When the people of Israel came in touch with the brilliant civilization of Egypt, Assyria, and Greece, they often became ashamed of the religion. of their forefathers, and embraced false gods; to-day we look upon their fancy of inferiority as foolishness, and we rank their religion high above the religious notions of the pagan Orient.

Thus has truth pursued its way through the centuries of human history, often unrecognized by the children of men, scolded for being obsolete, nay, more, driven from its home and forced to make room for delusion and error. Delusion fled, and error sank into its grave — but truth remained. Thus the Church has endured, and thus the Church will live on, with her doctrines and science misunderstood and repulsed by the children of a world unable to grasp them; they will pass away and so will their thoughts, yet the Church will remain, and so will her science. "She was great and respected" — this is the familiar quotation from a Protestant historian — "before the Saxon had set foot on Britain, before the Frank had passed the Rhine, when Grecian eloquence still flourished in Antioch, when idols were still worshipped in the temple of Mecca. And she may still exist in undiminished vigor when some traveller from New Zealand shall, in the midst of a vast solitude, take his stand on a broken arch of London Bridge to sketch the ruins of St. Paul's" (*Lord Macaulay*).

Then, perhaps, another observer, leaning against the pillars of history, and looking back upon the culture of this age, will realize that only one power of truth may rightly say: "Heaven and earth will pass away, but my words will not pass away" — Christ and His Church.

LAW AND FREEDOM

An Epilogue

The great Renovator of mankind, in whom the pious Christian sees his God, and in whom the greater part of the modern world, though turned from faith, still sees the ideal of a perfect human being, hence also of true freedom, once spoke the significant words: "*Et veritas liberabit vos,* and the truth shall make you free" (John viii. 32). As all the words that fell from His lips are the truth for all centuries to come, so are these words pre-eminently true.

There is in our times a strong tension felt between freedom on the one hand, and law and authority on the other; true freedom and true worth it sees too exclusively in the independent assertion of the self-will, and in the unrestrained manifestation of one's strength and energy, while law and authority are looked upon as onerous fetters. Our times do not understand that freedom and human dignity are not opposed to law and obedience, that no other freedom can be intended for man than the voluntary compliance with the law and the standards of order.

All creatures, from the smallest to the largest, are bound by law; none is destined for the eminent isolation of independence. The same law of gravitation that causes the stone to fall, also governs the giants of the skies, and they obey its rule; the same laws that rule the candle-flame, that are at work in the drop of water, also rule the fires of the sun and guide the fates of the ocean. The heart, like all other organs of the human body, is ruled by laws, and medical science, with its institutes and methods, is kept busy to cure the consequences of the disturbance of these laws. Every being has its laws: it must follow them to attain perfection; deviation leads to degeneration.

Thus the decision of the worth and dignity of man does not rest with an unrestrained display of strength, but with order; not with unchecked activity, but with control of his acts and with truth. The floods that break through the dam have force and energy, but being without order they create destruction; the avalanche crashing down the mountain side has force and power, but, free from the law of order, it carries devastation; glowing metal when led into the mould becomes a magnificent bell, while flowing lava brings ruin. Only ONE dignity and freedom can be destined for man, it consists in voluntarily adhering to warranted laws and authorities.

For him who with conviction and free decision has made the law of thought, faith, and action his own principle, the law has ceased to be a yoke and a burden; it has become his own standard of life, which he loves; it has become the fruit of his conviction, TRUTH has made him free. Ask the virtuoso who obeys the rules of his art whether he considers them fetters; indeed he does not, he has made them his principles. Let us ask of the civilized citizen whether he feels the laws of civilization to be a yoke; he does not, he obeys them of his own free will, they are his own order of life. Unfree, slaves and serfs, will be those only who carry with resentment the burden of the laws they must obey. Unfree feels the savage people fighting against the laws of civilization; unfree the wicked boy to whom discipline is repugnant. It is not the law that makes man unfree, it is his own lawlessness and rebellion.

Nor does submission to the God-given law of the Christian belief make man low or unfree; to those to whom their belief is conviction and life, the suggestion that they are oppressed will sound strange. On the contrary, they feel that this belief fits in harmoniously with the nobler impulses of their thought and will, like the pearl in the shell, like the gem in its setting. Man experiences this when his belief lifts him above the lowlands of his sensual life to mental independence, and frees him from the bondage of his own unruly impulses, that so often seek to control him.

> Freiheit sei der Zweck des Zwanges
> Wie man eine Rebe bindet,
> Dass sie, statt im Staub zu kriechen,
> Frei sich in die Lüfte windet.

(Freedom be the aim of restraint, just as the vine is tied to the trellis that it may freely rise in the air, instead of crawling in the dust.) This is the freedom of mind, knowing but one yoke, the truth; the freedom that does not bow to error, nor to high sounding phrases, nor to public opinion, nor to the bondage of political life; neither is true freedom shackled by the fetters of one's own lawless impulses. ET VERITAS LIBERABIT VOS.

INDEX